THE GOSPEL OF JOHN

The Gospel of John

A Commentary by
Michael Mullins

the columba press

First published in 2003 by
the columba press
55A Spruce Avenue, Stillorgan Industrial Park,
Blackrock, Co Dublin

Cover by Bill Bolger
Origination by The Columba Press
Printed in Ireland by ColourBooks Ltd, Dublin

ISBN 1 85607 427 7

Acknowledgements
Scripture quotations are taken from The New Revised Standard
Version, copyright (c) 1989, by the Division of Christian Education of
the National Council of the Churches of Christ in the United States of
America. Used by permission.

Contents

THE REACTION Jn 5:1– 2:50

THE RISEN AND GLORIFIED LORD Jn 20:1-21:25

This book is dedicated
with respect and gratitude
to the staff and students of
St John's College, Waterford
1807–1999

Foreword

Scholarly writing on the gospel of John is well-nigh boundless. Popularisations of scholarship abound, but the dependable writing on the fourth gospel suitable for the scholar, student and serious reader is regrettably small. In addition, the verse-by-verse exegesis imposed by the commentary format frequently had the effect of dulling the reader's attention to the literary data.

Dr Michael Mullins, however, presents his work as a text-book for students of theology and a guide for serious readers in the hope that it will deepen their spiritual and theological insight. The author aims to help us understand John so that we may respond to his appeal. In this he shares in the purpose of the gospel of John: 'these things are written so that you may believe that Jesus is the Christ, the Son of God, and that in believing you may have life through his name' (Jn 20:31).

To a theologian history without exegesis is empty; to a historian exegesis without history is blind. Unless supported by reliable historical information from various sources, no study of the gospel can be of more than fleeting interest.

Explaining John's gospel is one of the most challenging dimensions of biblical scholarship. Plumbing the depths of his message requires great spiritual openness. Origen claimed that no one can perceive the meaning of this gospel who has not leaned on Jesus' breast, who has not received Mary from him as his own mother. The study of the gospel also requires great respect for, and an ability to critically evaluate, the findings of those who have worked in this field.

This gospel was written out of, and for, a community locked in controversy with the Jewish synagogue, and so John reflects a historical conflict between the church and the synagogue. It is probably the product of a community of Christians who had undergone a traumatic exit or expulsion from a synagogue and this may well explain something of its distinctive character. A persistent motif in the gospel is the discussion of the relationship between the authority of the law and the authority of Jesus. Life-giving terms once applied to the law (water, light) now apply to Jesus. The authority of the law is never denied, but the authority of Jesus is made to supercede the law.

This gospel has attracted theologians and mystics. It stood close to the centre of christological controversy in the fourth century. In the last century and a half it has been at the heart of the debate about the relation between history and theology.

John's portrayal of Jesus emanates from the evangelist's ability to mix symbol and narrative, to play upon paradox and irony, suffusing historical description with exalted theological interpretation. Through core symbols the evangelist presents Jesus to us. Each of these symbols is an essential part of the context of life itself. Without light, water and food, there could be no life. This is a recurring theme in the fulfillment of Jewish expectations and the replacement of Jewish festivals and institutions.

Dr Mullins, fortified by his experience lecturing in the Old and New Testaments over a period of thirty years, leads us competently and confidently through these areas in a way which respects the complexity while not causing us to get lost in the detail. The author encourages us to read John's gospel on two levels. At one level it tells in a simple way the remembered story of Jesus of Nazareth against the background of the history of the people of Israel. On another level it tells the story of the faith and struggles of the Johannine community. Understandably, the evangelist makes abundant use of symbolic language, which enables his readers to get a glimpse into his faith convictions. Fr Mullins highlights this by allowing the gospel to speak for itself. For example, in presenting discipleship the fourth evangelist rings the changes on words like 'follow', 'seek', 'stay' and 'see'.

Many who have responsibility for God's word echo Mary Magdalen at the tomb of Jesus – 'the exegetes have taken away my Lord and I don't know where they have laid him'. Starting with the reality of the real life symbols that surround us, the evangelist is aware of its paradoxes and contradictions, attuned to its limitless potential for good, saddened by so much insensitivity, yet alive to the grace of God with whom nothing on earth is impossible.

Presenting the gospel is not just telling the truth but telling the truth in love, and to tell the truth in love means to tell it with concern not only for the truth that is being told but with concern also for those to whom it is being told.

In so far as it was the ultimately inexpressible that Jesus spoke about, in a sense he had no recourse but to preach in the way he did, not in the incendiary rhetoric of the prophet or the systematic abstractions of the theologian but in the language of images and metaphor, which is finally the only language.

No understanding of the gospel is possible without an appreciation of symbolism. It is used not just to elucidate that which is hidden but to make it come alive. The fourth evangelist suggests rather than spells out. He evokes rather than explains. He catches us by surprise. This gospel ranks among the most splendid treasury of Christian spirituality ever written. Whether privately or in the liturgy, whenever it is read, we continue to discover new insights which we missed before.

In this regard, Dr Mullins' work is not just a commentary but also an analysis of the rich background of the gospel. He communicates to a broader audience the results of contemporary scholarship on the fourth gospel. He has combined his scientific training as a historian, his theological and spiritual expertise, with his classical formation. The result of his work is a very readable, extremely informative and thoroughly researched commentary which will prove to be of enormous benefit to the student, scholar and serious reader.

✠ Michael Neary
Archbishop of Tuam

Preface

At a time when many people are taking a serious interest in the scriptures and looking for reading material to deepen their spiritual understanding of the inspired Word and broaden their knowledge of biblical scholarship, I offer this commentary on St John's gospel as a textbook for students of theology and as a guide for serious readers in the hope that it will deepen their spiritual and theological insight, and bring them to a level of academic competence. I offer it also to those many preachers who wish to underpin their preaching with serious reading and to the many people who practise *lectio divina* and other forms of spiritual reading. No prior technical knowledge of biblical scholarship is assumed and I explain technical terms and translate important Greek and Hebrew words and expressions as we meet them. Above all, I aim to share in the stated purpose of the gospel of John: 'These things are written so that you may believe that Jesus is the Christ, the Son of God, and that believing this you may have life through his name.'[1]

St John's gospel is often described as the mystical or most theological of the gospels, and from the time of Clement of Alexandria in the early third century it has been called the spiritual gospel. The evangelist has been called John the Theologian and is represented in art as the eagle because his gaze into the mystery of God reminds one of the eagle that flies directly into the sunlight. There is no transfiguration scene in John's gospel because the entire work is a treatment of the Father-Son relationship on a level with that of the transfiguration in the synoptics. In fact the words of the prologue 'We have gazed upon his glory' resemble the words used in the Second Letter of Peter to describe the transfiguration: 'For when he received honour and glory from God the Father and the voice was borne to him by the Majestic Glory, "This is my beloved Son with whom I am well pleased," we heard this voice borne from heaven, for we were with him on the holy mountain.'[2]

---

1. Jn 20:31.
2. 2 Pet 2:17f (Navarre Bible translation).

It has been said that John's gospel is like a pool in which a
child could swim and an elephant could drown, a fact that
brings out two essential aspects of this gospel. Like all scripture
it is an open book and not a secret document, but it is also an inexhaustible source of spiritual life and insight. Every section,
probably every verse, of St John's gospel is a storehouse of riches
any one of which could be the subject of a book in itself.

Over the years commentators have used many different
methods in the interpretation of St John's gospel and now some
of them point, with a degree of justification, to 'a conflict of
methods' in Johannine studies. This present commentary is *a*
commentary, *an individual reading* of the text and does not claim
to be *the* interpretation of the text or any part of it. It draws on
the insights of different methods but has three overall guiding
principles. Firstly, the text *as it now stands* (with its well known
variants), and not sources, hypothetical rearrangements or earlier
versions of the text, is the canonical gospel and, like any literary
work, it has its own structure and inherent dynamism, even if at
times they have been somewhat 'imposed' on traditional material.[3] Secondly, the gospel is part of the canon of scripture and has
its place within the greater understanding and interpretation of
the whole. Thirdly, the story of Jesus is more than any one
gospel, or any number of gospels or other writings, could ade-
quately express. The final words of the gospel of John declare: 'If
all were written down, the world itself, I suppose, would not
hold all the books that would have to be written.'[4] It is, however,
not only the volume of material that makes the story of Jesus
greater than the capacity of 'all the books that would have to be
written'. The glory of God revealed in Jesus could never be contained fully in any number of human descriptions.

Hans Urs von Balthasar expresses this very well with the
term *Gestalt* which he borrowed from Goëthe who used it to illustrate his understanding that a living organism is greater than
the sum of its parts, as the living leaf is more than its components. Similarly the mystery of Jesus' person is greater than the
sum of all the partial descriptions. Jesus '… is the one and only
exposition of God (Jn 1:18), infinitely rich and of a paradoxical
simplicity that integrates all the elements. He is absolute sover-

---

3. This 'imposition' can be seen from the 'aporias', that is the breaks, inconsisten-
cies and interruptions in the 'natural' flow of the text.
4. Jn 21:25.

eignty and absolute humility; he is infinitely approachable who can be reached by everyone and infinitely inaccessible, ever beyond reach.'[5] John's gospel attempts to capture the mystery of Jesus. Its many parts point us forward to the mystery that surpasses the sum of all parts. The impact of Jesus is essentially bound to a faith vision which is more than a 'sum of the parts' or the combined effect of various approaches to interpretation.

My special indebtedness to many scholars is acknowledged throughout the text, but there are levels of insight and understanding that cannot be easily quantified and acknowledged in a reference. For these too I owe a debt of gratitude to many scholars who have written on St John's gospel. In particular I wish to acknowledge the influence of two former teachers of mine, Ignace de la Potterie and Raymond E. Brown, and some authors whose very recent contributions greatly influenced my understanding and approach, as they brought fresh insight into well worn paths of interpretation. Their contributions will be obvious from the notes: R. A. Culpepper (1983, 1998), F. J. Moloney (1998), Sandra Schneiders (1999), W. J. Harrington (1999), Mary L. Coloe (2001), and Marianne M. Thompson,(2001).

My thanks are due to my colleagues in St Patrick's College, Maynooth, and my former colleagues in St John's College, Waterford, who have encouraged me throughout the writing of this book, and made many helpful suggestions. My thanks extend also to Columba Press for their professional competence in bringing this book to its readers.

Michael Mullins
St Patrick's College, Maynooth
Feast of the Transfiguration of the Lord
6 August 2003

---

5. H.U.von Balthasar, 'Theology and Aesthetic', *Communio*, 1(1981), 62-71; 64f.

Introduction

THE STORY OF JESUS

'Tell me a story' the child says at bedtime and the parent repeats again the favourite tale, careful to observe every last detail lest the child interrupt to adjust the current telling to ensure a repetition of the original impact. The fresh memory and stimulated imagination reach out like hands to grasp again the magic moment created by the story. The world is interpreted by the teller and the child experiences the telling from within the horizons of childhood. As the stories multiply and the horizons of experience expand an adult emerges with an individual identity and unique set of experiences. This individuality and unique grasp of the world will henceforth influence the interpretation of every story heard and inform every story told.

Story is perhaps the best and most effective form of communication. The reawakening of awareness in the power and impact of story has brought a whole new dimension to the interpretation of the gospels. After a period of oral transmission of the stories about the life, death, work and teaching of Jesus, the written gospels present the traditional material in an overall story or narrative. This change from oral to written medium had far reaching consequences for the story being transmitted.

When a story is written it takes on a life of its own and replaces the immediate dialogue between teller and hearer with the personally more 'distant' bond of author and reader. The reader has to approach the work on its own terms without immediate access to the mind of the author. Unlike the child listening to the story, the reader cannot interrupt the reading with: 'But what about …?' or 'You said last time that …!' The author may partially bridge this gap by creating a narrator within the text to tell the story or comment on it as it unfolds.[1] Reading becomes a dialogue between the reader and the work. The 'ideal' reader would be alert to all the aspects of the writing – its language, imagery and allusions and the horizons of author and reader would coincide within the work. However, the ideal reader probably never existed. The nearest to an ideal reader would most probably be the reader 'implied' in the text who

---

1. It can be difficult at times to differentiate between the author and the narrator.

would very likely be a contemporary who shared, at least in some measure, the horizons of the author.

Through the work itself the real or actual reader may construct a picture of the 'implied' author and the 'implied' reader. As the literary work itself takes on a life of its own and becomes independent of, and outlives, the author and the author's intended/implied readers, 'real' readers never envisioned by the author take their place.[2] Their horizons may be very different from those of the author and the 'implied' or intended readers. John B. Witherington comments on this 'problem' of horizons:

> If we are to bridge the two horizons, we must realize that we live with a post-Enlightenment worldview of history and the cosmos dominating our thinking, which is very different from the worldview reflected in these gospels....The fourth gospel must be evaluated on the basis of its own terms of reference, not on ours.[3]

Writing a story, be it fictional or historical, demands planning if meaning is to be conveyed and convincing. Two essential elements in such planning are *plot* and *character*. The author of fiction has unlimited scope to invent on both counts, the only constraints being credibility within the chosen genre. Writing history, however, the author is constrained by the known historical events, characters and outcome, and writes within the conventional boundaries of historical writing at the time of composition.

The *plot* of a story is the ordered sequence of events, showing causality from one event to another, in an overall unified structure, moving towards a goal or end point and achieving emotional, psychological, moral, religious or artistic effects in the process.[4] The plot is supported by action, characterisation and thought. In St John's gospel the plot is driven by conflict between belief and unbelief as responses to Jesus. The reader is being simultaneously led to identify with the desired goal of understanding and belief.[5] The plot of the gospel is summarised in the prologue: 'He came unto his own and his own did not receive him, but to those who did receive him he gave power to

---

2. Literary critics refer to 'the death of the author'.

3. Ben Witherington III, *John's Wisdom. A Commentary on the Fourth Gospel*, Westminster, John Knox Press, Louisville, Kentucky, 1995, 73f.

4. Aristotle's *Poetics* 1450b–1451b, speaks of order, amplitude, unity and probable and necessary connection.

5. This is highlighted by the fact that 98 of the 239 references to belief in the NT are in John's gospel.

become children of God.'[6] The integration of 'theme' or 'theolog-ical viewpoint' into the plot can slow the pace, as in the discourses, but it also intensifies the conflict, focuses further on the charac-ters and exposes a deeper meaning in the events, seeing them from the vantage point of revelation.

The characters in a story are the 'creation' of the author, who therefore is 'omniscient' in their regard. Since characterisation enables the 'omniscient' author to expose the character to the reader more profoundly and thoroughly than a person is exposed in real life, the readers of the gospel will have a better vantage point for observing and understanding Jesus than his followers and opponents had during his ministry.

Characters can be of two kinds. There are 'round' or 'auton-omous' characters with traits and personalities, whose strengths and weaknesses, thoughts and emotions, are like mini-plots in themselves. They are complex in temperament and motivation, in ways unpredictable and capable of surprising the reader with unexpected actions or patterns of behaviour. There are also 'flat' characters whose function is not to be interesting in themselves but to fulfil a role in the narrative. They are personifications of a single trait, or functionaries carrying out a task. These characters do not change, develop or suffer crisis.[7]

The characters in St John's gospel display interesting ele-ments of both types of characterisation. Jesus himself, unlike the main character in a novel or play, or indeed unlike the Jesus por-trayed in the synoptics, arrives on the scene fully developed. He does not learn, change, grow, or suffer crisis.[8] The events, dis-courses and disputes throughout the gospel serve to bring out what was true of him from the beginning. In this Jesus is closer to the static, ethical, Greek hero, whose inherent *pietas*, courage or wisdom brings him through all crises, than to the Old Testament heroes who were portrayed as characters developing, learning and changing in response to God's call.

Most of the characters in John's gospel appear for such a short time that 'roundness' of character is not always possible.

---

6. Jn 1:11f.
7. Characters carrying the main action, reactions and responses are referred to as *protagonists*. Intermediary characters who serve as plot functionaries, often with a symbolic or representative role, are referred to as *ficelles*.
8. The authors of the gospel stories, in the oral and written traditions, do not con-cern themselves with details of Jesus' personal appearance such as his height, colour of hair and eyes, or mannerisms in speech and general behaviour.

For the most part also, they do not interact with one another but fulfil a role in highlighting responses to Jesus.[9] Their characters are determined by these responses. However, they can have a very important representative value rather out of proportion to the brevity of their appearances.

Some of the characters are more or less autonomous, showing initiative, growth, learning and faith development. The Samaritan woman, for example, (who functions both as an individual and representative character) undergoes change and faith development, issuing in mission activity. The Beloved Disciple, (who also functions as an individual and representative character), comes to 'see and believe'. The blind man, healed at the Pool of Siloam, develops in faith and strength of character through the crisis of harassment and exclusion. Others like Thomas and Pilate represent a trait, that of the doubting disciple who comes to faith, and the scheming official evading responsibility. Others like the Mother of Jesus and the Beloved Disciple are typecast for a role or function, but they also display strong personal qualities. They are the two witnesses to Jesus who manifest understanding and a deep faith, prior to a sign that evoked faith in the other disciples – the Mother of Jesus at Cana and the Beloved Disciple at the tomb. There are also 'communal' characters constructed from the hostile authorities, usually 'the Jews'[10] and 'the Pharisees'. Sometimes 'the (chief) priests' are included (as in the trial before Pilate). These function mainly as a characterisation of the opposition to Jesus. 'The

9. The man born blind in chapter nine is a notable exception. His main exchanges are with the authorities, but concerning Jesus and his healing.

10. There are a number of shades of meaning in the use of the term 'the Jews'. At times the term refers to the inhabitants of Jerusalem or Judaea. At times it appears in phrases like 'festival of the Jews'. It can be an ethnic designation emphasising their difference from Samaritans or Greeks/Gentiles, as in the encounter with the woman at the well. In the account of the raising of Lazarus the Jews appear as the friends of Mary and Martha coming to console them in their bereavement. For the most part, however, the term is a characterisation of the forces hostile to Jesus within the Jewish people, especially among the authorities, but it must be remembered that Jesus himself, his family, friends, disciples and followers were also Jews. The term reflects the division between Jews (especially Pharisaic Jews) and Christian Jews and Gentiles during the post-70 division as both groups worked out a new self-definition. Sadly the term has been misunderstood and misused in a fiercely anti-Semitic way with disastrous consequences. Properly understood within its Jewish context in the Bible the tensions between Jesus and 'the Jews' in John's gospel should resemble the verbal battles between prophets like Jeremiah, Amos and Hosea and the religious and civil officials (and the people) of their time.

crowd' functions similarly as a characterisation of the forces of
opposition, support and division. They come in response to
signs, and are central to discussions and disputes about Jesus'
origins, identity and signs, being mentioned eighteen times during the various feasts in chapters six, seven and twelve. They are
a foil and a discussion partner for Jesus, at times articulating
what is going on in the background like the chorus in a Greek
play. The Pharisees disdain them as the ignorant crowd who
know nothing of the law.

The story of Jesus at one level fits the category of historical
story, in so far as it tells of a historical person, in concrete historical circumstances, surrounded by historical characters, the outcome of whose life left an enormous mark in human history. At
another level it is a story that history cannot confirm or assess.
His coming from the Father, his inner life and consciousness, his
promise of salvation and the second coming, and his resurrection and glorification are matters beyond the competence of the
historian. Yet they are a major part, in fact *the* major part, of his
story. 'No document that says it is written "in order that you
might believe that Jesus is the Christ" has purely historical aims,
and the document should not be assessed as if it did.'[11] Putting
the historical and ahistorical/transcendental together in one
story so that the reader can understand is, in the words of B.
Witherington:

> ... an exercise in hermeneutics, the science of the interpret-
> ation and application of a foundational narrative, the taking
> of the story of Jesus and putting it into a language and form
> of narrative that will convey the significance and meaning of
> the Christ event ...[12]

All aspects of plot, characterisation and thematic development
pass through the mind of the writers (authors and editors) as the
story or stories of Jesus are committed to the pages of a gospel
narrative. The acceptance of the gospel into the canon of scripture is the church's declaration that the inspiration of the Holy
Spirit was at work in its composition. Our belief in the presence
of the same Holy Spirit in the church leads us to believe in the inspired reception of the text in the official teaching of the church
(the *magisterium*) and the faith of the people (the *sensus fidelium*).

The story of Jesus in St John's gospel is really three stories

---

11. Ben Witherington III, *op.cit.*, 73f.
12. *Ibid.*

imposed one on the other. As the story of Jesus is told, the Old Testament story of God and the chosen people is retold in allusion, quotation and festal celebration, and at the same time the story of the Johannine Christians shapes, and shines through, the story of Jesus as it is told from their perspective and experience. Two other dimensions frame the story – the pre-existence of the Word with God and the future glory in the Father's house.

The gospels bear more than ample witness to the fact that the disciples, and others, did not understand Jesus. It is not surprising, therefore, and at the same time very fortunate, that we are spared the on-the-spot reporting of Jesus' words and deeds by his confused associates. The working of the Holy Spirit, the Paraclete, on minds and hearts in the believing community brought about in time the understanding now enshrined in the inspired books of the canon. The Paraclete inspired the community in its remembering of what Jesus said and did, and thereby led the community/church into understanding. This understanding has been articulated in the language and imagery of the authors and implied readers of the gospels, and written according to the literary standards of the time and place. We, the actual or real readers today, are at a great remove in time, place, language and culture from the horizons of the authors and original readers and have to come to an awareness, not only of the author's world but the world of the implied or intended readers for whom the authors wrote.

The Reader
John Ashton begins his book *Understanding the Fourth Gospel*, with the comment:

> There are many ways of approaching the fourth gospel. One may turn to it for enlightenment, for inspiration, for encouragement or consolation, for theological proofs … for evidence about early Jewish Christianity, for insight into the mind of Jesus, and much more besides. One may approach the work as an historian, a theologian, a simple Christian, or an enquiring unbeliever. What the gospel reveals of itself will be coloured, even controlled, by the interest one brings to it. There is no disinterested reading. Nor by the same token is there any disinterested writing …[13]

Every reader comes already programmed by life, experience, education, and faith to interpret the gospel. The story of Jesus,

---

13. J. Ashton, *Understanding the Fourth Gospel*, 3.

according to John, is read by me, the listening reader, two millennia after its composition. I read, hear and retell it. It is John's story, the early Christians' story, but now it is my story and my retelling, and the readers of my words will make it their story. But how do I read the story? What hermeneutical grid is functioning in me as I read? What factors determine my approach?

I read St John's gospel as a practising Catholic, a priest and teacher of scripture for more than three decades. I read it in the context of faith seeking understanding, a faith which has been nourished in the liturgy and prayer and enriched by art, music, ritual, processions and pilgrimages. My faith has been fed by a believing community of family, friends, teachers, colleagues and students. It comes as a gift, a pearl of great price. It is fed by the liturgy of the church and I believe it is guaranteed from error by the guidance of the Holy Spirit working through the *magisterium* of the church and the faith of the people. It has been enriched by the prayers and wisdom of the communities in which I have lived, and enhanced by the reading of the mystics and theologians. For me personally it has been further enriched and enhanced by the writings and personal contact with members and clergy of the other Christian traditions. It has been particularly energised and informed in recent times by reading the works of many feminist biblical scholars who have brought new insights and challenges since my time as a student. Above all it has been honed on the anvil of teaching and learning from students seeking truth and life in the scriptures. I come to the gospel then with all the fascination of one whose life has been an absorbing of the 'polyphony' of faith expression. Within, and supported by, this faith context I bring academic training, reading and teaching experience to the understanding of the text. I question and analyse the text, not to deconstruct it, much less to deconstruct Jesus himself, but to enrich the overall impression, the form or *Gestalt*, with awareness of the rich diet of components that make up the gospel. Hans Urs von Balthasar speaks of the faculty that allows one to see 'with the eye of faith':

> The fascination does not originate from the religious sense that subjectively exists in every person …The fascination is with Jesus Christ – if one sees Christ as he presents himself – with his uniqueness that cannot be compared to anything else in world history. The Fathers of the Church call this faculty to see the 'eye of faith'.[14]

---

14. H. U. von Balthasar, *op. cit.*, 64.

These are the co-ordinates on the grid of my hermeneutic as I set about commenting on the gospel according to John through the 'eye of faith'. That's me, the reader. But who is John?

The Author

The gospel itself does not identify its author. Irenaeus, writing probably about 180 AD and, following a tradition handed on by Polycarp, lent very serious credibility to the idea that John, Son of Zebedee, was author of the gospel.[15] It cannot be ruled out that the tradition about authorship on which Irenaeus relied was reliable, and though there is ample evidence of reluctance on the part of the author to reveal that identity, it may well have been known to others who spoke of it. Irenaeus had a serious motive for wanting to copperfasten the tradition of apostolic authorship of the gospel. It had been taken over by the gnostics and used by them to confirm their teaching about the myth of a redeemer who descended to impart to the unredeemed the knowledge (*gnôsis*) which would rescue them from ignorance and earthly entrapment. The first commentaries on John's gospel come from this gnostic background. Their positive attitude towards the gospel created in turn an attitude of suspicion on the part of the church. Irenaeus wished to rescue the gospel from both attitudes and did so by insisting on its apostolic origin and identifying the author as John, Son of Zebedee, one of the twelve. This remained the mainstream tradition for centuries and is widely testified in art and literature. But it poses a number of difficulties, not least of which are the facts that the gospel does not identify directly or indirectly the identity of its author and in addition it has all the signs of a document representing a tradition which evolved over a long period of time. Furthermore, scholars point out that there may be confusion with John the Presbyter, author of the letters, and John, author of the Apocalypse.

Though the gospel shows signs of a long period of formation, there is a dominant figure behind it, a person close to Jesus who first formed the tradition and gave it direction. Though the identity of that person is concealed in the gospel, the authenticity of the testimony is assured by the closeness of the chief witness to Jesus. This is stressed at the end of the gospel: 'This is the disciple who is bearing witness to these things, and who has written

15. Irenaeus lived from about 130 to 200 AD. Polycarp of Smyrna died in old age about 155-6 AD and was reputed to have known John.

these things; and we know that his testimony is true'.[16] This reference points to the witness of 'the disciple whom Jesus loved'. This Beloved Disciple is the one who reclined beside Jesus at the Last Supper and who conveyed Peter's question to him, seeking the identity of the betrayer.[17] He stood at the foot of the cross and Jesus commended his mother to his care, designating him as her son in his place.[18] The indications are that it was he who witnessed the blood and water flowing from Jesus' side.[19] He ran to the tomb with Peter and, observing the empty tomb and the position of the grave-cloths, 'he saw and he believed'.[20] He identified the Risen Jesus on the shore of the Lake of Galilee and because rumours that he would not die before the return of the Lord had circulated in the community, Peter put the question concerning his death to Jesus on the shore of the Lake.[21]

'The disciple whom Jesus loved' is identified with 'the other disciple' when the gospel tells us that Mary Magdalene 'came running to Peter and the other disciple, the one Jesus loved' with news of the empty tomb.[22] Here the Beloved Disciple is designated 'the other disciple'. This designation is then used twice in the description of Peter and himself running to the tomb. The indications therefore are that 'the other disciple' who arranged the admittance of Peter to the High Priest's courtyard, and even though some dispute the identification, 'the other disciple' who accompanied Andrew on the first visit to Jesus, may well be the same person.[23] 'The other disciple' therefore seems to be a well established and/or carefully contrived designation from the oldest stratum of the gospel which carefully concealed the identity of the chief witness to the tradition. He was later identified in the gospel as 'the disciple whom Jesus loved'.[24] His personal

---

16. Jn 21:24.

17. Jn 13:23-25.

18. Jn 19:25-27.

19. Jn 19:35. The masculine form is used both in the participle and possessive pronoun in the sentence. The Beloved Disciple is the only male mentioned in the group around the cross. Also the insertion into the narrative is very similar to that in 21:24 which refers to the Beloved Disciple.

20. Jn 20:2-10.

21. Jn 21:7, 20.

22. Jn 20:2.

23. If so, it would lend credibility to the identification of this disciple with John, Son of Zebedee.

24. One can only speculate why the name was concealed. Was it humility on the part of the originating figure in the tradition/community or was it to preserve the 'ideal' and 'representative' character of the disciple ?

contact with Jesus stands behind the witness of the gospel. The subsequent writers/editors were disciples of his and rooted in his tradition. They in turn shaped and moulded the tradition into the developed style and theology of the gospel.

However, at a time when the emphasis is on the text as it now stands, and literary critics speak of the 'death of the author', the personal identity of the 'real' author of the gospel does not seem quite so important. This 'other disciple' whose name has been withheld, but who had been subsequently identified as 'the disciple whom Jesus loved', stands behind the gospel as a link with Jesus and the ministry. He may or may not have been John, Son of Zebedee, one of the Twelve. The text does not tell us. The community/communities formed or influenced by him maintained his tradition and produced the author(s) who moulded it into its present form. The canon of scripture includes it in its list of inspired books, so on the authority of the church we can say that ultimately the author is God, who inspired the tradition in its formation, development, transmission, and commitment to writing. In this commentary, for practical reasons, I will follow the convention of speaking of John as the author.[25]

The Community
Stories are told in communities where they help to create and sustain identity and underpin religious and cultural development. Radical change in circumstances gives new life and new direction to old stories. The story of God and the chosen people sustained the life of the Jews for centuries but the terrible events of the year 70 AD changed their lives and forced them into a radical rethinking of the foundations of their faith. This radical reappraisal resulted in division and a parting of the ways between Jew and Christian as each worked out a new self-definition. The ensuing tension between them is reflected in St John's gospel in the telling of the story of Jesus. It is obvious in the accounts of the disputes with the 'Jews' and especially with the Pharisees. It is obvious also in the references to fear of being expelled from the synagogue and in the insistence on the superiority of Jesus over the pivotal figures of Moses and Abraham. The post 70 tensions have coloured both the content of the debates and the portrayal of the opposition.

---

25. Where it is necessary to avoid confusion I will use the term John the Baptist to distinguish the baptist and the evangelist, though the term baptist/baptiser is not used in the fourth gospel.

To understand the magnitude of the events of 70 AD, the reappraisal they occasioned, the tensions they provoked, and the new insight they brought to the story of Jesus, a historical note is required.

II
THE DESTRUCTION OF THE TEMPLE AND ITS AFTERMATH

It was the tenth day of the month Ab, in the year 70, a month falling in the July-August period of our modern calendar. After several battles and sieges throughout the land, the Romans had finally surrounded Jerusalem. The Zealots were besieged in the Temple which they themselves had desecrated by turning it into a fortress. The citizens were already devastated by the unspeakable horrors of the siege. Two days earlier the Romans torched the gates leading to the Temple area and the fire had been creeping around the colonnades, but the sanctuary itself remained intact. Titus, the Roman general, later emperor, ordered his men to put out the fire and retired for a rest, planning to storm the Temple next day. However, as the soldiers were putting out the fire they were attacked by the Zealots. The soldiers chased them back as far as the sanctuary. Josephus describes what ensued:

> Then one of the soldiers, without waiting for orders and without a qualm for the terrible consequences of his action but urged on by some unseen force, snatched up a blazing piece of wood and climbing on another soldier's back hurled the brand through a golden aperture giving access to the chambers built round the sanctuary. As the flames shot into the air the Jews sent up a cry that matched the calamity and dashed to the rescue, with no thought now of saving their lives or husbanding their strength; for that which hitherto they had guarded so devotedly was disappearing before their eyes …

> Yet more terrible than the din were the sights that met the eye. The Temple Hill, enveloped in flames from top to bottom, appeared to be boiling up from its very roots; yet the sea of flame was nothing to the ocean of blood, or the company of killers to the armies of the killed; nowhere could the ground be seen between the corpses, and the soldiers climbed over heaps of bodies as they chased the fugitives …

> However, two men of note, in a position either to save their lives by going over to the Romans or to face with the others

> whatever came their way, threw themselves into the fire and were burned to ashes with the sanctuary – Meiras son of Belgas and Joseph son of Dalaeus.[26]

The utter despair and unbelief that would descend on the Jews on seeing their sanctuary burned to ashes, and their holy city reduced to ruins, is anticipated in the action of Meiras and Joseph who preferred to perish in the flames than to face the future without the Temple and its atoning sacrifices. The Temple was the dwelling place of God in their midst and its sacrifices and rituals provided the ongoing means of holiness, repentance and right relationship with God. What were the surviving Jews to do now that they were gone? What precedent had they to follow in such a calamity?

There was such a precedent and it was remarkably obvious from the coincidence of date and circumstance, as Josephus reminds his readers.

> Grief might well be bitter for the destruction of the most wonderful edifice ever seen or heard of, both for its size and construction and for the lavish perfection of detail and the glory of its holy places; yet we find very real comfort in the thought that fate is inexorable, not only towards living beings but also towards buildings and sites. We may wonder too at the exactness of the cycle of fate: she kept, as I said, to the very month and day which centuries before had seen the sanctuary burnt by the Babylonians.[27]

On that former occasion in 587 BC the Jews were left to figure out how to understand their identity and re-interpret their religious experience in a completely changed environment. They pondered on the reason for the destruction as they sought the means of survival. The deuteronomistic historian, in the editing of the Books of Joshua, Judges, Samuel and Kings, explained the destruction of the Temple and the exile that followed as the result of 'doing what was displeasing to Yahweh', especially in the matter of idolatry.[28] In the wake of the collapse of the religious and civil institution it was the charismatic voice of the prophets that built on the one foundation that had not been destroyed – the promise of God to be covenant partner to the people. The prophet, known conventionally as Second Isaiah, based his

---

26. Josephus, *Jewish Wars*, Bk VI, iv,v. Penguin 1959 translation, 323-325.
27. Josephus, *ibid.*
28. 1 Kings 9:6-8.

message of hope for restoration on the belief that 'the word of our God endures forever' and the exiled visionary, the priest-prophet Ezechiel, promised new life to the scattered remnant of the nation.[29] After the destruction provoked by the Zealots and carried out by the Romans in 70 AD the people were again asking why it had happened and how they could continue their religious lives without the Temple and its atoning sacrifices. What were the foundations that had not been destroyed?

The famous Rabbi Simeon the Righteous, some two centuries earlier, had described the foundations of their belief and way of life. 'On three things does the age stand: on the Torah, on the Temple service and on acts of piety'.[30] The Temple service was now gone but Torah and acts of piety were indestructible and, building on these foundations, the Pharisees under the guidance of outstanding figures like Rabbi Johanan ben Zakkai gave the much needed leadership and hope to the survivors. As they set about reconstructing the religious life of the people the rabbis found the means of sanctification in the Torah, seen broadly as the law, the prophets and the oral tradition. 'Woe unto us,' Rabbi Joshua cried, 'that this, the place where the iniquities of Israel were atoned for, is laid waste!' Rabbi Johanan ben Zakkai replied: 'Be not grieved, my son. We have another atonement as effective as this ... acts of loving kindness, as it is said, "For I desire mercy and not sacrifice".'[31] Just as the rabbi's reflections on Hos 6:6 deepened his awareness of the importance of *hesed*, loving kindness, so too his awareness of the importance of ritual led him to organise a new calendar of feasts and festivals, centred now on the synagogue, and under the control of the Pharisees rather than the priests. Many of the priestly and Temple functions were thus transferred to home and synagogue. In the absence of the Temple and all it stood for, the synagogue now took on a whole new significance as the place where Jewish identity was focused and their religious life nurtured.

The Temple service was now gone and with it the priestly caste had lost their social position and power base. The Sadducees, Zealots and Essenes were mortally weakened in the destruction. The Pharisees survived as the most powerful group, and within the Pharisees it was the more liberal group in

29. Isa 40:8;Ezek 37:1-14.

30. trans. G. A.Yee, *Jewish Feasts and the Gospel of John*, 19.

31. Hos 6:6. *Avot de Rabbi Natan*, ch 6.

the tradition of the school of Hillel, rather than the more strict school of Shammai, that emerged in control. Their approach to scripture allowed them to adapt old laws and ways to new circumstances, and their teaching on life after death, retribution and recompense for suffering were ideal for the situation that presented itself after the great suffering of 70 AD. From the ruins of Jerusalem they removed their centre of learning and influence to Jamnia (Jabneh) on the coastal plain south of Joppa (Jaffa). There under the guidance of Johanan ben Zakkai they initiated and successfully carried through their thoroughgoing spiritual, liturgical, social and political reform which was designed to renew the spirits of the people and ensure their future identity.[32] Under the leadership of the Pharisees, the Jews thus redefined themselves along strict lines in a new situation. But the Pharisees had to overcome opposition from the survivors of the various other groups in order to have their reforms universally imposed. There were those who begged to differ with them, among them the Christian Jews, and especially those in the Johannine tradition with its Jerusalem roots and outlook.

The gradual and possibly spasmodic tensions between members of family and synagogue reached a turning point under Rabbi Gamaliel II, successor to Rabbi ben Zakkai, who took measures to preserve the identity and morale of the communities against any 'watering down' by 'heretical' groups. This occurred, according to the Babylonian Talmud,[33] when he commissioned a prayer, somewhere between 85 and 95 AD, to be added to the Eighteen Benedictions (*Shemoneh Esreh*) recited in the synagogue. Included as the Twelfth Benediction, the blessing against heretics, the *Birkat haMinim*, was aimed at those who were seen as 'heretical' and posed a threat to the ongoing reconstruction and preservation of Jewish life and identity. A version of the Benediction was found in the Cairo Genizah: 'let *ha-Notzim* (Christians) and *minim* (heretics) perish in a moment, let

---

32. Some of the surviving priests probably threw in their lot with their former rivals, the Pharisees, others may have converted to Christ. Acts 6:7 tells how at an earlier stage 'a large group of priests had made their submission to the faith', probably a pointer to an ongoing softening attitude towards Jesus and his followers among the priestly class as a whole.
33. *b. Berakoth* 28b-29a.

them be blotted out of the book of the living and let them not be written with the righteous.'[34]

Though primarily intended to unify Judaism along clear Pharisaic lines, the Twelfth Benediction effectively drove the Christian Jews (and some others), from the community, casting them out from the synagogue with its religious life and social network. How widespread the 'exclusion' from synagogue was practised is not known, but what seems certain from the emphasis given to it in John's gospel is that the community in which the gospel was formed experienced either such exclusion or the threat of it.[35]

Like the rest of the Jews these Christian Jews also had lost Temple and city and now they were excluded, or feared exclusion, from the synagogue, so they too had to re-define their identity in a new situation. As the Pharisees led the revival focused on the Torah and a comprehensive programme of Jewish religious life designed to replace the Temple and the sacrificial system, how could these Jewish Christians maintain their Jewish tradition with its rich cultic life and at the same time maintain their faith in Jesus?

As their Jewish neighbours gathered to pray and celebrate the festivals that recalled the great moments in their history, how could these Jewish Christians celebrate their heritage in the context of their faith in Jesus and their exclusion from the synagogue? They drew their inspiration from their own story, the story of Jesus. For these, especially those in the Johannine tradition with its roots in Jerusalem, the destruction of the Temple with its rituals, feasts and pilgrimages, brought home to them in a whole new way the realisation that in Jesus they had the presence of God and the saving work of redemption. Jesus was in fact the definitive Temple, altar and lamb of sacrifice. He had fulfilled the promise of the feasts and had appropriated to himself the cultic symbols of bread, water, light and sacred space associated with them.[36] With the coming of the Spirit-Paraclete

---

34. G. A.Yee, *op. cit.*, 23. The Genizah was the repository for manuscripts no longer in use because of damage or the wear and tear of age. The copy of the *Birkat haMinim* was found in the Cairo Genizah in 1898.

35. Jn 9:22 puts clear emphasis on the threat of excluding the parents of the blind man; Jn 12:42 speaks of the fear of expulsion which kept many from admitting to their belief in Jesus; Jn 16:2 contains Jesus' warning to the disciples that they will be expelled from the synagogue.

36. M. L. Coloe, *God Dwell With Us*, 3.

these Temple and cultic symbols passed to the community wherein Father, Son and Spirit dwell. In the gospel the Johannine Christians tell their story of Jesus from this deepening of theological perspective and from the standpoint of a group in tension with their erstwhile co-religionists and fellow citizens.

III

Study of the gospels has gone through many stages throughout history. Since the early days of the church, harmonisation of the gospels has been in vogue, putting the various accounts together to fill out a life of Christ. This is a noble and understandable endeavour. However, it tends to regard the gospels simply as biographies of Jesus and the exercise implies that each of the gospels is a defective biography needing to be supplemented by information from the other three. This approach can easily neglect the integrity of each account as a theological and literary whole. Since the Enlightenment a corresponding approach has been taken, though in a different guise. The various quests for the 'historical Jesus', defined differently by the different questers, have taken the focus off the gospels themselves in the search for the holy grail of a Jesus and his environment reconstructed from 'historical' data rather than a Jesus seen through the eyes of faith and the integral picture of a gospel.[37] Sources behind, and extraneous to, the canonical gospels have been sought. Much energy has been spent seeking these sources, from secular writings, archeological findings, and religious writings, including documents the early church regarded as lacking credibility, the so-called apocryphal documents. Furthermore, Mark's gospel was originally regarded as the most 'historical' gospel until it was rightly seen to be a very theological and subtly literary document.[38] Though a great deal was learned about Jesus and his times from these quests, no one 'historical' Jesus has emerged. The historical-critical method has given us a great deal of valuable information about Jesus and his world but it has given a fragmented jig-saw image.

Form Criticism came into vogue pointing to the literary

---

37. These two dimensions are conventionally referred to as the Jesus of History and the Christ of Faith.
38. W. Wrede's work on the Messianic Secret in Mark put paid to any ideas that Mark's gospel is a straightforward historical account. Written in 1901, an English translation *The Messianic Secret* was published in 1971 (London: Clarke).

forms in which the gospel material was cast during the process of oral transmission and to the social background in which they were developed. This further sharpened awareness of the complexity of the formation process. Then Redaction (or editorial) Criticism came to the fore. The mind of the author became the dominant goal of research. Comparison of texts for purposes of discovering editorial work further sharpened awareness of the production process, particularly in comparative studies in the synoptic gospels and between the synoptics and John. The spotlight then turned to communities in which the traditions were nurtured and applied to community needs and expressed in community language and thought categories. Again much was learned about the transmission process. On the negative side, no universally agreed sources, no agreed 'historical' Jesus and no agreed communities have emerged. On the positive side, great insight into the complexity of the process of transmission has been gained, and a positive reaction by way of a return to focusing on the text itself as a theological and literary whole has resulted.

I write this commentary from the standpoint of one who sees the work as a whole, the text as it now stands (with some well known variants). In dealing with sources, the 'historical' Jesus and the nature and composition of the communities in which the tradition was nurtured and transmitted, I do so only insofar as such information or speculation throws light on the text under examination and its place in the gospel as a whole. The author(s)/editors have shaped the final text from the sources, oral and written, at their disposal and in the process have produced a text that is a marriage of content and form. J. Ashton comments:

> ... no understanding of the book is possible if one loses sight of the simple fact that it is not a theological tract but a gospel. What the divine agent 'heard' from God is disclosed not in his words but in his life; the 'what' is displayed in the 'how'. The matter of the gospel, its true content, is indistinguishable from its form; the medium is the message.[39]

Furthermore, I see the gospel as an integral part of the whole canon of scripture, and consider exegesis as a science practised within the comprehensive view of the church. If one stands outside that comprehensive view one runs the risk of breaking up

---

39. J. Ashton, *op. cit.*, 553.

'the indivisible unity of the figure of Christ'.[40] Hans Urs von Balthasar states it very clearly:

> Jesus' word can be understood by all, but only in the light of his testimony of being the Son of God does it become truly clear. Moreover, only in relation to his death and resurrection does it attain the fullness of its meaning: Jesus' entire being is one single Word. This perfect being becomes manifest only from the testimonials of faith ... (which), all together, form a magnificent polyphony – not a pluralism in the contemporary sense ... The more facets we can view, the better we can grasp the unity of the inspiration. The possessor of this inspiration is the church, the early charisma of which was to compose the New Testament and establish its canon. Only her eye of faith, guided by the Holy Spirit, could see the whole phenomenon of Jesus Christ.[41]

IV

St John's gospel has its own particular *theology, style and structure*. Those familiar with the synoptic gospels[42] will notice immediately the 'high-descending' christology in John's gospel, that is, the portrayal of Jesus as the divine person who has descended from above and whose divinity shines through his life in the world. This christology is supported throughout by the titles used for Jesus and the metaphors applied to his life-giving relationship with his followers. His humanity, however, is also very much in evidence, particularly in his relationships. The portrayal of the Holy Spirit as the personal Paraclete is also unique to John among the gospels. The synoptic teaching about the kingdom of God/heaven is for the most part replaced by the emphasis on the Father-Son relationship and the life-giving teaching and work that the Son carries out on behalf of the Father. The emphasis on eschatology, the end of the world and the second coming of the Son of Man, are replaced in large measure in John's gospel by 'realised' eschatology, the teaching that eternal life has already begun in the here-and-now situation

---

40. H. U. von Balthasar, *op. cit.*, 65.
41. *Ibid.*
42. The gospels of Matthew, Mark and Luke, so called because they provide a 'synopsis' or common vision of Jesus and the ministry. It is possible to lay them side by side in parallel columns for purposes of comparison.

brought about by the saving work of the Father in Christ and through the gift of the Spirit-Paraclete.

The *structure and chronology* of the gospel is different from that of the synoptics. They have but one Passover feast and one journey of Jesus to Jerusalem. St John's gospel has three Passover feasts, from which the belief has emerged that Jesus' public ministry lasted approximately three years. This has facilitated, for example, the placing of the 'cleansing of the Temple' during his first visit to Jerusalem, and his words, deeds and controversies during many journeys to Jerusalem for the pilgrimage feasts. In addition, the synoptics describe the crucifixion as taking place on the feast of Passover, John has it taking place on the eve of the feast, a discrepancy that has given rise to a volume of literature about the date and the nature of the Last Supper, and whether or not it was a Passover meal.

St John's gospel has its own literary style. Instead of the parables and the short, memorable sayings (*logia*) of Jesus so typical of the synoptics, John's Jesus engages in lengthy discourses, dialogues and controversies which spell out the meaning of his teaching and actions. *Dialogues* sometimes become *monologues* as the partner fades out and Jesus keeps talking (as in the case of Nicodemus). There is great use of *irony* as the reader sees two contending levels of reality at work together. When the High Priest says 'it is good for one man to die for the people', his intention is to make Jesus a political scapegoat to ward off any threat from the Romans. The reader, however, is reminded by the narrator to hear the words on another level, where the death of Jesus is seen as gathering into salvation all the scattered children of God. *Misunderstanding* is another literary technique. The hearer misunderstands Jesus and so he has the opportunity to develop his point and explain himself further. Nicodemus thought he was saying that an adult must re-enter his mother's womb to be born anew, whereas Jesus was talking about total renewal of one's life through being born of water and the Spirit.

The *deeds* of Jesus are differently presented in John. First of all they are seen as an integral part of 'the Father's work' which Jesus has to 'bring to completion/perfection'. The two 'miracles' at Cana, the turning of water into wine and the healing of the royal official's son, are described as the first and second 'sign' (*sêmeion*). The term 'sign' therefore has been taken up and applied to the other 'miracle' stories in John's gospel. Whereas the synoptics describe many 'miracles' creating a cumulative effect and seeing them in the light of fulfilment of the prophecies such as those of Isaiah about giving sight to the blind, hearing to the deaf, freedom to captives and life to the dead, John on the other hand selects seven and uses them to explore more deeply and at greater length the significance of Jesus and his mission. The multiplication of the loaves, for example, leads to a multi-dimensional treatise on the Bread of Life, the healing of the blind man leads to a discussion about spiritual sight and blindness, and the raising of Lazarus provides the setting for Jesus to proclaim that he is the resurrection and the life.

St John's gospel is the gospel of the great *life-giving metaphors*. Jesus proclaims his life-giving relationship with the community in terms of his being the bread of life, the true vine, the way, the truth and the life, the light of the world, the good shepherd, the door of the sheepfold, the resurrection and the life and the giver of life-giving water.

The richness of St John's gospel, especially in its biblical allusions lies in the fact that it has an open-ended approach which introduces the reader to rich fields of imagery through allusions and 'generalising' or 'loose' quotations which often defy exact or exclusive location in the Old Testament. These allusions and 'quotations' function like the musical score of a film, keeping one's awareness sharpened to several levels of reality simultaneously, without defining and isolating them one at a time. The references to the Lamb of God are a case in point.[43] The paschal, apocalyptic and sacrificial lamb all come to mind as do the images of the servant who is led like a lamb to the slaughter and the prophet, innocent as a lamb, who is persecuted for his preaching. They are like threads running through a tapestry, at times very obvious, at other times rather subtle. Taken together, however, they produce the overall pattern which is greater than any single thread or group of threads. The richly revealing detail in imagery and allusions and the irony in the account serve as pointers to the invisible, as windows on the divine.

The gospel in many ways resembles a *trial* with the themes of *witness* and *judgement* running through it. Jesus is on trial throughout the gospel, but in keeping with the ironic stance of the gospel, it is those putting him on trial who are really under scrutiny. The themes of witness and judgement are all through

---

43. See the commentary on Jn 1:29, 36.

the gospel, but the accusations following the healing of the sick man at the Pool of Bethesda and the cure of the blind man at the Pool of Siloam, the meeting of the Sanhedrin following the raising of Lazarus, the Roman trial of Jesus by Pilate and the story of the adulteress, are particularly dramatic examples. These stories also illustrate the *dramatic* power and technique of St John's gospel.

The verbs of *perception* and *understanding* and how they open onto faith are also very much in evidence. So too is the *dual imagery* of light and darkness, truth and falsehood, life and death. This dualism is at the level of imagery dealing with spiritual and moral response and condition.[44] *Poetic structure* is in evidence in passages like the prologue and the final discourse and prayer of Jesus at the Last Supper. *Solemn oracular utterances*, especially in the 'Amen, amen, I say to you' pronouncements, play an important role in the gospel.

Passages which reflect one another in theme, language or location are placed at the opening and closing of the ministry, or used to section off a significant part of the text . These *inclusions* function like bookends at opposite ends of the entire text or serve to section off a significant portion within it. For example, the first and second miracles at Cana open and close a significant part of the early ministry. Similarly, the first miracle at Cana (the wedding) which introduces the Mother of Jesus and his *hour*, and the scene on Golgotha/Calvary with the Mother of Jesus and the Beloved Disciple who takes her into his home 'from that *hour*', open and close the public ministry of Jesus.

Literary structure or arrangement serves to highlight and interpret a text. In contemporary western society a storyteller, preacher or speechmaker tends to build up to a climactic finale and the punch line comes at the end. Even if the main point has already been introduced and repeated we expect a climactic moment of emphasis to conclude the story or discourse. In biblical literature, on the other hand, the emphasis is regularly placed at the central point of a discourse, allowing for a step by step approach to the central point and a parallel series of steps departing from it, like mirror images reflecting and interpreting each other. This *concentric* or *chiastic* structure could be represented as

---

44. It is not an ontological dualism springing either from the notion of good and evil as equally powerful and contending forces in the universe or from seeing spirit as good and matter as evil.

A-B-C-**D**-C-B-A. The trial of Jesus by Pilate is a case in point, where a series of scenes leads up to, and a corresponding series leads away from, the central scene, or pivot, which is the mock coronation of Jesus. The central scene focuses on Jesus as mock king and all the surrounding scenes deal with kingship and power. A simpler 'sandwich' approach highlights the central item between two parts of another story. For example, Peter's denials of Jesus are highlighted by the fact that the story of Jesus' interrogation by Annas is placed in the middle of Peter's denials. This sequence, known as *intercalation*, could be represented as A-**B**-A.

V

Ideally a serious study of any of the New Testament documents should be conducted from, and accompanied by, a reading of the Greek text. In reality, however, most students are still learning New Testament Greek and many general readers have little, if any, knowledge of the language. As every translation is but an approximation to the original, it is advisable, therefore, to follow more than one translation when making a serious study of the text. Words and expressions are very important in John and in translation they easily lose their impact and connotations. This is particularly true where a word group containing related noun, verb, adjective or adverb come from the same root, and are translated by very different words in English. In the commentary I frequently use italics for such related words. I also use italics for recurring words of particular significance, and for the transliteration into the Roman alphabet of Greek and Hebrew words and expressions. This last group I introduce gradually and translate until they should be quite familiar to the reader.

New Testament writers and readers knew the Old Testament from various sources. The Hebrew text had not yet been standardised as the Masoretic Text (MT) and so various traditions of the texts were probably available.[45] After the Exile the Jews for the most part became Aramaic speakers and, apart from scholars, seem for the most part to have become unfamiliar with

---

45. MT was produced by the Masoretes who were scholars of the Masorah (tradition). They gave the Hebrew text its final standard form around the eighth century AD. According to Jewish tradition this is exactly the same text as that edited by the rabbis in the period after the Fall of Jerusalem (70-100 AD).

Hebrew. The reading of Hebrew texts in the synagogue was therefore accompanied by an Aramaic translation-cum-interpretation of the text, known as a *Targum* (pl. *targumim*). Many Jews in New Testament times may have known their bible stories from these *targumim* and so they are often important for picking up allusions and references to the Old Testament as it was understood by the authors of oral and written material about Jesus.[46]

The Jews telling the story of Jesus against the background of the Old Testament stories were familiar with Jewish teaching and research methods and the commentaries they produced on Old Testament texts. The verb *darash* means 'to investigate, research, interpret' and the related noun form is *Midrash*, describing the commentary so produced. Two kinds of midrash were *Haggadah*, telling the story to inspire, and *Halakhah*, applying the text in a juridical and moral way.[47] These *midrashim* are very important for understanding how New Testament texts are woven around Old Testament themes and New Testament stories are told along parallel lines with stories in the Old Testament. A striking example is chapter six of St John's gospel which contains the story of the multiplication of the loaves and fishes, the coming of Jesus to the disciples over the water and the discourse on the Bread of Life. The chapter runs parallel to the events of the exodus and the gift of manna in the desert. In this sense it resembles in form a midrashic commentary, though it is dealing with another event and not just commenting on the Old Testament text.

Many readers of the New Testament were Greek speakers, Diaspora Jews and Gentiles who used the Greek translation of the Old Testament, known as the Septuagint (LXX).[48] This is particularly true in the case of the intended readers of St John's gospel. Many allusions in the text are to the Septuagint rather than a Hebrew text of the Old Testament. This was particularly apt as the gospel of John was used as a missionary document,

---

46. The *targumim* have been collected in the two great collections of rabbinic literature, the Palestinian Talmud and the Babylonian Talmud.

47. Haggadic Midrash is found in *Genesis Rabba* and Halakhic Midrash is found in *Mekilta on Exodus*.

48. So called because of the tradition that the Egyptian king, Ptolemy II (283-246 BC) brought seventy two scholars (six from each of the twelve tribes) to Alexandria to produce the translation for the library there and they produced it in seventy two days. It is usually represented as LXX. The Roman numerals LXX = 70.

both for the Greek-speaking Jews of the diaspora and for the Gentiles.

Though it is customary to include biblical references in the text itself, where possible I include them in the footnotes, to avoid breaking the flow of the text. At times, however, the text demands the inclusion of the references. Where a short passage is being studied I presume the reader is following the text of the gospel and so within that immediate passage I do not usually include the verse reference. Again this is for the purpose of smoother reading.

The Prologue Jn 1:1-18

1. THE FUNCTION OF THE PROLOGUE

The gospels preface their accounts of the public ministry of Jesus with theological reflections on his origin and identity. These highlight the source and nature of his ministry and foreshadow its course and final outcome. In so doing, they are in harmony with the classical practice of announcing the identity of the main character and giving essential background information concerning the events that are about to unfold. Matthew and Luke do this with the infancy narratives which contain the stories of Jesus' conception, birth and infancy, emphasising his human and divine origins, and with the genealogies which trace his human and spiritual heritage. Mark, on the other hand, employs a simple but profound christological formula introducing Jesus as 'Christ, Son of God'. John uses the prologue for this purpose.

The prologue in St John's gospel functions therefore as an overture, or promise of what is to come in the body of the gospel. It introduces the central character, establishes the main themes and provides a synopsis of the plot. It provides the reader with a privileged understanding of what is to follow. However, as this is not just a story acted out on the human stage, one asks: 'Who is the central character? Is it Jesus or the Father?' In fact it is both, since the unity of Father and Son functions as a single driving force throughout the gospel. '… the Father-Son language of the gospel of John is a prime example of the point that NT christology is formulated primarily in relational terms, and that it articulates the relationship of Jesus to God and God to Jesus'.[1] Throughout the gospel the attitudes and reactions of the other characters to the Son, mirror their attitude and reaction to the Father.

The prologue also introduces the themes of life, truth, witness, dwelling, glory and the world, together with the contrasting images of light and darkness, and the antithetical responses of acceptance and rejection, belief and unbelief, which are all pervasive in the story. As the themes introduced in the prologue subsequently unfold, the reader views the characters and events

---

1. M. M. Thompson, *The God of the Gospel of John*, 51.

with the all-knowing eye of one who has already been let in on
the secret of Jesus' origin and identity. This foreknowledge also
provides the ideal background for critical assessment of the
characters, and for the appreciation of the irony and dramatic effect in the various scenes and conversations.

> The omniscient prologue was almost indispensable in plays
> which exploited dramatic irony based on hidden identities.
> The revelation of Jesus' identity at the outset provides firm
> footing for the reader's reconstruction of hidden meanings
> and reception of suppressed signals behind the backs or
> 'over the heads' of the characters.[2]

This work of the prologue is continued throughout the gospel
by the explanatory comments of the narrator.[3]

Just as the first eleven chapters of Genesis serve as a theological, philosophical and anthropological introduction to the Bible
as a whole, and to the Pentateuch in particular, so also the prologue serves as a similar introduction to the gospel of John. It introduces the reader to the philosophical language, categories
and concepts of the time. It sets the scene for the theological,
christological and ecclesiological dimensions of the gospel. The
theological dimension is of two kinds. There is the general theology of the gospel in the sense of its religious concerns, language, concepts and categories. There is also the more focused
and specific *theo*logy, the portrayal of God, and this is facilitated
throughout the gospel by the high christology, both ontological
and functional.[4] 'There are unexpressed assumptions about God
present in the gospel, for Jesus' claim and significance is insepa-
rably connected with them'.[5] The ecclesiological outlook of the
gospel is the product of the faith-inspired vision, experience and
practice of those who received the Word-become-flesh and were
'given power to become children of God'.

It highlights also the negative response of the unbelieving
world and of 'his own people'.

---

2. R. A. Culpepper, *Anatomy of the Fourth Gospel,* 168, quoting P. W. Harsh, *A
Handbook of Classical Drama,* 316.

3. There are fifty nine such comments in all, ranging from straightforward translations of words to comments on the disciples' level of understanding and
knowledge of Jesus. cf R.A. Culpepper, *Anatomy,* 17, text and note 11.

4. High christology focuses on the divine dimension of Christ, his origin from the
Father, his 'coming down into the world' and the manifestations of the divine in
his ministry. 'Ontological' christology deals with the question of who he is and
functional christology deals with what he does.

5. W. Loader, *The Christology of the Fourth Gospel: Structures and Issues,* 140.

The prologue presents the main outline of the gospel narrative. It speaks of the pre-existence of the Word (*ho Logos*) in eternity and of his presence at creation, in the world, in his own place and finally among his own people. John (the Baptist) is sent by God to summon all to faith in the Word, the light of the world. Acceptance or rejection of the 'Word made flesh' provides a central dynamic of the gospel story. Those who accept the Word made flesh are empowered to become children of God and for them there is a new relationship of grace and truth, replacing the old covenant revealed through Moses, and based on the law. The Word, the unique Son, is ever in the Father's presence and he alone is the revealer who makes the Father known, for no one else has ever seen God.[6] In the subsequent discourses in the gospel Jesus speaks of knowing the Father because he has come 'from above' and the Father has sent him.[7] He is ever at the Father's side.[8] He speaks and acts in accordance with what he has learned from the Father.[9] He is the revealer *par excellence*. 'If you know me you will know my Father also … whoever has seen me has seen the Father.'[10]

As the prologue introduces the major themes it sets the scene and whets the appetite for what is to come. However, it cannot be properly understood until the work as a whole has been read. After one has read through the gospel, subsequent readings of the prologue can be much more rewarding, just as listening to the overture to an opera is more enjoyable, and has a more profound effect, when one has become familiar with the work as a whole. Great literature invites multiple reading.[11]

2. THE FORM OF THE PROLOGUE

Scholars have long argued that the prologue with its lofty language and poetic style has all the marks of a Christian hymn, one specially composed for the gospel or, more likely, of an older hymn already circulating in Johannine circles and now edited

---

6. Jn 1:18.
7. Jn 3:13, 17, 31, 34.
8. Jn 1:18.
9. Jn 3:31-36; 5:19f.
10. Jn 14:7,9.
11. James Joyce, for example, highlights this when he finishes his masterpiece *Finnegan's Wake* with the opening words of the work thus inviting a repeated reading. The first time reader may wish to read quickly through the commentary on the prologue and become more familiar with the body of the Gospel, then return to the prologue.

and adapted to deal with the main themes of the gospel.[12] Some
of these poems and related forms had their origin in worship
where careful theological reflection and artistic composition
prepared beforehand were further inspired by the promptings
of the Spirit. Psalms, hymns, and spiritual songs were central to
the theologising and worshiping activity of the Christians from
the earliest times right into the second century, a fact borne out
by Pliny the Younger who bears witness to the fact that that
which distinguished early Christians was 'the singing of hymns
to Christ as to a god'.[13] Christology in very large measure grew
out of worship with its hymns, credal statements, testimonia
and doxologies. It would not be too wide of the mark to say that
christology was conceived in liturgy and born in song. This
'worship-engendered' christology was a 'high' christology from
an early stage, that is, it looked to the glorified Christ, and celebrated his divine origins, life and glorification.

Keeping in mind the fact that the chapter and verse divisions
are not part of the original text, the reader looks for the 'natural'
divisions of the prologue by following the rhythm of language
and sequence of ideas.[14] One quickly notices that the poetic style
and rhythm are interrupted by the prose verses, some dealing
with John the Baptist,[15] others commenting on the contents of
the hymn.[16] Looking at the prologue without the prose verses
one can see a 'spiral' order of material when a new line opens
with the last word or idea of the previous one and sets that word
or idea in a new perspective, as for example, 'In the beginning
was *the Word*, and *the Word* was with God.'[17] However, in the

12. More likely because the language and concepts are not an exact match for
those in the body of the gospel. Some scholars have suggested a pre-Christian
gnostic style hymn, or a hymn about John the Baptist, as the source. However,
searching for an original source can be a distraction from the real task at hand
which is to look at the prologue as it now stands and examine its function in the
gospel as a whole.
13. Pliny, *Ep*. 10.96.7. cf Ben Witherington III, *John's Wisdom, A Commentary on the
Fourth Gospel*, 1995, 49f.
14. Chapter divisions were introduced into the bible by Stephen Langton,
Archbishop of Canterbury 1207–28, and the verse divisions were made by
Robert Estienne, French printer and publisher, for his 1551 edition of the New
Testament.
15. Jn 1:6-8, 15. He is not called the Baptist in John's gospel because his role as
witness is stressed. However, to avoid confusion with John the evangelist it is
expedient at times to use the term baptist.
16. Jn 1:13, 17, 18.
17. This spiral approach provides emphasis and clarity but it is not always easy
to maintain in translation.

final written text as we have inherited it, the prose verses are an integral part of the prologue, lending balance to structure and providing an interpretative key to the passage as a whole.

It must be noted also that no real agreement has emerged among scholars about the exact form and content of an original hymn. This has led commentators like C. K. Barrett and others to argue that there was no source and that the evangelist composed the prologue for its present setting and therefore the interpreter has only the present text as a guide in figuring out the structure and content of the prologue and how it relates to the rest of the gospel. He summed up his argument as: 'The prologue is not a jig-saw puzzle but one piece of solid theological writing. The evangelist wrote it all …'[18] Following this line of argument, R. A. Culpepper states: 'Even if the prologue contains an earlier hymn, attention needs to be paid to the structure of the present text apart from source analyses.'[19] T. L. Brodie argues that the hypothesis of a half-hidden hymn is unnecessary as the text was written originally as an interweaving of hymnic form, style and content with prosaic language, reflecting the soaring, poetic quality of the Word and the prosaic reality of human life. He states that the mixing of Word with flesh is reflected in the increasing mixing of poetry with prose, and the persistent failure of scholars to disentangle the poetry is a reflection of something more basic, that is, that God – insofar as God is known – cannot be disentangled from humanity.[20] Whether or not this hypothesis is correct, it makes practical sense in so far as the understanding of the text as it now stands is the primary concern of the interpreter, and as it stands it reflects a mixture of poetry and prose.[21]

Commentators view the structure of the prologue in different ways and there are differences in detail even between scholars following the same basic approach. Some see the prologue in a linear or chronological way with one point following the other, tracing the 'history' of the Word. R. E. Brown, for example, accepts the hypothesis of an original hymn, isolates the prose

---

18. C. K. Barrett, *The Prologue of St John's Gospel*, 27.
19. R. A. Culpepper, "The Pivot of John's Gospel", *NTS*, 27, 1.
20. T. Brodie, *The Gospel According to John: A Literary and Theological Commentary*, 134.
21. Other scholars who affirm the unity of the prologue are: P. Lamarche, M. Hooker, F. W. Schlatter, H. van den Bussche.

'additions' and divides the 'reconstructed original hymn' as follows.[22]

> I the Word with God, 1, 2.
> II the Word and Creation, 3, 5.
> III the Word in the World 10-12b.
> IV the Community's Share in the Word 14, 16.

> Explanatory verses added: 12c, 13, 17, 18.
> Inserts on John (the Baptist) 6-9, 15.

F. J. Moloney points out that the twofold reference to John the Baptist (vv 6-8 and15), 'which troubles most attempts to find a formal literary structure for John 1:1-18', may indicate a three-fold division of the prologue, with a statement and restatement of the same message, like waves following each other onto the shore, within each of the three sections.[23]

I the Word in God becomes the light of the world, 1-5.

II the incarnation of the Word, 6-14

III the revealer: the only Son turned toward the Father, 15-18. Also using the references to the Baptist as the dividing lines, Ignace de la Potterie divides the text into three parts (1-5; 6-14; 15-18) and sees a spiral arrangement in the complete text.[24] He sees the prologue as a triple spiral and considers the repetitiveness as a positive literary factor.

T. L. Brodie, assessing this division in the context of an overall acceptance of the approach of de la Potterie, makes the criticism that 1-5; 6-13; 14-18 would be a better division, because verse 14 introduces the 'final and climactic level' of the prologue, where the witness of John is now 'in the incarnation's shadow'.

Since the pioneering work by N. W. Lund in 1931 on the concentric or chiastic structural approach to the prologue, several scholars have followed his lead. M. E. Boismard, independently of Lund, also proposed a chiastic structure for the prologue. A chiastic structure is an arrangement of material whereby the same or parallel themes are reflected around a pivotal point. The emphasis is placed at the central point of a discourse, allowing for a step by step approach to the central point and a parallel series

---

22. R. E. Brown, *The Gospel according to St John*, Vol I, 22. A similar approach is followed by C. K. Barrett, *The Gospel According to St John*, 2nd ed, 149f, and G. R. Beasley-Murray, *John*. World Biblical Commentary 36, 5
23. F. J. Moloney, *The Gospel of John*, 34.
24. I. de la Potterie, 'Structure du Prologue du St Jean', *NTS* 30 (1984) 354-81.

of steps departing from it, like mirror images reflecting and interpreting each other. It could be graphically illustrated as A-B-
C-**D**-C-B-A, where D is the pivot around which the passage is
arranged. Scholars, however, have not agreed on locating the
pivot or centre of the concentric arrangement.[25] Lund regards v
13, 'who are born not of human stock or urge of the flesh or will
of man but of God' as the centre or pivot. R. A. Culpepper opts
for v 12, 'he gave authority to become children of God, to those
who received him, to those who believe in his name' as the
pivot. He points out that the climax of the prologue is, therefore,
neither a theological paradox ('the word became flesh') nor the
testimony of a privileged few ('and we beheld his glory'), but a
proclamation immediately relevant to every reader of the
gospel.[26] Interestingly, Boismard regards vv 12-13 together as
the pivot.

A different approach is that taken by Mary L. Coloe who
analyses the prologue as two interwoven strands, one reporting
the stages in the story of the Word in the third person, the other
witnessing to the same story in the first person, making it a personal testimony: the presence of the Word in the world (vv 3-5,
14), the witness of John the Baptist (vv 6-8, 15) and the arrival
and responses to the Word made flesh (vv 9-13, 16-17). In each
case there is a report in the third person followed by a personal
testimony in the first person. This reflects closely the witness
nature of the opening of the First Letter of John where there is
emphasis on 'seeing, hearing and touching with our hands'.[27]

In form and content the prologue resembles the hymns in
Philippians, Colossians and Ephesians.[28] These hymns are a
confession of faith in the risen and glorified Lord. Their 'high'
christology emphasises the divine status of Jesus, his coming
into the world and the consequences of his coming, especially
his salvific death and his return in glory to the Father.[29]
Although the return to the Father is not part of the prologue in St

---

25. N. W. Lund, 'The influence of Chiasmus upon the Structure of the Gospels',
A.T.R. xiii (1931), 42-46.
26. R. A. Culpepper. 'The Pivot of John's Prologue', *NTS* 27 (1981), 1-31; M. E.
Boismard, *St John's Prologue*, 1957, 15f.
27. M. L. Coloe, *God Dwells Among Us*, 18.
28. Phil 2:6-11; Col 1:15-20; Eph 1:3-14.
29. High christology emphasises the divine origins and status of Jesus. In John's
gospel the christology is 'high' also in its functions, as Jesus is doing the work of
the Father in a uniquely divine way. The descent into the world, a period in the
world and a return to the Father are often described as resembling a great
parabola.

John's gospel,[30] it becomes a major theme in the body of the gospel, where it is presented in terms of his 'departure' and his 'glorification'. This provides the crowd, his enemies and his disciples with the opportunity of questioning him about where he is going. The reader, however, knows from the start that he is returning to the Father. The theme of departure and return to the Father also supplies the narrative time frame as the story moves towards the hour (*hôra*) of Jesus, the appointed time (*kairos*) of his departure from the world and the return in glory to the Father.

The prologue also resembles the Wisdom tradition, especially the hymns, where God in God's knowability, visibility and audibility was to be encountered through the wisdom created at the beginning of God's work of creation. The hymns describe personified Wisdom accompanying God at creation as she delights in the work and then descends into the world and issues an invitation to her banquet.[31] This is graphically described in texts like Proverbs and Sirach (Ecclesiasticus) where Wisdom is said to come into the world to take up residence among the people of Israel.[32] She prepared a banquet and issued her invitation to all who sought wisdom. Acceptance or rejection of the invitation is a motif of the wisdom tradition just as acceptance or rejection of the Word is a central theme in the prologue and provides an all pervasive dynamic in the gospel proper. Like the *Logos*, Wisdom was with God at creation and remains forever with God.[33]

3. THE CONTENT OF THE PROLOGUE

Jn 1:1 In the beginning was the Word, and the Word was with God, and the Word was God. 2 He was in the beginning with God.

The gospels are rich in allusions to the Old Testament. They create an atmosphere and draw the reader's attention to horizons and experiences against which one can appreciate both the mystery of God and the divine presence in creation and history. For John this presence culminates in the momentous event of the Word becoming flesh, dwelling among us and our seeing his glory.[34]

John looked to the Old Testament writings for inspirational

---

30. Where the Son is described as being ever in the bosom of the Father, Jn1:18.

31. W. Carter, 'The Prologue and John's Gospel: Function, Symbol and the Definitive Word', *JSNT* 39 (1990), 47.

32. Prov 8:22-31; Sir 1:26; 19:20; 24:23. Wis 9:9

33. Prov 8:22f; Sir 1:1.

34. Jn 1:14.

passages and appropriate texts to articulate his faith in Jesus' divine sonship. The Genesis account of creation is his starting point. The opening words of St John's gospel, *in (the) beginning*, strike a chord and evoke a mood as they remind the reader of the first words of the Bible. Although the account of creation immediately springs to mind, the reader's attention is drawn beyond creation and directed into the life of God to encounter the eternal pre-existent *Logos*. The prologue begins its account in eternity with the Father before presenting the role of the *Logos* in creation and history, showing that the Word who was to become a human being, Jesus of Nazareth, already existed at the beginning. The pre-existence of the *Logos* 'with God' (*pros ton theon*), signifies not only 'accompaniment' or 'presence to' but a dynamic relationship with the Father.[35] This relationship continues after the Word became flesh, as is evident from the final verse of the prologue which describes 'the unique one' as 'existing in the bosom of the Father (*eis ton kolpon tou Patros*)'.[36]

Word/Logos

The choice of the term 'Word'/*Logos*, in the prologue is enriched by many strands of tradition. *Dabar (Word), Wisdom, Torah (Law)* and *Memra (Word)*[37] are all terms which speak of God's communion with creation and humanity, especially with the chosen people where God's presence and work in the world bring life and light. These traditions provide the theology and insight influencing the choice of the term *Logos* and contribute to the language, imagery and poetry of the prologue. In Hebrew *dbr* (word) signifies both word and deed. It can mean a spoken word, an action or an event. Word and deed together form a continuum in biblical thought – in speaking one acts and in acting one speaks. In the Hebrew scriptures the first creative action of God was to 'speak' and this creative word functioned as an action which brought all things into being. Thus all things came into being through the already existing Word which God voiced at creation. The Word ordered all things in creation and human affairs. Without it nothing came into or remained in existence. The psalmist affirmed: 'By the word of the Lord the heavens were

---

35. God, or as the Greek text puts it *ho theos* (the God), signifies the Father and *theos* (god) without the definite article points to the divinity of the *Logos*, emphasising 'divine being' while maintaining a distinction from the Father.
36. Jn 1:18.
37. *Memra* in Aramaic means 'word', but has a deeper significance as used in the Targumim, where it is used more or less as a surrogate for God.

made' and Solomon addressed the Lord in the words: 'O God of my fathers, lord of mercy who made all things by your word, and in your wisdom have fitted man to rule the creatures'.[38] The word gives life and has healing power.[39] It preserves the believer and restores those poisoned by the serpent.[40] But it is not only creative, it is also revelatory, making God's plan known for the world and the chosen people. The scripture declares solemnly that the Word of the Lord came to the prophets.[41] It not only revealed information, it challenged and transformed the prophets and they in turn challenged, supported, chastised or consoled the people. They regularly prefaced their sermons with 'Thus speaks the Lord', interspersed them with similar reminders that the word being spoken was the word of God, and closed with: 'These are the words of the Lord'.[42] Amos proclaimed: '... the Lord God does nothing, without revealing his secret to his servants the prophets' and highlighted its effectiveness when he said: 'The Lord God has spoken: who can but prophesy?'[43] In the call of Jeremiah the Lord promised: 'I have put my words in your mouth'[44] and the prophet complained later that the word was 'like a burning fire shut up in my bones. I am weary with holding it in ...'[45] Though the word is not personified in the Old Testament it is seen as having a quasi-substantial existence with its own power and energy. It comes from the mouth of God and returns only when it has achieved its purpose.[46] The Wisdom tradition speaks of the word in dynamic and almost personal terms. 'When peaceful silence lay over all, and night had run the half of her swift course, down from the heavens, from the royal throne leapt your all-powerful Word'.[47] Seen against this background, Jesus is now the incarnation of the creative and prophetic word and so he is the prophet *par excellence* who makes known the mind and life-giving work of God.

The Wisdom tradition celebrates the wisdom whereby God

38. Ps 33:6; Wis 9:1.
39. Deut 32:46f; Ps 107:20
40. Wis16:26, 12.
41. Hos 1:1; Joel 1:1 cf Is 6:1-13, Jer 1:4:19; 20:7-18; 30:1; 32:1 Ezek 2:8-3:3
42. Am 1:3, 6, 8, 9, 11, 13; 2:1, 3, 4, 6, 16; Jer 30:5, 12, 18; 31:2, 7, 10, 20.
43. Am 3:7f.
44. Jer 1:9. cf Ezek 3:1-3 'eat this scroll...'
45. Jer 20:9.
46. Isa 55:11.
47. Wis 18:14f (JB).

designed and sustains the heavens and the earth, directs history
and inspired the Torah. It celebrates God as creator and
Sovereign Lord of heaven, earth, history and humankind.
Wisdom was created to be the instrument or agent of God.
Wisdom is personified and described as an aura of the might of
God, a pure effusion of the glory of the Almighty.[48] Like an
omnipotent and all-embracing word, she came from the mouth
of the Most High and filled the earth like a mist. She dwelt in the
presence of God. Her tent was in the heights and her throne in a
pillar of cloud. She sought a place to pitch her tent and she
pitched it in Jacob, making Israel her inheritance.[49] Personified
Wisdom is an expression or manifestation of God's communion
with creation and humanity. The Wisdom literature responds to
the perennial human question about the knowability of God. In
seeking the fount of Wisdom, one seeks the accessibility of the
divine word and the knowability, visibility and audibility of the
creator. Wisdom is said to have come from the mouth of the
Most High, a concept that likens personified wisdom to a
word.[50] Wisdom was with God at the creation and remains forever with God, like the Word become flesh who is ever in the
bosom of the Father.[51] Wisdom and word are parallel concepts
in the prayer of Solomon: 'O God of my ancestors and lord of
mercy, who have made all things by your word, and by your
wisdom have formed humankind to have dominion over the
creatures you have made …'[52] The Qumran Community in its
Rule reflected on God's activity in creation in words reminiscent
of the treatment of Wisdom in the Old Testament and of the
Word in St John's gospel. They may well reflect a synthesising of
concepts of Word, Wisdom and Torah. 'All things came to pass
by his knowledge. He establishes all things by his design and
without him nothing is done.'[53]

Acceptance or rejection of Wisdom is a motif running
through the tradition. 'Wisdom came to make her dwelling
place among the children of men, and found no dwelling
place.'[54] Baruch states: 'You have forsaken the fountain of wis-

---

48. Wis 7:25f.
49. Sir 24:1-13.
50. However, the actual term 'word' is not used as a designation for wisdom.
51. Prov 8:22f; Sir 1:1; Jn 1:18.
52. Wis 9:1f.
53. 1 QS 11:11.
54. En 42:2

dom'.[55] The Wisdom tradition has numerous exhortations to learn from Wisdom who invites people to her banquet, to eat her bread, a metaphor for accepting learning and instruction. Light and darkness figure in the imagery of wisdom and folly. 'I saw that wisdom excels folly as light excels darkness.'[56] The fruit of wisdom is life. 'He who finds me finds life.'[57] In similar vein the Word is associated with light and life in the prologue, and throughout the gospel, and absence or rejection of the Word is seen as darkness. Although the wisdom hymns influenced the form, language and imagery of the prologue there is a very great difference in meaning. Personified wisdom is described as having been created, but the *Logos* of the prologue is no creature but *theos*, divine being which pre-existed. The *Logos* is not just a literary or theological concept. It is not just active in Jesus, like the word in the prophet or wisdom in the sage. It is embodied in him. The *Logos* became a human being.

In later rabbinic writings, the Torah/Law is idealised and Word and Wisdom are regarded as finding their ultimate expression in the Torah. Torah and 'the word of the Lord' are at times almost interchangeable terms as evidenced in the parallelism in Isaiah's prophecy: 'Out of Zion shall go forth the Law, and the Word of the Lord from Jerusalem'.[58] The identification of wisdom and Torah finds particular expression in Sirach and Baruch.[59] Sirach described wisdom as 'the law which Moses commanded us' and promised that 'whoever holds to the Law will receive wisdom'.[60] Baruch, speaking of wisdom, develops the theme in these terms 'the book of the commandments of God, the law that endures forever'.[61] Torah is described in Proverbs as light[62] and the psalmist in praising the Law says that God's word is a light.[63] Torah, like Wisdom, is associated with light and life, as is the *Logos* in the gospel. Just as word and wisdom deal with God's creation and sovereignty, so now the Torah is seen as having been created before all things and hav-

---

55. Bar 3:12.
56. Eccl 2:13.
57. Prov 8:35.
58. Isa 2:3 (JB).
59. Sir 24:23ff; cf Bar 4:1-4. In Sirach their functions are presented in similar order.
60. Sir 24:23; 15:1.
61. Bar 4:1ff.
62. Prov 6:23.
63. Ps 119:105. some LXX mss have 'Law' instead of 'Word'.

ing served as the pattern for creation. Those who observe the
Torah will live.[64] The rabbis taught that studying the Torah
leads one to the life of the age to come.[65] They also taught that
the Torah was the supreme example of God's loving kindness
and fidelity.[66] The text in the psalm which reads 'All your ways
are grace and truth'[67] is interpreted in the midrashic commentary: '*Grace,* that means God's acts of love; *truth,* that means the
Torah'.[68]

The rabbinic and targumic literature used various techniques
to avoid using the divine name, speaking of the divine presence,
and attributing actions or attitudes to God. A striking example is
to be found in the targumic tradition of Aramaic interpretations
of the Pentateuch, where the term *memra,* word, is used more
than six hundred times. It is not simply a translation of 'word' or
'word of the Lord' or a periphrasis for the divine name, but functions almost as a surrogate for God, signifying the presence and
power of God in the world. The *memra* is the way God becomes
present to Israel in a personal way. The *memra* creates, reveals
and saves. The targumic literature attributes to the *memra* divine
actions attributed to God in the biblical texts themselves. God is
said to create through the *memra*: 'From the beginning with wisdom the *memra* of the Lord created and perfected the heavens
and the earth.'[69] Commenting on the first light at creation, it
says: 'The *memra* of the Lord was the light and it shone.'[70] God is
seen to act on behalf of the people and communicate with them
by means of the *memra*. The biblical 'I will be with you' becomes
'My *memra* will be your support'.[71] In the biblical text Moses is
said to bring the people out of the camp to meet God. In the targum they are described as being brought to meet the *memra* of
God.[72] The function of *memra* in creation, presence and saving
action forms a close parallel with the functions already attributed to Word, Wisdom and Torah.

Logos was also a very meaningful term in Hellenistic culture

---

64. Bar 4:1-4
65. *Pirqe Aboth* 7:6
66. *hesed* and *emet*
67. *hesed* and *emet*
68. Midrash Ps. on Ps 25:10. cf Dodd, *Interpretation,* p. 82
69. *Tg. Neof.* on Gen 1:1.
70. *Tg. Neof.* on Ex 12:42.
71. *Tg. Onk.* on Ex 3:12.
72. *Tg. Onk.* on Ex 19:17.

and Greek philosophy where it carried the connotations of a
principle of order and finality, the primary power and rational
order in the world,[73] and the stable element in a world of flux.[74]
Many of the first readers of St John's gospel belonged to this cultural background. The term *logos* was therefore familiar to them
and proved an effective medium for conveying the theology of
the Word made flesh to believers of Gentile background as it led
them from the *logos* of philosophy, which was an impersonal,
created, principle of order and finality, to the biblical *Logos*,
which is not just a rational force or cosmic plan but the personal
communication of a personal God. 'The Logos of Philo is not the
object of faith and love. The incarnate Logos of the fourth gospel
is both lover and beloved; to love him and to have faith in him is
of the essence of that knowledge of God which is eternal life.'[75]

The concept of *Logos* facilitates the reader's understanding of
the nature of a God-centred universe and a God directed history.
Such an approach facilitated the Fathers in their portrayal of a
fruitful marriage between pagan and biblical use of the *Logos*. It
fits comfortably into the worldview of philosophers from Plato
to Plotinus who see a world beyond our own and the ultimate
and most important realities behind the visible and tangible.
These realities can be brought into the contemplative gaze of the
human attribute called *nous* (mind). The language that arises
from *nous* to articulate what it perceives to be true is well expressed by *logos* which represents the questing intellect, the
words articulating the quest and the reality discovered. The
logos produces the *logoi* (words or discourse).[76] In the prologue
we see how one's own *logos* can be illuminated by the *Logos* of
God.[77] This fits admirably the mindset of the Greek Fathers like
Origen but its fluidity is replaced in the Latin west by a more
static, technical understanding as for example where Augustine

---

73. Philo of Alexandria endeavoured to knit together Greek philosophy and the
biblical understanding of God's creative plan by his use of *logos*. This would
have been the understanding of persons who lived in the cultural milieu of the
diaspora Jews, like Philo, who used Greek language and ideas to express the
riches of biblical tradition. He saw God's *logos* giving meaning and plan to the
universe. Many of the first Jewish and Gentile readers of the gospel would have
shared this cultural milieu.
74. Heraclitus of Ephesus in the sixth century BC saw *logos* as the principle which
made all things an ordered *kosmos* in spite of constant change.
75. C H Dodd, *op. cit.*, 73.
76. C. Luibhéid, *Exploring John's Gospel: Reading, Interpretation, Knowledge*, 28f.
77. Ibid,40.

contemplates the meaning of *Verbum* (The Word) and asks: 'What sort of Word must that be which is both spoken and does not pass away? ... Look at what the Word has made and you will understand what the Word is.'[78]

To sum up, the term *Logos* draws together from many traditions a wealth of insight into the presence of God in creation and history.

God/ho theos/theos

The Greek word *theos* means 'god' and in its wide variety of uses it has many different connotations when it describes or defines a being as 'god'. The term *theos* was used broadly in the contemporary pagan world for all kinds of 'heavenly beings', major and minor divinities and human beings such as emperors and kings who possessed outstanding qualities or needed a great deal of flattery. It was applied in various ways to beings as different as the chief gods Zeus or Jupiter Capitolinus and emperors who were offered or claimed for themselves divine titles, like Alexander, Caligula, Nero and Domitian. Among the Jews who spoke Greek and used the LXX, the Greek translation of the Old Testament, one looks to the writings of Philo, who was contemporary with the early New Testament period, to examine the use of the term. One sees a sharp distinction between his use of the term *theos* with and without the definite article. For Philo, on the one hand, *ho theos* signifies the one true God, the God of Israel, the Creator and Sovereign Lord, God with the capital letter, so to speak. On the other hand, *theos*, without the article, can signify a being that reflects in some way the divinity of God through appointment as God's agent and possession of some divine prerogative or power. Philo is in line with Old Testament usage. The LXX used *theos* to translate *el, elim, elohim*. These terms had a broad application before *elohim* was marshalled into meaning the One God. Angels, judges, heavenly beings, Moses, Melchizedek,[79] all had these terms applied to them in certain circumstances. *Theos* is used to translate them and so can reflect this broader usage. In Exodus, for example, Moses is described as being 'god' to Aaron and Pharaoh. Moses is told: '(Aaron)

---

78. St Augustine, *Homily* 1:8,16. cf C. Luibhéid, *op. cit.*, 41.
79. 11 Q Melchizedek applies lines of Pss 7 and 82 to Melchizedek describing him in terms of the divine judge, and possibly associating him with Michael, one of the Elohim or heavenly beings. cf Thompson, *op.cit.*, 38.

shall speak for you to the people; and he shall be a mouth for
you, and you shall be to him as God'[80] and 'I shall make you
God to Pharaoh.'[81] But what does *theos* exactly predicate of
Moses? This is a classic example of the role of the agent or *shaliach*. It shows him to be the agent of God, authorised to speak and
act on God's behalf and in carrying out the task of agent he is
empowered and protected by God. He is in turn to be respected
and responded to with the same obedience and reverence due to
the one who sent him. To exercise such functions or claim such
honour without divine commission and approval was blasphemy.
Above all the agent was never to seek or accept worship except
that directed to the One who sent him. Only by way of reflection
of the divine and by divine commission could such prerogatives
be exercised. Commentaries and explanations of these passages
were strictly controlled by biblical precedent and the *targumim*
and *midrashim* and writers like Philo are careful to interpret
these texts in a way that does not lead to misunderstanding
about the absolute monotheism of Israelite religion.[82] Latin preserved a useful distinction between *deus* and *divus*, but Greek
tended to use *theos* with or without the definite article, rather
than an adjectival form such as *theios*.

Philo's understanding of, and language about, God is very
heavily influenced by his Platonism. He is concerned about
maintaining a distinction between *the One who is*, who is 'truly'
God, and who is immaterial, from the multiple manifestations of
the powers of God in the physical world. Philo's thought at least
demonstrates the way in which the term *theos* can be used to denote both the one true God, the Most High, and the manifestations of that God in visible and other forms.

Though John's gospel does not share the same philosophical
questions and speculations as Philo, it does, however, also use
'*theos*/God' to speak both of the one unseen God and of the

---

80. Ex 4:16. The LXX renders the Hebrew *w'atah tihyeh lô l'elohim* as *su de autôi esêi
ta pros ton theon, i.e. you shall be for him in things appertaining to God.*
81. Ex 7:1.
82. Targum (pl. targumim) was a free translation into Aramaic of the Hebrew
text of the Old Testament made for use in the synagogue when the people no
longer understood the original Hebrew. The targum tended to be a free translation incorporating a deal of interpretation. Midrash (pl. midrashim) was a teaching of doctrinal, legal or moral character which aimed at interpreting a biblical
text. Both throw light on how the scriptures were understood and interpreted in
a community. As such they can throw light on the early Christian understanding
of OT texts and how they were interpreted.

Logos, the Word of God, who in becoming flesh manifested God's glory (1:14).[83] To designate that 'visible' manifestation of God, Philo also employs the concept of the *Logos*, but there is quite a difference between the use of *Logos* in Philo and John. C. H. Dodd put it well:

> The Logos, which in Philo is never personal, except in a fluctuating series of metaphors, is in the gospel fully personal, standing in personal relations both with God and with men, and having a place in history. As a result, those elements of personal piety, faith and love, which are present in Philo's religion but not fully integrated into his philosophy, come to their own in the gospel.[84]

What does it mean to predicate *theos* of the Word in the context of the prologue? First of all, it should be noted that *theos* is used without the definite article when speaking of the Word and of the Son, but it is also used with and without the definite article even when referring to the God of Israel, the Father of the only Son. In verse one the Word is described as being with God (*pros ton theon*), using the definite article. However, there is no definite article in verse eighteen, 'no one has ever seen God (*theon*)', though the God of Israel, Father of the only Son is clearly meant. It is clear therefore that *theos* means the same as *ho theos* in this sentence. From this lack of a sharp distinction it can be seen that the use of *theos* and *ho theos* in the prologue is more fluid than in the works of the Jewish writer Philo. This fluidity of the term *theos* within the prologue, with *theos* without the article applied both to the One God and to the Word places the predication of *theos* with the Word in an entirely different category to any of the above examples from Old Testament and other writings. It serves not to draw a distinction between God and non-God, but between God and Word, and Father and Son within the sphere of the Divine.

The implications of this identification are in keeping with the emphasis on the pre-existence of the Word *pros ton theon* and the eternal existence *eis ton kolpon tou patros*.[85] They are further strengthened by the appellation *monogenês huios* (or *theos*), unique Son (or God).[86] The Word was *theos*, became *sarx*, exer-

---

83. cf M. M. Thompson, *op.cit*, 37.
84. C. H. Dodd, *The Interpretation of the Fourth Gospel*, 73.
85. 'with God' and 'in the bosom of the Father'.
86. variant readings.

cised divine powers and received divine honours. This divinity is emphasised throughout the gospel by the functional christology whereby the two powers reserved to God alone are exercised by the one whom the Father sent, the powers of giving life and exercising judgement. The divinity is further evidenced by the unity of purpose and activity of Father and Son as seen in the exercise of God's life-giving power on the Sabbath and Jesus' claim: 'My Father is working still and I work'[87] and his claim at the Feast of Dedication: 'The Father and I are one.'[88] The charge of blasphemy followed the obvious exercise of divine prerogative and power and the claim to be one with the Father. So too the acceptance of worship by Jesus from the man born blind and Thomas further illustrates the point.[89]

When the prologue states that the Word was God (*theos ên ho logos*), how is it to be translated? In the light of the preceding discussion, and of the fact that the noun form *theos* is used, not the adjectival *theios*, it is clear that an adjective such as 'divine' on its own is too weak a translation. Accurate translation demands at least a corresponding noun in this case, and in English it needs in addition a qualifying adjective as in 'The Word was *divine-being*', unless one uses the traditional translation 'The Word was God.'

3 All things came into being through him, and without him not one thing came into being. What has come into being 4 in him was life, and the life was the light of all people. 5 The light shines in the darkness, and the darkness did not overcome it.

In its origin all creation was shaped by the *Logos*. Human beings were enlivened and illumined by the *Logos* which was the source of life and light. The combination of life and light was so widespread in religious literature of early Christian times that one can speak of a 'liturgical formula that combines life and light'.[90] In the Wisdom tradition, both are seen as products of Wisdom. In the Wisdom of Solomon Wisdom is seen as the 'very life breath of God' and as 'the effulgence of pure light'.[91] The combination is commonplace in the Hermetic Literature, especially in the hymns, and in the Hellenistic Jewish outlook of

87. Jn 5:17-20.
88. Jn 10:30.
89. Jn 9:38; 20:28.
90. C. H. Dodd, *op.cit.*,19.
91. Wis 7:25-27.

Philo where light symbolism is found everywhere in his writing. The possible sources for this combination are Platonic philosophy and Old Testament passages such as Ps 26 (27) which proclaims: 'The Lord is my light and my saviour' and Ps 35 (36) which states: 'With thee is the fountain of life, in thy light we shall see light.'[92] Philo states that not only is the Lord 'my light' but he is the archetype of all light, more primitive and higher than every archetype.[93] The Johannine equivalent is: 'In him was life and the life was the light of human beings' and 'God is light and in him there is no darkness at all.'[94] The Philonic idea of *archetypon phôs*, archetypal light, is well matched in the Johannine writings by the phrase *phôs alêthinon*, 'true light', but whereas the former is an intellectual concept the latter opens onto the moral character and embraces the values of the covenantal relationship or communion between God and the people. The personal dimensions of the Father-Son relationship underpin this communion. The Son comes into the world as the Word who brings life from the Father and as the Light who reveals the Father and the Father's gift of eternal life.

Life/Zôê
The pre-existent life of the *logos* in eternity with God is highlighted by the repeated use in the prologue of the verb *ên* (was), the imperfect of the verb 'to be' in its absolute and predicative uses. Its significance is reflected repeatedly in the 'I am' (*egô eimi*) proclamations[95] of Jesus' ministry where he refers to himself in terms that recall the revelation to Moses of the divine name at the burning bush, a name which focused on the divine existence in the formula, regularly translated as, 'I am who I am'.[96] The revelation of the divine name is followed by the commission to Moses to go to Pharaoh and say '*I am* has sent me to you.' These are translated into Greek in the Septuagint as *ego eimi ho ôn* (I am the one who is) and *ho ôn apestalken me* (*the one*

---

92. Pss 26 (27):1; 35 (36):9.
93. Philo, *De Somn.* 1.75.
94. Jn 1:4; I Jn 1:5.
95. *ego eimi* is used in an absolute sense in Jn 8:24, 28, 58; 13:19; with understood predicate but absolute overtones in Jn 6:20; 18:5; in a participial phrase with absolute overtones in Jn 4:26; with predicates that deal with life and life-giving power in Jn 6:35, 51; 11:25; 14:6; 15:1, 5 and with the related predicates of light and light of the world in Jn 8:12; 9:5.
96. Ex 3:14

who is sent me).[97] The eternal existence of the Word with the Father is summed up in the final sentence of the Prologue in a similar participial phrase, *ho ôn eis ton kolpon tou Patros*, 'the one who is in the bosom of the Father'. This eternal existence stands out in contrast to *egeneto*, *gegonen* and *genesthai* (came to be) which illustrate the finite existence of all creation, and all human beings who 'came to be', a finite existence mentioned specifically in the case of John (the Baptist) and Abraham.[98] So too *egeneto* is used for the beginning in time of the human life of the Word made flesh, highlighting the contrast with the eternal pre-existence (*ên*) of the *Logos*.

A very significant aspect of the eternal pre-existence of the *Logos* is borne out in the statement 'in him was life'. It is emphasised in the body of the gospel in Jesus' declaration that 'as the Father has life in himself so he has granted the Son also to have life in himself'.[99] By command of the Father Jesus exercises sovereignty over his own life. This is borne out in the teaching about the ideal shepherd who lays down his life for his sheep. 'I lay down my life in order to take it up again. No one takes it from me, but I lay it down of my own accord. I have power to lay it down and I have power to take it up again. I have received this command from my Father.'[100] Similar emphasis is found in Jesus' declaration at the Last Supper: 'I am the Way, the Truth and the Life',[101] and on the occasion of the raising of Lazarus: 'I am the Resurrection and the Life.'[102]

The Word already existed when God spoke and all things came into being. All life flowed through the Word. Not alone has the Word made flesh, the Son (of God), the Son of Man, life in himself, but he has power to communicate that life to others.[103] 'As the Father raises the dead and gives them life, so also

---

97. Ex 3:14. The Greek translation of Isaiah makes frequent use of the *ego eimi* formula. Isa 41:4; 43:10; 46:4; 48:12 (cf 45:10). In Isa 51:12 *ego eimi* is followed by a participial phrase *ego eimi ho parakalôn se*, cf Jn 1:18 *ho ôn eis ton kolpon tou Patros* and Jn 4:26 *ego eimi ho lalôn soi*. In Hellenistic Judaism *ho ôn* and sometimes *to ôn* were used as designations for God.

98. In contrast to the multiple use of *ên* for the *Logos* (1:1), *egeneto and gegonen* are used of 'everything' (1:3), *egeneto* is used of John (Jn 1:2) and *genesthai* of Abraham (8:58).

99. Jn 5:26

100. Jn10:18ff.

101. Jn 14:6

102. Jn 11:25

103. In some texts Son, in others Son of Man.

the Son gives life.'[104] 'I have come that they may have life and have it to the full.'[105] This is borne out most dramatically at the raising of Lazarus when Jesus declares that he is the Resurrection and the Life.[106] He is the giver and sustainer of life and this is reflected in the metaphors of life-giving water, life-giving bread, and life giving-vine. As John speaks of living water and a fountain welling up to eternal life, the imagery of God as fountain of life springs to mind. God's accusation against the people in the sermon of Jeremiah, 'They have left me, the fountain of life', is commented on by Philo: 'God therefore is the primeval fountain ... For God alone is the cause of the soul and intelligent life. For matter is a dead thing, but God is something more than life; he is, as he himself says, "the perennial fountain of life".'[107] Jesus promises the Samaritan woman that if she asks he will give her 'living water ... a spring that wells up to eternal life' and at the Feast of Tabernacles he promised 'rivers of living water' for those who believe.[108] Putting this life-giving power in the overall context of his mission as revealer sent by the Father, Jesus says, 'I am the Way, the Truth and the Life.'[109] It is by revealing the Father who sent him that he leads his followers to eternal life. 'Eternal life is this, to know you the only true God and Jesus Christ whom you have sent.'[110] 'He who has seen me has seen the Father'.[111] In salvation as in creation all life comes through him. 'Through the gift of life given by the one sent by God there is the possibility of new life and the way to God is opened up'.[112]

Jesus' sums up the purpose of his ministry in the saying: 'I have come that they may have life (*zôê*) and have it to the full' and this is reflected in the stated purpose of the gospel which was 'written that you may believe that Jesus is the Christ, the Son of God, and that believing this you may have life (*zôê*) in his name'.[113] The significance of the theme of life is seen from the fact that *zôê* is used thirty-six times throughout the gospel, sev-

---

104. Jn 5:21.
105. Jn 10:10
106. Jn 11:25f
107. Philo, *De Fuga*, 197f.
108. Jn 4:10,14.
109. Jn 14:6
110. Jn 17:3
111. Jn 14:9
112. M. Hogan, *Seeking Jesus of Nazareth*, 131, Columba Press, Dublin, 2001.
113. Jn 10:10; 20:31.

enteen times combined with *aiônios*, eternal. The corresponding verb *zên* is used seventeen times and the verb *zôopoiein*, to give life, three times. *Zôê aiônios* is a favourite expression of the gospel and first letter of John. Elsewhere the New Testament tends to use *zôê* on its own. The tendency in the Old Testament is to see life in terms of earthly well being, prosperity and days blessed by God. Later the apocalyptic tradition began to speak of an age to come when life would be immeasurably better than in the present age.[114] Daniel spoke of eternal life in the sense of life beyond the grave.[115] Jesus responds to Martha's understanding of a future resurrection with the statement that he himself is the resurrection and the life and that those who believe in him have already begun to live eternal life: 'The one who believes in me, even if he should die, shall live, and whoever lives and believes in me will never die.'[116]

Light/*Phôs*
God's presence in creation and in history was a light in the world, particularly in the history of the chosen people. Creation, Wisdom and Torah reflected that light. The darkness of sin, disbelief and non-acceptance in the world did not overcome the light. In Christ, the true light, the Light of the World has come. This is the ultimate revelation and the ministry is full of references to the light and its acceptance or rejection. Those who reject him reject the light and are aligned to the unbelieving world. They come under the judgement because 'the light has come into the world and people loved darkness rather than light because their deeds were evil'.[117] The world continues not to accept the light but in the darkness of unbelief and rejection it will not overcome the light. Jesus accordingly warns and consoles his followers, 'In the world you will have tribulation, but be of good cheer, I have overcome the world.'[118] He prays for them saying: 'They do not belong to the world, just as I do not belong to the world.'[119]

Light is a universally acknowledged symbol of life itself and of the human mind with its self consciousness which makes pos-

114. 4 Ezra 7:12f; 8:52-4.
115. Dan 12:2.
116. Jn 11:25f.
117. Jn 3:19f
118. Jn 16:33
119. Jn 17:16

sible human reflection on life. In the biblical tradition the imagery of light is used to describe the existence, presence and abode of God, the creative and saving acts of God and the favour of the divine countenance.[120] The revelation of God in Creation, Wisdom and Torah is described in terms of light. 'Let there be light' were the first words of creation. The light shone in the darkness, and the darkness could not overcome it. The Word dwelling unrecognised in the world became, in the Word become flesh, the 'true light', 'the light of humanity', the Light of the World. The obvious contrast between John the witness to the light and Jesus the true light may conceal somewhat the underlying contrast between Jesus the true light and the Torah which was widely described as light, even as the light of the world. When Herod the Great put the rabbis to death he was told: 'You have quenched the light of the world.'[121] Dodd points out how even the priestly benediction, 'May the Lord make his face to shine upon you' is interpreted in terms of the Torah in the Siphre on Numbers with reference to Proverbs, 'The commandment is a lamp and the Torah is light'.[122] This further highlights the significance of the portrayal of Jesus, the Word become flesh, as the Light of the World. He declares himself to be the Light of the World during the Feast of Tabernacles in which there was great emphasis on the theme of light.[123] His followers are told to walk in the light. 'He who follows me will never walk in darkness but will have the light of life.'[124] St John's gospel reflects the widespread use of the imagery of light in the New Testament. In the synoptic tradition Jesus tells the disciples they are the light of the world and as such they must let their light shine for all to see.[125] Light is also widely used as an image to designate the status of the baptised and they in turn are seen as children of light.[126]

Jesus, the incarnate *Logos*, is the Revealer who illuminates existence. He says in the farewell discourse at the Last Supper: 'And this is eternal life, that they may know you, the only true

---

120. 1 Tim 6:16; Num 6:25; Pss 4:7; 31:17; 44:4; 62:7; 80:4; 8:20; 89:16; 119:135; Dan 9:17.
121. Dodd, *op. cit*, 84 quoting *Baba Bathra* 4a.
122. Dodd, *op. cit.*, 84, Siphre on Num 6:25, $41; Prov 6:23.
123. Jn 8:12
124. Jn 8:12
125. Mt 5:14ff; Lk 8:16; 11:33; Mk 4:21.
126. Rom 13:11ff; 1 Pet 2:9,12; 5:8; Col 1:13; Eph 5:8, 14; Heb 6:4.

God, and Jesus Christ whom you have sent.'[127] Jesus' life is the
revelation of the Father. 'He who has seen me has seen the
Father.'[128] This is the ultimate significance of the many references to Jesus as Light in the gospel. Darkness is seen as lack of
understanding, lack of faith, the sin of the world. 'Those who
walk during the day do not stumble, because they see the light
of this world. But those who walk at night stumble, because the
light is not in them.'[129] Nicodemus comes in darkness seeking
light.[130] The blind man comes into the light, the sighted authorities remain in darkness.[131] Judas departs into the night and returns in darkness with the arresting party carrying artificial
lights.[132] The unbelieving world rejects Jesus because they prefer
darkness to light.[133] The unbelievers remain in darkness lest
coming into the light their deeds might be exposed.[134] They prefer darkness to light because their deeds are evil.[135]

R. Bultmann put it succinctly when he spoke of Jesus as the
Revealer who illuminates existence:

> By making the world bright, it makes it possible for men to
> see. But sight is not only significant in that it enables man to
> orientate himself in respect of objects; sight is at the same
> time the means whereby man understands himself in his
> world, the reason he does not 'grope in the dark', but sees his
> 'way'. In its original sense light is not an apparatus for illumin-
> ation, that makes things perceptible, but is the *brightness* itself
> in which I find myself here and now; in it I find my way
> about, I find myself at home, and have no anxiety. Brightness
> is not therefore an outward phenomenon, but is the illum-
> ined condition of existence, of my existence ... Alongside
> this, the original sense of 'light' as the illumined quality of
> existence is preserved by its use to designate happiness and
> salvation; thus the word comes to designate the divine
> sphere in general; and its original meaning is preserved
> above all by the description of salvation itself, in its 'eschato-

---

127. Jn 17:3
128. Jn 14:9
129. Jn 11:9f
130. Jn 3:2
131. Jn 9:1-41
132. Jn 13:30; 8:2f
133. Jn 3:19
134. Jn 3:20
135. Jn 3:19

logical' sense, as 'the light' ... But the more completely *phôs* is regarded as something eschatological, the stronger grows the conviction that the definitive illumination of existence does not lie within human possibilities, but can only be divine gift. Thus *phôs* comes to mean revelation. And where one speaks of a Revealer, one can describe him as the 'Light' or the Giver of Light.[136]

Witness/Martyria/Martyrein

6 There was a man sent from God, whose name was John. 7 He came as a witness to testify to the light, so that all might believe through him. 8 He himself was not the light, but he came to testify to the light.

'There was a man sent from God.' This verse resembles the opening of an Old Testament Book, like the First Book of Samuel or the introduction to a cycle of stories, like the Elijah/Elisha cycle or the opening of one of the prophetic books. Like them it introduces a new phase in the history of God and the people. The statements about John the Baptist now contained in the prologue may well have been the opening verses of the gospel at an earlier stage in its composition before the prologue was added and they were detached from their original position. If so, the earlier opening of the gospel was very close to that of Mark which begins with the ministry of John.[137]

The narrator describes John as 'sent by God'. Even here the contrast between John and Jesus will be sharply drawn. Jesus does not put the primary emphasis on himself as 'the one sent', the *shaliach*, but rather turns the designation round so that the emphasis falls on the Father, the One who sent him (*ho pempsas me*). This sending by the Father is the origin of all mission. Jesus fulfils but far surpasses the role of the *shaliach*, the one sent. Later the Father, and the Son, *send* the Spirit to the disciples whom Jesus *sends* into the world.[138]

These verses dealing with John serve to punctuate the prologue and also to knit the prologue more closely into the body of the gospel which begins with an account of the witness of John. References to John and his mission continue to serve as major

---

136. R. Bultmann, *The Gospel of John*, 40-43.
137. This was probably the case also with Matthew's and Luke's accounts before the infancy narratives were added. This points to the solid foundation of the John the Baptist traditions as marking the beginning of Jesus' ministry in all gospel traditions. This is also reflected in Acts 1:22; 13:23ff.
138. Jn 14:26; 15:26; 16:7; 17:18.

punctuation marks in the first ten chapters of the gospel as they illustrate the progress of Jesus' mission and the declining role of John. Eventually they show the fulfilment of the prophecy of John that 'He must increase and I must decrease' when the crowds say: 'John performed no sign but everything he said about this man was true.'[139]

These verses also draw a sharp contrast between the true light and the witness to the light. During his ministry Jesus describes himself as the Light of the World[140] and John as 'a lamp burning brightly for a time', reflecting Sirach's designation of Elijah.[141] In this gospel John is not referred to as the Baptist/ Baptiser but as a witness. His witness to the light rests on the revelation of the one who sent him and on the manifestation of the Spirit.[142]

These verses point to John's role as witness to the light for the purpose of bringing all to believe in the light, and emphasise the fact that he himself is not the light.[143] Witnessing to the light, to the truth, to Christ, is a major theme of this gospel in which various witnesses are presented. It has been aptly described as a Book of Witnesses and a Trial of Jesus. Like Jesus, John 'was sent' by God. Their source of authority is one and the same so there is no clash of authority or competition of roles between them.[144]

Believe/Pisteuein

The purpose of witness is to lead people to faith, 'so that all might believe through him'.[145] The gospel itself was 'written that you may believe that Jesus is the Christ, the Son of God, and that believing this you may have life in his name'.[146] The prologue states that those who accepted him and believed in his

---

139. Jn 3:30; 10:40-42
140. Jn 8:12
141. Jn 5:35; Sir 48:1.
142. Jn 1:32-34
143. Jn 1:7, 8, 15, 19, 32, 34: *eis marturian ... hina marturêsê (x 2) .... marturei ... emarturêsen ... memarturêka.*
144. This would have been a necessary point of clarification in the event of ongoing confusion or competition between their followers. There may have been lingering doubts about the relationship of the two, which are being cleared up here and in subsequent passages.
145. *pisteuein* and its compounds are used 98 times in the gospel.
146. Jn 20:31.

name 'are given power to become children of God'.[147] The emphasis in the gospel is on 'believing' in the historical person of the Word made flesh, not on abstract belief in God. In St John's gospel there are different ways of speaking of belief, all using the Greek verb *pisteuein*, to believe. *Pisteuein* on its own has the meaning of 'having faith', more or less the same as having a spiritual vision, a personal awareness of God's presence and action in the world. *Pisteuein* used with the dative case refers to belief in the words spoken. *Pisteuein eis*, often translated as 'belief on the Lord Jesus', is a Johannine expression rarely found elsewhere in the New Testament. It refers to confidence in a person based on intellectual acceptance of the claims made for that person in relation to his identity and mission. *Pisteuein eis to onoma autou*, belief in his name, is a more specific example of this and may be originally related to a baptismal formula, 'baptised in his name'. *Pisteuein hoti*, corresponding to the Hebrew *h'min b'* means 'believe that', and it refers to belief in the nature, mission and status of Jesus, as for example, 'You believe that Jesus is the Christ, the Son of God.'[148]

Pisteuein in its various uses, therefore, sums up the various aspects of a disposition of trust in Jesus required of the onlooker or hearer. 'The encounter between Jesus and the individual is not something ... to be understood in generalities or symbolism but is to be seen as a most pressing, existential engagement.'[149] Accepting or rejecting the light is a motif providing the major dynamic of the gospel, just like accepting or rejecting the invitation of Wisdom or keeping or not keeping the law in the Old Testament. Those who reject the light pronounce their own condemnation. The reasons for their rejection are explored throughout the gospel. They are afraid of the light lest their deeds be exposed.[150] They do not know the Father, not ever having heard his voice or seen his shape, and his words find no home in them.[151] They do not have the love of God in their hearts.[152] They do not believe the witnesses.[153] They seek glory from one another

---

147. Jn 1:12.
148. Jn 20:31.
149. C. Luibhéid, *op. cit.*, 94.
150. Jn 3:20
151. Jn 5:37f
152. Jn 5:42
153. Jn 5:19-47

and do not seek the glory that comes only from God.[154] 'Seeing'
is an important verb throughout the gospel as it stands for the
various levels of understanding and believing. Chapter nine is a
dramatic account of the man born blind who received the gift of
sight and whose healing serves to show the lack of sight on the
part of those who claimed to see. On entering the tomb of Jesus
the Beloved Disciple 'saw and believed'.

Children of God/Tekna Theou

*9 The true light, which enlightens everyone, was coming into the
world. 10 He was in the world, and the world came into being through
him; yet the world did not know him. 11 He came to what was his own,
and his own people did not accept him. 12 But to all who received him,
who believed in his name, he gave power to become children of God, 13
who were born, not of blood or of the will of the flesh or of the will of
man, but of God.*

The hope of Israel was focused on *the coming one/the one coming into the world*, a phrase canonised in messianic expectation.
The Baptist speaks of *the one coming after him*,[155] the Samaritan
woman speaks of the Messiah who *is coming* and who will explain all things,[156] and Martha proclaims her faith in Jesus as 'the
Messiah, the son of God *the one coming into the world.*'[157] Here in
the prologue the *coming one* is described in terms of the true light
coming into the world. Another aspect of messianic expectation
was the belief that the messiah would be in the midst of the people but would be unknown. 'The Word was the true light ... he
was in the world ... and *the world did not know him.*'[158] The
Baptist testified that 'among you stands one *whom you do not
know*, the one who is coming after me',[159] and the Jerusalem
crowd speculate about the possibility of identifying Jesus as
Messiah in the face of their understanding that the Messiah
would be unknown.[160]

Accepting Jesus as the one sent from God, the one from
above who does and speaks what he has learned from his
Father, empowers those who accept him to become God's

---

154. Jn 5:44
155. Jn 1:27
156. Jn 4:25
157. Jn 11:27
158. Jn 1:9f
159. Jn 1:26f
160. Jn 7:27

children. They are born from above, born of water and the Spirit.
The Holy Spirit, the Paraclete, will come to them, and the Father
and Son will abide in them.[161] These are God's children, and
their becoming God's children is not like human generation, but
results from the salvific work of God. They 'were born, not of
blood or of the will of the flesh or of the will of man, but of
God'.[162] They shall see and enter the kingdom of God.[163]

The Word became Flesh/ho Logos Sarx egeneto
14 And the Word became flesh and lived among us, and we have seen
his glory, the glory as of a father's only son, full of grace and truth.

This verse forms a multiple contrast with verse one. Both
verses have a double *kai* (and) highlighting the contrast: '*and* the
Word was with God/*and* the Word was God' contrasts with:
'*and* the Word became flesh/*and* pitched tent among us'. The
eternal *Logos* is contrasted with the finite, earth bound, death
destined *sarx* (flesh). The eternal pre-existence, expressed by *ên*
(was) contrasts with the finite, time bound *egeneto* (came to be),
just as *theos* (God, divine being) contrasts with *sarx* (flesh,
human being). Furthermore, *ên pros ton theon* (was with God)
contrasts with *eskênosen en hêmin* (pitched tent among us) both in
time and place, as the eternal *ên* (was) contrasts with the temporary dwelling in a tent *(eskênôsen)*, and being in the presence of
God *(pros ton theon)* contrasts with being in the midst of humanity
(en hêmin). The temporary dwelling of the *Logos* in the tent of the
sarx will be further contrasted in the body of the gospel with the
post-resurrection indwelling *(menein)* of Father, Son and Spirit-
Paraclete in the believers. Though the *sarx* contrasts so radically
with the *Logos*, the *doxa* (glory) is now seen through the *sarx*, so
the glory is accessible to sensory human experience in the *sarx* of
Jesus, as Jesus tells the disciples: 'To have seen me is to have
seen the Father.'[164]

The Word which pre-existed in eternity 'became' flesh (*sarx*)
and began the finite existence of a human being. In contrast to
Wisdom which was the literary personification of a theological

---

161. Jn 14:16, 20; 23, 26; 15:26; 16:7, 13.
162. Some mss read 'who *was* born not of blood, or the will of the flesh, or the will
of man' in the singular and in this form it is seen to refer to the virginal conception of Christ.
163. Jn 3:3-7.
164. Jn 14:9.

concept,[165] the divine Word became flesh, a real human being, and dwelt among us. The Old Testament and its commentators used terms and concepts like *the word of the Lord, wisdom* and *memra* to speak of the wonder of God's immanence, that is, the divine presence and work in the world and especially among the people of the covenant. These same terms served also to protect the divine transcendence. That God should be present in the world and especially among the chosen people was a cause for wonder. This wonder is now compounded by the divine condescension in the mode of presence assumed by the Word, the flesh, subject to weakness and mortality. Thus the story leading to Jesus' death and its significance for salvation has begun. On the broader New Testament canvas, before this gospel was written, Paul wrote to the Philippians about humility and quoted the hymn celebrating the divine condescension, the *kenôsis* or self emptying: 'He emptied himself taking the form of a servant, becoming in the likeness of men, and being as all men are, he accepted death, even death on a cross.'[166] Writing to the Romans he pointed out that God's Son was descended from David according to the flesh, and marvelled that God sent his own son 'in the likeness of sinful flesh'.[167] John, however, does not focus on the *kenosis* or self emptying, in taking flesh and becoming a human being, but on the death and glorification to which it ultimately leads.[168]

To the Jews with their extraordinary reverence for the sacred and their traditions of avoiding the divine name in speech and veiling the divine presence in the Temple, the fact that 'The Word became flesh' was an extraordinary event beyond all expectation which posed an insurmountable obstacle for many. To the Gentile believers in the Greco-Roman world where many philosophies devalued the flesh and looked for a salvific purification in escape from the flesh and the world, the fact that the *Logos* not only dwelt in the flesh, but became flesh, posed a whole new challenge to their outlook on God, the world and salvation. It is well expressed in St Augustine's comment on his former teacher in the *Confession*:

You procured for me ... some books of the Platonists trans-

165. Sir 24
166. Phil 2:6-8
167. Rom 1:3; 8:3
168. There is no hint in John of the Pauline concept of *sarx*, flesh, as signifying the human proneness to sin.

lated from Greek into Latin. There I read, not in so many
words but in substance, supported by many arguments of
various kinds, that in the beginning was the Word and the
Word was with God and the Word was God ... Again I read
there that God the Word was born not of the flesh nor of
blood, nor of the will of man, nor of the will of the flesh, but
of God. But that the Word was made flesh and dwelt among
us I did not read there.[169]

The Word of God, the *Logos*, became a human being who speaks
to the world. Though the body of the gospel does not contain the
term *Logos* as a title for Jesus, the *Logos* theme continues with the
frequent repetition of the corresponding verb *lego* (speak),[170] in
the revelatory discourses[171] and particularly in the solemn declaratory formula, 'Amen, amen I say (*lego*) to you',[172] which
punctuates these discourses and highlights Jesus, the incarnate
word, as the ongoing presence of the divine *Logos*.

Dwelling/Presence/Glory/eskênôsen/Doxa

The *Logos* became *sarx*, flesh, a human being, and dwelt among
us. The divine and human polarities are held together in the context of one person. The Greek expression, *eskênôsen en hêmin*, literally means 'he pitched tent in our midst'. The references to
tent, glory, grace and truth (covenant love and fidelity) are the
language of the divine presence among the people chosen as
God's own. They recall the covenant at Sinai when the Tent of
Meeting became the locus of divine revelation. The God of the
covenant had fought on their side against the Egyptians at the
sea, had shown himself Lord of sea and sky, protector of the
people and victor in battle. He visited and watched over the people as a guiding and protecting presence during the wandering
in the desert, accompanying them as a cloud by day and a fire by
night. The narrative in Exodus speaks of their experience of the
glory (*kbd*) of God on the mountain at Sinai.[173] The glory covered
the mountain whither Moses was summoned to approach the

---

169. *Confessions*, VII, 9,
170. 44 times
171. Chapters 3, 4, 5, 7, 8, 13-17.
172. This formula 'Amen, amen, I say to you' as a solemn asseveration occurs
twenty five times in this gospel. The use of 'amen' at the beginning of an affirmation was peculiar to Jesus, and the double amen is peculiar to John's gospel. The
double 'amen' at the end of a sentence is found in Qumran, in liturgical usage,
e.g. in 1QS 1:20; 2:10, 18 after blessing and cursing.
173. Ex 24:16.

Presence.[174] 'The glory of the Lord settled on Mount Sinai, and the cloud covered it for six days; on the seventh day he called to Moses out of the cloud. Now the appearance of the glory of the Lord was like a devouring fire on the top of the mountain in the sight of the people of Israel.'[175] Moses sought the glory of God but was not permitted to see God's face. Like the people he had but a fleeting glimpse of the glory which was a manifestation of God's presence.[176] Still at the Tent of Meeting God spoke to him face to face as a man speaks with his friend.[177] On another occasion the cloud covered the Tent of Meeting and the glory of the Lord filled the Tabernacle so that Moses could not enter.[178] As they moved on from Sinai the Ark became the symbol or extension of God's presence, a reminder of the divine protection and a rallying point for the people. The Tent or Tabernacle, a moveable, temporary dwelling, that originally housed the Ark was not seen as a dwelling place of God, but as a place of meeting, of revelation, and the locus of prophetic inspiration.

The covenant with the house of David marked a seismic shift in the perception of God's presence to the people. When David occupied the Jebusite stronghold of Jerusalem, he gave the tribes a neutral capital, on an eminently suitable spot from the point of view of defence, and proceeded to develop it as a political, economic, military, cultural and religious capital. He brought the Ark to the city, to a temporary dwelling, and it proved a rallying point, a focus of religious identity and a cementing together of political and religious leadership. David's desire to build a permanent home for the Ark was fulfilled by his son Solomon. Now a permanent relationship or covenant replaced the former conditional bond assuring God's protection and blessing provided they kept the covenant. David is now seen as the adopted son of YHWH: 'I have found David my servant, with my holy oil I have anointed him ... my steadfast love (*hesed*) I will keep for him for ever'.[179] With the inauguration of the Temple of Solomon, the Judean royal ideology becomes closely bound up with the Temple and its cult. Kingship and Temple are divinely ordained. YHWH occupied the city and took over the mantle of the

---

174. Ex 24:16-18.
175. Ex 24:16f.
176. Ex 33:18-23.
177. Ex 33:7-11.
178. Ex 40:34f.
179. Ps 89 (Hb):20, 28f.

former god of the Jebusites, El Elyon. Now the God of Israel was seen to have a permanent dwelling place. Mount Zion, the Temple and City were the place that Yahweh had chosen, wherein he was pleased to dwell. 'The House of the Lord in Jerusalem replicates his cosmic Temple, giving *YHWH* a permanent place to dwell in the midst of his chosen.'[180] 'The Tabernacle creates space within the midst of a sinful people, wherein God's glory, the earthly manifestation of the divinity, can reside'.[181] Instead of God visiting the Tent-shrine of the Ark and his glory being manifest on such an occasion, the glory came upon the Temple at its dedication and remained there.[182]

The people felt the protection of God's presence in the Holy City and Temple. They went on pilgrimage to *the place where God's glory dwells,*[183] and the pilgrimage feasts became central to their religious life and identity. God was now present to hear their supplications and receive their homage. Blessings, law and divine authority emanated from the Temple. This faith experience of the people of Israel was so well grounded that, in the days of the double threat to Jerusalem and the House of David from the Syro-Ephraimite coalition and the Assyrian invader, the prophet Isaiah announced the forthcoming birth of the royal child Hezekiah as the sign of divine protection and gave the child the name, *Immanuel*, 'God is with us', as a permanent reminder of God's presence and protection.[184]

However, as throne and altar, palace and Temple were bound together, there was the ever present danger of over confidence in the divine presence and protection irrespective of their remaining faithful to their side of the covenant and its obligations. In this context there emerged the prophetic movement with its critique of royalty, Temple, priesthood and people. The prophets criticised many aspects of the Temple cult and the over assurance in the divine protection, irrespective of covenant fidelity. The conditional nature of the divine presence and protection again emerges and becomes a full blown motif in the deuteronomic reform in the time of Josiah and in the underlying

180. Coloe, *op. cit.*, 41.
181. Coloe, *op. cit.*, 51.
182. Ex 40:34; cf 1 Kgs 8:11. Ezekiel warned of the danger of a withdrawal of God's presence and glory from the Temple (Ezek 10:18-22).
183. 1 Kings 8:11ff; Is 6:3ff.
184. Isa 7:14

theology of the deuteronomistic history.[185] The Exile proved the point and the prophets described the terrible experience as 'punishment for crimes'.[186] The historian asserted that they were punished because 'They did what was displeasing to Yahweh.' 'They had broken his covenant ... they neither listened to it nor put it into practice.'[187]

However, because of the Exile, a new horizon opened up and they saw that God's presence was not confined to Zion and Temple worship. Prophetic insight and divine protection were available without the Temple. The exile experience renewed their insight into God's universal presence, and God's presence in the prophetic word, in the working of the spirit, and eventually in the presence of Wisdom and the law. The exile saw the emergence of the priestly tradition with its looking back beyond the davidic/solomonic covenant and theology to the older Sinaitic traditions. For the priestly writers the Sabbath and the festivals ensured sacred times while the Tabernacle (*mskn*) provided a sacred space. Together they enshrined the understanding and experience of God's immanence. At the same time the priestly tradition departed from the solomonic tradition of God's exclusive dwelling on Zion, to the idea of the glory (*kbd*) of the Lord inhabiting the tabernacle, thus ensuring the transcendence of God and the impossibility of containing the divine presence in any one place. A new futuristic vision was emerging already on the eve of the exile. Jeremiah and Ezekiel were looking to a new covenant, not expressed in a new national ideology, nor in a cult object like the Ark, nor in a sacred place like the Temple, but in the inner recesses of the human heart. The law will be written on the heart in a call to conversion and individual moral responsibility: 'Deep within them I will put my law'[188] and the heart of stone through the working of the Spirit will be replaced by a heart of flesh.[189] A new future became an ideal and the apocalyptic hope was born. 'In the days to come the mountain of the Lord's house shall be established as the highest of the mountains, and shall be raised above the hills; all the nations shall stream to it. Many peoples shall come and say, "Come, let us go

185. The books of Joshua, Judges, 1, 2 Samuel and 1, 2 Kings.
186. Isa 40:2 et al.
187. 2 Kings 15:9; 18:12 et al.
188. Jer 31:31ff.
189. Ezek 11:19; 36:26; 37:12.

up to the mountain of the Lord, to the house of the God of Jacob; that he may teach us his ways and that we may walk in his paths." For out of Zion shall go forth instruction, and the word of the Lord from Jerusalem.'[190]

Another futuristic vision was found in the apocalyptic literature, canonical and extracanonical, which held out the hope for a glorious future when the present historical order gives way to a totally new order created by God. This wicked age will come to an end in violent conflict and the reign of God will commence. Meanwhile the wickedness of the age makes the dwelling of God with the people impossible, so the apocalyptic seers have to ascend to heaven for the divine message. In the apocalyptic vision God's dwelling is in the heavens, and so the prayer for the new age is a plea that God 'will rend the heavens and come down'.[191] Yet another apocalyptic vision is that of Ezechiel's ideal Temple from which life-giving water will flow from under the sanctuary to give life to all that is dead in the land.[192]

The Targumic literature reflects the sensitivity of the deuteronomic and priestly writers and avoids anthropomorphic designations of God and God's earthly dwelling. Where the deuteronomic and priestly writers had used the idea of God's *shem*, (name) and *kbd*, (glory), respectively, the Targumic writers use *shekinah*, (presence, or numinous immanence).[193] Associated with the *shekinah* was *yichra*, glory. 'The glory of the *shekinah* of the Lord filled the Temple.'[194] Both terms are used as a periphrasis or alternative for 'God' and avoid anthropomorphic references to God's presence and activity among the people, thus preserving the divine transcendence.

Against the background of these rich traditions of reflecting on the presence and glory of God, the reader of St John's gospel is informed that the Word became a human being and 'pitched tent' among us. Jesus now becomes the manifestation of the glory of God, the tabernacle of divine presence and revelation, the place where *God's glory* dwells. At Cana Jesus manifested his *glory* and the disciples believed in him.[195]Prior to the raising of Lazarus he promised Martha that if she believed she would see

190. Isa 2: 2-4; Mic 4:1-3 (JB).
191. Isa 64:1.
192. Ezek 47:1-12.
193. *Shekinah* is a cognate of the verb *shkn*, to dwell.
194. *Tg. Neof.* Ex 40:30.
195. Jn 2:12.

the *glory* of God.[196] Summing up and commenting on the ministry, the narrator quotes Isaiah's remark about the blind eyes
and hardened hearts of those who had not seen the *glory* in
Jesus, a *glory* Isaiah had himself foreseen and which is now manifested in Christ.[197] Some did see it, and their faith is expressed
in the prologue: 'We have seen (gazed upon) his glory',[198] a profession of faith that draws the world of the believing reader into
the story.

Grace and Truth/Charis kai Alêtheia

As the Father is revealed in the Son, the glory of God is made
manifest and that glory is no longer a symbolic light or cloud
over Tabernacle or Temple but the outpouring of God's love in
the Son. The term 'covenant' is not used but the reality and
experience of covenant are at work in the language and thought
categories. However, the relationship is brought to a whole new
level, being no longer based on a 'legal' arrangement but rooted
in the Father-Son relationship into which the disciples are incorporated after Jesus is glorified. Covenant and Temple traditions
are united in the incarnate Word as the disciples 'contemplate
and interact with' (*etheasametha*) the 'the glory of the only Son of
the Father, full of *grace* and *truth*'.[199]

When Moses was denied seeing the face of God and commanded to approach the mountain with two tablets of stone, the
Lord descended in a cloud, passed before Moses and revealed
his divine attributes of *hesed* and *emet*.[200] '*YHWH, YHWH*, a God
of tenderness and compassion, slow to anger *rich in kindness and
faithfulness (rabh hesed w'emet).*'[201] *Rich in kindness and faithfulness*
is very close to the Greek *plêrês charitos kai alêtheias*, 'full of grace
and truth'. Covenant love in the Old Testament is expressed in
the frequently combined pair of nouns *hesed* and *emet*. *Hesed* signifies the faithful loving kindness whereby God is always faithful, even in spite of failure and betrayal on the part of the

196. Jn 11:40.
197. Jn 12:41; Is 6:4.
198. Jn 1:14; the verb *etheasametha* means 'gazed upon','contemplated', interacted
with. The word 'theatre' comes from the same root.
199. Jn 1:18. 'only', in the sense of 'unique', 'monogeneric', is the correct translation of *monogenês*. The Latin translation *unigenitus*, 'only begotten', was influenced by the debates surrounding the Arian crisis.
200. Ex 34:1-7.
201. Ex 34:6f.

covenant partner, and continues to seek out and call to repentance those who have strayed. *Emet* (related to the Hebrew '*mn*,
to fix, confirm, establish) signifies God's absolute credibility,
sincerity and utter reliability in dealings with humankind and
covenant partner. Truth, *emet*, is the sure foundation of all hon-
esty in relationship, and the divinely guaranteed correspon-
dence between perception, communication and ultimate divine
reality.[202] It has the sense of revealed truth, the teaching of wisdom with a moral significance. 'Knowing the truth' means
knowing the way God works with human beings generally and
the chosen people particularly, to bring about salvation. I. de la
Potterie points out that in St John's gospel the concept of truth is
specially indebted to late Jewish wisdom and apocalyptic literature where truth is revealed through God's agent such as
Wisdom or the Son of Man.[203] Now it is revealed in the Son, who
is both the revealer and the revelation. He *is* the truth. This pair
of words *hesed* and *emet* sum up the nature and blessings of the
covenant and are rendered into Greek here in the prologue as
charis kai alêtheia (grace and truth) where they connote the relational nature of the Hebrew background rather than the intellectual nature of the secular Greek philosophical concepts signified
by the words.[204] They now describe the new relationship
brought about in Christ, and form a contrast with the Mosaic
covenant and Torah.

John's Testifies/Iôannês marturei
15 *John testified to him and cried out, 'This was he of whom I said, "He
who comes after me ranks ahead of me because he was before me".'*

The one sent to witness to the light now bears witness in a
summary statement that highlights the superiority of 'the one
coming after him'. The one following him, his disciple, ranks
ahead of him. The follower taking over the leadership is a motif
in apocalyptic literature. In the animal allegory of history it is
the lamb who becomes the leader, shepherd of the flock, and de-
stroys the evil beasts, symbols of evil in the world.[205] Here the

202. The Hebrew expression *asah hesed w'emet* 'to do kindness and truth' emphasises the existential, practical dimension of the covenant relationship.
203. I. de la Potterie, 'The truth in St John', in *The Interpretation of John*, ed. John
Ashton, Philadelphia, Fortress Press, 1986, 53-55.
204. *Hesed* and *emet* are more often translated as *eleos kai alêtheia*, mercy/compas-
sion and truth. cf 2 Kgs 24 (25):10; 84 (85):11; 88 (89):15; Prov 3:3; 14:22; 20:22;
15:27; Hos 4:1 et al.
205. *Testament of the Twelve Patriarchs, Joseph* 19:8; cf Rev 7:17; 17:14.

reason for the superior role to be taken by the one following is given in terms of a summary of the profound truth already revealed in the prologue, that the one following already pre-existed in eternity. The one who 'was'(*ên*) outranks the one who 'came to be'(*egeneto*).

We have all received/hêmeis pantes elabomen
16 From his fullness we have all received, grace upon grace.

The *grace and truth* coming in the revelation of the Son establish a new relationship fulfilling and surpassing the covenant. The prologue presents the Word as the divine presence in the world, now become flesh. The *glory* of this presence is not perceived symbolically as a cloud or fire but as a real person, the unique Son, who establishes the two great covenant qualities of grace and truth (*charis* and *alêtheia/hesed* and *emet*). This signifies a radically new focus of relationship and a new locus of revelation and divine presence.

The synoptic tradition speaks of this in terms of the New Covenant foretold by Jeremiah and expressly named in the eucharistic formula at the Last Supper.[206] John uses the language of the Father-Son relationship and in the farewell discourse at the Last Supper he develops it into the language of communion of Father, Son, Spirit-Paraclete and disciple. From the fullness of the life and light present in the Logos we have received 'grace upon grace' or 'grace in return for grace'. These two possible translations of the Greek *charis anti charitos* reflect the debate as to whether the phrase means the adding of the new order to the old or the replacement of the old order with the new. Schnackenburg, however, puts it very clearly:

> John, however, is not just thinking of the superabundant mercy of God. He also means the riches of divine life which the Logos receives from the Father (5:26) and from which he enriches his own (10:10) … The *anti*, according to most modern commentators, indicates the ceaseless stream of graces which succeed one another. Perhaps the preposition also indicates the correspondence between the grace possessed by the Logos and that of those who receive him: what they possess they have received from him, and it corresponds to what he bears within himself in supreme fullness.[207]

---

206. Lk 22:20, Jer 31:31. cf Mt 26:28; Mk 14:24.
207. R. Schnackenburg, *The Gospel according to St John*, Vol I, 273f.

The Revealer/'Exegete' of the Father/ekeinos exêgêsato
17 *The law indeed was given through Moses; grace and truth came
through Jesus Christ. 18 No one has ever seen God. It is God the only
Son, who is close to the Father's heart, who has made him known.*

No one, not even Moses, has ever seen God. Moses approached the mountain with stone on which the words of the
law were to be written and though he did not see God, the *hesed*
and *emet* of God were proclaimed. Now the Word/*Logos* is described as the Son ever at the Father's side. He reveals God, not
in words on stone, but as the Word made flesh, full of grace and
truth.[208] His role as unique revealer in a special way answers the
question posed in the Old Testament about the revealer of Torah
and Wisdom: 'Who will go up to heaven for us and bring it (the
Torah) down to us, so that we may hear it and keep it?' 'Who has
mounted to the heavens and then descended (in search of wisdom)?' 'Who has ever climbed the sky and caught her (wisdom)
to bring her down from the clouds?' Who can discover what is in
the heavens?[209] The clear answer in St John's gospel is: 'No one
has ever gone up to heaven.'[210] This not only answers the older
question but it is a denial of the apocalyptic traditions in Jewish
literature, and also in Hermetic and Mandaean literature, of persons ascending to heaven to bring back a special revelation. At
the end of the ministry Jesus will proclaim, 'The one who has
seen me has seen the Father'.[211] I. de la Potterie states that for
John truth 'does not denote the typically Greek idea of divine
reality but the word of God, the revelation Jesus comes to impart'.[212] That revelation is both Jesus himself and his ministry –
he is revealer and revelation, and through him the divine plan of
salvation is made known and brought to fruition. The *hesed*,
faithful loving-kindness/grace, is brought to its ultimate expression in the love of the Father who gave his Son for the life of the
world. The *emet*, truth, finds its ultimate expression in the enfleshment of the Word, the divine communication in the gift of
the Son who, as Light of the World, is both the Revealer and the
Revelation of God's saving love. He is both the human face of
God and the source of life and resurrection for humanity. Jesus

---

208. The Greek *plérés charitos kai alétheias* reflects the Hebrew *rabh hesed w'emet*.
209. Deut 30:12; Prov 30:4; Bar 3:29; Wis 9:16-18.
210. Jn 3:13.
211. Jn 14:9.
212. I. de la Potterie, 'The Truth in St John', 55.

reveals the mystery of his person, that he lives in a unique rela-
tionship with the Father, and he invites us to share in his life as
Son.[213] The gospel about to unfold is the story of that revelation.
G.Rossé sums it up well:

> Precisely because Jesus is from eternity turned toward the
> Father, his revelation had an existential character that does
> not primarily consist in the teaching of a doctrine about God,
> but rather in letting the Father shine through him here on
> earth … Jesus shows himself as 'exegete' of the Father to the
> extent that he interprets his own existence and his own rela-
> tionship to the Father as he lives it out in everyday life. He
> says this in a loud voice at the end of his public life: 'Whoever
> sees me sees him who sent me' (Jn 12:45).[214]

4. CONCLUSION

The reader of the gospel now knows who Jesus is and where he
comes from, and will have no difficulty in understanding him
when he refers to where he comes from and whither he returns
when he departs from the world. Jesus for the reader is a fully
developed character from the beginning. The focus is on his relationship with the Father and carrying out the work the Father
gave him to do rather than on his psychological, emotional or intellectual awareness and development. Unlike the protagonist
in a drama or novel, he is not seen to develop or change and the
various crises that unfold around him do not alter his perception, action or character. However, as his identity, role and destiny are gradually revealed, many different perceptions are afforded and many a surprise sprung on the narrative audience.
Informed by the prologue, the reader now observes the other
characters in the gospel story as they struggle with the challenge
posed by Jesus and his mission from the Father.

---

213. G. Rossé, *The Spirituality of Communion*, 13.
214. *Ibid.*, 14.

The Inauguration Jn 1:19-2:25

The First Days (1:19-2:23)

1. THE PLOT

The prologue is followed by the earthly story of the Word made Flesh in Jesus of Nazareth, whose life, death and resurrection gave rise to, and continue for all believers, to inspire and under-pin the confession of faith that found such lofty expression in the prologue.

The historical figure of John ties together in an immediate way the prologue and the subsequent narrative in which a se-quence of days provides the framework for the inauguration of Jesus' ministry. The narrative contains the initial witness of John, the calling and faith confessions of the first disciples of Jesus and the inaugural statements and actions of Jesus himself. The Johannine technique of beginning a passage with *kai* (and) emphasises the link between prologue and narrative.

As the description of a series of days immediately follows the prologue with its references to creation and the accompanying imagery of life, light and darkness, the reader may well sense that the first days of a new creation are unfolding.[1] However, when the inaugural narrative comes to a climax at Cana it is said to be *on the third day* though six or seven days have already been indicated.[2] It thus becomes obvious that the text is enriched by more than the allusion to the days of creation.

A four day period comes to a climax with Jesus' promise to the disciples that they will see greater things with the rending of the heavens and the vision of the angels of God ascending and descending on the Son of Man. Then the climax of the inaugur-ation narrative comes at Cana 'on the third day' when Jesus manifests his glory and his disciples believe in him. Like the pro-

---

1. M. E. Boismard, *Du Baptême a Cana*, 14f.; H. Saxby, 'The Time-Scheme in the Gospel of John', 9-13.
2. Depending on whether one counts the fourth day, or the following day, as the first of the 'triduum' that climaxes at Cana 'on the third day'. In 'secular' Greek *tê tritê hêmera* means 'the day after tomorrow'. Its biblical use is determined by the symbolic character of the narrative and the rich allusions to OT passages.

logue the inauguration narrative is rich in allusions to the foundation events in the formation of Israel at Sinai, specifically the
story of Moses and his preparing the people in the desert for the
revelation of the glory of God *on the third day*.[3] 'Go to the people
and consecrate them today and tomorrow ... and prepare for the
third day, because on the third day the Lord will come down
upon Mount Sinai in the sight of all the people.'[4] *The third day*
subsequently became a 'canonised' term for the day of God's
presence in glory when he gave the people the gift of the law.
The memory of the event at Sinai came to be celebrated at
Pentecost following a three day preparation as described in the
Exodus narrative. Later still the three days of immediate preparation were preceded by four days of remote preparation.[5] Here
in John four days of witness and preparation of disciples precede Jesus' promise of their seeing 'greater things', and then 'on
the third day' Jesus revealed his glory at Cana and his disciples
believed in him.

John has already been introduced to the reader.[6] His presence ties the prologue immediately to the subsequent narrative.
The origin and nature of his mission have been stated. He was
sent by God. He came as a witness to the light.[7] In origin and
mission therefore there is no clash between himself and Jesus,
though the sharp contrast in person and mission, both originating from the same authority, are already stated. He was not the
light but the witness to Jesus, the true light. This witness is first
borne in the context of a challenge from the very authorities who
will later challenge the true light itself. The messenger sent by
God is challenged by the messengers sent by the religious authorities.[8] When they sense messianic expectation in the air they

3. Ex 19:9-25. The term 'the third day' occurs four times in the passage.
4. Ex 19:10f.
5. J. Potin, *La Fête juive de la Pentecôte*, 314-317.
6. If taken together and placed at the beginning of the ministry, the verses from
the prologue would serve to open the story of the ministry of Jesus just as Mark
does, or Matthew and Luke do after their infancy narratives. The account of
John's ministry would then begin just like the story of the commissioning of a
prophet in the Old Testament or the opening of a historical book like 1 Samuel.
Maybe that is how the gospel originally began before the detachment of these
verses and their insertion into the Prologue?
7. In John's gospel his role as witness overshadows his role as baptiser and so the
references to his baptising Jesus, to his ascetic life and to his garments and diet
are omitted.
8. His role is emphasised as that of 'witness' not as Baptist, a synoptic designation not applied to him in the gospel of John.

are suspicious and hostile to any possible challenge to their religious authority. The interrogation will be on their terms. But the
mould of their pre-conceived Messianic expectations is about to
be broken and something they cannot control is going to happen. They cannot mould to their own specifications *the one who is
coming into the world*.

John was introduced in the prologue with the definite clarification that he was not the light, that he was a witness to the light
and the stated purpose of his witness was that all might believe
through him. These three aspects are now spelled out in the account of his first days of witness. He first bears witness to himself in negative and positive terms before bearing witness to *the
one coming into the world*. The fruits of this witness are evident in
the faith of the first disciples.

The whole of the gospel of John can be seen as a trial of Jesus,
and John is the first witness in this trial. The encounter between
him and the priests and Levites sent by the Jews from Jerusalem
introduces the context, characters and mood of the opposition to
John that subsequently switches its attention to Jesus.[9] In situations of controversy in the gospel the term 'the Jews' is more a
literary device than an ethnic designation. It is a collective character created to represent the powerful element among the
Jewish authorities who formed the opposition to Jesus.[10]
Similarly the term 'the Pharisees' is a collective character representing the forces opposed to Jesus. Both terms are significantly
coloured by events contemporaneous with the writing of the
gospel. By that time the groups who formed the original opposition to Jesus had disappeared from the scene after the fall of
Jerusalem and the destruction of the Temple. These terrible
events destroyed the religious and social context of the priests
and Levites who had been the mainstay of the Sadducee party.
The Pharisees survived and subsequently became the dominant
influence in Judaism. The gospel sees the opposition to Jesus
through the lens of the disputes between the first Christians and
these Pharisees.

9. These messengers were the specialists in ritual, associated with the Temple
and its authorities. The Levites appear seldom in the New Testament and are
usually in a role inferior to that of the priests. This makes their appearance here
rather strange when one considers the tradition in Luke that the Baptist was son
of a priest. The rabbinic documents sometimes show them as temple police. cf
Brown, *op. cit.*, Vol I, 43f.
10. Seeing it as a global term for all Jews has led to disastrous anti-Semitic sentiment and activity and to the view of many Jews that this gospel is anti-Semitic.

2. THE LITERARY STRUCTURE

The public ministry is introduced with a quotation from Isaiah about preparing the way, just as it closes with another Isaian quotation commenting on the rejection of the one for whom the way has been prepared.[11] Like this reference to the Isaian voice, the reference to John's baptising in Bethany also functions as a literary *inclusion* with the close of the ministry when Jesus goes back across the Jordan to the place where John had been baptising.[12] John was baptising outside the promised land on the other side of the Jordan. From there Jesus enters the promised land where he will be rejected and will once more retreat beyond the Jordan. On that occasion the people will offer their assessment of his ministry by way of commenting on the fulfilment of John's predictions about him.[13] Location and movement play a significant part in the narrative, advancing the plot, supporting punctuation and thematic change, and reinforcing dialogue with body language.

There is yet another striking example of *inclusion*. At the beginning of the ministry John twice witnesses to Jesus, proclaiming him to be the Lamb of God who takes away the sin of the world, the one who baptises in Holy Spirit. John's presentation of Jesus to Israel as Lamb of God at the beginning of the ministry forms an inclusion with Pilate's presentation of him to the people as 'the man' and 'your king' at its close. At the crucifixion the Beloved Disciple witnesses the blood and water, the redeeming blood of the lamb and the life-giving water of the Holy Spirit, from the side of Jesus who died as the paschal lambs were being slaughtered for the Passover. Together these sets of witness form an inclusion or framework for the ministry and life of Jesus and hold the text together like matching bookends, drawing the reader's attention from the final outcome back to the initial promise and vice versa.

---

11. Jn 12:38-41.

12. The site has not been identified. Some commentators have read the name of the place as Bethabara, the place of crossing over, and have seen a parallel between the ministry of Jesus and that of Joshua. The Bethany mentioned here is definitely not the Bethany of Martha, Mary and Lazarus, which was near Jerusalem.

13. Jn 10:40. This may have corresponded with the conclusion of the public ministry of Jesus at an earlier stage in the formation of the gospel tradition. It points to the fulfilment of John's prophecy and to the successful outcome of his witness, evidenced by the many people coming to faith in Jesus.

3. THE WITNESS OF JOHN Jn 1:19-34

This passage is made up of two days equally balanced, each in two parts and contained within a framework of witness. The passage begins with 'This is the witness' and ends with 'I have witnessed', two references forming an inclusion or framework around John's initial witness.[14] The first day deals with the two sets of questions by the interrogators and John's 'negative' witness about himself; the second deals with John's public witness to Jesus.

The interrogation of John takes the form of two sets of questions, the first concerning his identity, the second concerning his baptism.[15] In both cases his authority is under scrutiny. His repeated response, 'I am not', strikes a chord which contrasts sharply with Jesus' repeated 'I am' statements, and reinforces the assertion of the prologue that he was not the light.[16] His denials afford the opportunity of identifying himself, as in the synoptics, in terms of the voice described in Isaiah as crying out to prepare the way of the Lord. The second question focuses on his baptism and affords John the opportunity of making a clear distinction between his own identity, mission and baptism and those of the one coming after him. Having testified to himself he testifies to the light as the *unknown one in their midst*, the *one coming into the world*, the *one greater than himself because he existed before him*, the *Lamb of God who takes away the sin of the world* and *the one who will baptise in Holy Spirit*. His witness culminates in the solemn recognition and profession of faith in Jesus as *Son of God*, revealed to him by the one who sent him.[17] Jesus is *the one on whom he saw the Spirit come down and rest (remain, dwell).*[18] He emphasises the superiority of Jesus, his mission, and his baptism.[19] All four gospels and Acts have John himself emphasising

---

14. Jn 1:19, 34.

15. Scholars debate whether the two sets of questions are put by the same interrogators, and why the priests and Levites, usually associated with the Sadducee party would have been emissaries of the Pharisee Party, their bitter rivals.

16. His denials reflect a decreasing order of length: 'I am not the Christ, I am not, No'; *ouk eimi ho christos, ouk eimi, ou*, a literary reflection of the whole presentation of John vis-à-vis Jesus whose *ego eimi* statements tend to increase in predication throughout the gospel.

17. Jn 1:34. Some mss read 'the chosen one of God'.

18. The verb *menein*, means remain/rest/dwell. Its predominant meaning in the gospel is 'dwell'.

19. Mt and Lk also elaborate on the superiority of Jesus over John. Matthew portrays John protesting that he is unfit to baptise Jesus, Lk presents two parallel

that he is unfit to carry, or untie, Jesus' sandals.[20] 'He is no more
than a slave whose task is to untie his master's sandal; and he
feels unworthy even of that.'[21] The baptism scene of the synoptics does not appear in the fourth gospel. It is replaced by John's
witnessing the Spirit coming on Jesus and remaining with him.
John's role as subordinate to Jesus is emphasised by stressing, in
contrast to the pre-existence of the Word who is in eternal relationship with the Father and the unique revealer of God the
Father, that his own existence is finite. He is a mortal human
being, and a messenger of God.[22]

The questions about identity reflect the messianic expectations current at the time.[23] The questioning initiates a series of
testimonies which continue on to 'the next day' when John bears
witness before some of his own disciples and points them towards Jesus, beginning a chain reaction of witness to Jesus resulting in the gathering of his first disciples. On encountering
Jesus they in turn reflect the messianic expectations of the time
as they bear witness to others who in turn become disciples.
They articulate their incipient faith in what could be described
as a roll call of New Testament christology. Their open attitude
to these messianic expectations stands out in sharp contrast to
the authoritarian and threatening attitude of the Jerusalem emissaries when they sensed messianic expectation in the air. The
new disciples are enthusiastic but their faith is incipient and still
determined by traditional categories. Jesus will point them forward to new horizons. In his response to their confessions of
faith in him, Jesus acknowledges Simon as 'the rock' and
Nathanael as 'a true Israelite without guile'. This process of witness, confession and discipleship comes to an initial climax

Infancy Narratives in which the marvellous circumstances of John's conception
and birth are surpassed by the even more marvellous circumstances of Jesus'
conception and birth at every point.
20. Mt 3:11; Mk 1:8; Lk 3:16; Jn 1:27; Acts 13:25. A disciple was expected to do for
the teacher what a servant does for his master except tend to his shoes and feet,
as this was too demeaning. Hence the significance of John's statement.
21. W. J. Harrington, John, Spiritual Theologian, 32. The remark about the sandals
may be a reminder to those who continued to see John as the messianic figure,
that John himself was the first to deny any such role for himself.
22. egeneto, anthropos, emprosthen mou, prôtos mou all reflect the subordinate status
of John..
23. The clarity of the roles of these expected messianic figures may be greater in
subsequent Christian reflection in the New Testament than in the historical circumstances of the ministry of John or Jesus.

when he promises the disciples that they will see greater things, and then the entire inauguration narrative reaches its climax at Cana when Jesus speaks of his *hour*, reveals his glory and his disciples believe in him.[24] Thus the inauguration of the ministry is complete.

The mixture of tenses in the narrative is interesting. In contrast to the straightforward narrative aorist, the historic present tense as in 'John sees Jesus coming towards him and says' sets the witness of John in the timeless framework of the ongoing believing community and its gospel. The historic present is used more than a hundred and fifty times in the gospel. Here it has the effect of making the reader feel included in the scene.[25] The use of the perfect tense at the end of the passage: 'I have seen and I have borne witness'[26] stands out against the historic present and aorist tenses to establish the once and for all historic nature of the witness of John.

Day One: John witnesses to the Authorities Jn 1:19-28
In terms of roles John denies that he is the Messiah, Elijah or the Prophet.[27] The interrogation by the authorities on the first day is articulated in terms of the generally held triple expectation surrounding the character of *the one to come* and the precursor figures. John the Baptist carried on much of his ministry in close geographical proximity to the Essene settlement at Qumran so he probably knew and reflected their expectations. Various beliefs were held as to whether these roles would be manifest in one, two or three persons. Moses and Elijah figure prominently in messianic expectation. In the synoptic tradition, for example, after Peter's profession of faith in Jesus as Christ/Messiah, Jesus goes to the mountain with Peter, James and John and is transfigured between the persons of Moses and Elijah. Both were intimately associated with expectations surrounding *the one to come* and both had Sinai/Horeb connections.

---

24. In referring to the *hour* Jesus introduces the narrative time frame of the ministry.
25. Jn 1:29.
26. The historic present is used 151 times in the gospel of John. cf John J. O'Rourke, 'The Historic Present in the Gospel of John', *JBL* 93 (1974): 585-90. Jn1:34
27. Such a testimony from the lips of John himself may have been particularly important if there were still groups who continued in the belief that John was the Messiah or had lingering suspicions in that regard.

The interrogators asked John if he was the Christ, Elijah or the Prophet. The *Christ/Messiah* was the anointed one, the expected royal prince of the House of David who would be a new David, the promised good shepherd-king. The shepherd imagery emphasised the care and integrity exercised by a leader and in reaction to bad leadership in the past God promised to look after the flock himself and provide a good shepherd-king. 'I will raise up a new David, a good shepherd' [28] who would re-establish the kingdom and rule wisely in justice and integrity.[29]

Elijah, the prophet, was expected to reappear in order to usher in the final time. This expectation was fuelled by the story in 2 Kings about his ascent into heaven in a fiery chariot and the account in 2 Chronicles which speaks of the reception of a letter from him after the event, suggesting that he was alive.[30] There was a strong post-exilic expectation of his return before the Day of the Lord. Malachi speaks of the angel coming to prepare the way of the Lord, and this angel is identified in a later addition as Elijah.[31] Sirach speaks of him as 'designated in the prophecies of doom to allay God's wrath … to turn the hearts of fathers towards their children, and to restore the tribes of Jacob.'[32] In Enoch the animal allegory of history portrays Elijah's return before the judgement and the appearance of the great apocalyptic lamb.[33]

The *Prophet* figured in the deuteronomic legislation drawn up for various functionaries such as judges, kings, priests and prophets. The text contains the statement: 'A prophet like me (Moses) will the Lord, your God, raise up.'[34] This came to be interpreted as a prediction of the coming of a 'Prophet-like-Moses'. The Essene community at Qumran were told to cling to the Torah and the laws of community till a prophet (like Moses?) comes.[35] The Samaritan woman at the well reflects a similar expectation among the Samaritans about the function of 'the one to come' when she hopes he will clarify the issue of the legality of

28. Ezek 34:23f; cf Jer 23:1-4.
29. Isa 9:6ff; 11:1-9.
30. 2 Kings 2:11; 2 Chr 21:12;
31. c. 450 BC; Mal 3:1; 4:5; 3:23f;
32. Sir 48:10f.
33. En 90:31; 89:52; cf Jn 1:29.36. The dress and behaviour of John, particularly as portrayed in the Synoptics, recall that of Elijah (Mk 1:6; cf 2 Kings1:8).
34. Deut 18:15-18
35. 4 QT; 1 QS 9:11; 4 QF.

the Temple worship on Gerizim.[36] In the Acts of the Apostles
Jesus is identified as the Prophet-like-Moses in Peter's address
in the Portico of Solomon.[37]

Having answered 'no' to the triple question about his identity
and role, the interrogators now ask John why he is baptising.
The fourth gospel narrows the focus of the traditional material
dealing with the Baptist to emphasise the witnessing role of *the
voice in the desert*. He replies with the Isaian quotation dealing
with the *voice crying out* to prepare the way of the Lord.[38] 'The
voice crying out' originally signified the voice of the prophet
calling on the people to prepare for their return home from exile
in Babylon.[39] It envisaged the end of the exile, a new exodus of
the people and a passage through the desert, under the protection of the angels of God. In the Hebrew text of the Old
Testament it was seen in terms of a physical journey, a real physical *path in the desert*.[40] In the New Testament (and the LXX) *the
voice in the desert* cries out to prepare a path for the Lord. This implies a new, spiritual, exodus, a calling of the people to the
movement of repentance being carried on by John in the desert.
The *voice in the desert* calls for a return from spiritual exile, a path
in the heart that makes possible the approach of God to his people, opening up their hearts, levelling their pride, filling in their
emptiness.[41]

In stark contrast to his own baptism John describes the baptism in Holy Spirit by *the one who is coming after me, unknown to
you*. Here are three messianic designations: *the one coming into
the world*, *the one following/coming after* (who is destined to take
over the leadership) and *the unknown one in your midst*. Of this
coming one John proclaims: 'I baptise with water, after me there

---

36. Jn 4:20-25
37. Acts 3:22
38. Isa 40:3; cf Mt 3:2f; Mk 1:2f; Lk 3:4f.
39. Isa 40:3
40. The MT has 'path in the desert', the LXX and NT have 'voice in the desert'.
41. John and the synoptics follow the LXX 'voice in the desert' rather than 'path
in the desert'. John takes an independent line from the synoptics when he con-
flates the two elements of the LXX, which read 'prepare the Lord's road, make
straight God's path' into 'Make straight the Lord's path'. The synoptics have the
two elements. The Qumran community used this text to explain their living,
waiting, preparing and studying in the desert (I QS VIII 13-16), another point of
contact between John and Qumran. The synoptics apply this text to John the
Baptist, in John's gospel he applies it to himself (another example of apologetic
against those who saw him as Messiah?).

is coming one who will baptise in Holy Spirit.' To appreciate the impact of the contrast between their baptisms and to highlight the distinctive features of the Johannine presentation of the role of the Spirit, it should be put in the context of the practice and understanding of baptism at the time.

The baptism of John fits into a wider context as is evident, for example, from the baptismal rituals of the Qumran community with which he may have had contact or by whom he may have been in some way influenced. Given the fact that he conducted his ministry in an area close to the monastery at Qumran it is quite possible that he was influenced in some measure by their asceticism, ceremonial practice and messianic expectation. Their Manual of Discipline is very definite, however, that mere washing cannot really make one clean. It can clean flesh, but only the submission of one's soul to God's ordinances can make one internally clean. It is only God who will finally purge all the acts of man and refine him by destroying every spirit of perversity in his flesh, cleansing him by a holy spirit and sprinkling upon him the spirit of truth like waters of purification to cleanse him.[42]The rite itself therefore was not seen as effecting forgiveness and purification and people could not use it to become like the holy ones. It was seen as an external expression of a sincere inner disposition of repentance. Josephus Flavius presents a similar view of John's baptism. He says that it was 'not to beg pardon for sins committed, but for the purification of the body, when the soul had previously been cleansed by right behaviour'.[43] This understanding highlights the preparatory nature of John's baptism and accentuates the contrast with the baptism of Jesus.

Contrary to the impression given by many works of Christian art, the Spirit was not conferred on Jesus by the baptism of John but the descent of the Spirit marks a completely new initiative of God in the economy of salvation. Mark and Matthew state that Jesus had already been baptised and had come up out of the water when the Spirit descended upon him.[44] Luke further emphasises the point when he says that he had been baptised and was at prayer when the Spirit descended on him.[45] The gospel of John omits any reference to the actual bap-

42. I QS 3:7-9; 4:20-22; I Q H 16:12; cf 7:6; 17:26; frag 2:9, 3. The influence of Ezekiel is evident here (Ezek 36:25-27) and is close to Mk 1:18.
43. Josephus, *Ant.*, 18:117.
44. Mk 1:10; Mt 3:16.
45. Lk 3:21.

tism of Jesus and refers only to the descent of the Spirit, an event witnessed by John who is portrayed as the key witness: 'I have seen the Spirit come down as a dove from heaven and rest (remain/dwell) upon him.'[46] The descent of the Spirit upon Jesus, shows him to be the Son/chosen one of God.[47] It signifies, too, the new creation symbolised by the dove hovering above the water, like the Spirit of God hovering over the waters at creation.[48] It is reminiscent of the dove sent out by Noah heralding the ending of the flood, the completion of the punishment and the inauguration of a new covenant. All these allusions point to the new initiative of God. Whereas the baptism of John was called a baptism of repentance[49] and could be graphically described as an empty hand stretched out to God for forgiveness, the baptism of Jesus, described as baptism in the Holy Spirit,[50] signifies the beginning of a new era, a pivotal point in the economy of salvation, a new and final initiative of God in Jesus. This new era will be marked by the gift of the Spirit. Baptism as an empty hand stretched out to God in repentance is now passed and the promise of baptism in Holy Spirit announces the beginning of the eschatological time, marked by the return of the Spirit and the work of the Messiah. Baptism has taken on a whole new significance.[51] In the synoptics the eschatological imagery of the rending of the heavens is described at the baptism of Jesus to announce the inauguration of this final definitive ac-

---

46. Jn Jn 1:32; the verb used is *menein* which means 'rest, remain, dwell'.

47. Jn 1:32. In the synoptics this descent of the Spirit signifies the anointing of the Messiah and is interpreted by the witnessing voice of the Father (Isa 42:1; Ps 2:7). It signifies also the return of the quenched Spirit in a Spirit anointed messiah (Isa 11:2; 42:1; 61:1) and the eschatological event heralded by the rending of the heavens (Isa 64:1). Furthermore the river has salvific significance in the biblical tradition where it can be seen to symbolise life (Ezek 47:1-12), forgiveness (LXX Ezek 47:3) and healing (2 Kings 5:14).

48. The hovering of the Spirit in Gen 1:2 is like the hovering of a bird above the nest inciting the young to fly. The bird in question was interpreted by the rabbis as a dove brooding above the nestlings.

49. Mk 1:4

50. cf Acts 19:1ff as a practical manifestation of the promised reality.

51. 'Baptism' can signify the beginning of a new life and a new state and similarly 'Baptism in a holy Spirit' signifies the beginning of a new state involving a new and critical 'religious' experience (cf Acts 1:5; 11:16). The conversation with Nicodemus speaks of such an experience in terms of new birth and birth from above which are a prerequisite for entry into the kingdom (Jn 3:5). It can signify a crisis and decision about one's response to the Messiah. Jesus himself used the metaphor of baptism for his impending passion and death (Mk 10:38; Lk 12:50).

tion of God. In St John's gospel, where the baptism of Jesus by John is not mentioned, the reference to the rending of the heavens comes at a climactic moment during the inauguration of Jesus' ministry when the first disciples are gathered and he promises them a future in which they would see 'the heavens opened and the angels of God ascending and descending on the Son of Man'.[52]

Day Two: John witnesses to all who hear Jn 1:29-34
In his solemn proclamation on the second day of witness John the Baptist uses a revelation formula, introduced with 'Behold … ', where witness is borne by one person about another to a third party who in turn responds to the personal revelation. In this formula the one who speaks is revealing the mystery of the special salvific mission that the one referred to will undertake.[53] John twice exclaimed: 'Behold the Lamb of God.'[54] The second time he uses the formula two of his disciples followed Jesus. The same formula was used by Jesus as he saw Nathanael approaching: 'Behold a true Israelite in whom there is no guile' and Nathanael responded with a confession of faith.[55] Pilate declared to the crowd: 'Behold the Man' and 'Behold your King' and the hearers responded with a call for crucifixion.[56] Similarly when Jesus announced. 'Woman, behold your son, Son behold your mother', the disciple took her into his home.[57]

Behold the Lamb of God
However, on this second day of witness, John testifies to an unspecified audience saying: 'Behold the Lamb of God who takes away the sin of the world.' No one is described as being present or responding. It is as though he is presenting Jesus to Israel and the world at large, just as Pilate presents him to the world at large with the inscription: 'Jesus of Nazareth, King of the Jews' in the local, international and official languages of the empire. Using the lamb of God image in this 'absolute' way at the beginning of the gospel leads the reader to see in it an umbrella image

---

52. Jn 1:51
53. cf R.E.Brown, *op. cit.*, II, 923.
54. Jn 1:29,36.
55. Jn 1:47.
56. Jn 19:5,14.
57. Jn 19:26f.

or term which holds together many of the strands of the gospel.

John declared: 'Behold the Lamb of God who takes away the sin of the world'.[58] Taking away the sin of the world is the mission of Jesus, the revealer *par excellence* of the Father who sent him because he 'so loved the world that he gave his only Son, so that everyone who believes in him may not perish but may have eternal life.[59] Sin is here described as *the sin of the world*. As one reads through the gospel it becomes clear that this sin of the world is the sin of disbelief, the non-recognition of the light and the preference for darkness over light. It expresses itself in the rejection of the one sent by the Father and of the gift of life which he brings. Consequently it is a rejection of the Father who sent him. The one whom the Father has sent is both the gift and the revealer of the gift of God. Accepting the gift through believing the one sent, who is the revealer *par excellence*, gives one power to become children of God. Alienation from God is thus ended and sin is taken away. The question arises: 'How does the imagery of the lamb illustrate the process of taking away the sin of the world?' The reference to the lamb leads the reader to an image field where several traditions spring to mind in reference to the lamb and the taking away of sin. Throughout the gospel the reader sees that several of these images are at work.

First of all the lamb is called 'the lamb *of God*'. When the reader hears later that 'God so loved the world that he gave his only Son so that those who believe in him may not perish but may have eternal life'[60] it becomes clear in retrospect that the lamb is above all the gift of God for the life of the world. *It is the lamb of God as a sacrificial offering provided by God.*[61] God has taken the initiative. It is the lamb *of God*, God's lamb. One thinks immediately of Abraham about to sacrifice his beloved son, sole heir to the promise and only hope for the future and prevented from doing so by the divine gift of a substitute sacrifice.[62] God praised Abraham saying: 'Because you have done this, because you have not spared your own son …'[63] Like Isaac, Jesus is bound and led away *to the place*, carrying the wood for his sacrifice on his back.[64] In this case, however, he himself is the sacrifice pro-

---

58. Jn 1:29.
59. Jn 3:16.
60. Jn 3:16.
61. cf Gen 22:8.
62. Gen 22.1-14.
63. Gen 22:16.
64. Gen 22:6.

vided by God, putting an end to all other sacrifices, and in this he is the lamb who takes away the sin of the world.

The paschal lamb springs to mind. The blood of the Paschal Lamb was sprinkled on the doorposts in Egypt to protect the Hebrews from the destroying plague. It marked them out as God's own first-born and so the marking of the doorposts with the blood of the lamb was in fact an anointing of the household as part of the people of God. It is very significant in St John's gospel that the crucifixion takes place on the eve of the Passover, a day earlier than in the synoptics. This means that Jesus is condemned and executed during the time when the lambs are being sacrificed for the Passover. Of significance too is the fact that only John mentions the hyssop stick on which the sponge soaked in vinegar was held to Jesus' mouth. Hyssop was used for sprinkling the blood of the paschal lamb and so the instrument associated with the saving and anointing power of the blood of the lamb was raised aloft as Jesus died. The blood flowing from his side is also the focus of particular attention. Following through on the imagery of the *paschal lamb*, the blood of Jesus protects the followers and anoints them as children of God. His death will deliver the world from sin just as the original blood of the lamb saved Israel from the destroying angel. When Jesus died on the cross the soldiers did not break his legs and so the narrator quotes the scripture: 'not a bone of his will be broken', recalling the prescription that the paschal lamb was to be spotless and unblemished.[65] Originally the paschal lamb was not seen as a sacrificial lamb, but by the time of Jesus the sacrificial dimension was present due to the fact that the priests had taken over the slaughter of the lambs and it took place in the precincts of the Temple.[66]

The lamb as servant of God also comes to mind. *The Servant* is presented in Isaiah as a Suffering Servant, and described as a *lamb* that is led to the slaughter house, like a sheep that is dumb

---

65. Jn 19:36; Ex 12:46. Breaking the legs hastened the death which otherwise could take several days. With the legs broken the crucified person could not lift the body in the attempt to breathe and quickly smothered. It was in the interests of all concerned that the executions would be over and the bodies removed before the Passover.

66. Jesus dies a day earlier in John's gospel than in the other gospels. This facilitates the timing of his condemnation and death to correspond with the slaughter of the paschal lambs for the feast.

before its shearers, never opening its mouth.[67] He takes away sin
by vicariously suffering on behalf of sinners, taking their sins on
himself as he prays all the time for sinners.[68] Also of significance
is the 'lifting up' of the Suffering Servant.[69] He is raised to great
heights by God, to the amazement of those who had seen his former humiliation and suffering.[70] When Jesus speaks of being
'lifted up', there is a play on his being raised up on the cross and
raised up in glory, as for John they are the same event. The quotation from Zechariah 'They will look on the one whom they
have pierced' serves to recall, among other allusions, this aspect
of the raising up of the Suffering Servant.[71] 'See my servant shall
prosper, he shall be lifted up, exalted, rise to great heights ... so
will the crowds be astonished at him and kings stand speechless
before him; for they shall see something never told and witness
something never heard before.'[72] The Baptist bears witness to
the Spirit of God descending upon and remaining with Jesus.
This is reminiscent of the description of the Servant of God, the
chosen one, on whom the Spirit is conferred. Though the relationship of Jesus to the Spirit is very different in John, still the
reference to Spirit in close proximity to the references to the
Lamb of God brings the Spirit-endowed servant to the mind of
the reader.[73] In the presence of Pilate Jesus, like the *Servant*, remains silent as the lamb before the shearers, when he was taken
by 'a perversion of justice'.[74] Under pressure from the Jewish
leaders and the crowd, Pilate, the official representative of the
Roman Law, disregards his own verdict of innocence in the face
of prejudice and political pressure. Elsewhere in the New
Testament, the Acts of the Apostles sees Jesus as the servant
'dumb as a lamb before his shearers'.[75] At his death the quotation 'not a bone of his will be broken' recalls also the divine
protection of the faithful servant.[76] According to some Aramaic

---

67. Isa 53:7. The servant is designated *the chosen one* in the First and Third Songs
of the Servant, Is 42:1; 49:6f, empowered by the Spirit.
68. Isa 53:11f.
69. cf The Fourth Song of the Suffering Servant, Isa 52:13-53:12.
70. Isa 52:12ff.
71. Jn 19:37; Zech 12:10.
72. Isa 52:13ff (JB).
73. Isa 42:1.
74. Isa 53:8.
75. Acts 8:32; Is 53:7.
76. Jn 19:36; Ps 33 (34):20.

scholars there may have been an underlying tradition in the Aramaic of the Baptist in which there was a play on the word *telêh/talyâ*, which can mean either lamb or servant.[77]

The lamb of apocalyptic tradition was portrayed as the one coming from behind, from among the followers to take over the leadership[78] and to lead the faithful to victory in the war on sin.[79] The idea of the follower (of John) becoming the leader brings out the apocalyptic notion of the lamb becoming the shepherd. The one from his own following proclaimed Lamb by John subsequently declares himself to be the Shepherd who lays down his life for his sheep.[80] The apocalyptic lamb takes away sin by leading the saints in the war against sin to destroy the power of evil.[81] Jesus defeats the ruler of this world and proclaims that he has overcome the world.[82]

The lamb as *symbol of innocence* and *victim of persecution* is highlighted in the prophetic tradition where Jeremiah is persecuted for his prophecy against the Temple. He described himself as 'a gentle lamb being led to the slaughterhouse'.[83] In fact the experience of Jeremiah may be an important factor in the thinking behind deutero-Isaiah's portrait of the Suffering Servant. The innocent lamb therefore is no sentimental image but the tragic figure of the one persecuted for the word. Jesus had a strong prophetic attitude towards the Temple and his first action in Jerusalem in this gospel is the cleansing of the Temple. This incurs the wrath of the authorities and puts him in serious danger. Jesus the prophet is three times declared innocent by

77. Scholars looking for an Aramaic background to the gospel have argued that underlying the idea of lamb in this context there may be the Aramaic word *talyâ*, (Hb *tâleh*) which can mean servant, child or lamb, cf W H Brownlee, 'Whence John?', *John and Qumran*, ed J. H. Charlesworth, 178. R. E. Brown argues against this on the grounds that the Hebrew equivalent *tâleh* is not used for the Isaian servant, but rather *ebed*, the Aramaic equivalent of which is *'abda;* and there is no precedent for using *talyâ*, and *tâleh* is not translated as *amnos* in the LXX. However it can be argued that imagery is more fluid than vocabulary and cannot always be so closely tied down to an exact choice of words.

78. Rev 5:8, 12f; 7:9f; 15:3; 22:1, 3 describe the lamb enthroned and glorified, and Rev 13:8; 21:27 portray the lamb as the judge who has the book of life, reflecting the judgement theme of the Johannine portrayal of the Son of Man.

79. En 90:31; 89:52. In Revelation the term is the diminutive *arnion*, not *amnos* as in Jn 1:29, 36, but the concept is the same.

80. Jn 10:11, 15, 17, 18.

81.Rev 17:4 portrays the lamb (*arnion*) as victorious in war.

82. Jn 12:31; 16:33.

83. Jer 11:19. *arnion* is used here for lamb in LXX, not *amnos* as in Jn 1:29, 36. The idea is the same.

Pilate during his trial, but is still flogged and handed over for execution.[84] At his death the quotation 'not a bone of his will be
broken' recalls also the divine protection of the suffering just
one.[85] In similar vein, the Jerusalem Targum on Ex 1:15, describes Moses as a lamb when it describes the threat to the
Hebrew infants.

The sacrificial lamb was offered twice daily as a holocaust in
the Temple, in the morning and between the two evenings.[86] At
the spot where the holocaust was immolated one could offer a
lamb as sin offering by placing one's hand on the head of the victim before immolation, dipping a finger in the spilled blood and
smearing it on the horns of the altar before pouring the blood at
the foot of the altar.[87] Elsewhere in the New Testament the First
Letter of Peter says: 'You were emancipated … not with perishable things such as silver or gold, but with precious blood, as of
an unblemished and spotless lamb, namely the blood of
Christ.'[88]

Describing Jesus as lamb therefore opens up an image field
that stretches right across the Bible, and provides an umbrella
term for many of the traditions woven into the fabric of the
gospel.

John's witness can be summed up as follows. He points to the
one who ranks before him because he existed before him; the
one in their midst whose shoes he is unfit to untie; the one who
is coming into the world; the one in their midst unknown to
them; the one who is following (and by implication will emerge
as leader); the one who is the Lamb of God who takes away the
sin of the world, a designation that opens up an image field with
many resonances throughout the text of the gospel. He testifies
to the fact that the one who sent him to baptise told him that the
one upon whom he sees the Spirit come down and rest (remain/
dwell) is the one who will baptise in Holy Spirit,[89] and so he testifies that he is the Chosen one of God/the Son of God.[90] John did

---

84. Jn 18:38; 19:4, 6.
85. Jn 19:36; Ps 33 (34):20.
86. Ex 29:38-46, *amnos* is used for lamb.
87. Lev 4:32ff, *probaton* is used for lamb.
88. 1 Pet 1:18f (JB).
89. Jn 1:32-34; cf Is 11:2; 42:1; 49:3, 7; Mt 3:16; Mk 1:10; Lk 3:22.
90. Jn 1:34: 'chosen one' or variant reading 'Son'.

not know him.[91] Only through divine revelation could he know Jesus' true identity. The Holy Spirit thus enters the story through descending upon Jesus and remaining upon him. John contrasts his own baptism in water with the coming baptism in Holy Spirit. The baptism of John was a sign of repentance for the people, symbolised by ritual washing. It is contrasted with the baptism in Holy Spirit which will be conferred by Jesus when his mission reaches its accomplishment on the cross.

The Descent of the Spirit Jn 1:32.
The Spirit is introduced in John's gospel as the primary witness to Jesus. It is the Spirit who witnesses to John (the Baptist), marking Jesus as the chosen one of God, or the Son of God. John then in turn becomes the witness to Israel. John *sees* the Spirit 'come down' and 'remain' on Jesus, as had been foretold to him by the 'one who sent him'. It is a manifestation of the divine, an epiphany, for the benefit of John.[92] The Spirit *comes upon* and *remains/dwells* with Jesus not just as an intermittent inspiration for prophecy or sporadic power for action as in the case of the prophet or charismatic figure, but as an abiding presence. This is quite different from the accounts in the synoptics and the Acts of the Apostles which speak of 'the pouring out of the Spirit', 'being filled with the Spirit', 'driven by the Spirit' and 'casting out demons by the power of the Spirit'.[93] The Spirit does not empower or drive Jesus in John or make him who he is, as he appears to do in the synoptics. Rather, the Spirit manifests Jesus for who he is and it is *because* of who he is that he has the Spirit.[94]He has permanent possession of the Spirit and will baptise by sharing the Spirit. In response to the epiphany John witnesses that Jesus is the one who will baptise in Holy Spirit. Jesus is thus seen to 'have' and to 'dispense/give/bestow' the Spirit. When Jesus is glorified and draws all to himself one will have access to the abiding presence of the Spirit in him.

Scholars identify two primary conceptions of the Spirit, quite

91. This 'knowing' does not refer to human acquaintance or knowledge of name, place of birth or kindred. This will be further developed in the gospel as those who *think* they know him refer to his origins and family etc.
92. In a somewhat similar way the promise of seeing the angels of God ascending and descending on the Son of Man will be a promise of epiphany for Jesus' disciples (Jn 1:51).
93. Mt 4:1; Lk 4:1, 17-19; Acts 10:38.The Johannine Epistles, however, do stress the Spirit-Prophetic link, cf 1 Jn 4:1-6.
94. cf Isa 11:2; 42:1.

different from each other, in the gospel of John. 'On the one hand, the Spirit has been understood, along with 'wisdom' and 'word,' as a way of speaking of God's activity or as the manifestation of a particular divine activity or power ... On the other hand, the Spirit has also been conceived of as a 'personal divine being distinct from and in some degree independent of God'.[95] On the one hand, in the narrative passages of the gospel (chapters 1-12; 20), the water imagery used portrays the Spirit almost as a substance poured out on the believers. One must be born of water and the Spirit, born anew, born from above through the activity of God (Jn 3:5f). The Spirit is seen as the source of life in the believer (Jn 3:36; 6:63; 7:37ff) and the gift of the Spirit empowers the forgiveness of sins and the resulting passage from spiritual death to life (Jn 20:22f). This is in keeping with the biblical tradition of the life-giving power of the Spirit as seen, for example, in Ezechiel's vision of the dry bones.[96] Corresponding to the play on the words 'spirit' and 'breath' (*ruach* in Hebrew, *pneuma* in Greek), this first conception conceives of the Spirit in terms of God's power, wisdom, or breath and to speak of the presence of the Spirit is to speak of the presence of God, since 'spirit' connotes the means of God's power or activity in the world. This is more or less the same as the synoptic understanding.

On the other hand, the Spirit-Paraclete is the one who will teach, recall, testify, accuse and convict. In the narrative section of the gospel the plain term 'Spirit' is used, but in the farewell discourse(s) (chapters 14 to 17) the terms Spirit-Paraclete, Holy Spirit and Spirit of Truth are used. This second conception of the Spirit owes much to an understanding of various figures proposed as patterns for the portrayal of the Johannine Paraclete, including particularly prophetic figures, such as Elijah and Elisha, and angelic figures, such as the archangel Michael or the interpreting angel of apocalyptic literature. 'On this model the Spirit-Paraclete can be conceived of as something like an angel, a quasi-independent figure summoned by God to carry out particular divine purposes or to complete a certain mission in the world.'[97]

95. M. M. Thompson, *op.cit.*, 147f; using phraseology (in parentheses) of J. D. G. Dunn, *Christology in the Making: An Inquiry into the Origins of the Doctrine of the Incarnation*, 2nd ed London, SCM, 1989, 131.

96. Ezek 37:14; inter alia.

97. M. M Thompson, *op. cit.*, 147f.

G. Johnston points out that the figurative speech in all these passages should be noted – spirit like water is a cleansing agent (1:33); spirit like breath is a vital element (20:22); spirit as teaching, guiding, defending, is a divine power (chs 16-17) and unifying them all is the concept of a Christlike power that is ultimately in the control of God, the heavenly Father.[98]

M. M. Thompson wisely cautions that scholars have often concentrated on the distinctively Johannine concept of the Paraclete in chapters 14 to 17 at the expense of the references to the Spirit in the narrative sections of the gospel. Often too they have concentrated on the pre-history of the text, seeking sources and influences outside the text, and in the process overlooking the overall theology of the gospel itself.

Explanations for the different functions predicated of the Spirit, and even for the different conceptions of the Spirit operative at various junctures in John, must also be sought within the narrative progression of the gospel and in light of the functions of the Spirit that arise from each passage. That is to say, the gospel ought not to be constructed as a hodgepodge of mismatched statements about the Spirit-Paraclete that John never quite finished sorting through. There are genuine differences between statements about the 'Spirit' in the narrative portions of the gospel (chs 1-12, 20) and statements about the 'Paraclete' found in the farewell discourse. These can, and indeed must, be accounted for by the narrative movement of the gospel itself, as well as by John's theological reflection upon the identity of the Spirit.[99]

The Spirit is, therefore, a much more dominant figure in the fourth gospel than in the gospels of Matthew and Mark where mention of the Spirit is infrequent. The fourth evangelist's perspective is that Jesus during his ministry is the bearer of the Spirit, on him the Spirit descended and remained (1:33). He will subsequently give the Spirit to his disciples after his resurrection and exaltation. Though Jesus possesses the Spirit and so has continual power to do signs and know God's will, the Spirit will be given to his followers only after he is glorified. At 3:5 Jesus says to Nicodemus that the Spirit is necessary for rebirth, and at 6:63 he says to the murmuring followers at Capernaum that only the Spirit gives life. This implies that the disciples before Jesus'

---

98. G. Johnston, *The Spirit-Paraclete in the Gospel of John*, SNTSMS 12, 31f.
99. M. M. Thompson, *op. cit.*, 155.

resurrection have neither of these and 'hence their constant misunderstanding and lack of spiritual perceptivity during the ministry'.[100]

4. THE FIRST DISCIPLES OF JESUS Jn 1:35-51

Witness, recognition and discipleship emerge as a pattern in the gospel. The two mentions of the Lamb of God bind together the two days – the general witness to an unspecified but all embracing audience on the first day and the specific witness to his own disciples on the second. This in turn results in two of his disciples approaching Jesus and so there begins a chain reaction of witness, recognition and discipleship. The initial 'leaving of all things' in the synoptic account of the calling of the disciples is replaced in John by the confessions of faith that now follow, expressed in traditional categories. Also the sudden and unexpected nature of the calling of Jesus' first disciples by the Lake of Galilee in the synoptic gospels is replaced here by an initial encounter in the context of the ministry of John the Baptist.[101] The story is brought to life and enhanced with typical Johannine attention to position, movement and body language. John was *standing*, Jesus was *passing*, the disciples *followed*, Jesus *turned* round, they *went* and they *stayed*.

The faith confessions of the disciples which emerge gradually and spasmodically in the synoptics, and reach maturity only after the resurrection, are focused in St John's gospel on the first moment of contact with Jesus and are articulated in traditional messianic terms. John has brought together in these verses almost every important messianic title. This proleptic approach, seeing the future development already present in the inauguration, serves the plot of the gospel. In short, John presents a great deal of the truth about Jesus' identity and mission in these initial encounters. The faith confessions move from acknowledging Jesus as rabbi, through Messiah, the one Moses and the prophets wrote about, to the Son of God and King of Israel. The imagery of the prologue which presents the Word as the Life and the Light of the World is being translated into a series of

---

100. B. Witherington, *op. cit.*, 253.
101. Historically this scenario in John seems quite plausible. Mark and Matthew omit a previous knowledge of Jesus on the part of the first disciples before the call by the Lake of Galilee. This is probably for the purpose of isolating and highlighting the uniqueness and once-for-all nature of the call to discipleship, together with its obligation of leaving family and livelihood.

titles which are a blend of the messianic expectations of contemporary Judaism and of early Christian proclamation. However, as presented here they fall short of the mature Johannine assessment of Jesus' identity. These traditional titles and expectations are inadequate and so just as John had pointed ahead to the Lord whose way was being prepared, now Jesus points ahead and promises 'greater things'.

The 'disciples' are mentioned seventy eight times in the gospel, the 'twelve' are mentioned four times, and the term 'apostles' is not used. In the narrative plot of the gospel the disciples do not have perfect faith in spite of their proleptic confessions. This will become obvious in their crisis in chapter six when so many forsake Jesus that he puts the question to Peter: 'Will you also go?' It will be obvious again in their troubled state as they question Jesus during the Last Supper and in their first confused reactions on Easter Day. However, they manifest positive responses and in the thematic/theological 'plot' of the gospel their proleptic confessions are vehicles of the church's faith. Their questions and misunderstandings provide Jesus with opportunities to clarify his teaching and typify the questions and misunderstandings of the implied readers. The disciples also provide the role models for those who come to believe through their word. As with many of the characters in the gospel, there is a certain tension between their representative roles as spokespersons for the Christian faith and their own personal faith journeys.

Day Three: Andrew, Another and Simon Jn 1:35-42
When two of John's disciples followed Jesus he asked them: 'What do you seek?'[102] This is a profound existential question posed by Jesus and heard by the prospective disciples and by the reader. They responded: 'Rabbi, where do you live?'[103] Calling him 'rabbi' shows that they already recognise and respect him as a teacher. They ask him: 'Where do you live?'[104] He responds with the invitation to 'come and see!'. In typical Johannine fashion this exchange takes place on two levels. The

---

102. A variant reading has 'Whom do you seek?' which emphasises even more the inclusion with the garden scene.
103. Jn 18:4, 7. There is a contrast in the arresting party's question. They name Jesus and where he comes from, 'where he dwells', and in the irony of the gospel they say more than they realise.
104. Jn 1:38.

disciples address him as 'rabbi, teacher', and ask about his
dwelling, a typical question put to a rabbi by potential followers
inquiring where his disciples gather together with him for instruction. The reader, by now familiar with the deeper reality of
the gospel unfolding on two levels, realises that this is a profound question and an even more profound answer. The 'where,
whence and whither' (*pou, pothen, hopou*) of the gospel refer not
primarily to spatial and geographical location but to community
of relationship between Jesus and God and Jesus and the disciples.[105] The prologue has stated that the Son is ever at the
Father's side/in the bosom of the Father.[106] The verb used for
'live/dwell' is *menein* used of the Spirit coming upon Jesus, and
remaining/dwelling on him (*emeinen/menôn ep' auton*). In the
farewell discourse(s) to his disciples Jesus will use the corresponding noun when promising them: 'Those who love me will
keep my word, and my Father will love them, and we will come
to them and make our home with them.'[107] The metaphor of the
vine and the branches elaborates at length on the life-giving
bond between Jesus and his disciples, a bond described repeatedly as 'remaining' in Jesus, remaining in his love, and having
his words remaining in them.[108] This is followed by repeated
references to 'indwelling' (*einai en* is a synonym for *menein en*)
which has the connotation of permanence of relationship.
Therefore the question 'Where do you live?' in the Greek of St
John's gospel means: 'Where is the source of your life, the inspiration of your living, the life-giving relationship?' In the broader
biblical context it is associated with living under the protecting
presence of God. Seeking the dwelling place of the Lord is a
theme associated with God's special presence in the Temple, a
frequent theme in the psalms. 'He who dwells in the shelter of
the Most High and abides in the shade of the Almighty says to
the Lord "my refuge, my stronghold, my God in whom I
trust".'[109] 'Dwelling' in this gospel has the connotations of tabernacle, Temple and the glory of God's presence, now residing in

---

105. *pou* (where)is used eighteen times , *pothen* (whence, from where,) eight
times and *hopou* (where, whither, where to) thirty times in the gospel, a total of
fifty six times.
106. Jn 1:18.
107. Jn 14:23
108. Jn 15:4; *meinate en emoi kagô en hymin ... mê menê ... mê menête*; Jn 15:5: *ho
menôn en emoi.* cf Jn 15: 6, 7, 10.
109. Ps 90 (91):1ff.

Jesus. Jesus' response, 'Come and see' sets the programme for
the whole gospel which is about *seeing*.

From a literary point of view this opening scene forms an inclusion with the arrest in the garden at the end of the ministry
when Jesus asks the police and soldiers: 'Whom do you seek?'
and they reply by giving his name and where he comes from, i.e.
where he dwells: 'Jesus of Nazareth.' They have failed to see
where he really comes from, and come in the dark to arrest him
– another example of John's irony.

In response to the disciples' question Jesus issues the invitation: 'Come and see!', literally, 'come and you will see', i.e. as
the revelation unfolds. They came and saw where he dwells
(present tense, *menei*) and they remained/dwelt (*emeinan*) with
him that day. The invitation to 'see' is extremely important in
the context of the gospel and its vocabulary. M. M. Thompson
has pointed out that, 'whereas hearing is typically a means to an
end, such as faith or obedience, "seeing" can be portrayed both
as a means to an end *and* as an end in itself.'[110] A number of examples illustrate the point. As a result of the incarnation of the
Word one may *see* his glory (Jn 1:14). Jesus promises his disciples
that they will *see* heaven opened, and the angels of God ascending and descending upon the Son of Man (Jn 1:51). He tells
Nicodemus that he must be born again to *see* the kingdom of
God (Jn 3:3). Of particular interest is the repeated framing of the
witness to the resurrected Lord in terms of *seeing*. Jesus' words
to his disciples in the farewell discourses are full of promises
that they will *see* him (Jn14:7-9; 19-22) ... Mary Magdalene reports, 'I have *seen* the Lord' (Jn 20:18). The Beloved disciple
looks into the empty tomb, and he '*saw* and believed' (Jn
20:20).[111] Here at the beginning of the ministry Jesus invites his
disciples to *see* where he dwells. The reader already knows that
he is ever at the Father's side. The disciples are beginning their
preparation for *seeing* the glory.[112] They came, remained/dwelt

110. M. M. Thompson, *op. cit.* 114f.

111. *Ibid.* Italics mine.

112. The mention of the tenth hour has suggested to some commentators that it
was the beginning of the Sabbath and the first disciples thus dwelt with Jesus on
the Sabbath. This opinion is further supported by some scholars with reference
to the fact that it was traditional to celebrate weddings on Wednesday.
(Mishnah, *Kethuboth* I prescribes that the wedding of a virgin take place on a
Wednesday.) Working back from the wedding at Cana would seem to point to
this day as the Sabbath, if one does not count the fourth day as the first of the
final three days leading up to 'on the third day'.

with Jesus and entered into faith and discipleship. The gospel is an account of their coming to see. The Beloved Disciple, who may well be the 'other disciple' referred to here, comes to the great moment of seeing and believing when he sees the empty tomb and the grave-cloths. 'He saw and he believed.'[113]

Andrew, the brother of Simon Peter was one of these two disciples of John. His companion on the occasion is referred to as the 'other' disciple. It is quite possible that this 'other' disciple is the same person mentioned as the 'other' disciple present with Peter when Mary Magdalene brought news of the empty tomb, and identified by the narrator on that occasion as the 'Beloved Disciple', the one who reclined beside Jesus at the Last Supper, and the one who on entering the tomb, '*saw* and believed'.[114]

Following, and in response to, the experience of 'coming and seeing' Andrew finds Simon his brother and witnesses to him in the words: 'We have found the Messiah (which translated means Christ).'[115] In his almost childlike enthusiasm he forgets that in fact it was John who had pointed Jesus out to them, having himself received a divine revelation, and that Jesus had invited them to come and see. The initiative was not with them. It was with the Father, and Jesus. 'We have found' will be roundly corrected at the Last Supper when Jesus says: 'You have not chosen me. I have chosen you'.[116] However, in his initial enthusiasm Andrew brought Simon to Jesus. Looking at him Jesus says: 'You are Simon, the son of John. You shall be called Cephas, (which means rock/Peter).' Here again, Jesus is asserting his own initiative, pointing out that he knows Simon, who he is and whose son he is, and promising him a change of name which signifies a new role, direction and destiny in his life, conferred by Jesus. The traditional messianic expectations are being surpassed. The 'rock' designation of Simon is anticipated here in St John's gospel, but it will be the confession of faith by Peter after the multiplication of the loaves and Jesus' coming to them on the water, which will function as the Johannnine parallel to the confession at Caesarea Philippi in the synoptics.[117]

---

113. Jn 20:8.
114. Jn 20:2, 8.
115. This is the only place in the New Testament where the Greek form of Messiah, *Messias*, is used. Elsewhere it appears in the Greek translation *Christos*.
116. Jn 15:16; cf 13:18. Note the sequence 'follow, seek, find' in the narrative. It will be repeated. 'Seek' is used 34 times in John.
117. Jn 6:67ff; Mk 8:27ff and //s.

Day Four: Philip and Nathanael Jn 1:43-51
On the following day, Jesus wished to go to Galilee and he
found Philip. Again the initiative is taken by Jesus. He said to
him 'Follow me.' Philip was from Bethsaida, the town of
Andrew and Peter. He is the only disciple actually called by
Jesus in the gospel. Philip found Nathanael and said to him: 'We
have found the one Moses in the law and the prophets wrote
about – Jesus, son of Joseph, from Nazareth.' Again the
Johannine irony comes into play with Philip's assertion, *we have
found* the one Moses wrote about in the law, and the prophets
(wrote/spoke about). The irony is carried through in the exchange between Philip and Nathanael about the origins of Jesus,
'son of Joseph from Nazareth', and Nathanael's reply: 'Can anything good come from Nazareth?' The reader who knows the
divine origins of Jesus sees the irony of such a 'worldly based'
discussion of Jesus' origins. Philip said to him: 'Come and see.'
The initial invitation issued by Jesus is now repeated by a disciple. Many people will speculate on Jesus' human origins during
the ministry, some emphasising the belief that the Messiah's origins will be unknown. Jesus, in turn, will challenge them to
recognise his divine origins, his coming from above, sent by the
Father. Nathanael is now about to make such a discovery.

Seeing him coming to him Jesus said: 'Behold a true Israelite
in whom there is no guile.' The ability of Jesus to read character
and not to need testimony about anyone is immediately evident
as the reader senses the contrast with the wily ancestor Jacob/
Israel who wrested the primogeniture and its blessings from his
brother Esau by pressing his advantage during Esau's desperate
hunger, and conspiring with his mother to obtain the blessing
due to the first-born by stealth and deception. The response of
Nathanael to Jesus' intimate knowledge of him, is to ask about
the source of his extraordinary knowledge. His question is introduced with the interrogative *pothen*, whence. It is an apparently
straightforward question but it can be understood in a theological sense; 'From where do you get the knowledge of me?' To this
Jesus replied that before Philip called him, he had seen him
under the fig tree. What did Jesus mean by that? The implied or
intended and ideal reader might have no difficulty in picking up
the reference, but the real readers ever since have had to speculate.

The rabbis used the phrase 'to sit under the fig tree' as a

description of the doctors of the law sitting under a tree studying the scriptures, especially the messianic passages. If this was
the intended meaning in Nathanael's case, then his immediate
response to Jesus and his messianic style confession of faith are
very understandable. The fig tree was also seen as an allusion to
the tree of knowledge in Paradise, which was believed to have
been a fig tree.[118] For the prophets Micah and Zechariah 'sitting
under the fig tree' was a symbol of messianic peace and plenty.[119]
Nathanael responded to Jesus: 'Rabbi, you are the Son of God,
you are the King of Israel.' Nathanael, however, may well have
traditional views of 'Son of God' in mind. Traditionally, the angels, the people, the just one, and in a very special way the
anointed king, were referred to as 'sons of God'. Already the
reader knows from the prologue that Jesus is the Son of God, the
pre-existent Word made flesh, ever at the Father's side. John the
Baptist knows it because he has had a special revelation made to
him by the 'one who sent him to baptise'. Nathanael, and the
other disciples, have yet to learn the deeper meaning of the title
he has just bestowed.

The concept of the Messiah as king receives great prominence in this gospel. It is probably the oldest element in messianic
expectation. Matthew and Mark use it only in scenes of mockery, but here in John it is one of the first expressions of a disciple's faith, evoking Jesus' praise and a promise of greater things
to come. It figures again in the excitement of the crowd at the triumphal entry, and during the trial before Pilate. It is proclaimed
on the execution notice at the crucifixion and motivates the
'royal' burial of Jesus.[120] Jesus will interpret his kingship for
Pilate as one of witnessing to the truth. 'My kingdom is not of
this world ... For this I was born, and for this I came into the
world, to testify to the truth. Everyone who belongs to the truth
listens to my voice.'[121] This is close to the Philonic idea of kingship. Philo reflects the Stoic doctrine that the wise alone are
kings and so they are true shepherds of the people. He quotes
the examples of Jacob feeding the flock of Laban, and Moses, the
all-wise (*ho pansophos*) as shepherd of Jethro. He sees them in al-

---

118. Midrash *Rabbah* on Eccl 5:11; R. Schnackenburg, *op.cit.*, I, 317; R. E. Brown,
op. cit., I, 83.
119. Mic 4:4; Zech 3:10; 'Under which tree' was also a test of right judgement and
knowledge of persons, following the Susannah story in Daniel.
120. Jn 19:19, 38-42.
121. Jn 18:37.

legorical terms as preserving the mind from delusion and unreality. The 'person disposed to truth', *pros alêtheian anthrôpos*, dwells in each person's soul and is at the same time ruler, king, judge, and arbiter and witness of accuser within.[122] This is not far removed from Jesus' assertion of the nature of his kingship as a bearing witness to truth for 'the kingship of the Messiah is the sovereignty of the truth which he reveals and embodies'.[123]

The messianic expectations of the disciples are brought to a whole new horizon in the promise of Jesus that they would 'see greater things' than they had expected. They would see 'the heavens open and the angels of God ascending and descending on the Son of Man'. There first comes to mind the apocalyptic imagery of the Son of Man at the right hand of God and coming in glory on the clouds of heaven with the angels surrounding him, a scene familiar from Jesus' prediction at his trial before Caiaphas in the synoptics and from his warning to those who are ashamed of him 'in this sinful and adulterous generation'.[124]

However, on reflection several other levels of meaning also enrich the imagery. Following the mention of the true Israelite, one thinks of Jacob, the original Israel and his dream at Bethel of the ladder joining heaven and earth with the free passage of the heavenly beings between heaven and earth. Bethel, in Hebrew, means house or dwelling place of God. Following the above comments on dwelling, this brings the passage to a climax seeing in Jesus the new dwelling place of God. Jewish exegetes were divided in their interpretation of the story of Jacob's dream. The Hebrew phrase describing the angels ascending and descending, *ôlîm weyordîm bô*, can be translated as 'ascending and descending *on him* (Jacob/Israel) or *on it* (the ladder). John accepts the 'on Jacob/Israel' interpretation and adapts it to the Son of Man. In this connection Burney states: 'Jacob as the ancestor of the nation of Israel, summarises in his person the ideal Israel *in posse*, just as Our Lord, at the other end of the line, summarises it *in esse*, as Son of Man'.[125] C. H. Dodd develops the idea further, pointing out that for John Israel is not the Jewish nation, but the new humanity reborn in Christ, the community of those who are 'of the truth' and of whom Christ is King.

122. Philo, *De Agricultura*, 41ff; *Quod Deterius Potiori insidiari soleat*, 22ff.
123. C. H. Dodd, *op. cit.*, 229.
124. Mt 26:64; Mk 14:62; Lk 22:68; Mk 8:38.
125. C. F. Burney, *The Aramaic Origin of the Gospel*, 115.

Furthermore he is not only their king, but in a deeper sense he is their inclusive representative as they are in him and he in them.[126] This corporate and representative role is reinforced by the promise: 'When I am lifted up from the earth I will draw all to myself', spoken in the context of the lifting up of the Son of Man.[127]

The angels ascend from him and return to him as in a bonding of earth and heaven, a manifestation of the dwelling place of God on earth. The tent of God's presence referred to in the prologue and the statement about Jesus' risen body as the new Temple are brought immediately to mind. The reference is not to the future apocalyptic return of Jesus in glory, as in the synoptics, but to the earthly presence of the Son of Man and its significance for salvation. This becomes clearer in the next references to the Son of Man, in chapters three and five.

Amen, amen, I say to you

The 'Amen, amen, I say to you' which introduces the 'oracular' statement is the first of many such statements in which the *Logos*, Word made flesh, speaks in the world with all the solemnity of the one ever at the Father's side.[128] This double 'amen' at the beginning of a sentence is peculiar to John where it occurs twenty-five times. It leads into a significant statement that is intimately connected with what went before. A single 'amen' occurs in the synoptics where Matthew uses it thirty-one times, Mark thirteen times and Luke six times. The double 'amen' is found at the end of a sentence in some Qumran texts, obviously under liturgical influence.[129] The Johannine usage strikes the solemn liturgical note, creating a context for divine revelation, before Jesus pronounces *legô hymin (soi)*, 'I say to you'. The use of 'I say to you', *legô hymin (soi)* immediately after the double 'amen' emphasises the *legô-Logos*, reveal-revealer connection, as the sentence in each case would be quite grammatically correct without the 'I say to you'. For example, 'Amen, amen, you will see...' is a perfectly clear statement without the 'I say to you'.

126. Dodd, *op. cit.*, 246.
127. Jn 12:32ff.
128. Many modern translations empty the oracular formula of its link to the uniqueness of the *Logos*/Word/Revelation by replacing it with a reinforced but very ordinary statement such as 'I tell you solemnly', rather than maintaining the 'unusual' but highly significant *Logos-lego* related formula, *'amen, amen legô...'*
129. I QS,1:20, 2:10, 18 (after blessings and curses); cf 1QS 1-17.

Son of Man

The Son of Man has been introduced into the story. Who is this Son of Man who figures prominently in this gospel and in the synoptics, especially in Mark's gospel? He is mentioned thirteen times by John and fourteen times by Mark. B. Lindars puts it succinctly when he says that John makes use of the title 'because it provides him with the means to express the relationship of Jesus to God'.[130] The Son of Man traditions in the New Testament are principally influenced by two Old Testament passages, Dan 7:15-27 and Isa 52:13-53:12. In Daniel the Son of Man is given royal power and honour. This is spelled out in the synoptics and John as power to be judge, life-giver, and deliverer of the kingdom. In the synoptics it is fused with the Isaian Suffering Servant theme of necessary abasement, obedience through suffering and final vindication by God. John does not have the abasement theme, but shares the teaching of a necessary 'raising up', a double play on crucifixion and glorification. Schnackenburg states that though the fourth evangelist is aware of the traditional view, his profounder theological contemplation has modified it for the benefit of his christology.

> The Son of Man on earth speaks only of his relationship to the heavenly world, with which the angels ascending and descending on him keep him in constant communication. It is only in the following revelation discourses that the reader learns that the Son of Man was once in heaven and returns there again. This first Son of Man *logion* also has another important aspect, in as much as it says that the Son of Man will disclose himself to believers, in further revelations.[131]

The Son of Man remains an enigma to unbelievers or to the weak of faith (cf 8:28; 12:34d). It might be said that the 'Son of Man' in John has the same function as the 'Messianic Secret' in Mark. B. Lindars sees the use of 'Son of Man' in John as evidence of John's unerring capacity to pierce through to the inner meaning of the primitive *logia*.[132] F. J. Moloney points out that scholars who show that 'the Son of Man' repeats throughout the gospel what was already said of the *Logos* in the prologue do not give the Johannine use of 'the Son of Man' its full importance.

130. B. Lindars, 'The Son of Man in the Johannine Christology' in *Christ and Spirit in the New Testament: Studies in Honour of Charles Francis Digby Moule*, 43-60, B. Lindars and S. Smalley (eds), 60.

131. R. Schnackenburg, *op. cit.*, I, 531.

132. B Lindars, 'The Son of Man in the Johannine Christology', 60.

He states further that it is true that 'the Son of Man' continues in the rest of the gospel, what has been said of the *Logos* in the prologue, but the Johannine Son of Man presupposes and builds upon the key ideas of pre-existence and revelation and does not merely repeat these ideas.[133] He agrees that there may well be a close link with the Wisdom traditions in this, but insists that there are Son of Man sayings which indicate that John wants to say more than this in his use of the title. He cites the important example of the crucifixion-elevation theme of 3:13-14; 8:28 and 12:34, and the judgement which the Son of Man is said to exercise in 5:27. Another important feature has been pointed out by C. H. Dodd. The Johannine Son of Man is a collective figure, embodying the people of God, possibly also another influence of the Isaian Servant. Unlike the Hellenistic archetypal man of metaphysical abstraction, the *anthrôpos*, the Johannine Son of Man is identified with a concrete historical person, the individual human being, Jesus of Nazareth, Son of Joseph.[134] M. Casey stresses the fact that the 'one like a Son of Man' was used as a corporate figure in New Testament times to represent Israel.[135] In this Jesus took on the Danielic role of the saints of the Most High, achieving authority through suffering. The gospel bears out this corporate dimension in the metaphor of the vine and the branches, the emphasis on mutual indwelling and the statement about 'raising up' and drawing all to himself. F. J. Moloney states:

> ... the Son of Man in the fourth gospel is the embodiment of 'new humanity'. He leads the whole community to union with God. John has taken the title from Jewish apocalyptic and uses it for his special theology of the cross which is at once a theology of revelation, judgement and glory. The elevated Son of Man on the cross is the place where all men can make their final decision for or against God.[136]

Jesus often uses the title to correct false messianic hopes, both in the synoptics and John. The passion predictions in the synoptics and the promise of seeing greater things at the opening of the heavens in John are cases in point, among others.[137]

133. F. J. Moloney, *The Johannine Son of Man*, 2nd ed. 8f.

134. C. H. Dodd, *op cit.*, 249

135. M. Casey, 'The Corporate Interpretation of 'One like a Son of Man' (Dan 7:13) at the time of Jesus', *NT* 18 (1976), 167-180.

136. F. J. Moloney, *The Johannine Son of Man*, 11.

137. Mk 8:31; 9:31; 10:33-34 and //s.

The witness of the Baptist, and the confessions of the first disciples have the cumulative effect of making a comprehensive
statement of the fulfilment of the messianic hope of *the one coming into the world*. Jesus' oracle lifts these expectations to a new
and unexpected plane. In doing so the Johannine emphasis on
the divine presence and the bonding of heaven and earth are
given full play.

The Wedding at Cana (Jn 2:1-12)

1. THE PLOT

The Wedding at Cana functions as the climax of the initial series of days which inaugurated the ministry. Its connection with what preceded is cemented by the opening 'and on the third day'. It also functions as the opening of the next major section of the gospel which is contained between the two signs/miracles performed at Cana. The second sign, the healing of the royal official's son, opens with a reference to Cana where the first sign had been performed and closes with a reference to the healing as the second sign in Cana. Drawing such particular attention to the two signs serves to punctuate the overall narrative by enclosing the intervening section in a frame. This intervening narrative concentrates on typical responses to Jesus. The nuptial and bridegroom imagery is very much in evidence in this section.

The Wedding at Cana functions also as an inclusion with the crucifixion scene where the *hour* introduced at Cana is fulfilled, the *glory* first manifested at Cana is established, and the *mother of Jesus*, the *woman*, figures prominently in the final scene of the public ministry as she did when it was inaugurated at Cana.[138] The scene contains the nuptial setting and imagery against which Jesus can be portrayed as the bridegroom of Israel.

The wedding is said to take place 'on the third day', though a six or seven day period (depending on how one counts the days) has just been described.[139] The mother of Jesus was there but her personal name is not given. Neither are the names of his disciples who were present.[140] Surprisingly, the names of the bride and groom are not given, nor is their relationship to Jesus and his family specified. The wine runs short but the reason is not given. The mother of Jesus notices the shortage and draws her son's attention to it. Addressing her as 'woman' and not as 'mother' Jesus makes an enigmatic reply, asking her: 'What is it

---

138. Jn 19:25-27.
139. Six days if one counts the fourth day as the first of the three day period ending 'on the third day', seven if one counts another three days after the fourth. The allusions to Exodus favour a six day interpretation, those to creation, a seven day period. Typical of this gospel, more than one set of references/allusions can be intended.
140. The personal name of the Mother of Jesus is not given anywhere in St John's gospel.

to me and to you?' and asks about his *hour* in a few words that can mean either 'has my hour not come?' or 'my hour has not yet come.' She orders the servants to do his bidding, an unusual and very determined gesture since the servants took their orders only from the chief steward. Then Jesus orders them to fill and carry out the water jars each containing a huge volume of water, twenty to thirty gallons.[141] The chief steward whose name also is not given speaks to Jesus as though he were the bridegroom and comments on the quality of the water made wine and on the tradition of serving the best wine first. It all sounds rather strange.

2. THE SIGN

Certainly as an account of an ordinary wedding the whole story seems very strange indeed. However, the mention of *the third day* and the suppression of the personal names of all except Jesus alerts the reader to the fact that this is a symbolic narrative in which a wedding is being regarded as a prophetic sign.[142] An ordinary event becomes the medium of divine revelation and represents something analogous to, but far greater than itself. It is a parable in action. Wedding feasts and wine figure prominently in Jesus' parables in the synoptics and in the broader biblical tradition. So do the vine, the vineyard, the vintage and the vintage and harvest banquet. The reader therefore realises, and is subsequently told, that this is a prophetic *ôt*, a Johannine *sêmeion*. However, although both the prophetic *ôt* and the Johannine *sêmeion* are called 'signs' they do not correspond to what today is conventionally known as a sign.[143] They are really symbols as the term is understood in our contemporary culture. A sign points to a reality beyond and extraneous to itself, in which it does not participate. A symbol participates in the greater reality it represents as it holds a sensory, perceptible reality and a transcendent, imperceptible reality together.

As this wedding banquet is lifted out of its particular historical circumstances it opens an image field that reaches right across the bible. *The third day*, has come. It recalls the gift of the

---

141. The text says 'two to three *metrêtes* , measures'. One measure equals 39.39 litres, about nine gallons.

142. *ôt* in prophetic literature.

143. The term 'sign', *sêmeion* is used in the gospel text itself for the wedding of Cana and the healing of the royal official's son, Jn 2:11; 4:54. It is also used in the expressions such as 'seeking signs', Jn 4:48; 6:30.

law on Sinai, the covenant and the manifestation of the glory of
the Lord.[144] The gift of the law and all that accompanied it by
way of God's manifestation of glory and protecting presence resulted in the covenant. This covenant was graphically described
as a marriage bond between God and the people.[145] The
Promised Land flowing with milk and honey came as an inheritance with the marriage. The ongoing fidelity to the covenant
guaranteed the inheritance. Just as the biblical writers had described how the disobedience of the first man and woman of creation had replaced Eden and its abundance with an unwilling
earth from which a living had to be wrested by the sweat of
one's brow, so too the prophets warned that neglect of the
covenant would lead to drought, famine and exile from the
land.[146] The promise of restoration in messianic times envisaged
another reversal when the hills would flow with new wine and
the harvest follow immediately after ploughing.[147] When the authority of God is acknowledged the covenant will be restored
and rendered secure with the virtues of justice and integrity. The
harmony of Eden will be restored when lion and lamb lie down
together and peoples beyond number will come to know the
Lord, accept God's authority and worship in Zion.[148] The
restoration of the divine authority and the attendant blessings
are encapsulated in the image of the reign/kingdom of God.
Jesus in his parables uses the wedding banquet as a metaphor
for the kingdom, with all it entailed by way of reconciliation,
restoration and abundance. The Book of Revelation looks forward to the final establishment of the reign of God in terms of
the eschatological banquet, the wedding feast of the lamb. Here
at the wedding feast in Cana the wine has run out and the
Mother of Jesus says, 'They have no wine.' The water for purification is there in abundance. The preparatory rites of purification, like the water baptism of John, have served their purpose.
Now Jesus provides the wine for the messianic banquet, and the
guest becomes the host as he assumes the role of the bridegroom
of Israel.

The new relationship replacing the covenant, the Johannine
counterpart to the kingdom in the synoptics, in which those who

144. Ex 19:16-20; 24:16f.
145. Hos 2:19f; Isa 25:6-8; 62:5; Jer 2:2; 3:14.
146. Gen 3:17-19.
147. Am 9:13.
148. Isa 9:1-7; 11:1-9; 2:1-4.

believe will be given power to become children of God, being born from above, has been proclaimed in the prologue. Here at Cana it is symbolically inaugurated. Jesus has supplied the wine. At the Last Supper he will tell his disciples that he is the vine and they are the branches and that they too will bear fruit if they remain in him. The vine and the branches constitute the vineyard, the long established metaphor for the people of God.[149] Now the preparatory ritual gives way to the celebration of the wedding feast as the water of purification becomes an abundance of the finest wine of the messianic banquet, just as John's baptism in water gives way to Jesus' baptism in the Holy Spirit.[150]

As reference to 'the third day' alerts the reader to the revelation of the glory of the Lord and the gift of the law on Sinai, so too the creation imagery of the prologue and the numbering of days that follows can dispose the reader to an understanding of the wedding at Cana against the background of the Genesis story of the Garden of Eden. In this perspective the scene is set for the man and woman of the new creation. The suggestion of the woman at Cana, unlike the suggestion of the woman in Eden, is true, perceptive and compassionate. The man, unlike the man of Eden, does not respond spontaneously to the human prompting, but commits himself to the will of God and its accomplishment in *the hour*. He presumes no miracle but leaves the water in the hands of God, wherein it becomes the finest quality wine, as the servants obey both the *woman*, the first disciple in faith, and the man of obedience. The servants become the agents, and the chief steward the witness, of something they never envisaged. Eden is reversed, dearth gives way to plenty. Creation is subjected to creator. The reign of God is acknowledged and the blessing of abundance is inherited.

3. THE STORY

The 'sign' transcends the 'earthly' story, but the 'earthly' story needs to be examined. The persons present, except Jesus, are not given their personal names, but described according to relationship to Jesus and function at the wedding feast - the mother and disciples of Jesus and the servants and chief steward of the feast. Scholars maintain that 'mother of Jesus' signifies both a relation-

---

149. Isa 5:1, 2, 7; 27:2, 3; Ps 79 (80):8, 9.
150. cf Isa 25:6; 55:1f; Am 9:13f.

ship and a function in this story. Representative figures such as Mother of Jesus, Samaritan woman, Beloved Disciple, Royal Official, are often nameless in the gospel. This enhances their power to represent religious, ethnic or social groups.

The reason for the mother's concern about the shortage of wine and her motive in drawing her son's attention to it is not stated. In a society whose culture was influenced by honour – shame considerations, the shortage of wine on such an occasion, a wedding feast which could go on for two days, would have been an extreme embarrassment, a cause of shame. The text states that the Mother of Jesus *was there*, but that 'Jesus *was invited*, and his disciples'. Does this mean that they were there in different capacities? Was she there as an older relation or friend sharing the obligations of hospitality (after all she did give orders to the servants) or was she also a guest, but an experienced one who quickly noticed the problem? Why did she address Jesus on the matter? Was she just upset about it and telling her son about her concern? Was she expecting a miracle? Did she think he was influential enough to have a word in someone's ear? Did the group of disciples have a common purse at that stage and access to immediate financial relief? Was she motivated by compassion or did she see an opportunity for further enhancing her important son's reputation and her own status as his mother? One can only speculate, and speculation on these points has been generated by considerations as different from each other as sentimental Marian devotion and rigorous feminist critique.[151]

Typical of his reactions to requests in this gospel, Jesus hesitates, as he will do in the case of the royal official's son, when he lamented the seeking after signs and wonders, and in the case of the summons to the dying Lazarus, when he waited another two days, saying it was for the glory of God. This hesitation on Jesus' part is reflected also in the synoptic tradition, as for example in the case of the Syro-Phoenician woman's plea for her daughter.

His reaction to his mother reflects another tradition also present in the synoptics. It emphasises the spiritual relationship of those in the kingdom, and points out that it transcends physical descent, as in the case of the children of Abraham, or relationship, as in the case of his mother, sisters and brothers. This is borne out by his remark, 'Who are my mother and my brothers?' and his pointing to those listening to his word saying that they

151. cf A. Fehribach, *The Women in the Life of the Bridegroom*, 23-43.

are his mother and sister and brother.[152] A similar response is given to the woman who proclaims: 'Blessed is the womb that bore, and the breasts that nursed you.'[153] Physical motherhood has no special place in the scheme of things. The synoptic tradition also emphasises this in the words of Elizabeth: 'Blessed is she who believed that there would be a fulfilment of what was spoken to her by the Lord.'[154] She is praised for the faith that enabled her biological motherhood. Now that same faith is in evidence here in Cana where the Mother of Jesus is represented as an exemplar of faith through her words: 'Do whatever he tells you.'[155]

The question: 'What is this to me and to you?' translates the Greek *ti emoi kai soi*, which in turn seems to reflect the Hebrew *mâh lî wâlâk*. This is a reply that 'is abrupt and draws a sharp line between Jesus and his mother'.[156] It is a Semitic idiom used for distancing oneself from the request or issue involved, 'an agreement to disagree ... (and) not to become involved with the specific concerns of the party addressed'.[157] In this case it is both a statement that the shortage of wine is not his responsibility and a refusal to do anything about it. R. E. Brown points out that in the OT the Hebrew expression has two shades of meaning, one in a situation of discord, the other when an inappropriate request is made. The second case is of interest here. Brown states: 'When someone is asked to get involved in a matter which he feels is none business of his, he may say to the petitioner, "What to me and to you?", i.e. that is your business, how am I involved? Thus, there is always some refusal of an inopportune involvement, and a divergence between the views of the two persons concerned; yet ... (this second case) implies simple disengagement.'[158]

Though the address 'woman', *gunai*, is a polite and formal way of addressing a woman, somewhat like the French 'Madame', and Jesus uses it regularly as an address, it is, however, rather strange and unprecedented in Hebrew and Greek litera-

152. Mk 3:33f.
153. Lk 11:27f.
154. Lk 1:45.
155. Jn 2:5.
156. C. K. Barrett, *The Gospel according to St John*, 2nd ed. London: SPCK, 1978, 191.
157. C. H. Giblin, 'Suggestion, Negative response, and positive action in St John's Gospel', *NTS* 26 (1979-80), 197-211.
158. R. E. Brown, *op.cit.*, I. 99.

ture for a son to address his mother in this way, and so one rightly
suspects a deeper significance in the address.[159]

The reply of Jesus which seems to be aimed at stopping his
mother in her tracks is followed immediately by her instruction
to the servants to 'do whatever he tells you!' These words to the
servants are reminiscent of the words of Pharaoh to the
Egyptians when famine was raging through the land. He told
the people to go to Joseph 'and do whatever he tells you'. Then
people from all over Egypt and all over the world came to
Joseph to buy grain when he opened all the storehouses of
Egypt.[160] Even in the face of apparent rejection or rebuke the
mother of Jesus trusts in his word, unconditionally. She understands the significance of his comment about his *hour*. She is the
first in the gospel narrative to do so and in keeping with her understanding she instructs the servants to do his bidding. In so
doing she takes an initiative in faith which begins the ministry of
the one who will provide the wine, the water and the bread of
life. In so doing, she also follows in the tradition of a series of
women who played key roles in furthering the history of salvation.

The 'patriarchal' narratives in Gen 12-50 give pride of place
to the male figures, Abraham, Isaac, Jacob and his twelve sons.
The role of the matriarchs is overshadowed, but when one ex-
amines the stories, there is ample evidence to show that had it
not been for their intervention the stories would have been far
different or have come to a full stop. Not only did they give birth
to the children of the patriarchs, they also intervened at critical
moments to ensure the continuation of the line of descendants
who would inherit the promises. Sarah secured Isaac's position
against the threat from Ishmael and his mother Hagar.[161]
Rebecca secured the blessing of primogeniture for Jacob, saved
him from the wrath of Esau and secured his future with his
uncle Laban.[162] Rachel, Leah and their handmaidens played out
their parts in the story of the sons of Jacob/Israel, the fathers of
the twelve tribes.[163] The mother of Moses and the daughter of
Pharaoh risked the wrath of the law for their biological and

---

159. Mt 15:28; Lk 13:12; Jn 4:21; 8:10; 20:13; 2:27.
160. Gen 41:55.
161. Gen 21:8-21.
162. Gen 27:1-45.
163. Gen 29-30.

adopted child.[164] The women in Matthew's genealogy Tamar, Rahab, the wife of Uriah (Bathsheba) and Ruth all took action to secure the line of the promise, and were referred to as mother of the sons they bore.[165] Matthew's account then leads on to 'Mary, and of her was born Jesus, who is called the Christ'. The mothers of the heir to the promise were formidable figures in the history of salvation, often left to take action to secure the future. Here at Cana the mother of Jesus does just that in the symbolic context of Jesus' inaugural sign. She intervened and did not take 'no' for an answer. Her intervention sets the ministry in motion by facilitating the first of the signs.

Being introduced into the story as Mother of Jesus, and addressed by Jesus, not as mother, but as 'woman', puts her in the context of the great women and mothers of the Bible. Not only is she mother of Jesus, she is woman in her own right. This picks up on the rich symbolism of the women in the Bible. Scholars debate the exact allusions. Perhaps several are at play together. The woman/mother imagery can be seen against the background of the Eden story. As such it portrays her as the new Eve, the woman of the new creation, soon to be designated mother of the Beloved Disciple who represents all disciples, as Eve was mother of all the living.[166] As woman in her own right and mother of an important son she can be seen in line with the great 'matriarchs' already mentioned. The mother of Jesus can also be seen as the representative of the people of Israel, embodying his natural and spiritual origins. She represents also the Jewish Christian community from which the Saviour, the gospel and the church emerged.

Two translations of the Greek *houpô êkei hê hôra mou* are possible: 'My hour has not yet come' or 'Has my hour not come?' The *hour* is introduced and mention of it will recur throughout the

---

164. Ex 2:1-10.

165. Mt 1:3, 5, 6; cf Gen 38; Josh 2:8-21; Ruth 3-4; 1 Kings 1:11-40.

166. From the early Fathers like Ambrose and Ephrem, through to modern commentators like R. E. Brown, E. C. Hoskyns, F. M. Braun, Max Thurian and others, scholars have seen the connection with Eve. Some, such as P. Gächter, J. D. Crossan, E. J. Kilmartin, M. Zerwick and others have seen this imagery together with that of the woman of Revelation 12. See A. Fehribach *The Women in the Life of the Bridegroom*, 23-25, A. Culpepper, *Anatomy of the Fourth Gospel*, 133, R. E. Brown, *op. cit.*, I, 107-109; R. Collins, 'The Representative figures of the Fourth Gospel', *Downside Review* 94 (1976),120, for a review and evaluation of the various positions. The topic of her motherhood will be further discussed in the commentary on the Golgotha/Calvary scene, Jn 19:25-27.

gospel until the *kairos* when the *glory* is fully manifested.[167] The hour refers to the passion, death, and resurrection of Jesus and his return to the Father. The mention of it here marks the opening of the ministry with the first sign. It also initiates the count down to *the hour*. Jesus' *hour* is not in his control but in the control of the Father. Hence his enigmatic reply to his mother.

The third day, the day of revelation, has come. It recalls the day of the revelation of the glory of the Lord and the divine presence on Sinai. The *hour* is introduced and mention of it will recur throughout the gospel until the *kairos* when the *glory* is fully revealed. The faith of the disciples reaches a significant point of development. The ministry is inaugurated. The challenge is about to come.

4. CONCLUSION

The disciples and their incipient faith have now been dealt with for the time being and the gospel can concern itself with its broader agenda. The disciples do not really figure again in the story of the ministry, until the multiplication of the loaves and its sequel on the lake, followed by the defection of many of the disciples and the confession of Peter.[168] After that they do not reappear until Judas complains at the anointing of Jesus by Mary of Bethany.[169] Finally, when Andrew and Philip approach him to say the Greeks wish to see him, Jesus proclaims that his *hour* has come.[170]

In typical Johannine form the story of Cana is concluded with a geographical reference. *After this he went down to Capernaum ...* Such references open and close various episodes in the gospel.[171] As often in the synoptic tradition, this reference to his mother describes her as accompanied by family members. This was a bonding of mutual affection, care and responsibility, especially in the context of travelling, which could be very hazardous, with danger from bandits and beasts.

---

167. Jn 7:6, 8, 30; 8:20.
168. Jn 6:67ff.
169. Jn 12:4ff.
170. Jn 12:20ff.
171. These geographic references opening and closing various passages are related to the theme of the passage. Attempts to harmonise them into an overall chronological or geographic plan in logical order sometimes can be difficult, and can miss the point of their immediate significance in the text.

The Challenge in the Temple (Jn 2:13-25)

1. THE PLOT

In St John's gospel Jesus begins his ministry in a context where the Jerusalem authorities have already flexed their muscles against John and his possible challenge to their monopoly on religious authority. In the synoptic tradition it is clear that their attitude to John proved to be an ongoing embarrassment to them, and that Jesus did not shrink from reminding them of their obtuseness in this regard when they began to question his own authority. His public question to them about the source of John's authority left them the stark choice of admitting their own failure or facing the hostility of the people.[172]

It is not surprising then that Jesus would take a position in relation to the Temple, their centre of power and influence, and the setting for a significant amount of his teaching and healing activity during the pilgrimage feasts. To readers familiar with the synoptics, however, it may come as a surprise that the incident commonly referred to as 'the cleansing of the Temple' takes place at the beginning of the ministry in St John's gospel. This contrasts with the synoptic accounts where it takes place at the end and is presented as the final challenge to official authority, bringing into sharp focus the question of Jesus' authority, and setting in motion the events leading to his trial and execution. By way of contrast the incident takes place at the beginning in St John's gospel and serves as a programmatic statement and a throwing down of the gauntlet to the establishment from the outset of the ministry. What really matters, however, is not the timing but the meaning of the event. The incident is a challenge on one level, but for John it has a far deeper meaning than just a 'cleansing' of the Temple and a 'purification' of its rituals.

The institutions of Israel were intended to reveal God, enabling the people to approach God and to be righteous before God. As Christians reassessed all these things in the early years of the church, the 'once-for-allness' of the revelation through Jesus encouraged a radical reassessment of many, if not all, the earlier means of mediation. Beginning here with the Temple and its sacrificial worship, the story of Jesus will unfold through the succession of Jewish feasts, showing how Jesus fulfils and sur-

---

172. When they questioned his own authority he responded with the question about their assessment of the authority of the Baptist, Mk 11:27-33 and //s.

passes the older promise of the institution or feast, and opens up
its meaning for the present and future in the context of his own
identity and mission. He begins the process here at the Temple
where he, the Lamb of God, passes judgement on, and replaces,
the sacrificial system. He proclaims a new temple in his resurrected body, which will ensure the divine presence among the
community of believers. This understanding is particularly important for Jewish Christians in the light of the destruction of the
Temple and the growing alienation from their mother Jewish
community with its institutions, feasts and various religious and
social celebrations and supports.

In St John's gospel the dramatic scene in the Temple functions as a symbolic narrative, especially in relation to the second
part of the scene where the *logion* (pronouncement) about destroying the Temple fits into the unfolding revelation of Jesus'
relationship to the Father, and opens onto the future divine
presence of the Risen Lord and the indwelling of the Holy Spirit,
the Paraclete, in the community.

Since there is but one journey of Jesus to Jerusalem in the synoptic gospels the reader can see that the event had to be placed
in the context of his final days. However, the fact that this action,
according to all four gospels and the Acts of the Apostles, attracted such hostile attention from the authorities and resulted
in their questions about Jesus' own authority, makes it likely
that if the event took place early in the ministry it would have
proved an obstacle to Jesus' continuing his ministry especially in
Jerusalem and above all in the Temple area. One therefore is inclined to think that the synoptic account towards the end of the
ministry is well placed historically. It is placed early in John's
gospel for theological and literary reasons where it functions as
a programmatic event setting the tone of the ministry and offering a challenge.[173] It is a catalyst provoking a reaction, a decision
for or against Jesus. Like the wedding at Cana it is a sign, even if
not a miraculous one, a Johannine *sêmeion* like a prophetic *ôt* or a
parable in action. As a symbolic narrative it provides an interpretative key and supplies a paradigm for other passages using
Johannine techniques of misunderstanding, prolepsis and symbolism.

---

173. John's gospel portrays the raising of Lazarus as the final 'straw' for the authorities. Here again theological concerns are uppermost.

2. BACKGROUND

To appreciate the Johannine account of Jesus' action and *logion* in the Temple the reader needs a broader look at the place of the Temple in the life of the people. This is a necessary extra text for a fruitful engagement between the reader and the gospel.

Jesus may well have had a strongly critical attitude to the Temple throughout his ministry which boiled over in the last days. In this he was not alone in his own day. The Hellenists, the Essenes and the Samaritans were all less than enthusiastic in its regard. In having such a critical attitude, Jesus would also have been in direct line of descent from the prophets. The four accounts of Jesus' cleansing of the Temple stand in continuity with this prophetic tradition. It was commonplace for them to adopt a critical stance on the Temple, its worship, its authority and its ongoing role in the life of the people. They issued stern reminders of the holiness of the Temple. It should be a place free from all kinds of corruption and venality, a place of true inner worship and a place which God would visit at some future time. Hosea had condemned rituals performed by unworthy people and stressed the need for proper inner dispositions on the part of those who worship. 'For I desire steadfast love and not sacrifice, the knowledge of God rather than burnt offerings.'[174] Exhortation at times gave way to warnings of dire consequences. Micah predicted the destruction of the Temple: 'Zion will become ploughland, Jerusalem a heap of rubble, and the mountain of the Temple a wooded height!'[175] Jeremiah said the Temple had become 'a den of thieves' and the Lord would destroy it as he did the sanctuary at Shiloh, making it 'a curse for all the nations of the earth'.[176] Furthermore Jeremiah paid dearly for his attitude with persecution and attempts on his life. The persecution of Jeremiah for speaking against the Temple foreshadows the persecution and passion of Jesus and supplies the New Testament writers with a storyline to emulate and a scripture to quote.[177] Such conviction, often leading to persecution, prompts the psalmist to say 'zeal for your house consumes me', a text which may well refer to the case of Jeremiah himself.[178]

174. Hos 6:6a;
175. Mic 3:12 (JB).
176. Jer 7:11; 26:6.
177. Jer 7:11 quoted in Mt 21:13; Mk 11:17; Lk 19:46.
178. After Ps 21 (22) this Ps 68 (69) is the most quoted psalm in the NT. Scholars see it as originally referring to the persecution of Jeremiah or of the Maccabees, or to the sufferings preceding the time of Ezra.

From the time of the Exile the prophets looked to an ideal future with a reformed, ideal Temple. Ezechiel spoke of a future ideal Temple from which the water of life would flow to bring life to all that was dead in the land.[179] Trito-Isaiah said the Temple would be a place of prayer for all.[180] Zechariah looked forward to the Day of the Lord when all would be holy and no merchant would be found in the Temple.[181] Malachi predicted that the Lord would suddenly enter his Temple after it was chastised for abuses in Levitical worship.[182]

Not alone did the Temple function as the central place for worship, the exclusive location for sacrifice and the goal of pilgrimage, it also played a crucial role in the socio-economic life of Jerusalem and its citizens and was central to the power, prestige and welfare of the Jewish religious and civil authorities.[183] Jesus' attitude would therefore have made a deep impression on the citizens and badly stung the establishment. The depth of feeling can be appreciated when one considers the role of the Temple in the life of the people and the status it afforded the Jewish authorities. All four gospels record and interpret the action in the Temple and the questioning of Jesus' authority which it provoked. Mark and Matthew record Jesus' attitude to the Temple as one of the accusations at his trial[184] and a source of mockery at his crucifixion.[185] The Acts of the Apostles records similar accusations about Jesus at the trial of Stephen.[186] The statements about destroying and rebuilding the Temple are heard on the lips of false accusers and mocking enemies. In St John's gospel, however, these statements are not heard on the lips of opponents, but form the basis for a high christological statement, or *logion*, on the lips of Jesus himself, and they serve the purpose of raising the issue onto another plane.[187]

---

179. Ezek 47:1-12.
180. Isa 56:7.
181. Zech 14:21.
182. Mal 3:1.
183. This socio-economic dependence was typical of all 'shrines', e.g. the centrality of the Temple of Artemis-Diana in Ephesus, as seen from the riot of the silversmiths, Acts 19:23-41.
184. Mt 26:61; Mk 14:58.
185. Mt 27:40; Mk 15:29.
186. Acts 6:14.
187. The many variations on the statement point to a widespread diffusion of the theme which therefore must have sprung from historical reminiscence rather than from the creation of a midrashic style commentator.

The synoptics record Jesus himself saying 'not a stone will be left upon another. All will be destroyed', but this is in response to the disciples' comments on the magnificence of the Temple buildings.[188] It is a prophetic warning in the context of the apocalyptic discourse and the rejection of the messenger of peace. Matthew uses another *logion* in the context of the dispute about breaking the Sabbath. Having pointed out that the Temple priests are blameless in 'breaking' the Sabbath by carrying on their ministry, Jesus makes a profound christological statement in the *logion* 'something greater than the Temple is here', and then goes on in true prophetic style to quote the text: 'What I want is mercy not sacrifice', before making a second christological statement in the *logion* 'The Son of Man is master of the Sabbath.'[189] The synoptics thus portray Jesus breaking the mould and transcending the institutions and practices of Israel's past. In all the gospels his attitude to Temple, Torah and Sabbath is of central significance and displays his greatest claims to divine authority.

3. THE ACTION

The scene in St John's gospel has two parts. There is the action, usually referred to as the 'cleansing' of the Temple, a generalisation that misses the main thrust and interpretation of the action in this gospel, and the pronouncement (*logion*) of Jesus in response to the questioning of the authority behind his action. The meaning of the action did not need explanation. It was so blatant to the onlookers and so obvious in its meaning that it caused them to seek not an explanation of its meaning but a confirmation of the divine authority behind it. Each of the two parts ends with a quotation from scripture and a comment by the narrator about the subsequent belief and understanding of the disciples in the light of the resurrection.

The first part of the story deals with the action in the Temple. Unlike the synoptics, John describes the making of a whip, the casting out from the Temple of the large animals, sheep and oxen, and the doves, in addition to the pouring out of the coins and the turning over of the money changers' tables. The distinctive character of the Johannine account highlights its meaning. The temple rituals are the target, so the focus is on the animals

---

188. Mt 24:1-3; Mk 13:1-4; Lk 21:5-7.
189. 1 Sam 15:22. Mt 12:6-8.

and the doves. The sheep and oxen were the animals used for sacrifice, the doves for offerings. In the presence of the one who has been declared Lamb of God, the sacrificial offering supplied by God, the gift of God, the definitive Passover and sacrificial lamb, these other rituals lose their significance. The merchants and the money changers who facilitate the rituals are thereby rendered redundant. Their transactions are henceforth devoid of religious significance and become simply commercial activity making the Temple itself an *emporion* or marketplace. 'The paraphernalia of Israel's cult are displaced, poured out, and overturned in anticipation of a new mode of worship.'[190]

The narrator draws attention to the reaction of the disciples, telling us first of all that the disciples remembered the scripture 'zeal for your house will consume me'[191] and subsequently that they believed the scripture. The quotation is from Ps 68 (69) which may have its origin as a reflection on the persecution of Jeremiah for his attitude to the Temple, or as a reflection on the fury of the Maccabees in the face of its desecration. It is the second most quoted psalm in the New Testament, after Psalm 21 (22), relating to the suffering of the Just One. Here in St John's gospel it is applied specifically to Jesus' death.[192]

4. THE PRONOUNCEMENT (*LOGION*)

The second part of the scene deals with the pronouncement or *logion* of Jesus, set in the context of the challenge to explain the authority behind his action in the Temple. Challenged about his action Jesus replies: 'Destroy this Temple and in three days I will build it up again.' The authorities react, with typical Johannine irony where the speaker misunderstands Jesus, saying that the Temple was forty-six years in the building and ask how could he rebuild it in three days. The reference to 'three days' reflects and forms an inclusion with 'the third day' of the wedding at Cana. The first glimpse of the glory was seen on the third day at Cana, the first instalment of Jesus' promise of greater things to come.[193] This reference to three days looks ahead to the final glorification. The narrator comments, saying that he was speak-

190. M. L. Coloe, *op. cit.*, 81.
191. Ps 68 (69):9.
192. After Ps 21 (22) this Ps 68 (69) is the most quoted psalm in the NT. Scholars see it as originally referring to the persecution of Jeremiah, or of the Maccabees, or the sufferings preceding the time of Ezra.
193. Jn 1:51; 2:1, 19, 20.

ing of the temple of his body, and that the disciples understood this when he was risen from the dead. As in the case of the psalm already quoted, the disciples subsequently remember, understand and believe. The symbolic narrative highlights this understanding at the outset of the account of Jesus' ministry. This understanding is the work of the Paraclete in the community, the fulfilment of the promise that Jesus will make in the last discourse(s) at his final supper with his disciples: 'The Advocate, the Holy Spirit, whom the Father will send in my name, will teach you everything and remind you of all I have said to you.'[194]

This is particularly striking when we remember that the gospel of John was written after the destruction of the Temple and the Holy City. For Rabbinic Jew and Christian Jew alike, the mother city was destroyed and the mother community dispersed. The Temple of God's glory was no more. Both communities had to rethink the meaning of God's presence. Rabbinic Jews emphasised the Torah. Christian Jews emphasised the person of Jesus and the promised Spirit dwelling in the community. M. L. Coloe comments:

> The Johannine community, in the midst of a Torah-centred Jewish community, also needed to reinterpret the meaning of the Temple's destruction. In this historical situation, the Johannine community transferred the meaning of the Temple to the person of Jesus. But this could be only a partial solution. For if the image of the Temple applied only to Jesus, then the Johannine community would be in exactly the same situation as Israel without their Temple, for Jesus is now absent ... The creativity of the community, or perhaps its leader is shown in the way it transfers the symbol of the Temple from the body of Jesus to the community of believers.[195]

A parallel development takes place in the Pauline writings in the teaching about the community as the Body of Christ, the household of God and temple of the Spirit. This insight must therefore have been deeply rooted in the community and their understanding of the teaching of Jesus.

Thus St John's gospel in its own inimitable way lifts the whole discussion from the physical action in the Temple, with its prophetic overtones, onto the theological/christological

---

194. Jn 14:26, cf 16:13.
195. M. L. Coloe, *op. cit.*, 7.

plane where it fits into the gospel's ongoing discussion on God's presence and dwelling place. The sacred place of God's dwelling is described as 'my Father's house', highlighting the dwelling of the Word, the only Son, 'with God' (*pros ton theon*) and 'in the bosom of the Father' (*eis ton kolpon tou patros*). The Word made flesh pitched tent among us and is now visible, audible and tangible so that through the 'flesh' (*sarx*) the 'glory' (*doxa*) is seen. The promised glory of the Son of Man on whom the angels ascend and descend as in a latter day Bethel indicates the glory of the *Logos* become *sarx*, and the bonding of heaven and earth in his person. The Temple incident now points forward to the divine presence in the resurrected and glorified Jesus, the New Temple, through whose glorification the community of his followers will enjoy the divine indwelling through the gift of the Holy Spirit-Paraclete. Through the Spirit the community becomes the *topos* or location of the divine dwelling.

> After the resurrection (Jn 2:17, 22) the full meaning of what Jesus did and said became clear to his followers. Jesus, the risen Messiah, had taken the place of the Temple and all it stood for. The centre of God's presence among his people is no longer a place; it is henceforth a person (see 4:21-24). The new sanctuary is the risen body of Jesus. In this new temple dwells the fullness of the Spirit. And that Spirit comes to those who believe and dwells with them so that they in their turn, become temples of God.[196]

The whole passage is framed by references to the Passover. 'Just before the Jewish Passover ...' and 'During his stay in Jerusalem for the Passover ...'[197] The first shadows of his major conflicts in the Temple on the occasion of the feasts, with a particular shadow of the Passover Feast, have been cast.

5. Transition

The narrator states that many people were impressed by the signs Jesus performed without coming to any real faith in him. Jesus had a profound distrust of a 'faith' based only on signs. Jesus does not 'trust himself' to those people. This is another shadow of things to come. This theme of 'faith' that depends on signs, in the sense of miraculous displays of power, surfaces a number of times in the ministry. Jesus tests the faith of the noble-

---

196. W. J. Harrington, *John, Spiritual Theologian*, 34.
197. Jn 2:13, 23.

man who comes to seek healing for his son with a challenge about faith based on signs and wonders, and he challenges the self interest of the crowd who follow him to Capernaum in the wake of the multiplication of the loaves.[198]

The narrator also assures the reader that Jesus needed no testimony about people because he knew what was in their hearts. This will be borne out many times in the ministry, especially in the case of Judas, but also in the case of Nicodemus, the Samaritan woman, Peter, Thomas and the crowd.

The remarks about faith and Jesus' knowledge of people's dispositions mark a transition in the narrative and form an immediate link between Jesus' initial appearance in Jerusalem and the stories of Nicodemus, the Samaritan woman and the royal official which follow, and illustrate these points.

---

198. Jn 4:48f; 6:26, 30.

The Response (Jn 2:23-4:54)

Three Representative Responses (Jn 2:23-4:54)

1. THE PLOT

The wedding at Cana functions as the climax of the inaugural narrative, but it also functions as the opening of the narrative that runs between the two signs performed in Cana (Jn 2:1-4:54). This section of the gospel deals primarily with friendly responses to Jesus of varying depths of faith and understanding. The reader has good reason to recall the words of the prologue: 'To those who accepted him he gave power to become children of God.'[1] These responses stand out in contrast to the subsequent narrative in chapters five to twelve which will be characterised by hostility and foreboding, recalling the words of the prologue, 'He came unto his own domain and his own people did not accept him.' This rejection has already been foreshadowed by the authorities' attitude to the Baptist, the action and pronouncement of Jesus in the Temple, and his wary response to miracle hungry faith.

The two programmatic actions of Jesus, one as bridegroom of Israel inaugurating his ministry with a messianic style marriage feast at Cana in Galilee, and the other as the Lamb of God issuing a fundamental challenge to the Temple sacrificial system in Jerusalem, are followed in the gospel by a series of responses. The disciples believed in him at Cana, and many of the crowd believed in him in Jerusalem because of the signs he performed. This elicited the narrator's remark about the enthusiastic, but utterly inadequate, response of a 'faith' that depends on signs and the comment on Jesus' ability to read people's hearts. These are followed by three representative responses, each foreshadowing a significant mission of the early church. They are arranged in geographical order representing local, social, cultural and religious distance from the centre of Judaism in Jerusalem. In typical Johannine ironic style the responses are in reverse order to the distance portrayed. The themes of marriage, bridegroom, gift, water, spirit and mission maintain the continuity of the

---

1. Jn 1:12.

overall story of the gospel as they facilitate the narrative in the exploration of the identity of Jesus. Like the wedding at Cana, the encounters with Nicodemus and the Samaritan woman are symbolic narratives in which the techniques of misunderstanding and irony are richly employed.

After the dialogue with Nicodemus in Jerusalem, Jesus 'had to' travel through Samaria on his way to Galilee, a journey symbolically representing distance from the centre of Judaism. The verb *edei*, 'he had to', reflects a divine plan rather than a geographic necessity.[2] The references to John the Baptist punctuate the overall narrative as they show the declining following of John and the increasing following of Jesus. John's earlier prophecy is being fulfilled but Jesus' success is already rousing suspicions among the authorities and he leaves Jerusalem for Galilee, and has to pass through Samaria on his journey there.

Nicodemus was Jewish in race and religion, a native of Jerusalem or the surrounding Judaean countryside, a member of the strict religious group, the Pharisees, who were the guardians of law and tradition, and are still remembered in Jewish circles as the saints and scholars of the period in question.[3] He was a male in a patriarchal and andro-centric society,[4] a learned man, a teacher in a society that put great value on learning, a member of the ruling class and very probably a wealthy man.[5] His encounter with Jesus seems to take place in Jerusalem, since there is no indication of a change of place from the preceding episode. He came to Jesus at night. Various connotations accrue to this nocturnal visit. Though there was a tradition of the diligent scribe studying the law and searching out the truth into the late hours of the night, it seems that here the late hour refers to the darkness in which he seeks the light of faith and understanding and the protecting cover of night against watchful enemies. 'He is a sympathetic Jewish seeker, "still in the dark", not yet a secret

---

2. In fact the route through the Jordan Valley would probably have been the more common one to take between Jerusalem and Galilee, so the choice of route is significant in itself.

3. *Judaios* may have the meaning 'Judaean' here, so Jn 3:1 means 'a leading member of the inhabitants of Judaea'.

4. In current usage 'patriarchal' focuses on the power structure operated by men, 'androcentric' indicates a society where the male is predominantly in evidence and everything is defined/described in relation to men.

5. His participation in the lavish burial preparations of Jesus suggests he was a wealthy man.

Christian, but remains in the synagogue.'[6] In response to Jesus, Nicodemus remains confused and falls silent. He is both a foil for Jesus and a character with conflicting understandings and allegiances. The dialogue becomes a monologue as Nicodemus fades from the picture leaving Jesus to deliver the first of the discourses which contain the high christology of the body of the gospel. This response foreshadows in the story and reflects in fact the historical reality of the difficulties of the early Christian mission among the Jews at the time the gospel was written. 'He is both individual and representative, a foil and a character with conflicting inclinations with which the reader can identify.'[7] He gets the emphasis he does in the gospel because he is representative of a certain type of Jew to whom Christians are being called on to bear witness, so the story is good for missionary or evangelical purposes.[8]

By way of contrast, the Samaritan woman is a member of a people whom the Jews regarded as ethnically half caste, religiously heretical, socially and culturally inferior and ritually unclean because of their former status as pagan worshippers and their refusal to acknowledge Jerusalem and the Temple as the only true place of sacrifice and goal of pilgrimage. In some respects the stories of Nicodemus and the Samaritan are parallel, one coming by night because of peer pressure, the other coming to the well at an unusual time of day, possibly because of rejection by peers due to her irregular marriage history. Both were anxious to seek the truth and concerned about religious matters. The parallels serve to heighten the difference between their responses. In contrast to Nicodemus the Jew, a teacher in Israel, who came by night and faded away letting Jesus talking to himself, the nameless Samaritan woman, member of a hybrid, heretical race in schism with the Jews, engaged in lively dialogue with him in the full light of day and in the sight of anyone who came along, including the disciples who were shocked to find him alone with a woman. Her response foreshadows in the story and reflects in fact the historical reality of the enthusiastic response of the Samaritans to the early Christian mission. The whole scene is one of growing recognition and witness. Jesus' attitude here to the Samaritans matches that portrayed in St

---

6. B. Witherington, *op. cit.*, 93.
7. A. Culpepper, *Anatomy of the Fourth Gospel*, 135.
8. B. Witherington, *op. cit.*, 92.

Luke's gospel in the stories of the Good Samaritan, the ten lepers among whom only one returned to give thanks, and he a Samaritan, and Jesus' strong rebuke to the disciples for asking him to call down fire from heaven on the Samaritans because of their inhospitality.[9] It matches also the enthusiastic response of the Samaritans to the preaching of Philip.[10] The underlying purpose of the story of the Samaritan woman in the gospel itself may very well be to legitimate the Samaritan mission and to establish the full equality in the community between Samaritan Christians and Jewish Christians. Sandra Schneiders sums up succinctly: '... the theological issues dividing Samaritans and Jews are faced and resolved with a re-affirmation of Jewish legitimacy as bearer of the covenant faith and a surprising recognition of the essential validity of the Samaritan faith tradition despite the very real failures in fidelity of these historical successors of ancient Israel'.[11]

The traditional approach to this story tended to focus on the fact that the Samaritan was a woman of loose living whom Jesus outwitted in spite of her wily ways of concealing her past, and her possible designs on himself as her next husband. This approach has been successfully challenged by feminist Bible scholars and theologians. It has been replaced with an understanding of her as a disciple and missionary in the story of Jesus and as a representative figure both of Samaritan religious history and of future Christian mission among the Samaritans. Her story has received a great deal of attention from contemporary feminist scholars who reject interpretations of gospel stories which either marginalise women or trivialise their role in the gospel stories. Such interpretations tend to focus on them only in so far as Jesus is shown to have saved them from their sexual sins and tend also to regard discipleship and missionary activity as the sole preserve of men.[12] The traditional treatment of the Samaritan woman fell into this category, where her marital history, Jesus' supernatural insight into it and her attempts to conceal it, were seen as the central points in the story. This is to miss the point that a much more significant event is taking place, and in fact is

---

9. Lk 10: 29-37; 9:51-56; 17:11-19.
10. Acts 8:5-25.
11. S. Schneiders, *Written That You May Believe: Encountering Jesus in the Fourth Gospel,* 134f.
12. S. Schneiders, *ibid.,* 126-148; A. Fehribach, *The Women in the life of the Bridegroom,* 45-81.

well under way before there is any mention of her husbands. In fact many of the commentators who highlighted the woman's initial inability to see beyond the physical level of 'earthly' water, fell into the same category themselves as they failed to see beyond the 'earthly' relationships of the woman.[13]

Even reading the story with the emphasis on the woman's marital history, there was no serious attempt to portray the woman as oppressed and victimised rather than promiscuous and sinful. She had five husbands/men in her life. Did this mean she was a loose living person? It is difficult to see it that way in a patriarchal and andro-centric society. She would never have got away with it, at least if the customs in Samaria reflected those in neighbouring Judaea or Galilee, all being rooted in the same Mosaic tradition. One could argue the case that she was a rejected or abused person, victim of a male controlled divorce culture based on Mosaic prescription of simply handing a document of dismissal to the one being driven out, in circumstances where a woman could be divorced for any reason, however trivial, if she was displeasing to her husband.[14] Such a practice was the source of the Shammai and Hillel debates about the grounds for divorce in neighbouring Judaea, a debate into which some Pharisees tried unsuccessfully to draw Jesus.[15] However, the woman's marital history is not the main point of the discussion but it facilitates the use of a long established biblical metaphor for the religious history of the Samaritans.

The royal official, *basilikos*, lived in Galilee, the most distant part of the 'Holy Land', seen in New Testament times as Galilee of the Gentiles, a place where Jews lived in the midst of pagans. The term *basileus*, king, was applied in the New Testament to the Herods and the term *kaisar* was used for the emperor.[16] The term *basilikos*, an adjectival cognate of *basileus*, seems to refer to an official of the Herodian court. In Josephus' writings the relatives and officials of the Herods are called *basilikoi*. In a broader context *basilikos* was used of any civil or military official of the state. This royal official may well have been a Gentile, a view supported

13. The traditional interpretations say the same about the interpreters as the interpreters say about the woman and her failure to understand.
14. Deut 24:1; cf Mt 19:3-6.
15. The practice in neighbouring Judaea of casting off a wife for a matter as trivial as spoiling the food was the source of a heated debate between the leading rabbis Shammai and Hillel.
16. Mt 2:1, 9; Lk 1:5; Jn 19:12, 15.

by the fact that the conversion of the 'whole household' is a phrase regularly applied to Gentile conversions throughout the New Testament. This may be another version of a similar story in the synoptics which deals with a centurion[17] (*hekatônarchos*) who was obviously a Gentile.[18] He too was a person of exemplary faith who had a grievously ill servant (or child)[19] whom Jesus healed with a word from a distance. He too sought Jesus out, entered into a lively dialogue with him which clearly demonstrated his faith, and persisted in his request. For these reasons the reader tends to associate John's story with the head of a Gentile household rather than with a Jew living in a pagan place. The royal official sought Jesus out, and instead of feeling rebuffed by Jesus' remark about inadequate faith based on signs, he reciprocated the challenge displaying to Jesus the desperation of a distraught parent. Then he obeyed the word spoken by Jesus, signifying that he believed before any sign was given. This response foreshadows in story and reflects in fact the response of the wider world of Galilee, the Gentiles, and possibly also of Jews of the Diaspora, to the Christian mission.

2. NICODEMUS

There are three sections to the encounter with Nicodemus. It begins with the report of the inadequate faith of the people in Jerusalem (Jn 2:23-25) which serves as a conclusion to the preceding narrative and as an introduction to the dialogue between Jesus and Nicodemus (Jn 3:1-11/12), and this in turn leads to the monologue (Jn 3:11/12-21).The section dealing with John (the Baptist) which follows immediately has the same outline, a report (Jn 3:22-24), a dialogue (Jn 3:25-30) and a monologue (Jn 3: 31-36).

The Character: Background
He was a good man, a devout Jew who searched for the truth,

---

17. B. Witherington, *op. cit.*, 127f, does not see that it is necessarily another version of the same story, but sees 'healing at a distance' as a story type, and quotes also the extra biblical example of the healing of R. Gamaliel II's son by the healer Hannina Ben Dosa. It makes no difference to the import of the story in John's gospel whether it is a variation of the synoptic story or not.

18. Mt 8:5-13; Lk 7:1-10. The centurions were drawn from the Italica cohort, most of whom were from Italy, some from Cisalpine Gaul, and therefore from a pagan background.

19. Mt 8:5-13 speaks of *pais*, which can mean 'servant' or 'child'. Lk 7:1-10 speaks of *doulos*, a slave or servant which may have been one interpretation of *pais*.

demanded justice and fair play for Jesus when he was under
suspicion and risked the hostility of the authorities and the
crowd in giving Jesus a fitting burial, in the absence of his more
prominent disciples.[20] He was impressed with the signs Jesus
worked and wanted to investigate further. Though a leading
member of the Jews he showed no hostility or rejection towards
Jesus and, like the first disciples and many people in Jerusalem,
showed incipient faith in him as rabbi, teacher and worker of
signs. Though he tells Jesus he knows he comes from God, he
has not yet come to terms with the full reality of Jesus' origins.
Maybe it was in reaction to the criticisms of Jesus and in conse-
quence of his own desire to ensure that he got fair treatment that
he came seeking conversation with him. Later in the gospel he
protested to the chief priests and the Pharisees that Jesus had a
right to a fair hearing before any judgement was passed on
him.[21] However, Nicodemus falls silent in the discussion and
the reader senses that he departs without having seen the light,
at least at this point in the narrative. His approach to Jesus,
nonetheless, shows how a certain admiration for him was
emerging even among the circle of his critics and enemies.
Nicodemus will re-emerge in the story when he protests to the
chief priests and the Pharisees that Jesus has a right to a fair
hearing and again when he comes to assist at his burial.[22] He
represents here the devout Jews who had difficulty in coming to
faith in Jesus and accepting the claims made either by himself or
subsequently on his behalf by his followers.

The Dialogue (Jn 3:1-11/12)
The dialogue opens and closes with a recognition of sorts and an
ironic reversal of roles. Nicodemus begins by addressing Jesus
as rabbi, a term of respect but not of real faith, and acknowledges that his signs prove that he is a teacher come from God
and that God is with him. He speaks as one who knows and who
belongs to the group who know. '*We know* that you are a teacher
who comes from God.'[23] This *we know* will be re-echoed later in
the chapter, this time on behalf of the followers of Jesus.[24] In a
great twist of irony the dialogue ends with Jesus' statement to

20. Jn 7:50; 19:39.
21. Jn 7:50. Maybe this was the original historical background to his visit to Jesus.
22. Jn 7:50ff; 19:39.
23. Jn 3:2.
24. Jn 3:11.

Nicodemus that he is a teacher in Israel 'who *does not know* these things'. He is one of those people who is still trapped by 'definitions they know too exactly'.[25] This is an extended version of the mutual recognition scenes, such as those described already between Jesus and Simon, and Jesus and Nathanael.[26] Here, however, the mutual recognition falls short on both sides.

In a series of Semitic style parallels, saying the same thing in two different but related ways, Jesus speaks about 'seeing' and 'entering' the kingdom of God. As in the solemn pronouncement about seeing the heavens open[27] both statements about the kingdom, how to see and enter it, are introduced with the solemn declaratory formula: 'Amen, amen, I say to you.' Thus the *Logos* dwelling in our midst reveals the divine order. The power to 'see' the kingdom results from being born 'from above' and the power to 'enter' comes from 'being born of water and the Spirit'.[28] The phrases *born from above* and *born of water and the Spirit* are in apposition, interpreting each other. They recall the statements in the prologue about 'power to become children of God' and 'being born not of blood, or urge of the flesh or the will of man but of God'.[29] This birth into a new situation where believers become children of God as a result of the initiative and action of God, has already been described in the prologue as a result of receiving, that is, believing in Jesus. 'Being born of the flesh' and 'living in the flesh' signify entering on, and remaining in, a way of life in which people are content with what can be observed and controlled, making their judgements and choices according to what is perceived with the senses and learned from the 'definitions they know too exactly' and which they can master and control.

Water and the Spirit can be understood in a number of ways. Most simply it can be seen as a hendiadys, using two different terms to express one reality. Water in St John's gospel is predominantly a symbol of the life-giving power of the Spirit and so water and the Spirit may be a double indication of the same

---

25. J. Bishop, 'Encounters in the New Testament' in Kenneth R. R. Gros Louis, ed., *Literary Interpretation of Biblical Narratives*, 2 vols, Nashville, Abingdon, 1982, 2:285-294.
26. Jn 1:41ff; 1:47ff.
27. Jn 1:51.
28. *dunatai idein; dunatai eiselthein*
29. Jn 1:12f.

reality.[30] Water is also used as a symbol of repentance in the baptism of John and of purification at the wedding in Cana. There
was an established tradition of combining both symbols.

New birth through the life-giving power of water and spirit
is associated in biblical tradition with purification and cleansing.
Ezekiel paints a striking picture of God making a new covenant
with the people. Beginning with purification or cleansing he
goes on to speak of new life forces and a newly formed people.

> I shall pour clean water over you and you shall be cleansed. I
> shall cleanse you of all your defilement and all your idols. I
> shall give you a new heart and put a new spirit within you; I
> shall remove the heart of stone from your bodies and give
> you a heart of flesh instead. I shall put my spirit in you, and
> make you keep my laws and sincerely respect my obser-
> vances ... You shall be my people and I will be your God.[31]

Following this account in Ezekiel there is the vision of the valley
of dry bones. The power of the word, accompanied by the life-
giving power of the *ruach*, breath or spirit, brings new life to the
dry bones, signifying the resuscitation of the dead remains of
the people.[32]

Isaiah uses similar imagery which compares the life-giving
power of the Spirit to that of water. 'I will pour out my spirit on
your descendants, my blessing on your children. They shall
grow like grass where there is plenty of water, like poplars by
running streams.'[33] The obedience of a renewed people, empowered by the Spirit is attested in the Second Temple period in texts
like Jubilees, a text not only emphasising the purifying role of
the Spirit but also speaking of a 'counter' Spirit, a category later
developed in the Qumran documents. Moses prays: 'Do not let
the spirit of Beliar rule over them ... and ensnare them ... Create
a pure heart and a holy spirit for them'.[34] The Lord responds: 'I
shall create for them a holy spirit, and I shall purify them so that
they will not turn away from following me from that day and

---

30. B. Witherington, *op. cit.*, 97, and 'The Waters of Birth: John 3:5 and 1 John 5:6-
8', NTS 35 (1989):155-60, shows how the water metaphor was used for various
facets of procreation – insemination, the child in the womb, childbearing and
childbirth; Prov 5:15-18; Song 4:12-15; m Aboth 3:1; 3 Enoch 6:3; I QH 3:9f.
31. Ezek 36:23-29.
32. Ezek 37:1-10.
33. Isa 44:3-6.
34. Jub 1:20f.

forever.'[35] Similarly the prayer of Joseph for Aseneth pleads that
Aseneth be given new life and numbered among the chosen
people.[36] The Qumran community believed that God would
finally purge all human acts and refine humanity by destroying
every spirit of perversity in the flesh, cleansing with a holy spirit
and sprinkling with a spirit of truth like waters of purification
for cleansing humanity.[37] From these examples it can be seen
how prominently water and spirit figure together in the divine
action which achieves the purification, gathering, and home-
coming of the people, resulting in their obedience and the renewal or strengthening of the covenant relationship with God. It
is therefore very apt that the gospel promising the believers
power to become children of God would use the combined imagery of water and spirit for the process of seeing and entering
the kingdom.

Nicodemus misses the point about being born again or from
above, *anôthen*, and thinks only of physical birth as he understands 'born again' to mean re-entry into his mother's womb
rather than being 'born from above'. This use of a misunderstanding is a Johannine literary technique which affords Jesus
the opportunity to explain himself further. The mysterious
power of God is like the wind (*pneuma/ruah*). It blows where it
will. Qohelet and Sirach both use this imagery of the wind.[38]
Playing on the double meaning of wind and spirit, the earthly
phenomenon of wind is used to illustrate the fact that the heavenly mystery of God's plan, its origin, operation, finality and
comprehension are beyond human control and understanding.
As in the case of the wind one feels the effects without understanding the full reality. There is a call to a fundamental re-
orientation, a repudiation of merely human origins and being, in
favour of a new birth from spirit (*pneuma*). 'Any other kind of relationship is doomed to be false because, devised humanly, it
must be locked into the only context which human beings ordi-
narily know.'[39]

Nicodemus is familiar with this world, its milieu and operations, a world summed up in *sarx*, and he does not relate to the
other worldly milieu and its operations summed up in the term

---

35. Jub 1:23.
36. *Joseph and Aseneth* 8:9-11.
37. I QS 3:7-9; 4:21; I QH 16:12; cf 7:6; 7:26; frag 2:9, 3.
38. Eccl (Qoh) 11:5; Sir 16:21.
39. C. Luibhéid, *op. cit.*, 97.

pneuma. R. Bultmann points out that: 'There can be no true relationship between God and man unless it first be grounded in
God's dealings with man.'[40] This calls for a fundamental option
and re-orientation of life which looks beyond human origins to
new birth from *pneuma*. All other relationships are trapped within
the limited parameters known to human beings. That which is
born of *sarx* is *sarx* and that which is born of *pneuma* is *pneuma*.
What is at stake is the discovery and acceptance of one's status
in a God-created and God-directed world.

There is a sacramental dimension to the text, reflecting the
sacrament of Christian baptism with its cleansing power and en-
dowment of the Spirit. Being given the power to become children of God is a gift *from above* in response to accepting the Word.
It enables one to be spiritually born again 'of water and the
Spirit'. This rebirth enabled people to *see* and *enter* into the kingdom of God. 'From its beginnings the gift of the Spirit "from
above", which enabled this passage, was accompanied by a ritual
of rebirth solemnised by water baptism (3:5)'.[41] Picking up on
the use of water and Spirit already encountered in the text, one
sees how John contrasts his baptism in water with Jesus' baptism in Holy Spirit. This is the contrast between a ritual of repentance which is a washing clean and stretching out of the hand to
God for forgiveness, and the baptism in Holy Spirit which is the
definitive, divine act of salvation. So too here, both factors are
included. Baptism as repentance and a ritual washing pointing
to a turning away from sin on the one hand, and as the gift of the
life-giving power of the Spirit on the other, empowers one to
enter the kingdom, and to become one of the children of God.

Baptism can also be used as a metaphorical term for the beginning of a new life and a new state. Baptism in a holy spirit can
be used metaphorically to signify the beginning of a new state
involving a new and critical experience (cf Acts 1:5; 11:16). The
conversation with Nicodemus deals with such an experience in
terms of 'new birth' and 'birth from above', prerequisites for
seeing and entering the kingdom. It signifies a crisis and decision about one's response to Jesus. In his study of baptism and
confirmation, T. Marsh points out that the distinctive character
of the Christian rite is indicated by the formula 'in the name of

---

40. R. Bultmann, *op cit.*, 192.
41. F. J. Moloney, *The Gospel of John,* 93. I. de la Potterie, 'Naître de l'eau et naître
del'Esprit', cf *ScEc* 14 (1962) 351-74.

Jesus Christ'. His examination of the texts in the New Testament where it occurs (Acts 2:28; 8:16; 10:48; 19:5; 22:16; cf 1 Cor 1:13; 6:11) causes him to conclude that the formula had a technical status in the early church. In keeping with the line followed by A. Oepke and G. R. Beasley Murray, he points out that the expression was an idiom in both Greek and Aramaic, with basically the same meaning in both languages, though used in different contexts. In Greek it was a commercial or banking term, like a modern 'to the credit of/to the account of', and expressed ownership. In Aramaic the phrase was used to express a personal relationship or the purpose or result of the action establishing the relationship. He quotes the example of the slave entering the household and receiving a baptism 'in the name of slavery', and thus becoming a slave of the master of the house. Statements about baptism 'in the name of Jesus' focus not so much on the ritual as on the acceptance of the claims made by, or on behalf of, Jesus, and a decision to unite oneself with the group of which he is the founder, leader and saviour.[42] The final words of chapter 20, which were probably the final words of the gospel in an earlier stage of its composition, sum up the purpose of the gospel as: 'These things are written so that you may come to believe that Jesus is the Christ, the Son of God, and that through believing you may have life *in his name.'*[43] *In his name* is a key expression in the context of 'spiritual' and 'sacramental' baptism.

The Monologue (Jn 3:11/12-21)
After the dialogue proper, there follows a monologue where Nicodemus has faded from the picture.

Opening the monologue with a solemn 'Amen, amen I say to you' proclamation, Jesus, the Word made flesh, reveals the mind and loving purpose of God, as he sums up the central theological, christological and soteriological purpose of the gospel as: 'God so loved the world that he gave his only Son that those who believe in him may not perish but may have eternal life.'[44] This gift of God's saving love for the world, is a reality so profound that its motive, purpose and destiny are beyond human knowledge. The one who 'has come down from heaven' reveals it.

---

42. T Marsh., *Gift of Community, Baptism and Confirmation. Message of the Sacraments*, 2, 49f.
43. Jn 20:31. In many ancient religions the devotees tattooed the name of the divinity on their skin.
44. Jn 3:16.

After the solemn 'Amen, amen I say to you', the singular subject 'I' changes to the plural 'we', signifying the followers of
Jesus. It re-echoes Nicodemus' original 'we know', speaking for
the Jews and the Jewish authorities. This collective 'we' foreshadows in the story and reflects the historical reality of the ongoing dialogue between the followers of Jesus and the Jews in
the period of the gospel composition. *We know ... we have seen, we
have witnessed ... you have not accepted our witness.*[45]

Jesus immediately switches back to speaking in the first person singular but continues to address his audience in the plural.
He poses a question which goes directly to the heart of the matter. 'If you do not believe when I speak about things in this
world, how are you going to believe me when I speak to you
about heavenly things?'[46] This rhetorical question harps back to
the image of the wind whose effects can be felt but whose origin
and destination cannot be fathomed. It points to the infinite
chasm between God and humanity, a chasm that can be bridged
only by God. Having read in the prologue that 'no one has ever
seen God', the reader is informed here that 'no one has ever
gone up to heaven.'[47] The need for a revelation by God is made
absolutely clear. Such revelation demands a revealer. Jesus
Christ is the revealer, and as such is styled both Son (of God) and
Son of Man in the body of the gospel. The titles 'Son (of God)'
and 'Son of Man' bear the weight of the evangelist's interpretation of the person of Christ and his role as revealer.[48] The prologue stated that the Only Son, ever at the Father's side, has
made God known. Here the revealer is presented as *the one who
has come down from heaven*, and he is called the Son of Man, but
the language of the prologue quickly reasserts itself in speaking
of the Father-Son relationship.

Son (of God) and Son of Man
The title 'Son', signifying Son of God or Son of the Father, nearly
always expresses a direct relationship between Jesus and the
Father. It is not used by John in a qualified sense as in the Old
Testament where it can refer to the prophets, the king or the people as a whole, but in an absolute sense where it signifies the relationship of the Son to the Father from all eternity. It refers to

45. Jn 3:11f.
46. Jn 3:12.
47. Jn 3:13.
48. C. H. Dodd, *op. cit.*, 230.

the inner life of God, now made visible in Jesus. It not just a static privileged relationship, but a dynamic one characterised by salvific activity. He is sent to bring salvation to those who believe in him. In the synoptic tradition the absolute use of 'Son' is used only at three points.[49] In John's gospel, however, Jesus speaks of his Sonship twenty times, others refer to it four times, and there are five other comments about it, one in the prologue and four throughout the body of the gospel. The Son is the revealer of the Father. He is the pre-existent Son, ever at the Father's side, the human Son and the glorified one who returns to the Father's presence. Three times Jesus speaks of the glory of the Son. Through the raising of Lazarus and the return to the Father the Son of God will be glorified.[50] There is a concentrated focus on Sonship in Jn 3:16-21 and this is further developed in Jn 5:19-26, with emphasis on the life-giving role of the Son and the resulting judgement if it is not accepted. The theme is repeated in Jn 6:40 where Jesus declares: 'Yes, it is my Father's will that whoever sees the Son and believes in him shall have eternal life, and that I shall raise him up on the last day.' Here in Jn 3:16-21 and in the parallel passage Jn 3:34-36, the purpose of Jesus' mission is explained in terms of the gift of the only Son for the life of the world, 'because God so loved the world'.[51]

Concerning the revelation that 'God so loved the world...', M. M.Thompson observes:

Curiously, none of the synoptic gospels ever speaks explicitly either of God's love for Jesus or for his disciples. Jesus of course calls upon people to love God, to love their neighbours as themselves, and to love their enemies. He also speaks of loving him (Mt 10:37) ... By contrast, the Father's love for the Son and the Son's love for the Father, as well as the Son's love for the disciples and their love for him and for each other, are programmatic in John ... While the primary characteristic of the Father-Son relationship is the life that constitutes their relationship, that relationship is further characterised in John in terms of love. Even as the life of the Father is given to the Son and so through him to others, so

---

49. Mt 11:27 // Lk 10:22; Mt 24:36 // Mk 13:32; Mt 28:19. cf 1 Cor 15:28; Heb 1:2:8; 36; 5: 8; 7:28.
50. Jn 11:4; 14:13; 17:1.
51. Jn 3:16.

too the love of the Father is bestowed on the Son and through him to others.[52]

The interplay of the titles Son (of God) and Son of Man in this monologue raises the question of their relationship. They have distinct functions and are not just variations of one christological title. They are, however, complementary and at times overlap. The Son of Man title highlights the human state of Jesus, between the incarnation of the *Logos* and the crucifixion. It deals with the earthly span of Jesus' life. It emphasises the *hour*, and the *hypsôsis*, the raising up, when he will be raised up (*hypsô-thênai/hypsoun*) in crucifixion and glory. The Son of Man is referred to throughout the gospel in the third person until Jn 12:32 where the 'I' of Jesus and the Son of Man are identified together as the one who will be raised up/exalted. With its roots in the Danielic Son of Man the title is closely associated with life-giving power (*zôopoiêsis*) and judgement (*krisis*). In this it overlaps in function with the role of the Son (of God). However, unlike the Son (of God) title it does not emphasise the Father-Son relationship but stresses the unique role of the revealer who has 'come down from heaven'. As such the Father has put his seal on him, guaranteeing the truth of his revelation.[53]

His role as unique revealer in a special way answers the question posed in the Old Testament about the revealer of Wisdom. In the Book of Proverbs Agur, son of Jakeh, in his search for Wisdom, asks: 'Who has mounted to the heavens and then descended (searching for Wisdom)?'[54] Solomon asks in his prayer for Wisdom: 'Who can discover what is in the heavens?' and pleads with God to 'despatch her (Wisdom) from the holy heavens', and 'send her forth from your throne of glory'.[55] Baruch asks: 'Who has ever climbed the sky and caught her to bring her down from the clouds?'[56] Deuteronomy comments on the folly of asking: 'Who will go up to heaven for us and bring it (the Torah) down to us, so that we may hear it and keep it?'[57]

---

52. M. M. Thompson, *op. cit.*, 98-100.

53. Jn 6:27.

54. Prov 30:4.

55. Wis 9:16, 10.

56. Bar 3:29.

57. Deut 30:12, 14. Deut goes on to say: 'The word is very near to you; it is in your mouth and in your heart for your observance.' The Johannine emphasis on the rejection of the Word, the light, the One sent, is very much a reflection of the fact that the word was not in their mouth or in their heart.

The clear answer here in John is: 'No one has ever gone up to heaven.' This not only answers the older question but is a denial of the apocalyptic traditions in Jewish, Hermetic and Mandaean literature, of persons ascending to heaven to bring back a special revelation.

In this gospel the Son of Man was first introduced as the figure surrounded by angels and joining earth to heaven at the rending of the heavens.[58] For the rest of the gospel, the 'eschatological' imagery is replaced by the eternally present Only Son, ever at the Father's side, who is here and now present to offer eternal life and to exercise judgement. These are the prerogatives of the Son of Man.[59] So here the roles of the Son of Man and the Son of God overlap. However, in the Johannine perspective the gift of life and the exercise of judgement or condemnation are not imposed on the individual by the Son (of God) or the Son of Man, but result from the acceptance or rejection of the one sent by the Father. Such acceptance or rejection results from one's inner disposition. This is the fundamental option leading to eternal life or death.

The Son of Man must be raised up like the serpent in the desert, as a sign of healing from sin and reconciliation with God. Both the promise of glorification and the foreshadowing of death are here introduced with their salvific power, but for the moment they are left unexplained. The idea of being raised up and exalted which is introduced here and continues throughout the gospel, will return with the promise that, 'When they have lifted up the Son of Man, then will they know that *I am*'[60] and 'When I have been lifted up from the earth, I shall draw all to myself.'[61] This promise/prophecy will be fulfilled at the crucifixion when Jesus is lifted up from the earth and the allusions to the healing serpent, the Suffering Servant and the rejected Son are all gathered under the rubric of the quotation from Zechariah as those gathered around the cross are said to 'look on the one they had pierced'.[62] On the physical level 'being raised up' refers to crucifixion, but to the eyes of faith there is the deeper meaning of 'exaltation' and 'glorification'. In this gospel, particularly, the 'raising up' on the cross is presented as a public

---

58. Jn 1:51.
59. Dan 7:13-28.
60. Jn 8:28.
61. Jn 12:32.
62. Jn 19:37; Zech 12:10.

proclamation of Jesus' kingship following his mocking enthronement and coronation.[63] The 'raising up' is the central and
most dramatic expression of the revelation of God in Jesus.

When Moses made the brazen serpent and put it on a standard (*epi sêmeiou*) the people who had been bitten by the fiery
serpents looked at it and were healed.[64] The exact symbolism of
the brazen serpent itself as it is described in the original incident
in the desert is difficult to pinpoint. Different understandings
probably emerged subsequently. Some of them may have been
less than orthodox and this may account for the fact that the
brazen serpent in the Temple, reputed to be the serpent placed
by Moses on the standard, came to a bad end when it was
smashed to pieces in the reforms of Hezekiah.[65] The Wisdom of
Solomon avoids any direct interpretation of the serpent itself or
any ascribing of healing power to it, calling it simply a token of
salvation and focusing both on the people's act of 'looking' at it
and on the saving act of God:

> When the savage rage of wild animals overtook them and
> they were perishing from the bites of writhing snakes, your
> wrath did not continue to the end. It was by way of repri-
> mand, lasting a short time, that they were distressed, for they
> had a saving token (*symbolon sôtêrias*) to remind them (*eis
> anamnêsin*) of the command of your law. Whoever turned to
> it was saved, not by what he looked at, but by you, the uni-
> versal saviour.[66]

The Targums also focus on the 'looking', interpreting it as a
turning of the heart towards the *memra* of God.[67] However, it appears that the main point in the Johannine use of the imagery 'is
not the serpent but the lifting up. As in the old Jewish interpretation the uplifted serpent drew the hearts of Israel to God for
their salvation, so the uplifted Jesus drew men to himself and so
gathered to God those who were his children.'[68] When Jesus dies
on the cross 'they look on the one they have pierced'.[69] Looking

63. In Jn12:31f the 'raising up' follows immediately on Jesus' statement that the
ruler of this world has been cast out, (some mss read 'cast down'), in effect, de-
throned.
64. Num 21:4-9.
65. 2 Kings 18:4.
66. Wis 16:6f (JB).
67. *memra*, a surrogate for God, emphasising the Divine Presence.
68. C. K. Barrett, *The Gospel According to John*, 178.
69. Jn 19:37.

on they see the saviour, the source of salvation for all as he draws all to himself[70] and seeing the Son, they see the Father.[71] His death reveals the complete gift of the Father who 'gave' his only Son because he loved the world so much. T. Brodie states: 'Death, therefore, the process of being lifted up, is not something to be run away from. It may be destructive at one level, as were the fiery serpents, yet, paradoxically, it is by facing the thing that most terrifies – by putting the fiery serpent on a standard and looking straight at it (Num 21:8-9) – that greater life is achieved.'[72] The gaze of faith looks beyond the suffering and death of Jesus to the saving work of the Father which is brought to completion in Jesus' death. 'Looking at he cross, the gaze of faith discovers the identity of Jesus ... (which) is here expressed in the unqualified "I am" formula, which in John's language signifies the divinity of Jesus.'[73]

Whereas the MT and Targums speak of placing the serpent on a standard-bearing pole or on an elevated place, the LXX speaks of Moses placing the serpent on a standard, *epi sêmeiou*. John's gospel uses this term *sêmeion*, sign, for the revelatory actions of Jesus. The implied or intended readers of the gospel may well have been familiar with the imagery and language of the biblical story from the Greek of the LXX and so they could well have seen the cross as a *sêmeion*. If so, the crucifixion, with its Saviour, reconciling death, and exaltation, would be seen as a major *sêmeion* in the Johannine sense of a great revelatory event.

The coming of the Son of Man as revealer, life giver and judge, God's gift of the Only Son for the life of the world, provokes a crisis, demanding a decision. God sends 'the only son' because he so loved the world, so that those who believe in him might not perish (as a result of judgement, condemnation) but have eternal life. Believing or not believing, accepting or not accepting him leads on the one hand to eternal life, on the other to judgement. Here the gospel emphasises personal decision and the factors motivating it. The encounter between Jesus and the individual in the gospel is a vital existential engagement. What is at stake is the discovery of one's true self and status before God and one's place in a God-directed world. The incarnate

70. Jn 12:32.
71. Jn 14:19.
72. T. Brodie, *op. cit.*, 199.
73. G. Rossé, *op. cit.*, 29f.

Logos is the Revealer who illuminates existence.[74] This choice is
now presented in terms of accepting or rejecting the light. Those
'doing the truth' come into the light. Evil deeds are the opposite
to 'doing the truth' and rejection of the light results from fear of
having one's evil deeds exposed.

3. INTERLUDE ON JOHN: ADVANCING THE PLOT (JN 3:22-30)

The monologue is followed, or interrupted,[75] by a story of John
and his baptism, affording the opportunity to introduce into the
plot a progress report on Jesus' increasing following, and a re-
iteration of John's own testimony. This story of the Baptist follows
the same outline as the Nicodemus story, a report (Jn 3:22-24), a
dialogue (Jn 3:25-30) and a monologue (Jn 3: 31-36).

The report supplies information about the whereabouts of
Jesus and his disciples and the baptising activity of John. It refers
to his subsequent imprisonment and to the fact of a dispute
which took place between the disciples of John and a certain Jew
(or Jews)[76] about purification.

Some of his disciples commented to John about the great
numbers of people going to Jesus: 'Rabbi ... the one to whom
you bore witness ... everyone is going to him.' John responds by
emphasising the fact that no one can take other than what has
been given by God (from heaven). He then reminds them of his
earlier witness that he was not the Christ but was the one sent
before him. He uses the imagery of the bride and bridegroom for
Jesus and his following, an imagery long established for the
covenant relationship of God and Israel. The one who has the
bride is the bridegroom, the friend (the best man) stands by and
rejoices at the voice of the bridegroom. 'My joy is fulfilled,' is a
statement of John the Baptist which in some way parallels Jesus'
final remark about his own ministry: 'It is accomplished.'[77]
John's joy is to see the stage set for that accomplishment as the
bridegroom of Israel receives his bride, and so this time he concludes his remarks with the words: 'He must increase and I must
decrease.'[78]

The necessity of carrying out God's plan is again seen here in

---

74. C. Luibhéid, op. *cit.*, 93f. cf R. Bultmann, *op. cit.*, 43.
75. Depending on one's understanding of who the speaker is in Jn 3:31-36.
76. variant readings.
77. Jn 19:30.
78. Jn 3:30.

the use of 'it is necessary' (*dei*): '*it is necessary* that he increase and I decrease'. Just as *it is necessary* for the Son of Man to be lifted up/exalted, as stated already, so too *it is necessary* for John to decrease as he increases.

This increasing following of Jesus will provoke the suspicion and hostility of the Jerusalem authorities, making it necessary for Jesus to return to Galilee. On that journey he will pass through Samaria and converse with the woman at the well. The wedding imagery, already encountered at Cana, has surfaced again with reference to the bride, the groom and the friend of the groom (the best man). In the scripures the marriage bond was used as a metaphor for the covenant relationship between God and the people. Here the imagery is transferred to Jesus and his following. The prophetic figure of John prepares the nuptials and rejoices for his friend the bridegroom. This wedding imagery, already introduced at Cana, is continued in the dialogue with the Samaritan woman.

The final section of the chapter (Jn 3:31-36) further addresses the question posed earlier, and interrupted by the interlude about John. 'How will you believe if I speak to you of heavenly things?'[79] Scholars wonder if the speaker here is Jesus, John the Baptist or the narrator. It is almost as if a series of apt and pithy sayings had been collected and added to the end of the chapter either to sum up what had been said or because a place for them had not been found in the text. The one coming from above has heavenly knowledge, and can witness to what he has seen and heard, but no one accepts his testimony. The one God sent announces the words and deeds of God, the one from the earth has but earthly knowledge. The Father loves the Son and has given everything into his hand. This is a Semitic idiom for saying he has given him power and authority. Furthermore the Father gives the Spirit without measure to the Son who thereby 'has' the Spirit, and he too 'gives' the Spirit.[80]

---

79. Who is the speaker here? Jesus, John, or the narrator?
80. There has been a debate about the subject of the sentence 'He gives the Spirit without measure.' Is it the Father or Jesus who gives the Spirit? Here in this sentence it appears to be the Father, judging by the proximity of 'the Father loves the Son and he gives all things into his hands'. However, elsewhere in the gospel Jesus is seen to give the Spirit. Origen and Cyril *et al* regard the Son as the subject of the sentence. cf Schnackenburg, *op. cit.*, I, 386f.

4. THE SAMARITAN WOMAN

Literary type scene

The nameless Samaritan woman with a past enters the narrative after the named, privileged male of Jewish religious life. The story follows the lines of a well established biblical type scene. The bridegroom-to-be or his agent travels to a foreign land, meets a woman (or women) at a well, drawing water. A drink is sought or offered, the woman returns home with the news of the stranger and an invitation to hospitality is issued by her people. This is regularly followed by a celebratory meal and a betrothal. The reader familiar with bible stories immediately recalls scenes like those of Abraham's servant seeking a wife for Isaac and seeing Rebecca at the well of Nahor, Jacob seeing and falling in love with Rachel at the well in Haran and Moses meeting and protecting the daughters of Reuel (Jethro) when they were being harassed by shepherds at the well in Midian and subsequently marrying one of the daughters, Zipporah.[81] These are human stories of romance and matchmaking leading to marriage, but they are also central to the continuation of the line of descendants who inherit the promise to Abraham. These people are the agents of the divine plan of salvation.

Here in St John's gospel Jesus encounters and seeks a drink from a woman at the well of Jacob in Samaria. The scene is charged with nuptial symbolism. Jesus has been presented already in the role of the bridegroom of Israel, supplying the wine at Cana, and was further described as the bridegroom by John the Baptist. The woman fills the same role as the future bride in the biblical stories of Rebecca, Rachel and Zipporah. Her fellow townspeople issue an invitation to the hospitality of the town at the end of the scene. But the woman is nameless. The reader asks if the storyteller is reluctant to name her for posterity through respect and sensitivity because of her personal past, as in the case of the woman of ill repute in Luke's gospel.[82] That may be true on one level, but typical of this gospel there is a deeper significance. Nameless, like the Beloved Disciple, the Mother of Jesus and the royal official, the woman of Samaria fulfils a representative function. She represents the people of Samaria, the former Northern Kingdom, now the estranged bride of the covenant God. As her ethnic and religious background shines

---

81. Gen 24:15ff; 29:9ff; Ex 2:15ff.
82. Lk 7:36-50.

through her personal story, the woman's marital history becomes a metaphor for the Samaritans' religious history.

Background
The story is therefore much more than a personal history of the woman. The issue of her husbands only emerges in the midst of a theological discussion. It is not the opening point of a conversation which is then awkwardly avoided by reference to theological matters, as has often been asserted. It emerges between her growing awareness that Jesus may be even greater than Jacob and her hope-filled references to the expected prophet-like-Moses, a messianic figure who was expected to clarify matters of theological and legal dispute. The two burning issues for the Samaritans were those of *belonging* and *worship*. Did the Samaritans belong to the people of the covenant and was their worship 'on this mountain' (Mt Gerizim), legitimate and true worship? They were awaiting a 'prophet like Moses', not the political messiah of Jewish expectation, but one who would clarify these major issues.[83]

In spite of Jewish objections the Samaritans considered themselves part of the covenant people and followed the law of Moses and worshipped the God of the covenant. They regarded Mt Gerizim, and not Mt Ebal, as a Mosaic shrine commemorating the place where the first worship was offered on entry into the promised land.[84] It was more important than Ebal and significantly more important that Mt Zion, a shrine dating back only to David's time. They honoured Moses and regarded the Pentateuch as sacred scripture. As such they could claim to be part of the 'marriage' covenant with the God of Israel. This was denied by the Jews who kept in mind their former status as pagan worshippers when they arrived in Samaria, five separate peoples, with their seven pagan gods, transplanted from different parts of the Assyrian Empire after the Fall of Samaria in 721 BC.[85] As two of the ethnic groups had two gods, the second god in both cases was probably a divine consort, and so the imagery

---

83. They did not accept the prophetic books and other literature of the Hebrew scriptures, so their expectations were determined by the promise of a prophet-like-Moses in the Pentateuch (Deut 18:18) and they were untouched by the prophetic expectations of a messianic Son of David.
84. Deut 27:4-7.
85. 2 Kings 17:24-41. The ethnic groups were from Babylon, Cuthah, Avva, Hamath and Sepharvaim.

of the five peoples with their five 'male' gods forms a symbolic background to the Samaritan Woman's story of five husbands.[86] The division between Jews and Samaritans was greatly acerbated two centuries later when the Jews refused to allow them to take part in the rebuilding of the city and Temple after the Exile and they in turn tried to have the enterprise stopped by the Persian authorities.[87] Ever afterwards a state of mutual hostility existed which allowed no contact between them. The Jews had even burned the Samaritan temple on Mt Gerizim.[88] They regarded vessels or implements used by the Samaritans as unclean and untouchable. They reinforced their prejudice and protected their separate identity with the theory that Samaritan women were always ritually unclean.[89] The Samaritans, however, claimed to be worshippers of the God of Moses and so part of the marriage covenant with the God of Israel and descendants of the original inhabitants of the Northern Kingdom.

S. Schneiders states that if the scene itself is symbolically the incorporation of Samaria into the New Israel, the bride of the new Bridegroom, which is suggested by the type scene itself, then the adultery/idolatry symbolism so prevalent in the prophetic literature for speaking of Israel's infidelity to *YHWH* the Bridegroom would be a most apt vehicle for discussion of the anomalous religious situation of Samaria.[90] The reader conscious of the broader biblical traditions remembers the Book of Hosea, written in the Northern Kingdom before Samaria became contaminated with the foreign gods of the Assyrian colonists. Hosea wrote then of the covenant between God and the people as a marriage bond, exploring the depths of *hesed*, the faithful loving kindness of God which endures in spite of the infidelity of the covenant partner, like the husband seeking the wife until she returns to her first husband and rediscovers her first love and happiness. 'Then she shall say: "I will go and return to my first husband, for it was better with me then than

---

86. G. Sloyan, 'The Samaritans in the New Testament', *Horizons* 10 (1983), 10.

87. Ezra 4:1-23.

88. The Samaritan Temple was burned by the Jewish High Priest, John Hyrcanus.

89. Their prejudice against Samaritan women seems to have been reinforced by the belief, as recorded in a Jewish regulation of 65-66AD, that a Samaritan woman could never be trusted to be ritually pure since they were menstruants from the cradle. cf R. E. Brown, *The Gospel According to John*, I, 170.

90. S. Schneiders, *The Revelatory Text*, 190f.

now"... Therefore, I will now allure her and bring her into the wilderness, and speak tenderly to her ... There she shall respond as in the days of her youth, as at the time when she came out of the land of Egypt.'[91] Against this religious background the woman's marital history is used as a mirror reflecting Samaria's religious history and relationship to the covenant God of the Jews. Her remark 'I have no husband' and Jesus' response 'You have said rightly "I have no husband", for you have had five husbands and he whom you now have is not your husband' reflects the denunciations of idolatry and religious syncretism of the classical prophets, and could sum up the plea of Hosea: 'Plead with your mother, plead – for she is not my wife, and I am not her husband.'[92] Now at the well in Samaria in a traditional courtship and matchmaking scene, Jesus seeks to win back the lost bride of Samaria. Following the witness of this woman to her fellow townspeople, he proclaims 'the fields are ripe for harvest' as he notices the Samaritans coming towards him.[93]

The Dialogue
As seen from the following chiasm, the main emphasis of the dialogue is on the place and nature of true worship, resulting from the two great questions of the Samaritans, whether they belonged to the people of the covenant and consequently whether their own worship was valid. The emphasis is brought out clearly by looking at the chiastic structure of the passage with the discussion on the place and nature of true worship as its pivot:[94]

    A. Jesus in Samaria as he journeys to Galilee (4:1-6).
      B. Jesus asks for drink. Dialogue on two waters (4:7-15).
        C. Woman told to bring her husband (4:16-18).
          D. Place and Nature of true Worship (4:19-26).
        C. Woman goes and brings the villagers (4:27-30).
      B. Disciples ask Jesus to eat. Dialogue on two foods (4:31-38).
    A. Jesus in the village and journeys to Galilee (4:39-45).

Like the dialogue with Nicodemus this is a theologically laden conversation following the lines of a symbolic narrative. It is facilitated by themes that run right throughout the gospel such as

---

91. Hos 2: 7, 14-17.
92. Hos 2:2.
93. Jn 4:35.
94. cf M. L. Coloe, *op. cit.*, 87, agreeing with F. Manns, *L'Evangile de Jean à la lumière du Judaïsme*, 124-127.

bridegroom, husband, marriage, water, spirit, worship, gift and life. Unlike the dialogue with Nicodemus, it takes place in the full light of day for all to see and hear, should anyone come along. This symbolically highlights the woman's courage, openness and transparency. Unlike Nicodemus, and the disciples and others who often function only as a foil to feed Jesus 'cue lines' in his discourses, this woman engages in a serious religious dialogue touching on all aspects of Samaritan religious belief and practice and their theological disputes with Judaism. 'She is a genuine theological dialogue partner gradually experiencing Jesus' self revelation, even as she reveals herself to him.'[95] This step by step recognition of Jesus' identity is central to the dialogue. It focuses on Jacob, Moses, the Prophet and the Messiah.

At first the Samaritan woman reacts to Jesus' approach, then challenges him, investigates further and finally bears witness about him to the people of the town. In her response to Jesus she begins with curiosity about the man who speaks to her unaccompanied, a Jew who asks her, a Samaritan, for a drink and may have to use her drinking vessel. She then progresses through the stages of asking if he is greater than Jacob, asking for the living water, remarking that he is a prophet, questioning him about the rival claims of Jews and Samaritans about places of worship, and expressing the hope that the coming Messiah will answer these questions. Finally she brings the people of the town to Jesus.

Jacob, has already been alluded to in the gospel in the references to a true Israelite and to the heavenly ladder and Bethel images. He now looms large in the conversation, in three verses, as Jesus and his gift of living water emerge as greater than Jacob and his gift of the well. The setting of the dialogue at Jacob's well and the opening references to drawing and drinking water reflect a field of biblical allusions. These allusions to Jacob's dream, Bethel, Haran, and the miracle water of the well enrich the text of John in which they are embedded. Jacob's well is not actually mentioned in the Old Testament. There is, however, mention of his gift of land to his son Joseph around Shechem.[96]

---

95. S. Schneiders, *Written That You May Believe*, 141.
96. Gen 33:19; 48:22. The name of the well is sometimes given as Sichar. This may be due to a confusion in the writing of the final letter in the word in Semitic alphabet.

The targumic and rabbinic literature more than make up for the absence of any Old Testament references to the well. They reflect the tradition of the travelling well, a belief based on the promise in Numbers that the Israelites would always have water on their journey though the desert.[97] They relate how Jacob's presence in Haran caused the water to bubble up (*allomai*) for twenty years and how the stone from the mouth of the well was erected as a pillar and caused Jacob to travel miraculously to Haran.[98]

Jesus meets the woman at Jacob's well in a foreign country. He is tired and thirsty and seeks the traditional hospitality of a drink of water from the well. Surprised at such a request from a Jew, the Samaritan woman points out that he has no bucket, which means he would have to use hers, in contravention of the rules and customs of segregation between their two peoples. Jesus points out that if she knew the identity of the one seeking her hospitality she would seek from him something far greater than well water. He offers her the gift of living water. The guest is now becoming the benefactor, a well established biblical theme.[99] He will supply 'living' water, 'bubbling up' to eternal life and whoever drinks it will not be thirsty again. Just as the well of Jacob was a gift of God for the people so now Jesus offers the gift of water that bubbles up to eternal life.[100] The Samaritan faith and identity were deeply rooted in patriarchal tradition. Jesus' alignment with Jacob therefore was very significant for her thinking and his offer moved her to see him as more than a Jew on a journey, and she asks: 'Are you greater than our father Jacob who gave us this well and drank from it himself with his sons and his cattle?' Thinking only of an endless supply of ordinary water, she asks Jesus to give her some of that water so that she may never be thirsty again, and not have any need to come to draw water. Drawing water may have been a particularly difficult task for her if she could not be part of the social scene in the mornings when the women came to draw water and had to

---

97. Num 21:16-18.

98. *Tg. Neof.* Gen 28:10, 11-22; 29:1-10.

99. Gen 18:1-15; Lk 24:28-31.

100. The verb 'bubble up' (*allomai*) is used in the LXX of the activity of the Spirit in Samson, Saul and David (Judg 14:6, 19; 15:14; 1 Sam 10:10; 17:13.). Jesus is now promising the activity of the same Spirit in the lives of those who accept his offer of living water. Water was long established as a symbol of the life-giving power of the word of God, of wisdom and the law. All these will be gathered together in the symbolism of the Spirit in John's gospel.

come alone at mid-day in the heat because her peers shunned her due to her personal history.

Jesus replied to her question about his being greater than Jacob with the request: 'Go call your husband and come back here.' She replied: 'I have no husband.' Jesus then said: 'You are right to say, "I have no husband," for although you have had five the one you now have is not your husband.'[101] At this, the woman moves to a deeper appreciation and greater curiosity about the identity of the one speaking to her and says: 'I see you are a prophet, sir.' She obviously has in mind a 'prophet like Moses' as the Samaritans did not acknowledge the prophetic writings with their expectation of a messianic royal Son of David.[102] She then goes on to ask him the burning question about the value of worship 'on this mountain' (Mt Gerizim) and the Jewish belief that the only true worship was in Jerusalem.

Picking up on this Jesus reinforces the legitimate claims of Jerusalem with his statement 'salvation is from the Jews', but then he transcends both sides of the argument by lifting the dispute onto another plane as the woman questions him about the place of true worship. Jesus responds with a solemn statement, twice referring to an *hour* which is coming (*erchetai hôra*).[103] The *hour* will see a seismic shift, when true worship will not be judged in terms of place but in terms of its nature as worship 'in spirit and truth'. This is not a contrast between 'external' worship in public rituals and 'internal' worship in the recesses of one's mind and heart. Jesus' own ministry is well punctuated with rituals, feasts and public prayers. The prophets, even in their most scathing condemnations of the cult, never wished to abolish it, but to purify it. Purification of the worship through purification of the disposition of the worshippers had been a long established prophetic tradition. The Qumran community had broken away from the Temple and its worship, not to put an end to rituals but to distance themselves from the corruption of the system as they saw it. But they proceeded to establish their own rituals. Their rule pointed out that God pours out the spirit

---

101. Jn 4:18 (JB).
102. The term *Taheb*, which means 'restorer', is used of this expected figure, but it is not certain if it was in use as early as NT times.
103. Jn 4:21, 23; cf Jn 5:28f; 4:21, 23. The use of the term '*hour*' in ' an *hour* is coming ...' *erchetai hôra hote* ... could be translated 'the' hour, since the qualifying temporal clause gives the value of a definite article retrospectively to the antecedent noun.

on their members and purifies them for service of God. The Spirit of Truth instructs them in divine knowledge and observance of the law and so the community is a temple of God, 'a house of holiness for Israel, and an assembly of the Holy of Holies for Aaron'.[104]

Jesus follows on in this tradition about the internal dispositions necessary for worship and his teaching in this regard takes on a whole new dimension as it incorporates and reflects the theology, christology and pneumatology of the gospel as a whole. The *hour* of Jesus will bring about a whole new relationship between God and the followers of Jesus as they are re-born of water and the Spirit and become children of God and worship in a whole new way. The prologue had spoken about power to become children of God and Jesus spelled this out to Nicodemus in terms of being 'born again, born from above, born of water and the Spirit'. In his resurrection message to the disciples, Jesus will designate them his *adelphoi*, brethren,[105] and will speak of 'ascending to my Father and your Father'. St Paul had a similar statement about the Spirit teaching the believer to say 'Abba, Father': 'The proof that you are sons (and daughters) is that God has sent the Spirit of his Son into our hearts; the Spirit that cries, "Abba, Father", and it is this that makes you a son (or daughter), you are not a slave any more'.[106] The new worship will be the worship of the children of God, 'born from above, of water and the Spirit'. In the Temple he had spoken about himself as the new Temple, and in the Last Supper discourse(s) he will speak of the Father, Son and Spirit-Paraclete coming to dwell with the believers. Just as Jesus is the new Temple, his followers will be the Temple where Father, Son and Spirit-Paraclete will dwell.

The Spirit is coupled with truth. It is best explained as a hendiadys, two terms signifying one reality. Spirit and truth could well be spoken of as Spirit of truth. The Son describes himself as the truth,[107] he speaks the truth[108] and bears witness to the truth.[109] Jesus asks the Father to send his followers the Spirit of truth to be with them forever,[110] and he promises to send the

104. I QS iv 19-22; viii: 5f, ix: 3-5.
105. An inclusive term for brothers and sisters.
106. Gal 4:6f; cf Rom 8:14-17.
107. Jn 14:6.
108. Jn 8:45.
109. Jn 18:37.
110. Jn 14:17.

Spirit of truth from the Father to be his witness forever.[111] The
Spirit will enable them to recall all that Jesus, the truth, had said
and done. The community among whom the Spirit of truth
dwells, will be the new Temple of the divine presence. In this
Temple there will be worship in Spirit and truth.

Jesus' comment on the true nature of worship further con-
firms the Samaritan woman's growing intuition that someone
very special is here. She probes Jesus on another great tradition
of the Samaritans, the expectation of a non-political messiah, a
prophet like Moses who would settle the theological and liturgical arguments between themselves and the Jews. This pivotal
section of the dialogue is brought to a climax as he responds to
her question about the messiah with the solemn pronouncement, his first *egô eimi*, 'I am' proclamation in the gospel. '*I am*,
the one who is speaking to you' (*egô eimi ho lalôn soi*).

The fact that Jesus does not respond with a straightforward
reply 'I am the Messiah/Christ', but uses a stylised formula
alerts the reader to the fact that something deeper is being asserted. The implied reader who shared the conceptual world of
the implied author would have known what was intended but
the real reader today needs an explanation. D. M. Ball states the
case clearly as he points out how the single phrase containing
egô eimi may alert the implied reader to an entire thought world,
which is shared with the implied author since they are within a
shared cultural framework as the implied reader would automatically understand the implications of the words *egô eimi*,
which is clear from the the the fact that they are not explained.
Furthermore when Jesus uses these words, it is not only the
words themselves but the *thought world* to which they point
which helps to explain what he means.[112] He also points out that
'The absolute use of "I am" in the Old Testament is striking as the
only conclusive parallel to the use in the New Testament.
However ... it is not only in the words *egô eimi* that John points
back to Isaiah, but also in the way that those words are
presented.'[113]

When God's name was revealed to Moses in the words usually translated as 'I am who I am', the revelation was followed

---

111. Jn 15:26.
112. D. M. Ball, '*I Am' in John's Gospel: Literary Function, Background and
Theological Implications. Journal For the Study Of The New Testament. Supplement
Series, 124*, Sheffield Academic Press, 1996, 177.
113. *Ibid.*

by the command to go to the people and say: 'I am sent me to you.'[114] I am is subject of the sentence, just as here 'I am the one talking to you', or perhaps better translated: 'I am is the one talking to you.' Isaiah develops this I am designation for God in several passages, and the LXX use of *ego eimi* for the divine name springs immediately to mind,[115] as for example, 'I am, I am, the one comforting you' (Isa 51:12), and 'therefore my people will know my name on that day because I am he, the one (who is) speaking to you (Isa 52:6).'[116] Speaking to the Samaritan, Jesus responds to her 'knowing' that the Messiah is coming, with the words of YHWH which he applied to himself. 'That day' picks up on the promise of 'that day' which is coming when there will be true worship in spirit and in truth. The whole passage rather than the isolated phrase throws light on the meaning.

The I am proclaims the divine presence in Jesus, mediating the Father and promising the gift of the Spirit. Here is the encounter with the divine, making Jesus the locus of the divine, the Temple, the place of presence and worship.[117]

At the end of the dialogue the Samaritan woman brought the townspeople to see someone who has told her 'everything she has ever done', symbolically representing everything the Samaritans had ever done, and speculating about the possibility of his being the messiah.[118] Her faith and fruitful witness to her fellow townspeople prefigure the Christian mission to the Samaritans and their enthusiastic response. The theological thrust of the dialogue is the mission to the Samaritan townspeople. Ironically the woman's words of witness are being spoken to the Samaritans just as Jesus is telling his disciples that he has food to eat they know not of, that is, doing the work of the Father in carrying on the mission, in this case to the Samaritans. He then speaks of the fields being ripe for harvest and reminds them that they are being sent to reap what others have sown. This obviously refers to the immediate context of the missionary

---

114. Ex 3:14f.

115. Isa (LXX) 41:4; 43:10; 46:4; 48:12; 51:12.

116. Isa 51:12 *ego eimi ego eimi ho parakalôn se*; Is 52: 6 *dia touto gnôsetai ho laos mou to onoma mou en tê hêmera ekeinê, hoti egô eimi autos ho lalôn soi. (egô eimi autos, in Hb ani hû).*

117. A chiastic structural analysis of the chapter, and of vv 19-26, seeing the concentric or chiastic order of the dialogue, places this at the centre of the chiastic structure on both counts. cf M. L. Coloe, *op. cit.*, 87, 100.

118. Jn 4:28ff.

activity of the Samaritan woman even if it also refers to a greater
plane of missionary activity.

The Samaritan woman is portrayed also as a disciple. She
came to believe in Jesus because of his knowledge of her, just as
happened in the case of the disciple Nathanael. She has a serious
religious/theological discussion with Jesus, like a disciple with
the teacher. She was invited by the teacher to believe and to ask
for the living water. She was sent to call her husband and went
to call the townspeople. As the disciples in the synoptics left the
boats and the nets, symbols of their life and livelihood, to follow
Jesus, and become fishers of people, she left her jar, symbol of
her life and livelihood, at the well and went to call others to
Jesus. As Philip called Nathanael with: 'Come and see (*erchou kai
ide*)', one disciple calling another, she calls the Samaritans with
similar words, *deute idete,* 'Come and see'. Both these expressions echo the call of Jesus to the first two disciples: *erchesthe kai
opsesthe,* 'Come and you will see.'[119] The Samaritan brings others
to Jesus *through her word* and Jesus later reflects on the disciples'
role when he prays for those who believed *through their word.*[120]
He told her that God seeks (*zêtei*) worshippers in spirit and
truth. The disciples wonder what he seeks (*zêteis*) of the woman,
the implication being that he is seeking the lost bride of Samaria
and returning her to true worship.[121] Now she is seen as one of
the sowers whose work the disciples are entering.[122]

As she is leaving to call the townspeople, the disciples return
and are surprised to see him talking to a woman. The woman
was surprised that he spoke to her, because she was a Samaritan,
They were more surprised to see him talking to her because she
was a woman and no rabbi would be alone with a strange
woman. He has been talking to her about drinking the living
water bubbling up to eternal life. In typical Johannine irony the
disciples are concerned about his eating 'earthly' food. He responds with his remark about having food to eat that they know
not of. The harvest is ripe. The woman has been one of the sowers. The townspeople are coming. 'Come/coming' is almost a
technical term for 'first steps in faith'. They ask him to remain,
he remains two days. 'Remain' (*menein/meinai*) also is a quasi

119. Jn 1:39. It will be re-echoed in the invitation to Jesus at the tomb of Lazarus,
'come and see', *erche kai ide,* Jn 11:35f.
120. Jn 4:39, 42; 17:20.
121. Jn 4:23, 27.
122. Jn 4:38.

technical term for 'dwell' and for 'union with Jesus'. They came because of the word she spoke to them (*dia tôn logôn tês gu-naikos*). Then like the other disciples having encountered Jesus their faith becomes rooted in their own experience which she has facilitated. 'It is no longer because of what you said that we believe, for we have heard for ourselves ...' The change of term from *logos* to *lalia*, referring to the 'word of the woman' is not meant to be derogatory of her witness, as is sometimes claimed, and translated in terms of 'babble' or 'gossip'. Rather, the change signifies the deeper experience when one encounters Jesus personally. This was the way the first disciples came to him. It is a typical ending to a recognition scene. They proclaim him 'the saviour of the world'. This may well be a reflection of the Johannine community's articulation of their faith in Jesus in a title highlighting their faith as a countersign to the emperor worship which saw the emperor, since the time of Augustus, as *restitutor orbis terrarum*, a title recognising the emperor as the re-storer/saviour of the world after the disastrous series of Roman civil wars. 'Saving the world' is, however, beyond the power of any Roman emperor. John is encouraging his readers never to be swayed or intimidated by the aggrandising claims of the Roman emperors who styled themselves as saviours. He is laying stress on the fact that no other figure was comparable to Jesus for the saving of the world.[123]

5. THE GALILEAN NOBLEMAN/ROYAL OFFICIAL (JN 4:46-53)

This is a short but extremely significant story in the gospel. It brings to a climax the three stories of emerging faith in Jesus. It rounds off the opening of the ministry with the reference back to the first sign at Cana, forming an inclusion with it, and contain-ing the intervening material in a literary frame. Maybe also the indication 'after two days' points to 'the third day', as at the first Cana sign, with its promise of divine blessing. It also forms an inclusion with the raising of Lazarus where Jesus sets out after two days to perform his miracle on the third day. The gift of life to a dying boy following the desperate plea of his father, is the first of Jesus' healing miracles, and the restoration of life to Lazarus after the desperate pleas of his sisters, is the last, and

---

123. cf R. J. Cassidy, *John's Gospel in New Perspective: Christology and the Realities of Roman Power*, 85, cf 34f. A similar case can be made for the imperial use of the titles Lord and God.

climactic miracle at the end of his ministry. It reflects and surpasses this second sign at Cana.

A number of stories in the New Testament show people coming to Jesus for healing for themselves or a loved one, and meeting with what appears to be a less than friendly response. The
rebuff serves to test the faith and resolve of the petitioner who
then redoubles the appeal, matching Jesus' own tough stance
with resolute faith. The evangelists highlight the test of faith for
the believers of their own day. The Syro-phoenician woman and
her response about the house dogs eating the crumbs that fall
from the children's table is perhaps the best known example.[124]
Here in John's gospel the nobleman's request is greeted by
Jesus' reaction of exasperation at people whose faith depends on
signs and wonders. The nobleman matches Jesus' exasperation
with the desperation of a parent. 'Come down before my child
dies!' In the midst of such desperation he obeys Jesus' command
to return home and trusts in his promise that the child will live.
Whatever his initial level of faith, he came to believe Jesus' word
without seeing any evidence or sign and went home. This is the
authentic belief that leads to life, the stated purpose of the
gospel, that those who believe may have life in his name.[125] The
Johannine setting of the miracle in Cana thus lengthens the distance between the healer, the healed and the petitioner and thus
heightens the dramatic effect. The attestation of the witnesses is
strengthened by meeting him on the way and confirming the
time of the healing. This act of faith brings this series of responses
to Jesus to a climax.

R. Bultmann states: 'Chapters three and four showed the
coming of the Revealer as the *krisis* by which the possibility of a
new existence and a new form of worship is brought to man'.[126]
To date the gospel has shown examples of emerging faith in
Jesus. The responses are positive but at various stages of development. From here on in St John's gospel there will be greater
emphasis on the lack of faith, division among the crowd, and
overt hostility to Jesus, especially on the part of the authorities.
The reader will have good reason to recall the words of the prologue: 'He came to his own domain and his own people did not
accept him.'[127]

124. Mk 7:24-30.
125. Jn 20:30f.
126. R. Bultmann, *op. cit.*, 203.
127. Jn 1:11.

The Reaction (Jn 5:1-12:50)

The Sabbath Controversy (Jn 5:1-47)

1. THE PLOT: CRISIS AND JUDGEMENT: SABBATH AND THE FEASTS

Until now there has been a predominantly positive tone to the narrative. John the Baptist, the disciples, Nicodemus, the Samaritan woman, her fellow townspeople and the royal official all have had positive, even if inadequate, reactions to Jesus. From now on, however, the emphasis is largely on the negative reactions. These reactions focus on the central question of the locus of revelation – whether it is Jesus' revelation or Moses' Torah.[1] What A. E. Harvey says about the gospel as a whole is more and more in evidence from here on in the narrative:

> The underlying pattern ... is of two parties in dispute, Jesus and the 'Jews'; and the dispute has to be presented in such a way that the reader is persuaded of the justice of Jesus' cause ... Hebrew practice, and consequently Hebrew literature, allowed more matters to come to court, or at least to be discussed as possible subjects of litigation, than would naturally be the case in the western world. Not only so, but this fundamental model of two parties in dispute at law entered the realm of religious thought ... This tendency to present an issue under the literary form of a trial or dispute (a *ribh*) must be borne in mind when we come to consider how far the disputes recorded in John's gospel are intended to be understood as records of actual legal proceedings, or how far they are rather literary elaborations of issues which were known to be in dispute between Jesus and the Jews (that of healing on the Sabbath for instance).[2]

Beginning with the dispute about the Sabbath in chapter five, Jesus' claim to be God's agent on earth, acting and speaking on God's behalf, gathers momentum in the following chapters as he makes profound claims about his identity and authority. These claims to authority, pre-existence and unity with the Father take

---

1. This dispute reflects the post 70 AD divisions and tensions between Jews and Jewish Christians.

2. A. E. Harvey, *Jesus on Trial: A Study in the Fourth Gospel*, London: SPCK, 1976, 15f.

expression in statements like: 'my Father is working still, and I work', 'before Abraham came to be I am' and 'the Father and I are one'.[3] The 'forensic' character of the discussions is obvious as these utterances of Jesus give rise to charges of blasphemy to which he responds with further words giving rise to attempts to arrest and kill him (by stoning). The charge of blasphemy after the healing at Bethesda, resurfaces during the Feast of Tabernacles, and from then on Jesus is really on trial for his life and has to defend himself with 'polemics'. The divine plan is an obstacle in the way of arrest until the *hour (hôra)* or *time (kairos)* has arrived.

Several times it is said that the Jews desired to kill Jesus. The first such mention is on the Sabbath during an unspecified feast when Jesus healed the invalid at the pool of Bethesda (Bethzatha).[4] During the Feast of Tabernacles there are seven such indications of a threat to his life. On one such occasion when they picked up stones to throw at him, he hid himself and slipped out of the Temple.[5] Finally at the Feast of Dedication he left the Temple definitively, never to return.[6] These displays of hostility take place for the most part during the celebration of the feasts of the Jews in Jerusalem, in the Temple area. The events at the approach of the Passover feast in chapter six, however, take place in Galilee.[7] The section that begins here in the Temple reaches a turning point at the end of chapter ten with Jesus' final withdrawal from the Temple to the far side of Jordan where his mission originally began. Maybe this marked the end of the public ministry in an earlier stage of the gospel formation. As the text now stands, however, the threats to Jesus reach a climax

---

3. Jn 5:17; 8:58; 10:30.
4. Jn 5:16-18. The pool is variously named in the mss as Bethesda, Bethzatha, Belzatha and Bethsaida.
5. Jn 8:59.
6. Jn 10:31, 39f.
7. Because it interrupts the sequence of arguments and is set in a different place some scholars, like Bultmann, think chapter six should be placed before chapter five, and that it was mistakenly placed in its present position. However, no mss have such an arrangement. cf Schnackenburg, Vol 2, ad loc. The order of the events in the text makes logical sense when seen in the context of the order of the feasts in the yearly calendar. Passover was celebrated in the first, Tabernacles in the seventh, and Dedication in the ninth month. Furthermore, the fact that Jesus performed a healing in Jerusalem in chapter five would make it very unlikely that the brothers would be putting pressure on him to go to Jerusalem to perform a sign immediately afterwards, it if were placed where chapter six now stands in the text.

at the end of chapter eleven with a trial *in absentia* after the raising of Lazarus.[8]

The passage begins: 'After these things there was a feast of
the Jews', and goes on to speak about a healing on the Sabbath.[9]
This most likely refers to a Sabbath which fell during an unspecified feast of the Jews, but it could also refer to the Sabbath itself
as a feast of the Jews, along the lines of the description of the
Sabbath in Leviticus where the days of the sacred assemblies,
the festivals of the Lord, are introduced with the description of
the Sabbath.[10] It signifies a special time set aside for worship by
the people bound to God in covenant. Placing the Sabbath at the
head of the list creates the impression that the other feasts in
some respects grow out of or flow from the Sabbath. The *mekilta*
on Ex 16:25 states: 'If you will succeed in keeping the Sabbath,
the Holy One, blessed be he, will give you three festivals:
Passover, Pentecost and Tabernacles.' Whether the setting in
this chapter of John's gospel is simply the Sabbath, treated as a
festival of the Jews, or a Sabbath actually falling during one of
the festivals really makes no difference. Not specifying the feast,
if such were the case, avoids the possibility of a clash of meaning
and significance between the Sabbath and the feast. In either
case, the emphasis is on the dispute which arose about proper
observance of the Sabbath. This dispute provides the opportunity
for exploring further Jesus' relationship with the Father and the
nature of his mission.

There follows a series of feasts in the order in which they
occur during the year. Naming a feast creates an atmosphere for
the reader, conjures up a mood and provides a religious and theological framework for presenting the claims of Jesus and his
ministry. Celebrating the feasts enabled the participants to share
in the history of God's dealings with the people, revive their religious memory, sharpen their focus and heighten expectation for
God's saving action in the present and the future. The Hebrew
name for a feast is *zikkârôn*, from the verb *zâkar*, to remember.
'Remembering' in the context of the Sabbath or a feast is not just
a recalling of the past, but a making present for every subsequent generation of the experience of those who originally

---

8. Jn 11:47-53.
9. Chapters five, six and seven, begin with '(and) after these things', (*kai*) *meta
tauta*, showing the editorial technique of connecting the sections of this part of
the gospel.
10. Lev 23:1-3.

partook in the saving event. Liturgy makes the participants contemporaries of the events they remember in their celebration.
The feasts collapsed time into the present time of the festival.
Jesus now steps into the context of the feasts, fulfils their
promise and opens up the future. As he manifests himself in the
context of the feasts he fulfils the promise embodied in the
Temple, the institutions and the feasts of the Jews. In so doing he
appropriates to himself the cultic symbols of sacred time,[11]
bread,[12] water,[13] light,[14] sacred space,[15] and shepherding,[16]
associated with Sabbath, Passover, Tabernacles and Dedication.

The struggle between Jesus and the Jerusalem authorities
takes place largely in the context of the feasts which are celebrated
at the Temple in Jerusalem. Describing them as 'feasts of the
Jews' highlights the fact that by the time the gospel was written
there was a real division between Christians and Jews. Divisions
had taken place in the Jewish community between those who accepted and those who rejected the claims made by, or on behalf
of, Jesus. The fall of Jerusalem left the Jews who at the same time
had lost the mother city, community and Temple, rethinking
their position with regard to Torah and synagogue. Hardening
of attitudes took place after Jamnia (Jabneh) and some expulsions from the synagogue, occasioned by the addition to the
eighteen benedictions of the prayer against heretics, had taken
place.[17] This was painful for the expelled who lost their mother
community, and for those doing the expelling as they lost their
religious and family brothers and sisters. Both groups were now
working out a new self-definition. The tension between them is
evident in the story of Jesus as it is told in the gospel where his
experience is seen to foreshadow in story, and reflect in fact, the
subsequent experience of his followers. Although Jewish
Christians in the Johannine tradition had lost their mother community as well as the Temple and holy city, they kept the calendar and the feasts, now, however, with a new perspective, focused on Christ.

Growing hostility towards Jesus on the part of the authorities

11. Jn 5:17.
12. Jn 6:35, 48, 51.
13. Jn 7:37-39.
14. Jn 8:12.
15. Jn 2:19f; 10:36.
16. Jn 10:1-18.
17. The date and extent of these expulsions and of the addition to the benedictions is not clear.

and discussion of his origins, identity and credibility on the part of the crowd, together with unbelief on the part of his brothers, are a feature of the ministry from now on. An increasing sense of foreboding permeates the story from the time they desired to kill him after the healing on the Sabbath at Bethesda to their finally persuading Pilate to hand him over for crucifixion. This sense of foreboding combined with rumours of arrest and plots to kill him punctuate the narrative from here on and form a parallel with the more focused and stylised passion predictions in the synoptics.[18]

2. JESUS ON TRIAL

Chapter five, which opens this lengthy section of the gospel, has all the marks of a trial. It presents in forensic fashion Jesus' challenge to Sabbath observance and its interpretation, which in turn opens up the discussion of how he is doing his Father's work. From here on Jesus' judging and being judged are counterpoints in the irony of the gospel. His healing action on the Sabbath and his defence of his conduct result in two charges being levelled at him. He is accused of breaking the Sabbath for telling the healed man to carry his bed, and of blasphemy for speaking of God as his own Father and making himself equal to God by claiming to work on the Sabbath just as God does. For this blasphemy they want to kill him. Jesus conducts his own defence by answering these charges with his second great monologue in the gospel, containing some of its highest christology, in which he equates his own work with the work of the Father, that is, with the work that God alone does on the Sabbath. Having spoken in his own defence, Jesus then summons as his witnesses, the Father, the Baptist, Moses, the scriptures and the works he does.

The aftermath of this trial continues in chapters seven and eight with continuing emphasis on judging and judgement.[19] The story of the adulterous woman, long without a fixed home in the New Testament text, finds an appropriate setting in this context and serves to highlight the difference in judging standards between Jesus, the healing and reconciling judge who thwarts the sentence of death against the woman, and those wishing to pass judgement of death on the woman (and on him-

---

18. Mk 8:31; 9:31; 10:32ff and //s.
19. Jn 7:15-24; 8:13-20.

self).[20] The Sabbath is again the subject of controversy in Jn 7:14-24 where the reference is most likely to this healing at Bethesda and then a fresh controversy follows the healing of the blind man at the Pool of Siloam in chapter nine.

The Healing (Jn 5:1-9)
The cure at Bethesda[21] is a healing story like many similar stories in the synoptics, particularly the story of the healing on the Sabbath in Mk 3:1-6 and the healing of the cripple lowered through the roof to whom he gave a similar command as to the healed man in Bethesda: 'Pick up your bed and walk.'[22] Set in the Johannine gospel it takes on many levels of meaning. Listening to the conversation between Jesus and the Samaritan woman at the well in Samaria the reader heard both Jesus' offer of the gift of water bubbling up to eternal life and the enthusiastic response of the woman in asking for that gift. The whole conversation took place beside the well of Jacob with all its connotations of the gift of God providing miraculously for the needs of the people. That was in Samaria and the Samaritan woman asked about worship there and in Jerusalem. Now we are in Jerusalem when the people have come to worship at a feast. In the first part of the story, far from a well of living water we are presented with a magnificent pool large as a football field with four porticoes along its periphery and one cutting it in two across its middle. But in spite of its magnificent setting it is a stagnant pool surrounded by a multitude of 'weak' people (*asthenountôn*), blind, lame and withered, waiting in desperation for a movement of the waters. There is a kind of exhausted silence, nobody seems to react to the coming and presence of Jesus, though by now he was well known in Jerusalem as well as in Galilee and Samaria. One man, thirty eight years in his 'weakness', was there. Jesus asked if he 'willed' to be cured. He did not quite know. He seems to have lost the 'will'. All he could do by way of answer was complain that nobody would put him in the pool when the waters were disturbed, and that someone else always got there before him. Maybe a movement of the waters in the cisterns from time to time caused a momentary flow of cura-

---

20. Jn 8:1-11.
21. The name of the pool is variously given as Bethesda, Betzatha/Bezatha, and Bethsaida. It is identified with the excavated site beside the Church of St Anne, near the present Lion Gate.
22. Mk 3:1-6; 2:1-12.

tive elements for those able, or aided by others, to avail of them before they disappeared.[23] The helpless condition of these people depending on the movement of waters and on someone's aid in reaching the pool before the curative elements passed, is a piteous sight, and stands out in stark contrast to the promise of living water which one would drink and never be thirsty again.

References to the sheep pool, may also conjure up the image of the flock of God languishing in need of a shepherd. The man is not named, just referred to as 'a certain man', and so he may well be seen as a representative figure for the helpless flock. The thirty-eight years of the man's illness recalls the thirty-eight years the people spend in the desert, languishing around Kadesh-Barnea, unable to help themselves. They murmured, complained and shed tears before YHWH.[24] This sad individual, and the whole group, recall those unhappy times and people. Now the word of Jesus heals him, like an act of creation itself. Jesus tells him to take up his bed (mat) and walk.

Perhaps also there is an intended allusion to the Torah, symbolised often by life-giving water, and the five magnificent porticoes recalling the five books of the Torah, the Pentateuch. The healing, life-giving power of Jesus is being contrasted with the magnificence of the Torah and its expected life-giving power which, however, has not brought life and healing to these people.

The Accusation (Jn 5:10-16)

The second part of the story happens as the man is on his way with his bed (mat). Carrying it was seen as an infringement of Sabbath observance. The Jews point this out and he replies by way of defence that the one who healed him told him to carry it. This could mean 'Don't blame me, blame him!' or 'He obviously has divine authority if he performed this healing, so don't rush too quickly to judgement!' He was unable to tell them the name of his healer. Was this ingratitude on his part, that he had not even found out the name of his benefactor, or was it due to the fact that Jesus, as the text says, had slipped into the crowd, possibly to avoid the attention of a sign-seeking crowd?

Jesus later, in the third scene, found him in the Temple where he had obviously come to worship and, significantly drawing

---

23. Some texts have a verse about the angel touching the waters. It is a later gloss.
24. Deut 2:14f; 1:1-46, esp: 45, 46.

attention away from the 'wonder' of the miracle itself, Jesus set it in the context of salvation and the destructive power of sin: 'Sin no more lest something worse befall you.' This command to sin no more may well reflect a dimension of early tradition in the re-counting of the miracles of Jesus. In the healing of the man let down through the roof on a stretcher Jesus forgives his sins and as a proof of his power to forgive sin he heals his physical infirmity.[25] This association of sickness and sin was part of pop-ular religious thinking at the time, as seen here in Jesus' remark and later when the question was put to him about the cause of a man's blindness: 'Who has sinned, this man or his parents, that he was born blind?'[26]

The healed man went and told the Jews. Did he ungratefully report the name of the Sabbath-breaker or naïvely proclaim the name of the one who had healed him? Whichever way one reads it, the result is that Jesus is now in serious trouble. The emphasis moves from the man carrying his bed (mat), to the healing activ-ity on the Sabbath for which the Jews start persecuting Jesus.

If one reads the reactions of the healed man negatively, then this story forms a striking contrast with the healing of the blind man which follows in chapter nine. At first glance he shows no gratitude, no faith, no curiosity about the one who has healed him after so long an illness. In fact he stoops so low as to identify his benefactor as the Sabbath-breaker to the authorities. If one reads his reactions more positively, one is still left with the feel-ing that there was no real conversion in the sense of a faith com-mitment and desire to witness in the face of hostility. Perhaps this response represents an attitude to healing on the part of those who saw the signs and still were not moved to full faith in Jesus, either during his ministry or in the early church. The blind man in chapter nine, on the other hand, responds to harassment by authority and distancing by neighbours and family, with ever growing faith and resolve, and finally worships his healer. The telling of these stories may well reflect the differing re-sponses to healing activity in the early Christian community.

The Charges (Jn 5:16-18)
As the whole of John's gospel can be seen as a trial of Jesus in which the role of witnesses is crucial, so too here in chapter five the whole of the chapter is organised as a trial or *rîbh*. The dram-

25. Mk 2:1-12.
26. Jn 9:2.

atic character of the symbolic narrative is a *rîbh*, resembling a plea for the defence in court. It begins with a challenging action, a healing on the Sabbath, accompanied by the explanatory statement that 'My Father works until now and I work.'[27] When the authorities charge Jesus with breaking the Sabbath, they do so on the level of the law. He responds on the level of God and God's work. Two charges are brought against Jesus on this account, breaking the Sabbath and making himself equal to God. His opponents viewed this as blasphemy and so they wanted to kill him. In response Jesus presents his defence, outlining his commission from the Father, and then calling his witnesses.

3. BACKGROUND: SABBATH OBSERVANCE

However, the story of the healing at Bethesda is told not so much as a comment on Jesus' power of healing by word alone or on the ingratitude of the man healed, but rather as an introduction to the subject of Sabbath observance and Jesus' defence of his activity on the Sabbath which is a major statement about his identity, mission and authority. The healing and his defence 'my Father works until now and I work'[28] together form the basis of a double charge against him. He has broken the Sabbath and made himself equal to God. This defence knits the activity and the discourse into a single symbolic narrative revealing the identity of Jesus and the divine authority of his mission.

The origins of Sabbath are obscure. Scholars have looked for evidence of such an observance among the Babylonians, the Canaanites and the Kenites. The decalogue as it is now presented in Exodus and Deuteronomy, reflects the priestly and deuteronomic traditions and theology.[29] Maybe the earliest form of the decalogue did not have the theological rationale with which the practice was subsequently invested. As with the feasts, older institutions were gradually historicised and invested with the memory of what God had done in creation and history.

The priestly tradition reflected in Exodus opens the Sabbath commandment with the injunction to 'remember' the Sabbath day, to keep it holy. The Hebrew *qds*, holy, emphasises separation, keeping person, place, object or time separated from the world and its pursuits, for the worship and service of God. The

---

27. Jn 5:17.
28. Jn 5:17.
29. Ex 20:7-11; Deut 5:12-15.

version of the command in Exodus emphasises the creation motif, recalling the priestly creation account, the first account in Genesis, describing how God rested from his creation and saw it was very good. This priestly theology is further evidenced in Exodus with the command, accompanied by the death penalty for infringement: 'Therefore the people of Israel shall keep the Sabbath, observing the Sabbath throughout the generations, as a perpetual covenant. It is a sign forever between me and the people of Israel that in six days the Lord made heaven and earth, and on the seventh day he rested and was refreshed.'[30] The Sabbath is a sign of God's perpetual covenant with the people. This 'sign' value was of particular importance especially during the Exile when other institutions giving expression to their identity and facilitating their life of worship were destroyed.

The deuteronomic tradition emphasised the dramatic event of God's intervention on their behalf in liberating them from the house of slavery in Egypt. They are exhorted in the deuteronomic version of the decalogue to 'remember', that is, to experience for themselves, the enormity of that event, as they celebrate the Sabbath.

Sabbath observance was therefore at the heart of the Torah and prescriptions for its observance were spelled out in great detail. Thirty-nine works were forbidden. These represent a certain relaxation of the practices such as those found in the Book of Jubilees and the Zadokite fragment.[31] Nine prescriptions referred to farming tasks, thirteen related to wool and thread tasks, seven to hunting and related tasks, two to writing, three to building and hammering, two to fires, two to baking, and finally one to 'taking out anything from one domain to another'.[32] Of immediate relevance to the healing at Bethesda was the prohibition on carrying a burden, 'taking out anything from one domain to another'. Each of these prescriptions was subdivided to cover many activities. One could carry objects in one's private domain or four cubits in the public domain. Carrying a bed with an invalid on it was allowed, but carrying an empty bed was forbidden. Challenging these prescriptions, Jesus opened a debate on the whole nature of the Sabbath and on the relationship of

---

30. Ex 31:15-17.
31. Jub 50:8-12; Zadokite Docm 10-11.
32. *m. Sabb.* 7:2.

God to creation, to salvation history, to the chosen people, to social justice and humanitarian concerns.

Rabbinic interpretation, however, allowed three classes of exception where situations took priority over Sabbath obser-vance. They were cultic duties such as circumcision and work required for the Temple service like baking cakes for the cereal offering.[33] Matthew's gospel refers to this: 'Have you not read in the law how on the Sabbath the priests in the Temple profane the Sabbath and are guiltless? I tell you, something greater than the Temple is here.'[34] Defensive warfare, to defend oneself, was allowed, following the case where Mattathias decided the Jews could defend themselves if attacked on the Sabbath after he heard of a group of Jews, a thousand men, women and children, who were massacred because they refused to fight on the Sabbath.[35] Saving life was also permitted. Rabbi Eleazar stated that since circumcision which concerns one of man's 248 mem-bers, overrides the Sabbath, how much more must his whole body (if in danger) override the Sabbath.[36]

The rabbis also noted the fact that God works on the Sabbath in sustaining creation, giving life and administering judgement, since children are born and people die on the Sabbath. When rabbi Akiba was challenged by Tinneus Rufus, the Roman Governor about the Sabbath, using the argument that God stirs up the wind and causes the rain to fall on the Sabbath, he refuted the argument by pointing out that the world is God's private do-main and God could cause anything to move about in it as it was not taking anything from one domain to another. Similarly the world is God's Temple and so God's work in the universe is like the work permitted in the Temple on the Sabbath.[37]

The synoptics and John all show Jesus challenging an inter-pretation of the Sabbath which failed to see it as a day for the cel-ebration of creation, life, liberty and salvation. In the gospel of John Jesus' defence of his conduct is based not on an argument about the actual prescriptions of the laws of observance and their detailed interpretation, but he raises the issue onto another plane. He claims to be doing the Father's work on the Sabbath. This is an extremely solemn claim to work as God does on the

33. *m. Sabb.* 18:3; 19:1; *m. Tem.* 2:1.
34. Mt 12:5-8.
35. 1 Macc 2:29-41.
36. *b. Yoma* 85b; cf *Mek. Sabbata* 1.
37. *Gen. Rab.* 11:5; *Mek. Sabbata* 2.

Sabbath and it is blasphemy to those who hear him. G. A. Yee
puts it succinctly:

> By transforming the tradition into a Sabbath controversy,
> John is able, on one hand, to articulate Jesus' mysterious rela-
> tionship to the Father, a theological affirmation that was
> bound to alienate the Jewish community. On the other hand,
> John is able to develop two related christological themes
> through this Sabbath dispute: Jesus as the one who gives life
> and Jesus as the one who judges ... As Jesus' discourse
> makes clear, Jesus' healing work on the Sabbath reveals that
> he carries on the same life-giving/life-judging activity as his
> Father. As God's son, Jesus must work on the Sabbath.[38]

Sabbath is a remembering (*zakôr*) of the creative and redeeming
action of God. Celebrating it is a public acknowledgement of the
sovereignty of God in creation and history. Though God has to
work on the Sabbath lest creation fall apart and history come to
an end, such work is the sole prerogative of God. To usurp such
a prerogative is blasphemy. When Jesus says, 'My Father is
working still (*heôs arti*) and I work', he is associating himself and
his work with this prerogative of God, and compounding it in
this 'explosively blasphemous' context by referring to God as his
Father. This raises the issue of the exact nature of the relationship he is claiming to have with God.

   The healing of the man at the pool brings forward the developing understanding of Jesus' life-giving power. To Nicodemus
Jesus had spoken about birth, entering into a life empowered by
the Spirit. To the Samaritan woman he had spoken about the gift
of water that bubbles up to eternal life. To the Galilean nobleman he restored his son to life from the threat of imminent
physical death. At the pool he restores wholeness of health and
physical life. In the ensuing discussion he speaks of life in a combination of eschatological and 'here and now' terms. He speaks
of those in their tombs who will hear the voice of the Son of Man
and live. Life after physical life in the body and fullness of
'spiritual' life in the body are now held in tension. In chapter
eleven, at the raising of Lazarus, the restoration of physical life
will point forward to Jesus' own resurrection and the sharing of
the believer in that resurrection, both in the 'here and now' life
in the world and in the life to come.

   This unfolding role of Jesus as life-giver will continue in the

---

38. G. A. Yee, *Jewish Feasts and the Gospel of John*, 41, 42.

developing hostility and threat to his own life. Mark's gospel shows Jesus being lured into a situation of healing on the Sabbath and the murderous intent of those he outwitted by his questioning about its true nature.[39] This is a similar reaction to the desire and ongoing attempts to arrest and kill him after the healing at Bethesda.

4. THE DEFENCE (JN 5:19-30)

The charges have been brought. Now Jesus offers his defence. Three times he uses the solemn proclamatory formula 'Amen, amen, I say to you', introducing each of the three main aspects of the argument.[40] The Word made flesh is speaking. First of all he declares that the Son does the Father's work for which the Father has instructed him. 'The Son can do nothing of himself, he can only do what he sees the Father doing and whatever the Father does the Son does too.'[41] It is because the Father loves the Son that he shows him everything and empowers him to do great things, and even greater things to come. This repeats the senti-ment of the former discourse: 'He whom God has sent speaks the words of God ... The Father loves the Son and has placed all things in his hands.'[42] As in the discourse in chapter three, the two fundamental powers of giving life and pronouncing judge-ment (zoôpoiêsis and krisis) are treated. The Father has given these powers to the Son. Secondly, the Son who exercises these powers is due honour as is the Father, and to refuse it is to refuse honour to the Father who sent him. This emphasises the union between Father and Son which demands the same honour for the Son as for the Father. Whoever listens to the words of Jesus and believes in the one who sent him has eternal life and does not come to judgement (condemnation). In this is found life and favourable judgement. Thirdly, in a statement that brings to-gether the final and realised eschatology of the gospel, and the roles of Son, Son of God and Son of Man, this promise of eternal life will touch those already in their tombs, for the Father, source of life, has made the Son source of life. Now the Son of Man im-agery is used for the supreme judge. The dead will rise to judge-ment, to life or condemnation. The judgement is just because it is

---

39. Mk 3:1-6; cf. Mt 12:9-14; Lk 6: 6-11.
40. Jn 5:19, 24, 25.
41. Jn 5:19.
42. Jn 3:34f.

in keeping with the will of the one who sent him. The two great powers of giving life and judgement associated with the Son of Man are emphasised here as they were in the monologue in chapter three. H. Ridderboss puts it very clearly:

> ... we are dealing with neither just a 'programme' that the Father has given the Son once for all to carry out nor with incidental *ad hoc* instructions, but with the continuing agreement of the Son's speech and action with the Father, agreement rooted in his oneness with the Father (cf 1:1a) and in the absolute authority bestowed on him as the beloved Son (cf 3:35; 5:21ff). Hence it can be said that the Son speaks and acts in accord both with what he *has* seen and heard from the Father and with what the Father *will* show him.[43]

Like the many agents of God in scripture, the judge, king, and prophet, the Son, in a very special way, is to be honoured as the one who sent him. M. M. Thompson describes very succinctly 'the theological grounding for the predications of the authority and work of the Father given to and embodied in the Son', but she cautions against a too easy description of the Father-Son relationship in this context as fitting the 'apprentice model'.[44] She says:

> The element of the Father's discipline or correction of his Son is absent from John. Similarly, the note of learning in apprenticeship does not capture the tenor of the Johannine depiction of Father and Son. The Son is never said to learn; rather, he speaks what he hears from the Father, and he does what he has seen the Father doing ... Perhaps one may wish to call this 'apprenticeship' for a son learns by imitation to model what he sees his father doing ... the picture that emerges is closer to the view of a prophet who becomes a mouthpiece of God, or a 'seer' who has a vision or heavenly journey and reports what he has seen. However ... John does not credit Jesus' doing and speaking to the work of the Spirit as though he were an inspired prophet, but rather to the unique relationship of the Father and Son, perhaps best summarised in the pithy statements of John 5.[45]

This is Jesus' defence of himself and his activity. Having thus stated his case he now summons the witnesses to support his defence and testify on his behalf.

43. H. Ridderbos, *The Gospel of John*, 192.
44. M. M. Thompson, *op. cit.*, 98; cf Brodie, *op. cit.*, 247.
45. M. M. Thompson, *op. cit.*, 97.

5. THE WITNESSES (JN 5:31-47)

In law there must be another witness to validate one's testimony. There is an implied suggestion on the part of the opposition that Jesus cannot produce another witness, or if he can, then he is being challenged to do so. The introduction of the 'other' witness is somewhat confusing as it leaves one asking the question whether the Father is one of a number of witnesses mentioned, or the witness who empowers the others. Jesus' response could be read as: 'Of course there is a witness other than myself, in fact there are several.' It could also be interpreted as: 'The "other" witness is the Father who empowers the works of Jesus, sent John (the Baptist), inspired the scriptures and appointed Moses, all of whom are witnesses.' The opponents' rejection of the one about whom Moses wrote exposes their actual non-belief in what he wrote. John (the Baptist) was a witness. He is described as a light burning brightly for a time. This description recalls the depiction of Elijah in the Book of Sirach: 'There the prophet Elijah arose like a fire, his word flaring like a torch.'[46] The works his Father gave him to do testify on his behalf. The Father bears witness, but they do not accept his witness, because they have not seen or heard him and his word finds no home in them, as is obvious from the fact that they rejected the one whom he sent. The scriptures witness to him and though his opponents believe that they find life in the scriptures yet they refuse to come to him for life. They place their hope in Moses. If they had really understood Moses, however, they would have discerned the continuity between the writings of Moses and the words of Jesus. Since they do not believe what he wrote how can they believe what Jesus proclaims?[47] 'In the event, he who should have been their advocate will be their prosecutor.'[48]

Jesus does not need human approval. They look to one another for approval. They accept people who set themselves up in their own name, but they refuse to accept him because the love of the Father is not in them, and they are not concerned about the approval that comes from the one God.[49] The gospel plays on the secular meaning of *doxa*, reputation, to say that some

---

46. Sir 48:1.
47. The Greek here *tois emois rhêmasi* signifies more than just speaking in words, but in deeds that speak as well, hence the translation 'proclaims'. Note the contrast with *ton logon mou* above in v. 24.
48. W. J. Harrington, *op. cit.*, 45.
49. Jn 5:44.

were more interested in their own *doxa*, reputation or image, than in the unique opportunity of seeing the glory revealed in Jesus. The Greek term *doxa* means both glory and reputation. In the prologue the statement that 'we have seen', or more accurately, 'we have gazed upon' his glory, shows that the Old Testament *k'bôd YHWH* (usually translated as *doxa to theou*), is now applied to Jesus, the *Logos* become *sarx*. As this cannot apply to his glory 'in heaven' which we do not see, it applies to what was seen and experienced in Jesus, especially as seen in his 'miraculous' activity, as at Cana and the tomb of Lazarus.

The Outcome

The trial initiated in this chapter is ongoing. A sense of foreboding and rumours of arrest and plots to kill him continue until chapter eleven when the Sanhedrin meets after the raising of Lazarus and definitively decide on his death.[50]

Meanwhile attention is drawn to the Passover Feast, the first of the feasts in the year.

---

50. Jn 11:47-53.

The Passover in Galilee (Jn 6:1-71)

1. THE PLOT: SURPASSING THE MIRACLES OF MOSES

With the now familiar Johannine phrase for introducing a new section or situation, *meta tauta*, 'after these things', the scene switches from Jerusalem to Galilee.[51] This is the only part of St John's gospel that has an extended section set around the Sea of Galilee (Tiberias) during the pre-Easter ministry. Rather than the usual context of Jerusalem and the Temple as a setting during a pilgrimage feast, the location is Galilee at the approach of the Passover.

As in the introduction to the Sermon on the Mount in St Matthew's gospel, Jesus, on seeing the crowd, ascends *the mountain*, an unspecified mountain in Galilee familiar also to readers of the synoptics[52] and reminiscent of Sinai/Horeb with its connotations of the presence and glory of God, the gift of the Law to Moses and the gentle breeze heralding the word of the Lord to Elijah.[53] Reminiscent of Moses too is the sitting position of Jesus who teaches like the scribes who occupy the chair of Moses.[54] This is a typical gospel setting for a teaching, healing or feeding sequence.[55] It reflects the role of the shepherd caring for the flock in the desert, an image spelled out explicitly by Mark in his introduction to the teaching and feeding of the multitude. '... He had compassion on them, because they were like sheep without a shepherd; and he began to teach them many things.'[56] The various multiplication accounts refer to green grass, their need to rest after a long journey lest they faint on the way, and the fact that they ate, were satisfied and had food left over. All these elements recall Ps 22 (23). 'The Lord is my *shepherd* I shall *not want*, fresh and *green* are the pastures where he gives me *repose* ... he

---

51. This section opens with the mention of Jesus crossing the Sea of Galilee, then after the multiplication of the loaves the disciples cross again to Capernaum and the crowds in turn cross the following day. These geographical references can be confusing, especially since they often serve principally as connections to smooth a transition between passages linked by themes. The connections can differ between mss and scribal efforts to smooth them can lead to even greater confusion.
52. Mt 5-7, the Sermon on the Mount; Mk 3:13-19//Lk 6:12-16, the appointment of the twelve; Mt 17:1-8//Mk 9:2-8//Lk 9:28-36, the Transfiguration; Mt 28, the final appearance of the Risen Lord – all are on the mountain in Galilee.
53. Ex 19-20; 1 Kings 19.
54. Mt 5:1; Mk 6:1; 9:35; Lk 4:20.
55. cf Mt 5:1ff; Mk 6:33f; Lk 9:12.
56. Mk 6:34.

prepares a *banquet* for me ... my cup is *overflowing*.' John mentions the green grass, eating their fill and gathering the fragments left over. Here too in St John's gospel the shepherding imagery of the psalm is in the background. However, at the beginning of the account of the multiplication, the reader's attention is
drawn to the approach of the Passover. Mentioning the feast so
pointedly at the beginning of the chapter creates a mood and
provides a frame of biblical reference for Jesus' action and teaching about the life-giving bread. It is an interpretative rubric for
the whole chapter. It conjures up reminiscences of the mighty
deeds of God whereby the covenant people were brought into
existence and how they responded by complaining and murmuring throughout their time in the desert. It sets the figure of
Jesus and describes his actions and words against the background of Moses and in the context of the expectation of the
'prophet like Moses'. Among other expectations there was an
opinion abroad that the Messiah would repeat the miracle of
Moses' feeding the people in the wilderness.[57] It taps into the
various expectations about 'the one who is to come into the
world' and excites the messianic hopes of those who want to
proclaim him king.

The open spaces around the Sea of Galilee provide a setting
reminiscent of the events of the Exodus-Passover. The green
grass points to the advent of spring and the time of the Passover.
The two accounts in Matthew and Mark seem to refer respectively to a messianic banquet for the Jews and a messianic banquet for the Gentiles.[58] John has one multiplication and, given its
location in Galilee of the Gentiles and close to the pagan cities of
the Decapolis, it possibly signifies a messianic banquet for a
multitude made up of both Jews and Gentiles. The Jerusalem
crowd and the authorities of the previous scene are replaced by
the disciples and the multitude, many of whom have come because they saw the signs Jesus performed for the sick.
Introducing the crowd as 'having seen the signs' the narrator is
making a negative comment on their sign-dependent faith, like
that of the Jerusalem crowd on Jesus' first visit there.[59] Jesus

57. 2 Bar 29:8 foretells a second feeding in the desert as the sign of the Messianic
Age.
58. Scholars draw this conclusion from the symbolic numbers of the crowd and
of the baskets of left-overs as well as from the locations of the multiplications.
59. Jn 6:2; cf 2:23. Some scholars have seen this reference to 'signs' (in the plural,
though only one sign has been described here) as an argument for a sign source
edited for use in the gospel.

himself will solemnly remind the crowd on the day after the multiplication that they have come out to him in Capernaum because they had their fill of the bread, not because they saw (i.e. understood) the sign of the multiplication. Their failure to understand that it was a sign is further emphasised by the fact that they go on to demand yet another sign.[60] Their reactions throughout recall the murmuring of the crowds during the Exodus and wandering in the desert.

Chapter six tells the story of Jesus in Galilee at the approach of the Passover festival against the background of the events surrounding the foundation of Israel as a people. These events are 'remembered' in the celebration of the feast as hope for the present and future is renewed and enthusiasm is enkindled through the festivities. On this occasion, however, Jesus, rather than the Temple or domestic ritual, occupies the central spot. The promise of the feast is fulfilled and the future anticipated in his person and mission. It was expected that the Messiah would repeat the miracle of Moses and feed the people in the desert. This Jesus does, but he reinterprets the latter-day manna as bread from heaven and food for eternal life, not just as sustenance for physical life. Furthermore, Jesus not only *gives*, but *is* that bread come down from heaven.

The institution of the Eucharist is not described during the Last Supper in this gospel but the eucharistic teaching is contained here in chapter six. The eucharistic dimension is reflected in the stylised liturgical words and actions of the multiplication and is further developed in the instruction in the synagogue in Capernaum about 'eating my flesh and drinking my blood'.[61] Flesh and blood are the elements of the sacrifice and the sacrificial communion meal in the sharing of which the partakers drew life from, and became one with, the sacrificial victim. In addition, the close association of Judas' betrayal with the institution of the Eucharist, recounted in the synoptics, is reflected here in chapter six with the reference to the betrayal following on the eucharistic teaching, as the chapter draws to a close and reaches a climax with Peter's confession of faith.

The circumstances of Jesus' own life, and the lives of his followers, are highlighted in this chapter, particularly in regard to the 'temptations' put in his way by the curiosity of some, the un-

60. Jn 6:26, 30.
61. Jn 6:53-58.

belief of others and the political and religious agenda of friend and foe alike. Matthew and Luke deal with these factors neatly and imaginatively in the three temptations in the desert at the beginning of the ministry. There they are stylised and presented proleptically at the beginning of the ministry in the form of temptation and response with apt biblical quotations from Deuteronomy.[62] In St John's gospel, however, these same factors, the temptations to gratify physical need, to grasp at power and to impress with signs, are encountered in the practical everyday circumstances of Jesus' ministry. Here in chapter six all three are present as the crowd follows Jesus because of the 'physical' food they have received, as they desire to carry him off to make him king, and as they demand from him a sign.

2. BACKGROUND TO THE FEAST

Originally the Passover (*Pesah*) probably combined an older nomadic, pastoral feast celebrated with the slaying of a sheep or goat and a settled agricultural feast of the grain (barley) harvest. *The Passover sacrifice* has its origins in the nomadic times when the shepherd sacrificed an animal and sprinkled the blood on the tent pegs to ensure fertility for the flock and safety for the inhabitants. *The sacrificial meal* was then eaten with bitter herbs gathered in the desert, in the nomadic style of someone ready for a journey. *The feast of Unleavened Bread* had its origin in an agricultural celebration of the barley harvest when all the old leaven was got rid of, and a new beginning was embarked upon with bread made from the new grain. *The consecration of the first-born* began as a feast recognising the gift of life from the Deity, with the sacrifice of the first born of the animals and the consecration of the first born of the children. The first born was believed to embody the best qualities. These older pastoral and agricultural festivals were eventually combined and historicised into a festival celebrating the Passover, Exodus and wandering which brought the people to Canaan. The slaying of the lamb recalled the escape from the plague of death visited on the first-born in Egypt. 'It is the sacrifice of the Lord's Passover, for he passed over the houses of the people of Israel in Egypt, when he slew the Egyptians but spared our houses.'[63]The sprinkling of the blood of the lamb symbolised the gift of life, and the sealing

---

62. Mt 4:1-11; Lk 4:1-13.
63. Ex 12:27 (JB).

or anointing of the Israelites as the first-born of God. The blood became a sign of life given and protected by God, an anointing, symbolising Israel's position as God's children 'The blood will be a sign for you upon the houses where you are; and when I see the blood, I will pass over you, and no plague shall fall upon you to destroy you.'[64] 'The blood is the life.'[65] 'The life of the flesh is in the blood. This blood I myself have given you to perform the rite of atonement for your lives at the altar; for it is blood that atones for a life.'[66] The doorposts and lintels were anointed with the blood of the lamb, using sprigs of hyssop. The unleavened bread recalled the haste in which they began their journey from Egypt, not giving the bread time to rise and God's providence in feeding the people in the desert until they received the gift of the manna, the bread from heaven. The unleavened bread also celebrated the new beginning unfolding at the escape from Egypt as they left the old leaven behind. In this process of historicisation all the elements of the Passover meal were eventually interpreted in historical terms. The celebration was communal, not individual, and all Israel was united in the remembering of God's mighty deeds in forming a people.

Many major events in the history of the people were marked by the celebration of the Passover. When Joshua led them across the Jordan to the Promised Land they encamped at Gilgal and kept the Passover in the plains of Jericho. On that occasion the manna ceased and they ate the grain, a bringing together of the feasts of Passover and Unleavened Bread. When Josiah completed his far reaching religious reform programme he celebrated the Passover, and when the returned exiles worshipped for the first time in the newly constructed Temple, they too celebrated the Passover.[67]

The Passover in Jesus' time was celebrated as one of the three great pilgrimage feasts. A hundred thousand people crowded into the city on these occasions, adding to the fifty thousand inhabitants. Zealots and revolutionaries could easily enter in the shadow of such crowds. In the afternoon of the day before the Passover the paschal lambs were ritually slaughtered and offered to God in the Temple. The liturgical instructions for the Passover feast in Ex 11-13 cover three of its ceremonies, the

64. Ex 12:13 (JB).
65. Deut 12:23 (JB).
66. Lev 17:11.
67. Josh 5:10-12; 2 Kings 23:21-23//2 Chr 35:1-18; Ezra 6:19-22.

Passover sacrifice, the feast of Unleavened Bread and the consecration of the first-born. The sacrificial meal was eaten, if not in the precincts of the Temple, at least within the boundaries of the city. The meal had three main components, the sacrificial meal itself, the Haggadah or Passover instruction, and the Hallel or songs of praise, usually the psalms. The intense religious atmosphere added to the general political awareness of the time and often resulted in revolutionary activity and heightened messianic expectation. It was a time for political activists and revolutionaries to play on that expectation and a time for the Roman authorities to take special precautions. It was a time when a Jewish king, a son of David, might appear.

However, between the lifetime of Jesus and the time when the gospel was written a change of seismic proportions had taken place. The Temple and its sacrifices were destroyed, Jerusalem was no longer the great focus of pilgrimage, and the Passover sacrificial meal evolved into the non sacrificial Seder Meal celebrated in a domestic setting. The loss of Temple and sacrificial ritual occasioned the further development of symbolic interpretation of the feast and its elements. As Christian Jews reassessed their position in the wake of the destruction of the Temple and the growing alienation from their mother Jewish community with its institutions, feasts and various religious and social celebrations and supports, the 'once-for-allness' of the revelation through Jesus encouraged a radical reassessment of many, if not all, of the earlier means of mediation. The story of Jesus came to be told with an emphasis on showing how he fulfills and surpasses the older promise of the institutions and feasts, and opens up their meaning for the present and future in the context of his own identity and mission.

Through the leadership of Moses whom God had commissioned to say to the children of Israel, '*I am* has sent me to you',[68] God led the people from the slavery of Egypt, saved them from the waters of the sea, made a covenant with them in the desert, accompanied them as a cloud by day and a fire by night, sustained them with manna from heaven and water from the rock, and promised them an inheritance in the land flowing with milk and honey. But the same narratives which tell this story in Exodus and Numbers also describe the obdurate response of the people, a response highlighted and kept alive in the sermons of

---

68. Ex 3:14.

Deuteronomy and in the historical psalms.[69] They murmured and complained. They demanded food and drink in the desert, and wanted to return to Egypt. They worshipped a golden calf, a god made by their own hands and to their own liking. They rebelled, disobeyed and provoked Moses and deserted the God who looked after them.[70]

These aspects of the Passover event which reveal God's dealings with the people and their response are now re-run in a new context in the Johannine story of Jesus in Galilee at the approach of the Passover when he repeated the miracle of Moses and fed the people in the wilderness. On the one hand there is the miraculous feeding in the desert followed by the miracle on the water with its experience of the protecting *I am* presence and the teaching about the gift of food from heaven. All these are reminiscent of the mighty deeds of God in the desert but the response of the crowd in Galilee also recalls the response of the Israelites. That response was one of murmuring, quarrelling, fault finding, division, and apostasy. Throughout the chapter in John's gospel the crowd act like the chorus in a Greek play, filling in the background, raising issues, acting as dialogue partner, and like the Israelites in the desert, complaining, reacting and falling away. The Jews have not understood Moses and the Torah, and now they misunderstand Jesus. The repeated 'how?' highlights their lack of understanding here and throughout the gospel.[71] The disagreements, murmuring, and apostasy spread from the crowd to the disciples, provoking the crisis among the disciples in which Jesus asks Peter if he too is going to leave him. Following closely on the crisis is the reference to the future betrayal and the naming of the betrayer. The earlier optimism of the narrative has collapsed. The reader has serious questions about the future of the mission. The disciples who remain now appear to be a remnant of the original larger group, among whom were the twelve.[72]

3. THE MULTIPLICATION (JN 6:1-15)

The multiplication of the loaves and fishes is one of the few miracles recounted in all four gospels.[73] In fact it is recorded twice

---

69. Pss 77 (78); 105 (106); cf Ps 94 (95).
70. Ex 16; 17; 22; Num 11; 12; 14; 16; 20; 21. Pss 77 (78); 105 (106); 94 (95).
71. Jn 3:4, 9; 6:42, 52; 7:15; 8:33; 9:10, 15, 16, 19, 21, 26; 12:34; 14:5.
72. Jn 6:67-71. Only here (three times) and in 20:24 is there reference to 'the twelve'.
73. Mt 14:13-21; 15:32-39; Mk 6:35-44; 8:1-10; Lk 9:12-17.

by Matthew and Mark. The accounts reflect a strong influence of
the liturgy of the first Christians with the use of the eucharistic
formula 'took the bread, gave thanks or said the blessing, and shared
it around'. Both Matthew and Mark have two 'bread sections' in
their gospels, containing the multiplication of loaves and fishes,
sea crossing, request for a sign, teaching about bread, and a be-
trayal/passion theme leading to a demonstration of Peter's
faith.[74] The Johannine account has all these themes or elements
in chapter six. In John's gospel, as in the second accounts in
Matthew and Mark, it is Jesus who takes the initiative. Matthew
and Mark state that Jesus felt sorry for the crowd because they
were with him for three days and had nothing to eat.[75] As in the
case of the invalid at the Pool of Bethesda, and later in the case of
the blind man at the Pool of Siloam, Jesus takes the initiative in
relation to the marginalised, the excluded and the suffering.
(This makes his 'slow' response to the call to the dying Lazarus a
very significant gesture and focus for serious theological comment).

Where shall we buy bread for these people to eat?
When Jesus puts the question to Philip: 'Where shall we ever
buy bread for these people to eat?', the circumstances of the
Exodus-wandering with its large groups of people needing food
in the wilderness and the dominant figure of Moses are recalled.[76] One remembers the desperation in Moses' questions to
the Lord in the desert: 'Where am I to get meat to give all these
people?' and 'If all the flocks and herds were slaughtered would
that be enough for them ? If all the fish in the sea were gathered
(LXX *synagein*) would that be enough for them?'[77] This same
theme is reflected in the psalm: 'They even spoke against God.
They said, "Is it possible for God to prepare a table in the

74. Luke's account stands alone among the six accounts in not having a sea crossing following the multiplication.
75. Mt 15:32; Mk 8:1-3. In their first accounts of the multiplication Matthew and
Mark, like Luke, mention the concern of the disciples/apostles for the people.
The disciples/apostles said to Jesus, after healing (Matthew) and teaching at
length (Mark), and after teaching and healing (Luke), to send the crowds away
to buy food. Mt 14:15; Mk 6:35; Lk 9:12.
76. Jn 6:5. Jesus' question to Philip is interesting in the light of Luke's statement
that Philip came from Bethsaida. It may well point to a historical reminiscence of
Jesus' consulting his local knowledge.
77. Num 11:1-3, 13, 22 (JB).

desert?".'[78] According to the prediction of deutero-Isaiah the miracle of feeding the people during the Exodus-wandering would be repeated during the return from exile in Babylon: 'They shall be fed along the way ... they shall not hunger, nor shall they thirst.'[79] Jesus is portrayed in biblical fashion like Moses, posing the question to heighten the awareness of the problem and create an appreciation of the gift which follows and its sign value. The theological concern of the narrator that, in the event of these biblical allusions being lost on the reader, it might detract from Jesus' omniscience, probably prompted the remark that Jesus asked Philip in order to test him.[80] Philip hears and responds on the 'earthly' level. But the reader can sense another level of meaning in Jesus' question about food for the people and where it can be obtained. He had told the disciples when they were concerned about his conversation alone with the Samaritan woman that he had food to eat of which they were unaware. Carrying out of the will of his Father by doing the work of his Father is his real sustenance. Jesus will subsequently talk to these Galileans in similar vein about working for food that does not perish.

Eucharistic formula
Jesus, in this account of the multiplication, unlike the account in the synoptics, passes the bread around himself, as he did at the Last Supper in the synoptics. This is obviously a theological 'simplification' to highlight the word and action by then established in the eucharistic liturgy. The Greek term 'giving thanks', *eulogêsas*, is in line with Lucan and Pauline usage and contrasts with the more semitic 'blessing' as used by Matthew and Mark.[81] The focus of attention is on the bread rather than the fish, because the allusion to the eucharistic celebration is highlighted and also because the discourse on the bread of life is to follow.[82] The use of the verb *bibrôskein*, 'to feed on', prepares the

78. Ps 77(78):19.
79. Isa 49:9ff (JB).
80. Philip and Andrew figure here at 6:18 where they procure the bread from the little boy, and again they are the ones approached when the Greeks want to see Jesus at 12:21f. They appear as the 'handlers' of Jesus.
81. Mt 26:26; Mk14:22; Lk 22:17; 1 Cor 11:24.
82. Bread was not usually eaten on its own but would have some 'filling' as in a sandwich. *opsarion*, a double diminutive, was used to describe such a filling. It literally means 'a small, little fish'. Combined with bread such a 'filling' is referred to as 'food' or, in the more general sense of the term 'bread'. The' fish' is not therefore left 'redundant' in the narrative.

reader, by using a related word, for the discourse on 'food (*brô-sis*) that endures to eternal life' and for Jesus' statement that 'my flesh is true (or real) food (*alêthê brôsis*)'.[83]

Gathering

The verb *synagein* 'to gather', is used for gathering up the fragments (*klasmata*). This usage is peculiar to this gospel, and emphasises the fact that the fragments are not a remnant, but a surplus. The gathering of the fragments recalls the gathering of the manna and with it the desert scenario of Moses and the Exodus-wandering when the people gathered the manna each day, until they had what they needed.[84] In fact the same verb is used in the LXX for the *gathering* of the manna. Unlike the manna, however, which was not to be stored, and any manna hidden away perished, the *klasmata* are gathered after the multiplication so that none may be lost. Unlike the food people work for which does not last, it is to continue to be available to future believers who want to share in the food which Jesus provides.[85] The noun *klasmata* has overtones of the breaking into shared pieces of the eucharistic bread and is so used to signify the eucharistic fragments in the Didache.[86] The mention of *twelve* baskets, however, shifts the focus of attention from the food to the people, pointing to the complete number of the tribes of Israel, thus referring to the completeness of God's people, used also in the choice of twelve apostles, like the twelve sons of Israel (Jacob), and now signifying the full number of believers in Jesus.[87] The verb *synagein* carries these overtones into the liturgy as it signifies the gathering of the liturgical assembly to celebrate the Eucharist.[88]

Barley bread

The reference to barley bread conjures up the imagery of the Elijah-Elisha cycle with its promise of the return of Elijah. The barley bread, cheaper than wheaten bread and so regarded as the bread of the poor, recalls the multiplication of the barley bread by Elisha, successor to Elijah: 'Give it to the people to eat', said Elisha to a man from Baal-Shalishah, 'they will eat and have

---

83. Jn 6:27, 55.
84. Ex 16:18, 8, 12, 16, 21.
85. Ex 16:19f; 27.
86. *Didache* 9:3, 4.
87. Mt 14:20; Mk 6:43; Lk 9:17.
88. *Didache* 9:4; *1 Clement* 34:7; Ignatius, *Letter to Polycarp* 34:7.

some left over.' They ate and had some left over.[89] As the Elijah-Elisha tradition is recalled, the prophetic and Mosaic traditions go hand in hand in the mix of festal allusions. The coming of the prophet like Moses[90] and the return of Elijah both spring to mind. This double allusion probably reflects the conflation in the popular opinion of first-century Jews, especially in Galilee, who did not share the clear division of personalities and roles of 'the coming one' unlike the educated Pharisees and Qumran devotees. Even as early as the writing of the First Book of Kings there was a merging of the Mosaic, Messianic and Elijah figures.[91] Also the popular expectation was that the Messiah, the anointed Davidic King, may well come at Passover.

Diminutives

On the literary level the Johannine penchant for using the diminutive and sometimes a double diminutive is in evidence. The word *paidarion* used for the boy who had the loaves and fishes is a double diminutive of *pais*, and could be translated as 'a small little boy'. Similar diminutives are the words for fish, *opsarion* and boat, *ploiarion*. Later on in the passion narrative Peter cuts off the *ōtarion* of Malchus, another diminutive, probably signifying the earlobe.[92]

Response/Reaction

The aftermath of the multiplication is a display of limited faith, expressed in terms of belief that Jesus was 'the one who was to come into the world'. As Jesus became aware of their desire to carry him off and make him king he removed his disciples from the temptation and escaped himself into the mountain. This is reminiscent of the synoptic accounts of the temptation on the mountain overlooking the kingdoms of the world.[93] A similar expectation will break out among the pilgrims and the Jerusalem crowd at the triumphal entry of Jesus into the city before his trial and execution.

4. THE SEA CROSSING: EPIPHANY (Jn 6:16-21)

After the attempt to make him king Jesus removes the disciples

---

89. 2 Kings 4:42-44.
90. Deut 18:15-18; 1 Macc 4:41-50; 14:41; 4 QT; Acts 3:22.
91. 1 Kings 19.
92. Jn 18:10.
93. Mt 4:8-10//Lk4:5-8.

from the temptation, and himself from the disciples, as he escapes into the mountain alone. The episode on the lake which follows may be a variant of the story of the calming of the storm in the synoptics or of Jesus' walking on the water and, in Matthew's account, inviting Peter to join him on the storm tossed waves.[94] In John's gospel the detail of the storm and the distress of those in the boat are described only sufficiently to put the event at a dangerous distance from the shore and create the setting for what follows. The 'Mosaic' action of feeding the multitude is thereby followed by another great miracle reminiscent of the Passover-Exodus event, the safe passage through the life threatening sea, guaranteed by the divine name and presence. The focus is not on the miracle of calming the storm but on the epiphany conveyed through the divine name, *I am*, and the accompanying reassurance *do not be afraid*.

This epiphany reflects the biblical awareness of the divine presence in, and power over, creation, especially as manifested in the case of the angry sea. Job proclaimed: 'He and no other stretched out the skies and trampled the sea's tall waves', and the psalmist proclaimed: 'You strode across the sea, you marched across the ocean but your footsteps could not be seen.'[95] Deutero-Isaiah says: '… the redeemed pass over the depths of the sea … *I am, I am*, the one comforting you, how then can you be afraid …'[96] Ps 106 (107) reflects the Passover ritual which connected the passage through the waters with the gift of manna. It celebrates the saving power of God who saved the people wandering hungry and thirsty in the desert and heard the cry of those terrified in the gale at sea and led them to a safe haven. 'He satisfies the thirsty soul; he fills the hungry with good things … They rejoiced because of the calm, and he led them to a safe haven.'[97]

I am. Do not be afraid.
The *egô eimi* statement of reassurance is inextricably linked to the words 'Do not be afraid'. This injunction not to be afraid is a recurring feature of Old Testament theophanies. *YHWH* spoke

---

94. Mt 8:23-27; 14:22-33; Mk 4:35-41; 6:45-52; Lk 8:22-25.
95. Job 9:8; Ps 76 (77):19.
96. Isa 51:10, 12. *I am, I am*, the one consoling/comforting you. LXX *ego eimi, ego eimi ho parakalôn se*.
97. Ps 106 (107):9, 30. For similar references to God's power over the sea cf Ex 14; 15; Deut 7:2-7; Job 38:16; Pss 29:3; 65:8; 77:20; 89:10; 93:3f; 51:9f; Isa 43:1-5; 51:9f.

to Abram, saying: 'Do not be afraid, Abram, I am your shield' and went on to promise him the land from the Wadi of Egypt to the Great River.[98] In the apparition to Isaac at Beersheba, *YHWH* said; 'I am the God of your father Abraham, *do not be afraid* for I am with you.'[99] To Jacob *YHWH* said: 'I am God, the God of your fathers, *do not be afraid* of going down to Egypt, for I will make you a great nation there.'[100] The injunction not to be afraid is found in Isaiah, 'I am holding you by the right hand; I tell you *do not be afraid*, I will help you', and '*Do not be afraid* for I have redeemed you; I have called you by your name, you are mine. Should you pass through the sea I will be with you, or through rivers they will not swallow you up … *do not be afraid* for I am with you.'[101] Several times Jeremiah is assured that he has no need to fear his enemies, because *YHWH* will be with him.[102]

Jesus fulfils the role of the comforting saviour, pronouncing the 'I am' and exhorting the disciples not to be afraid. Having repeated the miracle of Moses in feeding the people in the desert, a sign expected to herald the arrival of the messianic age,[103] he proceeds to repeat the other Mosaic miracle of leading his followers through the angry waters. However, unlike Moses, it is Jesus himself who pronounces the 'I am' and issues the exhortation not to be afraid.

The effect of the epiphany on the water was to move the disciples to invite Jesus to join them in the boat, that is, to be with them. Again in this story, location and movement are important. The crowd were still stuck fast at the location of the miracle and on the morrow had to go frantically in search of the miracle worker at another location after scrutinising the traffic on the lake. They are still stuck in the same mould, unchanged by any transforming power of the sign. Jesus has meantime escaped to the mountain. The disciples, without him in the boat, were tossed about on the sea making little progress towards the point where they were heading. Jesus comes to them over the water. They react to his epiphany with a desire to receive him into the boat. Then the boat immediately arrived at its destination.

---

98. Gen 15:1, 18.
99. Gen 26:24.
100. Gen 46:3.
101. Isa 41:13f; 43:1-5 (JB).
102. Jer 1:8, 17; 42:11; 46:28.
103. 2 Bar 29:8.

Location, movement, stagnation, adverse forces, swift arrival, all add to the dramatic effect of the story.

5. DISCOURSE ON THE BREAD FROM HEAVEN (JN 6:22-59)

Three introductory verses set the scene for the discourse on the bread from heaven. They deal with the reassembling of the participants in the events of the previous day – Jesus, the disciples and the crowd.[104] The partial faith of the crowd is seen again in their desire to find the wonder worker. There is a sense of compulsive urgency in their search. The reference to the bread and the 'giving thanks' are further clear eucharistic overtones pointing to the deeper meaning of the event. The reader may ask if those now searching for Jesus are in pursuit of the *klasmata* gathered up after the multiplication, or seeking another similar or possibly even greater miracle. When they find Jesus he responds to their questioning with a discourse that could well be described as a homiletic midrash on the biblical theme of 'bread from heaven'.

Bread was a longstanding symbol for the nourishment given by Word, Torah and Wisdom. The symbolic interpretation was not really new. Already in the Old Testament the manna was associated with God's word: 'You shall remember all the way which the Lord your God had led you these forty years in the wilderness ... and fed you with manna, which you did not know; that he might make you know that one does not live by bread alone, but one lives by everything that comes from the mouth of the Lord.'[105] The books of Nehemiah and Wisdom of Solomon similarly associate manna and 'bread from heaven' with Torah, and the rabbinic tradition associated the 'bread' with the Torah that lady Wisdom offered to those whom she invited to her banquet.[106] The concept of bread from heaven, manna, was a particularly apt symbol for the Torah.[107] Torah became closely associated with Wisdom as it came to be seen as the great repository of divine Wisdom, and both are symbolised by

104. Probably a representative number of the crowd is meant, as conveying the whole crowd would have required far more than a few fishing boats.
105. Deut 8:3 (JB).
106. Neh 9:13, 15, 20; Wis 16:26; *Gen. Rab* 70:5.
107. Borgen, P., *Bread from Heaven: An Exegeical Study in the Concept of Manna in the Gospel of John and the Writings of Philo*, 111f; cf Malina, B. J., *The Palestinian Manna tradition: The Manna Tradition in the Palestinian Targums and Its Relationship to the New Testament Writings*, 1968.

the manna. The gift of the manna was seen as the greatest of Moses' miracles. In fact it was not the gift of Moses, but of God. The divine origin of the manna is emphasised in the biblical accounts and in writers like Josephus and Philo who were contemporary with the New Testament. One reads in Exodus: 'I shall rain loaves from heaven on you' and 'This is the bread the Lord has given you to eat.'[108] The psalmist says: 'He rained on them manna to eat and gave them the bread of heaven.'[109] Wisdom of Solomon states: 'You fed your people with the nourishment of angels and you sent them from heaven bread that took no labour.'[110] Speaking of the manna, Josephus describes it as 'divine and miraculous food'.[111] Philo allegorises the manna as the divine gift of wisdom and even used the words *manna* and *sophia* (wisdom), interchangeably.[112]

Word, Torah and Wisdom provide nourishment. Deutero-Isaiah invites all who thirst, even those who have no money, to come to the water and drink, to buy corn, wine and milk, without money. Then he advises them: 'Why spend money on what is not bread, your wages on what fails to satisfy? Listen to me and you will have good things to eat and rich food to enjoy.'[113] He compares the word coming from the mouth of God with the rain and snow that produce seed for the sower and bread for the eating. The text from Deuteronomy, quoted by Jesus in the Temptations, 'not by bread alone does man live but by every word that comes from the mouth of God', compares listening to the word with eating food.[114] The Wisdom tradition developed this in a personified way. Personified Wisdom issues an invitation to her banquet. The invitation comes in Proverbs in the words: 'Come and eat my bread, drink the wine I have prepared' and in Sirach, 'Come to me you who desire me and eat your fill of my fruits.'[115] Sirach says of Wisdom: 'She will give ... the bread of understanding to eat, and the water of wisdom to drink' and speaks of the creation of an appetite for wisdom: 'They who eat me will hunger for more, they who drink me will

108. Ex 16:4, 15.
109. Ps 77 (78):24.
110. Wis 16:20.
111. Ex 16; Num 11; Ps 77 (78); Wis 16:20; Josephus, *Ant.* III 1. 6. 30.
112. Philo, De *Mutatione Nominum*, 258-260.
113. Isa 55:1-3 (JB).
114. Isa 55:10f; Deut 8:3 (JB).
115. Prov 9:5; Sir 24:19.

thirst for more.'[116] The Wisdom of Solomon promises nourishment and immortality by way of a reputation that will never die: 'The various crops are not what nourishes man, but your word which preserves all who trust in you.'[117] 'By means of her, immortality (memory) shall be mine.'[118] The invitation to eat and drink is a metaphor for the call to hear, learn and obey the word of God, the commands of the law and the dictates of Wisdom. Just as eating and drinking sustain physical life, so hearing, learning and obeying sustain 'spiritual' life, and lead one along the paths of life. 'The one who finds me, finds life ... all who hate me are in love with death.'[119] The repeated invitations to eat and drink in the Bread of Life discourse and elsewhere in St John's gospel, reflect these traditions. In St John's gospel Jesus reflects this understanding as he repeatedly invites his listeners to eat and drink.

The Discourse (Jn 6:25-59)

The use of 'I am', *ego eimi*, with a predicate, unlike the absolute use of 'I am', signifies not who Jesus is in himself, but his relationship with humanity, his followers and his disciples. These are the great metaphors for Jesus' life-giving power in the gospel. Here in chapter six the dominant metaphor is: 'I am the Bread of Life.' Elsewhere Jesus proclaims himself the Way, the Truth and the Life, the Resurrection and the Life, the Good Shepherd, the Door of the Sheepfold, the Vine and the Light of the World.

The discourse is punctuated throughout with questions and remarks from the crowd which are the cues for Jesus' ongoing explanations. They are convenient headings for arranging comments on the discourse.

When did you come here? Jn 6:25-29

After the narrator's introductory remarks about the whereabouts of Jesus and the attempts of the crowd to find him, the spotlight shifts to their motives for seeking him. Their 'faith' is seen to be inadequate and based solely on the physical food they enjoyed, missing the point that the multiplication was a sign of

---

116. Sir 15:3; 24:21.
117. Wis 16:26 (JB).
118. Wis 8:13 (JB).
119. Prov 8:35f (JB).

deep significance. In asking Jesus, 'When did you come here?' they address him as 'rabbi', a respectful address for a religious teacher, but a far cry from their earlier calling him 'the prophet who is to come into the world' and wanting to make him king.[120]The reader senses a deeper meaning, typical of Johannine irony, in the question, as though more than 'when did you come from the other side of the lake?' is being asked, even if inadvertently, by the crowd. This question will dominate some future discussions about Jesus' identity and origins. He responds with a solemn 'Amen, amen I say to you', declaring that they sought him not because they saw (i.e understood) the signs but because they ate their fill of the loaves. Accordingly he goes on to instruct them not to work for food that does not last and draws a sharp contrast between perishable food and food that lasts to eternal life. This food will be given by the Son of Man, the one credited throughout the gospel with life-giving power.[121]

The unique role of the Son of Man is highlighted by the affirmation: 'On him the Father, God himself has set his seal.'[122] The verb, *sphragizein*, to set a seal, is used in Jn 1:33 to show that the believer, in accepting the testimony of Christ, attests to the truth of God himself. Here the verb is used in the context of the Father's attesting to the Son of Man. The form of the sentence lays particularly heavy emphasis on the authority of the one doing the testifying. *ho Patêr ... ho Theos esphragisen* could be translated as 'The Father, who is none other than God himself, has set his seal.' The aorist tense *esphragisen*, 'has set his seal' seems to point to a past action/event, and so scholars look to the incarnation or the descent of the Spirit as the divine act of 'sealing'.[123] In the context of 'the bread of life', a metaphor picking up on the biblical traditions of revelation in Word, Torah and Wisdom, God has set the seal of ultimate truth and absolute reliability on the revelation of the Son of Man. 'Setting his seal' also has the overtones of setting aside for sacrifice, or 'consecration', setting aside for the exclusive service of God, as in the reference

---

120. Maybe this points to a different crowd from the previous day, and to two different traditions edited together in the text.

121. cf Mt 4:4; Lk 4:4; quoting Deut 8:3.

122. Jn 6:27.

123. The concept of 'sealing' (*sphragis/sphragizein*) is used in the texts dealing with early Christian baptism, cf 2 Cor 1:22; Eph 1:13; 2 Clement 7:6; Acts of Paul and Thecla 25.

to consecrating Jesus, like the altar at the Feast of Dedication, and sending him into the world.[124]

When the disciples found Jesus alone with the woman in Samaria and encouraged him to eat, he replied that he had food to eat of which they were not aware. He explained that food in terms of doing the work of the Father. Here the crowd ask Jesus what 'work' they should do to 'work for' eternal life. 'Work' in the question posed here by the crowd reflects the idea of doing the 'works' of the law which give access to God. Jesus proclaims that the only access to God is through the one God has sent and so he responds to their question with the injunction to believe in 'the one sent'. Just as Jesus' own food is to carry out the work that God, the Father, sent him to do, so the people's food is to believe in the one sent to carry out the Father's work. The reader is again reminded of Jesus' response to the tempter in the synoptics: 'Not by bread alone does man live, but by every word that comes from the mouth of God.'[125]

What sign do you do that we may see it and believe you? Jn 6:30-34
Asking Jesus for a sign, the miracle-hungry crowd quote the biblical example of the manna in the desert. In a solemn 'Amen, amen I say to you' proclamation he tells them it was not Moses who gave their ancestors the bread from heaven in the desert, and goes on, with a change of tense in the verb, to say that it is his Father who *gives* the true bread from heaven. It is the true, the real bread, Jesus goes on to say, because it is the bread of God which comes down from heaven to give life to the world.[126] The crowd respond by asking him to give them this bread always. The dialogue with the crowd about food for eternal life parallels the dialogue with the Samaritan woman about the 'water bubbling up to eternal life'. Both dialogues build up to a request. The crowd ask Jesus to 'give us this bread always' just the Samaritan woman asked him to 'give me this water so that I won't get thirsty again'.[127]

124. cf Jn 10:36.
125. Mt 4:1-4; Lk 4:1-4.
126. Jn 6:32f; cf Jn 6:27, 35, 39, 40, 44, 47, 48, 50, 51, 53-58. The Greek sentence emphasises 'from heaven' (*ek tou ouranou*) and 'true' (*alêthinon*).
127. Jn 6:25-34 and Jn 4:9-14. The opening questions are: 'When did you come here?' and 'How can you, a Jew, ask me a Samaritan for a drink?' There follows a comment on food that perishes and water that only satisfies for a time. Then in both cases there is a comparison/contrast between the Old Testament food and drink, the manna in the desert and the water from the rock, and what Jesus is offering by way of the bread of life and the water bubbling up to eternal life.

Give us this bread always ... Jn 6:34-40

The request of the crowd to Jesus to 'give us this bread always' is the cue for him to proclaim: 'I am the bread of life' and to say that whoever comes to him will never hunger, and whoever believes in him will never thirst.[128] This stands in stark contrast to the assessment of Wisdom in Sirach: 'He who eats of me will hunger still, he who drinks of me will thirst for more.'[129] The ongoing search for wisdom is now replaced by the fully satisfying bread and the life-giving water from heaven which will put an end to human hunger and thirst. The bread – revelation in Word, Torah and Wisdom brought to its fulfilment – is now enfleshed in Jesus. He does not just 'speak' or 'teach' the word, he *is* the Word. God's gift of revelation in Jesus surpasses the revelation in the law, the prophetic utterances, and the Wisdom tradition.

After proclaiming himself to be the Bread of Life, Jesus elaborates on its significance in terms of life, here and hereafter. Being bread of life he is carrying out the Father's will which is to give life to those who come to him, and to raise them up on the last day. Those whom the Father gives him he will not turn away. The gift of the law through Moses gathered a people for Yahweh. Now the gift of revelation in Jesus draws people to him. Those who come will not be lost. They will have life here and hereafter. F. J. Moloney points out that this reflects the concern of third generation Christians for the ultimate fate of their loved ones who had believed in Jesus and had since died.[130] Jesus has been sent to carry out the will of the one who sent him, and that will is precisely to ensure that all he has been given will not be lost, and that all who see the Son and believe in him may have eternal life. This is spelled out in terms of resurrection on the last day. In spite of his promise, however, they do not believe in him, though they 'see' him.

Is this not Jesus the son of Joseph? Jn 6:41-51

The discourse is interrupted with a reference to the Jews who are complaining and murmuring, like the Israelites in the desert.[131] They discuss his origins and wonder how he can say

128. Jn 6:35.
129. Sir 24:21 (JB).
130. F. J. Moloney, *The Gospel of John*, 215.
131. Ex 16:2. *goggusmon*, the nominal equivalent of *egogguzon* is used in Ex 16:7, 8 (LXX).

that he came down from heaven, because they know his father and mother. Here John is close to the account in the synoptics where Jesus is rejected in Galilee, by his own people in Nazareth, where he was brought up. In Mark one reads their comment: 'Is not this the carpenter, the son of Mary and the brother of James, Joses, Jude and Simon? And are not his sisters here among us?' In Matthew the question is: 'Is not this the son of the carpenter? Is not his mother called Mary and are not his brothers James and Joseph and Simon and Jude?' Luke gives the version: 'Is not this the son of Joseph?' Here in John's gospel the crowd say: 'Surely this is Jesus, son of Joseph. We know his father and mother.'[132] Mark reports the reactions as: 'Where did the man get all this? What is this wisdom that has been granted him, and these miracles that are being worked through him?'[133] John, however, raises the question to another level, playing on the irony of his divine and human origins. The reader has read the prologue and has the advantage over the Jews and the crowds, and so can appreciate the irony.

Jesus responds to the murmuring (not yet outright hostility) by saying no one can come to him unless drawn by the Father who sent him.[134] This resembles the rabbinic teaching about conversion, which is seen in terms of being drawn, brought nigh, to the Torah. It is the natural desire of the one who loves his fellow man to bring him nigh to the Torah, to share with him the knowledge of God.[135] Deutero-Isaiah promised: 'They shall all be taught by God,'[136] and Jeremiah promised in regard to the New Covenant that God would be the teacher of all, implanting the law within them, upon their hearts.[137] This is now fulfilled through Jesus whose life and mission teach that God so loved the world that he sent his only Son so that those who believe in him might have eternal life. This love of the Father draws people to the Son. This is done through the teaching of the Father. 'Everyone who has heard the Father and learned from him

---

132. Mk 6:3; Mt 13:55; Lk 4:22;
133. Mk 6:2//Mt 15:54; cf Lk 4:22, 28-30.
134. The verb 'helkuein' to draw, is used here of the drawing power of the Father, it will be used of the Son of Man who draws all to himself when raised up (Jn 12:31f), and it will be used of Peter drawing the nets ashore without breaking them(Jn 21:11).
135. *Pirke Aboth* 1:12.
136. Isa 54:13.
137. Jer 31:33f.

comes to me. Not that anyone has seen the Father – only the one who is from God has seen the Father.'[138] The note of universality is sounded by the word *pantes*, all. No longer is the life-giving instruction of God meant only for Israel. Moses, the gift of the law and the manna, have now been opened up to all believers. Their promise has been fulfilled and surpassed in the bread that came down from heaven.

A solemn declaration : 'Amen, amen I say to you' introduces a summary of what has been said. The believer possesses eternal life. Jesus is the bread of life. This bread is contrasted with the manna which sustained physical life for a time but whoever eats this bread come down from heaven will never die. Jesus has already identified himself as 'the bread of life', 'the bread that came down from heaven'. Now he speaks of himself as 'the living/life-giving bread that came down from heaven' and goes on to speak of the bread from heaven in terms of his flesh (*sarx*) for the life of the world. This reference to flesh, *sarx*, introduces a new element into the discussion on food and bread, as *sarx* is mentioned in tandem with *haima*, blood, introducing a different concept of *sarx* to that in the prologue where it signifies a human being.

How can this man give us his flesh to eat? Jn 6:(51) 52-59
The discourse is interrupted by reference to 'violent quarrelling' among the Jews about how Jesus could give them his flesh to eat. He responded: 'The bread that I shall give for the life of the world is my flesh.' A solemn proclamation: 'Amen, amen, I say to you' warns that 'if you do not eat of the flesh of the Son of Man and drink his blood, you have no life in you'. The warning is followed by the assurance that 'the one who feeds on my flesh (*sarx*) and drinks my blood (*haima*) has eternal life'. Here again the figure of the Son of Man emerges as the donor of the gift of life (*zôopoiêsis*). This life is described in terms of 'remaining' or 'abiding' (*menein*) in Jesus and the life Jesus has from the Father is communicated to the one abiding in him. This is similar to the statement in the defence he made after the healing of the invalid at Bethesda: 'Just as the Father possesses life in himself so has he granted that the Son possess life in himself.'[139] Again there is a

---

138. Jn 6:45f.
139. Jn 5:26. The term 'Living Father' is a hapax in the NT. The usual term is 'Living God', Jn 6:57.

contrast with the food the ancestors ate (the manna). They are dead physically.[140] There is general agreement among scholars that this passage is eucharistic. Some maintain that in an earlier stage of the gospel formation it was not present at this point. It may, however, have formed part of the Last Supper account in an earlier stage of the formation of the tradition. The expression 'the bread that I shall give is my flesh for the life of the world' (*ho artos de hon egô dôsô hê sarx mou estin hyper tês tou kosmou zôês*), may even have been the eucharistic formula ('words of institution') used in the Johannine tradition. Be that as it may, as the text now stands it complements the other dimensions of the life-giving food. The term *sarx* on its own refers to the fact that Jesus is giving himself, using *sarx* in the sense in which it is used in 'the Word became *sarx*', a human being.

The blood on its own signifies his life-giving death. In the celebration of the Exodus-Passover, the blood became a sign of life given and protected by God, an anointing, symbolising Israel's position as God's children. 'The blood will be a sign for you upon the houses where you are; and when I see the blood, I will pass over you, and no plague shall fall upon you to destroy you.'[141] 'The blood is the life.'[142] 'The life of the flesh is in the blood. This blood I myself have given you to perform the rite of atonement for your lives at the altar; for it is blood that atones for a life.'[143] Jesus now interprets this tradition in relation to his saving death.

Taken together, flesh and blood are the elements of sacrifice and Eucharist. This emphasis on eating flesh and drinking blood corresponds to the eucharistic teaching found in the synoptics in the context of the Last Supper when Jesus interprets the elements of the meal as his body (*sôma*) and blood in relation to his saving death and the new covenant in his blood.[144] Apart from the fact that flesh (*sarx*) and blood (*haima*) together signify the whole person, the use of *sarx* rather than *sôma* as partner to *haima* here in John is probably influenced by the sacrificial language of separation of flesh and blood in sacrifice and sharing in the sac-

---

140. Some Jewish traditions believed that they were dead spiritually as well and would not have a place in the world to come.
141. Ex 12:13 (JB).
142. Deut 12:23 (JB).
143. Lev 17:11.
144. Mt 26:26-29; Mk 14:22-25; Lk 22:14-20; cf 1 Cor 11:23-25.

rificial communion meal in which the partakers identify with, and draw life from, the victim.

The consuming of blood was forbidden to the Jews and accounts in part for the strong reaction to Jesus' statement about eating his flesh and drinking his blood. The prohibition on blood is contained in the command to Noah, 'You must not eat flesh with life, that is to say blood, in it', and in the prescriptions in Leviticus, 'never eat either fat or blood', and Deuteronomy, 'take care not to consume the blood, for the blood is the life, and you must not consume the life with the flesh ... but pour it out like water on the ground.'[145]

6. REACTION AND RESPONSE (Jn 6:60-71)

The focus of attention now shifts from the reactions of the crowd to those of the disciples and the twelve. Many of the disciples said 'this is a hard (*sklêros*) saying' and went on to ask 'Who can hear, that is, who can understand and accept it?'[146] The same verb *akouein* is used for 'hearing' in the sense of hearing only at the level of the ear and also for hearing in the sense of understanding, accepting and believing. This is in keeping with the various verbs of perception, knowing and believing throughout the gospel which function on these different levels.

Jesus was aware that they were complaining. The verb *gogguzein* signifies grumbling, whispering, displaying an attitude of smouldering discontent. It is used in the LXX for the discontent of the people in the desert. Jesus asks them if this teaching 'scandalises' them. The verb *skandalizein* means causing one to stumble, putting an obstacle in one's path. A rhetorical question, powerful in its non-completion, comes from the lips of Jesus: 'What if you were to see the Son of Man ascend to where he was before?' Does Jesus mean: 'Would that satisfy you?' or 'Even if you did see someone ascend like Moses to receive the law, or Abraham, Isaiah or Enoch who were also associated with ascensions to heaven to acquire divine revelation, would you still be unconvinced?'[147] The Son of Man has come from heaven. He is

---

145. Gen 9:4; Lev 3:17; Deut 12:23. Ezekiel, however, has a symbolic passage of a sacrificial banquet in which the people will eat the flesh of heroes and drink the blood of princes, a metaphor for a victory celebration.

146. *sklêros* means hard, tough, unyielding. It is used in the compound noun *sklêrokardia*, 'hard of heart'.

147. *Ex Rab*, 28:1; 40:2; 41:6f; 43:4; 47:5,8. *Deut Rab* 2:36; 3:11; 11:10; *Pesiqta Rabbati* 20:4.

the revealer *par excellence*. Now he is in their midst but they must have a spirit-filled vision to see him and understand where he came from. As long as they have a flesh-based life and knowledge they cannot appreciate the spiritual dimension. They continue to await the fulfilment of their human expectations. This is reminiscent of the dialogue with Nicodemus which expressed the need to be born *anôthen*, from above, of water and the Spirit, and reminiscent also of the prologue and its teaching about becoming children of God who are born not of blood, nor of (the) will of the flesh nor of (the) will of man, but of God.[148]

Disbelief and Betrayal (Jn 6:60-66)
Jesus knew those who did not believe and the one who would betray him. He remarked that only those drawn by the Father come to him. They are those who hear the word and accept the revelation in Jesus, as coming from God. They are drawn to Jesus, whom the Father has sent, by their knowing and having faith in God. After Jesus' first visit to Jerusalem the narrator remarked on Jesus' ability to read people's hearts without needing anyone to inform him. His conversations with Nathanael, Nicodemus, and the Samaritan woman well illustrate the accuracy of the remark. Now he speaks of the disciples' unbelief, pointing out that one of the twelve has a devil and will eventually betray him. Many of the disciples left him and went their own way.[149]

7. PETER'S PROFESSION OF FAITH

Turning to the twelve, Jesus questioned them as to their intentions. He was testing their resolve to stay with him. Peter professes his, and their, faith in Jesus. He proclaims that Jesus has the message of eternal life and that he is the Holy One of God.[150] This parallels Peter's profession of faith at Caesarea Philippi in the synoptics. B. Witherington comments on this profession of faith, highlighting how it is influenced by the Wisdom tradition:

... the context of this confession is critical: various disciples

---

148. Jn 3:1-10; 1:12f. Flesh here refers to the merely human capacity, unaided by the Spirit.
149. This reflects also the kind of situation that arose among the Christians in the Johannine tradition, when people left the community because of its christology, as is obvious from situations like that reported in the First Letter of John.
150. This title is used by 'supernatural' beings, the demons, of Jesus. It is the first 'title' given to him in Mark's gospel, by a demon. Mk 1:24.

have just rejected and abandoned Jesus, and so 'the events of John 6 therefore resemble an enacted parable in which there are some who find Wisdom, and others who reject it' ... The point is, in light of this wisdom tradition, which closely associates wisdom with the holy, the title 'the Holy One of God' is perhaps the most appropriate title for one portrayed as Wisdom come in the flesh to earth, both rejected by his own and received by a few to whom he gave eternal life, and then ascending again into heaven (cf 1 Enoch 42).[151]

The chapter ends with a further prediction of the betrayal, and a statement of Jesus that he himself had picked the one who would betray him. In the light of the gospel teaching that Jesus knew what was in everyone's heart, it can be concluded that he knew his betrayer, Judas, son of Simon Iscariot,[152] and still chose him. The references to betrayal anticipate the third and final Passover in Jesus' public ministry.

---

151. B. Witherington, *John's Wisdom*, 161, including quotation from W. R. Domeris, 'The Confession of Peter according to Jn 6:69', *Tyndale Bulletin* 44.1 (1993), 155-67.
152. The name 'Iscariot' has been interpreted in two ways, as '*ish Kerioth*, man of Kerioth', or as a Semitic version of *Sicarii*, 'men of the dagger', a name for revolutionaries working to overthrow the Romans and their Jewish collaborators. This latter background would align Judas with Simon Zealot.

The Feast of Tabernacles (Jn 7:1-10:21)

1. THE PLOT

The hostility to Jesus grows. Already in chapter five the menacing attitude towards him was manifest, together with the intention to kill him.[153] The murmuring of the crowd, their disbelief and violent disagreements, and the falling away of the disciples were increasingly evident in chapter six. Now as the opposition to Jesus hardens there are repeated statements about the desire of the Judaean Jews to kill him. The accounts of the Temple pilgrimage feasts of Tabernacles and Dedication are punctuated with threats to his life from the opening of the section where the narrator tells us: 'He could not go about openly in Judaea because the Jews sought to kill him' to his final, definitive leaving of the Temple, never to return, after the attempts to stone and arrest him.[154] The division (*schisma*) among the crowd hardens and those who are beginning to have faith in him are in dread of the Jews. Even his brothers do not believe in him. It is becoming obvious that the *hour* of Jesus signifies the *hour* of his arrest, trial and death.[155] However, it is becoming equally obvious that the opposition will be able to arrest him only when his time (*kairos*) or hour (*hora*) has come and this realisation is already setting the tone for the passion narrative where Jesus is seen to be in control of the events as they unfold.

The theme of light, with its stated or implied opposite, darkness, is a major controlling category between chapter eight where Jesus proclaimed himself the Light of the World and said that those who followed him would never walk in darkness but would have the light of life, and chapter eleven, where he tells the disciples, as he sets out for Lazarus' tomb, that those who walk during the day do not stumble because they see the light of this world, but those who walk at night stumble because the light is not in them.[156]

Jesus' identity is set in relief against the main symbols and historical figures associated with the feast. The rituals of water and light provide the main symbols while Moses and Abraham

---

153. Jn 5:16-18.
154. Jn 7:1, 19, 25; 8:59; 10:31-42.
155. Jn 7:30.
156. Jn 8:12; 11:9f.

are pivotal figures associated with the Feast of Tabernacles.[157] In the context of the water and light rituals Jesus proclaims himself the source of life-giving water and the light of the world. In discussions about Moses and Abraham he reveals his own superior origins and authority. As the feast brought the role and identity of Moses to the forefront of people's minds, so too the ancestral origins and ancient character of the feast were kept in mind. As the Book of Jubilees reminds its readers, it was Abraham who first celebrated the feast.[158]

As the threats to Jesus' life and the likelihood of his arrest and execution grow stronger, his claims about his origin and his power 'to lay down his life in order to take it up again' become more insistent. At the end of the Feast of Tabernacles he proclaims: 'No one takes (my life) from me; and as it is in my power to lay it down, so it is in my power to take it up again.'[159] Throughout the account of the feast the Johannine use of irony is at its most potent as the crowd pit their 'knowledge' of Jesus' origins and their life threatening words against Jesus' own claims and self-assurance. Having read the prologue the reader has a privileged view of developments and can appreciate the irony in the christological claims of Jesus against this background of hostility and purely earthly assessments of his identity and mission.

2. BACKGROUND TO THE FEAST

Tabernacles was celebrated five days after the Day of Atonement (*Yom Kippur*). Deuteronomy prescribes a seven day feast.[160] Leviticus prescribes an eight day feast beginning with a solemn day of rest on the 15th Tishri, and ending on the eighth day with another solemn day of rest dedicated to worship and sacrifice.[161] It was probably the oldest, most joyful and popular of the pilgrimage feasts. Associated with the vintage there was much merrymaking and dancing, as seen in the Book of Judges where the men of the tribe of Benjamin laid in wait in the vineyards for the dancing girls in Shiloh and carried them off as wives.[162] The

---

157. Ex 16-17; Jub 16:30.
158. Jub 16:30.
159. Jn 10:18.
160. Deut 16:13.
161. Lev 23:39. Tishri is the seventh month, falling during the September-October period.
162. Judg 21:19-23.

priest Eli thought Hannah had celebrated too much during the feast and reprimanded her, mistaking for intoxication the distress which drove her to a great intensity of prayer.[163] Josephus records how sacred and important the feast was for the people. He described it as 'the holiest and greatest of the Hebrew Feasts'.[164] The feast had several names. Its ancient name was *asîp*, ingathering.[165] It is more commonly called *Sukkot*, meaning Booths, Tents, Shelters, which was translated into Latin as *Tabernacula*, giving rise to the English term 'Tabernacles'.[166] It is sometimes called simply 'The Feast',[167] or 'The Feast of the Lord', a designation which highlights its importance in the calendar of feasts.[168]

As seen from the ancient name *asîp,* ingathering, the Feast of Tabernacles obviously had its origins in an ancient autumnal harvest festival which celebrated the harvest of grapes, olives and autumnal fruits. The building of huts or booths in the vineyard during the feast may have emerged from such an autumnal festival and the building of huts to protect the harvest. From this practice came the name *sukkot*, the root meaning of which is 'protection'. Early on in history the feast began to be historicised and theologised as it became associated with the gift of the promised land, inherited after the hazards endured in the wilderness in which *YHWH* protected the people from enemies and provided the manna, quail and water in the desert. This desert experience is recalled in the prophetic literature as the honeymoon period of God and his bride Israel. Calling the people back to covenant observance, Hosea speaks of God in terms of the husband caring for and seeking after his estranged wife and refers back to the period in the desert: 'That is why I am going to lure and lead her out into the wilderness and speak to her heart … There she will respond to me as she did when she was young, as she did when she came out of the land of Egypt.'[169] He also describes that period in terms of the caring Father who liberated his son and looked after him as he grew to maturity: 'When Israel was a child I loved him and called my

---

163. 1 Sam 1:14-18.
164. Josephus, *Ant.* VIII iv I *100.
165. Ex 23:16; 34:22. cf Deut 26:4ff
166. Lev 23:34; Deut 6:13, 16; Ezra 3:4; Zech 14:16, 18f.
167. 1 Kings 2, 65; 2 Chr 7:8; Neh 8:14; Isa 30:29; Ezek 45:23, 25.
168. Lev 23:39; Judg 21:19.
169. Hos 2:14f (JB).

son out of Egypt … I myself taught Ephraim to walk, I took them in my arms … I was like someone who lifts an infant close against his cheek; stooping down to him I gave him his food.'[170] Side by side with this caring action of God there was the memory of the murmuring and complaining of the people in the desert.[171]

As the harvest festival became the occasion of recalling the period of wandering in the desert, the huts of willow, myrtle, and palm branches which they erected and occupied in the vineyards during the feast were now seen to recall the temporary dwellings in the desert and the tent dwelling of the Ark.[172] Probably under the influence of the Canaanite Ba'al cult there entered into the celebration of the feast the mythological language of *YHWH* the warrior on his victory march. The conquest of Israel's enemies along the way led to the taking possession of the land and entering into sovereign rule for the purpose of taking up residence in Jerusalem and the Temple and celebrating the enthronement of *YHWH* in Zion. With the replacement of the temporary dwelling built for the Ark by David, Solomon's Temple marked a new era. The dedication of his Temple took place at Tabernacles ensuring for the future the special relationship of the Temple and the feast.[173] The emphasis of the celebration moved decisively to the foundation of the Davidic House and the Solomonic Temple.

However, the stark realities of life, the failure of monarchs, priests and people in their covenant obligations and the perceived insincerity of worship led the prophets to a critical assessment of the Jerusalem partnership of palace and Temple, throne and altar. As they criticised the status quo they opened up a vision for the future. After the Exile, the feast was renewed and celebrated with great joy on the occasion of the reading of the law by Ezra.[174] Even before the Exile Ezechiel and Jeremiah were already looking to an ideal future. Earlier still Isaiah and Micah had spoken about the nations gathering in Jerusalem and coming to the Temple of the God of Jacob.[175] This hope is further

---

170. Hos 11:1-4 (JB).
171. Ex 16:1-3; 17:1-7; 17; 22; Num 11; 12; 14; 16; 20; 21; Pss 77 (78); 105 (106); 94 (95).
172. It seems that palms were brought from the Jordan valley near Jericho for the feast as they did not grow in Jerusalem.
173. 1 Kings 8:2.
174. Neh 8:1-18.
175. Isa 2:2-5; Mic 4:1-5.

developed with the experience of the Exile and Return. Ezechiel spoke of a future, messianic time when the Temple would be the source of life giving water flowing from the divine presence, out from under the right side of the Temple, south of the altar, bringing life from the divine presence to the whole land and the sea, south to the Arabah.[176] Zechariah spoke of the Day of the Lord when the messianic king would come to Jerusalem, triumphant and riding on an ass. On that day the Lord would pour out a spirit of compassion and supplication on the city, and open a fountain for the house of David to cleanse Jerusalem and waters would flow out from Jerusalem to the Mediterranean and the Dead Sea.[177] After the defeat of their enemies people would come every year to Jerusalem to celebrate the feast properly.[178] Then there would be an ideal celebration, everything in Jerusalem would be holy and no merchants would be found in the Temple.[179] The Book of Revelation describes the New Jerusalem as having trees of life on either side of the river in the messianic city of Jerusalem.

The name Tabernacles (*Sukkot*) thus gathers together the allusions to harvest booths, tents in the wilderness, traditions of the Ark and Tent of Meeting, David's temporary shelter for the Ark and the dedication of the Solomonic Temple. At the same time it looks ahead to an ideal messianic future. These various dimensions celebrate the divine presence, protection and revelation.

3. RITUALS OF THE FEAST

The three main rituals of the feast in Jesus' time focused on water and light. Each morning just before dawn the priests went to the eastern wall of the Temple facing the Mount of Olives and, turning their backs on the rising sun, faced westwards towards the Temple in a gesture of atonement for a past act of sun worship. The act of idolatry is recorded in Ezechiel. 'There were about twenty five men with their backs to the sanctuary of Yahweh and their faces turned to the east. They were bowing to the east, towards the sun.'[180] During the feast the priests now made atonement for this act of betrayal as they turned their

---

176. Ezek 47:1-12.
177. Zech 9:9; 12:10; 13:1; 14:8.
178. Zech 14:16.
179. Zech 14:20f.
180. Ezek 8:16.

backs on the rising sun, faced the Temple and proclaimed: 'But as to us, our eyes are to the Lord.'[181]

Another important ceremony was the bringing of the water in a golden flagon in solemn procession from the pool of Siloam through the Water Gate to be poured into one of the two silver bowls placed above the altar. Into the other bowl the priest poured a libation of wine. The bowls were perforated with spouts and this resulted in a great flow of water and wine over the altar down into the cisterns below and down the steps of the Temple. Rabbinic interpretation compared this to the water flowing from the rock of Horeb.[182] Processing through the Water Gate was significant because it was identified with the gate through which the waters of life would flow from under the threshold of the Temple.[183] Life-giving water thus figures prominently in the traditions associated with the feast and provides a central metaphor for describing the life-giving power of Jesus and the Spirit.[184]

An instruction for the celebration in Leviticus states: 'On the first day you shall take choice fruits, palm branches, boughs of leafy trees and willows from the river bank, and for seven days you shall rejoice in the presence of *YHWH*.'[185] Rabbinic interpretation of this verse emphasised the important cultic significance of 'the four species'. Three of these, myrtle (a leafy branch), willow and palm were tied into a bouquet called the *lulab*. During the procession the pilgrims waved the *lulab*, in their right hand, while carrying a citron (a choice fruit), symbol of harvest, in the left. As they processed they sang the Hallel, waving the *lulab* aloft at the beginning, during and at the end of Ps 117 (118) which, significantly, mentions the Tabernacles themes of light and festal procession with branches to the altar.[186]

At nightfall the four great menoras (candelabras), on which were great golden bowls, reached by ladders, containing oil and wicks were lit on the Temple Mount giving light to the whole city, where no other fires were lit prior to the illumination.[187] This recalled the period of wandering when God was with the

181. *m. Sukk.* 5:4.
182. Ex 17:1-7; Num 20:8-13; *t. Sukk.* 3.11-12.
183. *m. Seqal.* 6:3; *m. Mid.* 2:6.
184. Rev 22:2.
185. Lev 23:40.
186. *m. Sukk.* 3:9.
187. The wicks were made from the cast off girdles and undergarments of the priests from the previous year.

people in the desert as a pillar of fire by night. During this celebration the celebrants danced and the Levites chanted the
Psalms of Ascent (Pss 120-134), a psalm on each of the fifteen
steps leading down to the Court of the Women. The *Mishnah* recalls that 'there was not a courtyard in Jerusalem that did not
reflect the light of the *Beth hashe'ubah*, the House of Water
Drawing'.[188]

It was the ideal time to pray for rain and if rain fell during the
feast it was seen as a blessing and a good omen for the next harvest. The *haftarah* or reading from the prophetic books on the
feast gave Zechariah's instructions for praying for rain and a
warning that there would be no rain for those who did not go to
Jerusalem for the ideal feast of Tabernacles.[189]

Two significant persons recalled during the feast are Moses
and Abraham. Moses dominates the stories of the desert wandering commemorated in the feast. His gift of the well is used as
a metaphor for his gift of the Torah, just as digging the well and
drawing water have connotations of giving and studying the
Torah. The expected Messiah or Prophet in the tradition of
Moses can be seen as one who will draw from the Torah, the
well of God.[190] The earlier history of the feast in patriarchal
times is not forgotten. Abraham is described in the Book of
Jubilees as the first person to have celebrated the feast.[191]
Discipleship of Moses and descent from Abraham are used as
weapons of self righteousness by the opponents of Jesus.

The account of the feast in the gospel of John comes in three
distinct stages: the approach of the feast, the middle of the feast
and the last day of the feast. In each scene the speculation and
misunderstanding of the crowd about Jesus' identity, mission,
departure and destiny are highlighted.

4. AT THE APPROACH OF THE FEAST (Jn 7:1-13)

After mentioning the threat to Jesus' life in Judaea and his consequent remaining in Galilee, the narrator draws attention to the
unbelief of the brothers. The unbelief has spread from the crowd
to many earlier disciples and now to his brothers. This lack of
belief is quite evident from their attitude to signs. They do, however, recognise that Jesus does marvellous deeds and they want

188. *m. Sukk* 5:3.
189. Zech 10:1; 14:17.
190. F. J. Moloney, *Signs and Shadows*, 68. cf Targum on Gen 49:10.
191. Jub 16:30.

him to show these off to the disciples (because of the crisis they were suffering?) and the world. They wish him to come to the Feast of Tabernacles in Jerusalem for this unworthy purpose. Jesus did not trust himself to the crowd in Jerusalem because of this unsound 'belief' and had also complained in Galilee that 'unless you see signs and wonders you will not believe'.[192] The demand for 'signs' is an indication of an unbelieving attitude in all four gospels.[193] The temptation accounts in Matthew and Luke describe a dramatic and imaginative dialogue in which the tempter is answered with the authority of scripture when he puts forward in symbolic form the type of temptations that Jesus actually faced in a more prosaic way during his ministry.[194] The same temptations surface in a practical and experiential way in John as seen in the build up to the Passover in Galilee. The attempt to make him king, the request for miraculous bread and the desire for a sign were cases in point.[195] As the brothers of Jesus 'tempt' him to go to Jerusalem for the purpose of performing a sign there on the occasion of a major pilgrimage to the holy city and Temple, the reader is reminded of the synoptic account of the temptations in the wilderness where the tempter asks Jesus to go to Jerusalem to perform there in the holy city itself, the great miracle of throwing himself from the pinnacle of the Temple.[196]

The rather stylised passion predictions in the synoptics are similarly paralleled by concrete circumstances in John, especially in the contexts of the celebration of the feasts. The threats to his life, the attempts to arrest him, and the fear of the authorities engendered in those who were coming to believe in him, create a sense of foreboding similar to that surrounding his going up to Jerusalem in the synoptic gospels.[197] This atmosphere combined with Jesus' response about going away and returning to the One who sent him, and his comments, combined with those of the

---

192. Jn 2:23; 4:48.
193. Mt 4:1-11; Lk 4:1-13; Mt 12:38f; 16:1-4; Mk 8:11; Lk 11:16; Mt 27:43ff; Mk 15:29ff; Lk 23:35.
194. Mt 4:1-11; Lk 4:1-13.
195. Jn 6:15, 31; 7:3.
196. Mt 4:5-7//Lk 4:9-12. Throwing someone from the pinnacle of the Temple or some other height onto the rocks below was a form of execution by stoning as, for example, the attempt to throw Jesus over the brow of the hill in Nazareth, Lk 4:29f.
197. Jn 7:1, 13, 25; 8:40; 10:33, 39.

narrator, about the coming *time* or *hour* of arrest, are very reminiscent of the synoptic predictions of the passion.[198]

Jesus refuses the temptation to go to the feast for the unworthy purpose proposed by his brothers, as his 'time' (*kairos*) was not come.[199] His time, *kairos*, is the decisive salvific moment of his return to the Father. Its timing is not his but the Father's, for he does the Father's will. 'Going up' (*anabainein*) to Jerusalem has the double meaning of going up to the festival and 'going up' or returning to the Father. Jesus' time is determined by the Father. His judgement unsettles the world in its evil ways and so it is hostile to him. The brothers, on the other hand, belong to the (unbelieving) world and so they are always at home in it and accepted by it and so their time, their opportunity for their plan of action in their world is now and always.

He follows later, arriving in the middle of the feast. His 'second thought' is reminiscent of his reaction at Cana when he responded to his mother by setting his ministry in the context of the *hour*, an *hour* determined by the Father.[200] He will again react similarly in delaying his response to the urgent appeal to go to the terminally ill Lazarus.[201]

While the authorities search for Jesus in an attempt to arrest and silence him, the crowd enter into debate about him resulting in a division of opinion among them, some saying he is good, others that he is deceiving the crowd. These discussions and the fear of the authorities on the part of those who would believe in him, have already set the tone beforehand for the discussion, division and hostility when he arrives in Jerusalem. The charge of deceiving the crowds is reminiscent of the charge against Jesus in Luke's account of his trial and in Matthew's statement that the Pharisees regarded him as a deceiver.[202] The statement about fear of the Jews in the context of Jesus' ministry means fear of the authorities since those who were afraid were in fact Jews themselves. Also it is very likely that the statement reflects subsequent conflict between Christians and Jews at the time of the writing of the gospel. The charge of deceiving the crowds was an ongoing Jewish argument even in the time of Justin.[203]

198. Mt 16:21; 17:22f; 20:17 and //s.
199. Jn 7:6, 8, 10.
200. Jn 2:4f.
201. Jn 11:1-7.
202. Lk 23:2; Mt 27:63.
203. Justin, *Dialogue with Trypho*. LXIX. 7.

5. IN THE MIDDLE OF THE FEAST (Jn 7:14-36)

When Jesus goes up to the feast, it is his last journey from Galilee to Jerusalem.[204] The ensuing disputes focus on his teaching authority, his identity and his departure. The attempts to arrest him fail because his time (or hour) has not come. The threats and attempts to arrest him heighten the dramatic character of the story, and function as punctuation marks between the various points of dispute.

Jesus' Teaching Authority: Sabbath controversy (Jn 7:14-24)

Jesus' teaching in the Temple precincts provoked a discussion among the people about how he came by his education since he had no formal training as a rabbi. Again the dialogue between Jesus and his interlocutors takes place on two levels. They are talking about a human teacher. Jesus is talking about his Father from whom he has learned everything. If one knows God and desires to carry out God's will, then one will be disposed to identify and accept the one God has sent. This is the point Jesus makes when he tells them that anyone wishing to do the will of the Father will discern whether his teaching is from God or himself. Discernment depends on one's religious disposition. Anyone speaking on his own behalf seeks his own glory, but the one seeking the glory of the one who sent him is true and there is nothing false in him. There is a word play here in the Greek, between *doxa* meaning reputation or image, and *doxa* meaning glory.

Jesus' combined question and accusation: 'Did not Moses give you the law? Yet none of you keeps the law' reflects ongoing discussions between Christians themselves and between Christians and Jews in New Testament times on the relative claims of Moses and Jesus, about salvation through the law or through Christ. The debate in Galatians, and subsequently in Romans, points to the failure of the Jews to obey the law, and the necessity for a saviour independently of the law. That argument is reflected here in Jesus' statement: 'Did not Moses give you the law and not one of you keeps (does) the law?' Paul wrote to the

---

204. The mention of palm at his triumphal entry into the city, only in the fourth gospel, may recall his entrance at Tabernacles, since palm did not grow in Jerusalem, and was brought there from around the Jericho area for the Feast of Tabernacles. cf R. E. Brown, *John*, Vol I, 456 c. The material contained in the last week of Jesus' ministry in the synoptics is spread over the rest of the ministry in John.

Galatians: 'Scripture says: "Cursed be everyone who does not persevere in observing everything prescribed in the book of the Law",' and to the Romans he wrote: 'By boasting about the law and then disobeying it, you bring God into contempt.'[205] This controversy here in St John's gospel reflects that broader controversy between Christian and Jew at the time of the writing of the gospel.

The mention of wrongdoing provides Jesus with the cue for recalling the charge against him for breaking the Sabbath and making himself equal to God when he said: 'My Father goes on working, and so do I' after the healing on the Sabbath at the Pool of Bethesda.[206] This now results in Jesus' challenge to them for wanting to kill him. This they deny and accuse him of being demented. He uses their own favourite style of argument against them and appeals to Moses. Like any rabbi, he appeals to Moses, the great teacher of the law and the person central to the events in the wilderness now being remembered in the celebrations of the feast. A rabbi's teaching was based on scripture and traced back to some great teacher of the law, ultimately going back in an unbroken line to Moses himself. Jesus appeals to scripture, to Moses, and back beyond Moses, to the Father.

Jesus now uses a rabbinic style argument, arguing from the lesser to the greater good, from the circumcising of one part of the body without infringing the law to the healing of the whole, to justify his action on the Sabbath.[207] Sabbath was instituted for 'remembering/making present' the mighty works of God in creation and redemption. The letter of the law caused them to 'forget' the practical humanitarian dimension of God's creative and redemptive work.

As a climax to this polemical exchange Jesus emphasises the

---

205. Jn 7:19; Gal 3:10; Rom 2:23.
206. cf Jn 5:17ff. Because of the similarity of points in the argument some scholars think that Jn 7:15-45 originally followed after what is now the end of chapter five. It could be equally well argued that the account of events on the Sabbath during the feast was originally here in chapter seven and put back before the Passover in Galilee to reflect the order of feasts in Leviticus. However, our interest is in the text as it now stands and not in a hypothetical reconstruction of an older stage of development. The points of similarity are Jesus' dependence on the one who sent him, the references to Moses, to the 'work' (ergon), to one's own glory and God's glory, and to the plot to kill him.
207. Rabbi Eleazar stated that since circumcision which concerns one of man's 248 members, overrides the Sabbath, how much more must his whole body (if in danger) override the Sabbath.

recurring theme of judgement telling them not to judge by appearances but to judge justly. The related words judge and judgement (*krinein* and *krisis*) occur three times in the sentence and are reinforced by the adjective 'just' (*dikaia*). This is another favourite word of Paul's in his discussions in Galatians and Romans about the justice of God, the just one living by faith and the success or failure of the law in making one just before God. This further reflects the wider Christian-Jewish debate on law, justification and judgement.

Jesus' Identity (Jn 7:25-31)

The fact that the authorities have allowed Jesus to speak in public and have not attempted to stop him makes the crowd wonder if they have begun to believe that he is the Christ. This is the cue for a discussion on his identity and origins. They question whether he could be the Christ because they know where he comes from, but there is a strong tradition that the origins of the Christ will be unknown. Again the discussion takes place on two levels. The repeated self assured opinions of the crowd are reminiscent of the *we know* in the dialogue between Jesus and Nicodemus and the subsequent monologue, where the initial 'We know' of Nicodemus is rebuffed by Jesus' remark 'You do not know.' Here, too, Jesus ironically says: 'You know me and where I come from' and he goes on to say 'I have not come from myself, but the one who sent me is true, whom *you do not know.*' 'I know him, I am from him and he sent me.' Again the *we know* of the crowd is challenged by Jesus' *you do not know*. In all these cases the Johannine irony is at its best as Jesus' opponents perceive and argue on the level of physical reality, while Jesus talks about the divine, and the reader of the prologue observes the discussion from a privileged position. Jesus has come from God. They do not know him because they *do not know* the One who sent him. They are being challenged to see in Jesus a new gift from a God who loved the world so much that he gave his only son.[208] The narrator tells us that they wanted to arrest him but nobody laid a hand on him because his *hour* had not yet come.

Jesus' Departure (Jn 7:32-36)

The schism among the crowd grows, sparking another debate about whether the Messiah would perform more signs than this

---

208. Jn 3:16; 4:10.

man. On hearing this the chief priests and Pharisees sent the temple police to arrest him. Jesus then talks about his going away. They will seek him and not be able to find him. In a sentence reminiscent, by way of stark contrast, of the first request of the disciples 'where do you live?', and Jesus' reply, 'Come and see', he now tells the crowd, 'where I am you are unable to come'. In typical fashion the listeners think in physical terms about his going to the Diaspora to teach the Greeks, outside the jurisdiction of the authorities who are harassing him. The reader knows he is talking about his going to the Father, 'to the one who sent him', as he will tell the disciples during the farewell discourse at the Last Supper. On that occasion, however, he will promise not to leave them orphans, and assure them that he goes to prepare a place for them, to return to take them with him and to send them the Paraclete.

6. ON THE LAST DAY OF THE FEAST (Jn 7:37-52)

On the last and greatest day of the feast the priests passed through the Water Gate in procession and encircled the altar seven times with water from the pool of Siloam. Against the background of this impressive scenario Jesus calls out: 'Let anyone who thirsts come to me and let the one who believes in me drink.'[209] He follows this invitation with a quotation about 'rivers of living (life-giving) water'. His announcement of a new source of living water has left readers debating whether the living water is portrayed as flowing directly from Jesus or from the one who believes in him.[210]

Life Giving Water (Jn 7:37-52)

Looking at Jesus as the source of living water to whom one comes to drink because rivers of living water flow out of his very being, the reader can see Jesus as the new temple from which the waters of life will spring forth, as promised by Ezekiel. Jesus can also be seen as the new rock in the wilderness that quenches the people's thirst as he invites those who believe in him to satisfy their thirst now with the water he provides. This outpouring of

---

209. Jn 7:37-39.
210. In favour of seeing Jesus as the source of the living water were Justin, Hippolytus, Tertullian, Cyprian, Irenaeus, Ephraem. It is sometimes referred to as the 'western' interpretation. In favour of seeing the believer as the source of the living water were Origen and most of the Eastern Fathers. The debate continues among scholars.

water signals that the messianic age has arrived in his own person as the new Moses. This will be graphically and symbolically illustrated by the water that pours forth from Jesus' pierced side (Jn 19:34). When Jesus is glorified in his death and resurrection the Spirit (which the water represents) will be bestowed. This fits the gospel's repeated emphasis on Jesus as the one who gives the Spirit, foreshadows the later scenes in which blood and water flow from the crucified Jesus (1 9:34) and in which he breathes the Spirit upon his disciples (20: 22).[211]

The 'rivers of living water' can also be seen as flowing from within the heart (*koilia*) of the believer. Interpreting the verse in this way one sees Jesus not only promising that those who drink will have their thirst quenched, but also that they shall have within them 'rivers of living water'. On this reading, the passage has a clear parallel to Jesus' promise in Jn 4:14: 'Those who drink of the water that I will give them will never be thirsty. The water that I will give will become in them a spring of water gushing up to eternal life.'[212] The interpretations are not mutually exclusive. In fact they are complementary. As one comes to Jesus for the living water one replenishes the wellspring within. The narrator points out that he is speaking about the Spirit which those who came to believe would receive. The Spirit, however, will be given after, and because of, Jesus' death and glorification.

Further discussion among the crowd ensues when some speculate that he might be the prophet-like-Moses, others that he might be the Messiah. They focus on his known identity, and his place of origin and how they are at variance with the view that the Messiah would be from the line of David and from the town of Bethlehem. The schism deepens among the crowds. Again some wanted to arrest him, and did not. The police sent for that very purpose failed to do so and proclaimed to their superiors by way of explanation for not carrying out the order: 'Never has anyone spoken like this.'[213] It is a prelude to their judgement which is the total dismissal and condemnation of Jesus. The police are told they have been deceived, that none of the rulers or the Pharisees have believed in him, the only ones who have believed are the mob who know nothing of the law. At this point, Nicodemus calls for fair play by way of due

211. cf G.A.Yee, *op. cit.*, 80.
212. cf M. M. Thompson, *op. cit.*, 177f.
213. Jn 7:46.

process, only to be taunted as a ' Galilean' and reminded that prophets do not come out of Galilee.

7. THE ADULTEROUS WOMAN (Jn 7:53-8:11)

This well known story of Jesus and the woman taken in adultery has been part of John's gospel in the standard Greek text from about 900 A.D. There are no commentaries on it by Greek writers in the first millennium. It is not in the Old Syriac, Old Georgian, Armenian or Coptic texts. However, Ambrose and Augustine regarded it as scripture and Jerome included it in the Vulgate.[214] Acceptance into the Vulgate made it canonical in Catholic circles, irrespective of its late arrival into the canon. It is in the 5th century Codex Bezae. In the West it was accepted as a liturgical reading for the feast of St Pelagia in the fifth century. The majority of Christian churches now accept the story as canonical in spite of its late arrival into the canon. It is generally accepted as an ancient and well founded traditional story about Jesus, a stray piece of Lucan or Johannine tradition. Maybe the strict discipline of the early church in regard to adultery regarded the apparent ease with which Jesus dealt with the case as open to misunderstanding and so this ancient story about Jesus took time to get its due canonical recognition. It contains what is now in the popular usage of Christians and of the world at large one of the most quoted lines of scripture: 'Let the one without sin cast the first stone.'

Possibly the story has Johannine origins, but it is very like a Lucan story. Jesus is portrayed in similar fashion to the healing, forgiving, merciful Jesus of Luke, where the women figure prominently in his ministry, and the sinful woman in chapter seven stands as a model of love and forgiveness. In fact it would fit very neatly into Luke's gospel after Lk 21:38.[215] In its

---

214. The Catholic Church has regarded the story as canonical principally because of its acceptance into the Vulgate, the undisputed official text in use in the West prior to the Reformation.

215. Following closely on a series of challenges to Jesus and attempts to trap him, the actual setting following Lk 21:37f would be very similar. If it were placed here in Luke, omitting the verse in brackets which may be an editorial joining, the combined Lucan and Johannine verses would read: 'In the daytime he would be in the Temple teaching, but would spend the night on the hill called the Mount of Olives. And from the early morning the people would gather round him in the Temple to listen to him' (Lk 21:37f). '(Then each went off to his own house while Jesus went out to the Mount of Olives). But at daybreak he again made his appearance in the Temple precincts; and when all the people started

Johannine context, however, the story takes on and further high-lights the surrounding christology. It is placed here in the section of the gospel dealing with the feasts where there is an on-going emphasis on the Jews' judgement and condemnation of Jesus, set in ironic counterpoint to his own role as divinely ap-pointed judge and Son of Man with power over life and death, judgement and acquittal.[216]

He is not pressurised by the would-be execution squad into passing judgement or sentence (it is unclear which is required of him). This stands out against the judgement passed on Jesus himself in Jn 7:51 when Nicodemus protested against the lack of due process. It illustrates the statements in Jn 8:15 where Jesus says: 'You judge by human standards; I judge no one' and Jn 8:46 where he asks: 'Can any of you convict me of sin?' in the face of the repeated condemnations of himself, possibly by some of the same crowd whom he confronted about their own sinful-ness when he challenged them about throwing the first stone.

Why did they bring the woman to Jesus? Was it for judge-ment or sentence? It is not clear. What is clear, however, is their intention to trap him, as in the synoptic controversies about the payment of tribute to Caesar or which husband the woman would have in the resurrection after she had seven husbands in this life.[217] How would they do this? Whether they brought her for judgement or for sentence, either case could put him in ten-sion with Roman or Mosaic Law. If the Jews had already lost the power of capital punishment then it was a dangerous situation to advocate or participate in a stoning. The date of the loss of capital punishment on their part is uncertain. The only piece of evidence is written at a later period in the Jerusalem Talmud and may be dependant on a particular reading of Jn 18:31. It states that: 'Forty years before the destruction of the Temple the trial of capital cases was taken away from Israel.'[218] Did that cover the time of Jesus? If so, the trap set here could involve Jesus with the Roman law. Aside from the Roman Law, it could show Jesus either as not complying with the Mosaic Law and so losing credibility with strict observants or alienating his follow-ing among the people if his rigorous approach was seen to un-

---

coming to him, he sat down and began to teach them. Then the scribes and the Pharisees led forward a woman ...' (Jn 7:53; 8:1-3).

216. Some mss have the story after Jn 7:36, 7:44 or at the end of the gospel at 21:25.

217. Lk 20:20ff; 20:27ff.

218. *j. Sanh.* 1.1; 7:2. This is crucial for assessing the trial of Jesus.

dermine his teaching on mercy and forgiveness (especially in a synoptic style context). The Mosaic Law, according to Lev 20:10, prescribed the death penalty, leaving the manner of execution open. Deut 22:21 specified stoning for a betrothed woman (was the woman in the story betrothed, and not yet living with her intended husband?). The LXX version of the Susannah story mentions death by mangling on, or by, rocks. Stoning often meant being thrown from a height onto rocks. This was the case in the threatened throwing of Jesus from the brow of the hill in Nazareth.[219] Ezek 16:38-40 shows stoning as the normal penalty for all types of adultery. In post Maccabean Judaism the zeal of Phineas was greatly admired, as seen from 1 Macc 2:26. Phineas had punished the debauchery of Zimri, son of Salu, an Israelite who was caught sinning with a Midianite woman called Cozbi, during the rites of worship of Baal-of-Peor. Both were impaled with a spear through the groin by Phineas and the anger of YHWH was thought to be purged.[220] Stoning was meant to be carried out by the people, in the name of the people, and so a stoning often began with a representative laying on of hands on the one about to be stoned, signifying the involvement of the people in the rooting out of the evil in question.[221]

If, on the other hand, Jesus was seen to comply with the very rigorous interpretation of the law it could have cost him his following, because of a loss of his reputation for mercy, forgiveness and reconciliation of sinners, illustrated above all in the table fellowship and its accompanying parables (in a synoptic setting). In the Johannine setting it would contradict the picture of a God who loved the world so much that he gave the gift of his only Son that those who believe in him may not perish but have eternal life, a God whose gift was the Lamb of God who takes away the sin of the world.[222] Whether one sees a synoptic or Johannine origin to the story, the practical dilemma posed by a carefully laid trap is evident. As it now stands, however, the story is set in the Johannine context.

There are echoes of the Susannah story and the wicked

---

219. It was also a mode of execution at the Tarpeian Rock in the city of Rome.

220. After Jesus' time, the Pharisees replaced stoning with strangulation as punishment for adultery.

221. cf Deut 13:9-10 which prescribes a stoning for idolatry with the involvement of the people. After Jesus' time the Pharisees replaced stoning with strangulation as punishment for adultery.

222. Lk 15:1-32; Jn 3:16; 1:29, 36.

judges shown up by the young Daniel. As Daniel, the great example of a wise, just and God fearing judge, outwitted the wicked old men who falsely accused Susannah, because of their own frustrated lustful desires, so Jesus frustrates the intent of those who brought the woman to him, by writing on the ground. Maybe the reader is meant to think of Susannah and wonder if in this case too the charge is a trumped up one or if there had been connivance of some kind, since there is no reference to husband or co-adulterer. What did Jesus intend by writing on the earth? Was he reminding the accusers of the sentence in Jeremiah: 'Those who turn away from you will have their names written on the earth'?[223] Even if the writer did not have this in view, the reader with a biblical background and sensitivity can see the connection. Maybe this is why Jerome and medieval scholars surmised that he was writing or pretending to write the sins of the accusers, a tradition that has turned up in a tenth century Armenian manuscript.[224] Or was he imitating the practice in Roman jurisprudence where the judge wrote out the sentence before reading it aloud? Was he recalling the judgement involved in the writing on the wall in the Book of Daniel?[225] Or was he just showing complete disinterest, displaying his annoyance with their tactics? However one views the writing on the earth, the challenge that followed by way of an invitation to the one without sin to cast the first stone was a decision truly in the tradition of a wise judge like Solomon or Daniel.

The casting of stones was a ritual in itself. It was meant to represent the punishment of the people as a whole on the offender, partly to rid the community of the guilt lest punishment be exacted on the community, and partly because certain crimes were seen as breaches of the covenant with YHWH. These crimes, like idolatry, blasphemy and profanation of the Sabbath, were serious breaches of the covenant and so offended not only God but the people of the covenant. According to Lev 24:14 and Sus 34, the witnesses were to lay their hands on the head of the condemned person before stoning, showing that they took responsibility for the execution of the guilty party. The witnesses were to throw the first stones, in order of seniority. In the case of the woman brought to Jesus, the would-be stone throwers, chal-

---

223. Jer 17:13 (JB).There is a variant reading, 'recorded in the underworld'.
224. cf R. E. Brown, *John* I, 333, note on v. 6.
225. Dan 5:24. cf R. E. Brown, *ibid*.

lenged by Jesus, realised their own sinfulness and departed in order of seniority (*seniores priores*), the order in which they would have given evidence (thus passing judgement) and thrown the stones.[226] Left alone with the woman Jesus acts as the serene judge balancing forgiveness and the injunction not to sin again. This final scene is poignantly summed up in Augustine's famous comment: *Relicti sunt duo, misera et misericordia*.[227]

8. AT THE TREASURY: JESUS THE LIGHT OF THE WORLD (Jn 8:12-20)
Jesus declared himself the source of living water earlier in the festival and now in his discourse at the Treasury he declares himself the Light of the World. Both major symbols of the Feast of Tabernacles, water and light, are now applied to him. Proclaiming himself Light of the World is very significant in the context of the feast itself and the imagery of light throughout the Bible. First of all the great fire on the Temple Mount as the four huge candelabras were lit at nightfall, illuminating the courtyards of Jerusalem, celebrated the light of God's presence as a pillar of fire with the people during the wandering in the desert. The priests atoning for the historic act of sun worship turn towards the Temple and the light of God's presence. These ceremonies of light resonate with many of these allusions to God's presence and work in the world and among the people. The first words of creation were 'Let there be light'. The presence of God in glory on Sinai was described in terms of light, a light which was reflected in the countenance of Moses. That light shone through the teachings of prophets, Wisdom and Torah as the mighty deeds God worked for the people resulted in the gift of the law, the prophets and the writings. Light figures in the prayer of the psalmist: 'You are a light for my path.' As they reflected on the gift of water from the rock to sustain them and the pillar of fire to guide the people in the desert, the sustenance and guidance were interpreted in terms of the gift of Torah. The Wisdom of Solomon describes the pillar as 'the imperishable light of the Torah'.[228] When Herod the Great massacred the scribes he was condemned for having quenched the light of the

---

226. J.Blinzer, 'The Jewish Punishment of Stoning in the New Testament', in *The Trial of Jesus*, ed E.Bammel, 147-161.
227. Augustine, *In Joh* xxxiii 5; PL 35:1650. A literal translation would be: 'Two are left, the wretched woman and mercy.' The verve and alliteration of the Latin are lost in translation.
228. Ex 13:21; Wis 18:3f.

world. The promise of future glory is also made in terms of light. The servant of God will be 'a light to the nations'[229] and Jerusalem will be summoned to 'Arise, shine out, for your light has come.'[230] Zechariah looks to the future when there will be continuous day and the Book of Revelation speaks of a time when there will be no need for lamplight or sunlight for the Lord God will be shining on them. Jesus now draws all these images to himself as he fulfils, absorbs and replaces the light ceremonies of the feast, just as he had earlier replaced the water ceremonies. He publicly and solemnly proclaims himself the source of this light through the revelation he brings. 'I am the Light of the World.'

Jesus transfers some of this imagery to his followers both in the synoptics and in the Johannine tradition. 'The one who follows me will not walk in darkness but will have the light of life.'[231] In the synoptics he tells them, 'You are the light of the world', and compares them to a city on a hilltop, and reminds them that the light is not to be hidden under a bushel but to shine for all the world to see. In St John's gospel he admonishes them to 'walk in the light'. The prologue declared that the light was coming into the world and that John was the witness to the light. In response to its coming some people came into the light but others preferred to remain in darkness because of their evil deeds.[232]

Witness and Judgement (Jn 8:13-20)
The criticism of Jesus now articulated by the crowd is reminiscent of that voiced already at the Feast of Tabernacles and earlier in the ministry after the healing at Bethesda in chapter five. On that former occasion Jesus defended himself with the claim: 'My Father works until now and I work', and in response to the ensuing charge of blasphemy he called on the Father and other witnesses to testify on his behalf. Here at Tabernacles he is again accused of being his own witness. Here again he invokes the Father as the guarantor of his witness. 'I bear witness to myself and the Father who sent me bears witness to me.'[233] He appeals

---

229. Isa 42:6; Lk 2:32.
230. Isa 60:1-3.
231. Jn 8:12.
232. Jn 3:19-21.
233. Jn 8:18.

to his origins and final destiny – both central themes in the gospel – as he speaks of where he came from and where he is going, and this makes his witness and judgement 'true' as it sets him in a different category entirely from his critics, lending divine authority to his witness.

This authority is borne out in verse 18 with the *ego eimi* sentence construction which alerts the reader to look for a deeper meaning than might be expected at first glance. Instead of the straightforward *egô marturô*, ' I bear witness', the periphrastic *egô eimi ho marturôn peri emautou*, declares not only the bearing of witness but also the solemn identity of the person bearing the witness. The sentence does not lend itself to easy translation into English if its full meaning is to be preserved. It therefore has to be rendered 'awkwardly' as: 'The one bearing witness to myself (is) *I am*' or '*I am* is the one bearing witness to myself.' Here Jesus is identifying himself as one of the two witnesses required by Jewish law and he identifies his Father as the other. However, Jesus presents himself as a very exceptional type of witness, using the *ego eimi* of self identification, attributed to God in the Isaian passage: 'You be my witnesses, and I (am) a witness, says the Lord God, and my servant whom I have chosen, so that you will know and believe and understand that *I am*.'[234]

He also makes a similar point to that made in chapter three about ' things above' and ' things below'. His critics judge according to the flesh, that is, according to merely human standards. He accuses them of not knowing either himself or the Father. His assertion about knowing *where* he comes from and *where* he is going, and their question, '*Where* is your Father?' reflect the repeated use of *where* throughout the gospel, especially in relation to divine presence and dwelling and the origins and destiny of Jesus. The term *judge/judging* again has a dominant place in the discussion, carrying on the theme begun in chapter five. And again the theme of the *hour* is mentioned. They do not arrest him because his *hour* has not yet come.

It is a point worth noting that Jesus says 'in *your* law it is written that the testimony of two witnesses is valid'. Speaking of *your* law reflects the division that had occurred between Christians and Jews by the time of writing the gospel. It is similar in effect to the expression ' a feast *of the Jews*'.

---

234. Isa 43:10. There are many similarities between Isa 42-43 and Jn 8-9 – the servant, light for the nations, sent to open the eyes of the blind, to set captives free etc.

Jesus' Departure (Jn 8:21-24)

Jesus talks to his critics about his forthcoming departure, telling them that they will seek him and not find him because where he is going they cannot come. They wonder where he is going. Again the word *where* serves an important theological function in the passage. They wonder if he is going to kill himself. They already asked if he was going to the Diaspora. He tells them that *where* he is going they cannot come and they will die in their sins. Here a sharp contrast is being set up between these critics and the disciples who will ask Jesus similar questions during the Last Supper discourse. The disciples will ask him *where* he is going. They will also ask him to show them the way, and to show them the Father. These are similar questions to the ones now posed by his critics, but they are asked in very different tone, and answered by Jesus in very different vein. He will tell the disciples that he is going to the Father, to prepare a place for them, that he is the Way, and that he will return and take them with him so that *where* he is they may be also.[235]

In this discussion with the unbelieving crowd Jesus uses the distinction 'from above' (*ek tôn anô*) and 'from below' (*ek tôn katô*), to highlight the difference of origin and operation between himself and his critics. Summing up the nature of belief required he says to them: 'Unless you believe that *I am* you will die in your sins.' This is the required christological faith in the terms of John's gospel. It is the acceptance of Jesus as the eternal *Logos* now become *sarx*, sent by the Father to accomplish his work as the unique, transcendent revealer of God. Jesus is now present as the enfleshment of the Father's saving love and offer of salvation. In this Jesus is the one who takes away the sin of the world and empowers those who receive him to become children of God, born from above, *anôthen*, so they are now *ek tôn anô*, having been born 'again' of water and the Spirit. Those who refuse to receive him remain *ek tôn katô*, of the world, and refuse to accept the one who comes to take away the sin of the world. They therefore remain in that sin. Receiving Jesus implies believing the implication for salvation of his *ego eimi*, 'I am', claim.

Who are You? (Jn 8:25-30)

The *ego eimi* of verses 24 and 28 speaks of Jesus' identity in terms of his own divine life and his life-giving mission. It reproduces

---

235. Jn 13:33-36; 14:1-10; et al.

the formula used in the Old Testament for speaking of the unique God of Israel. Jesus is now being presented as the life-giving presence of God to humankind. Being absolute, without predicate, the *ego eimi* statements leave the Jews questioning, 'Who are you?' when he tells them that unless they believe 'that I am' they would die in their sins, and they will come to know 'that I am' only when the Son of Man has been 'lifted up'. The implied reader, sharing the thought world of the implied author, probably had immediate access to the meaning and did not need an explanation, but the real reader today is left looking again to the biblical background for such an explanation.

As already noted, chapter 8 of John reflects chapters 42 and 43 of (Deutero-)Isaiah. The context in Isaiah is *YHWH's* claim to be the only God and the call to Israel to acknowledge that God is the only saviour of Israel. The Hebrew expression *ani hû* lies behind the Greek *egô eimi* as it emphasises the exclusive claim of *YHWH* to be saviour of Israel as portrayed in the Isaian statement: 'I am God and also henceforth I am he (*ani hû*) ...'[236] The clause 'to know and believe that I am' carries the soteriological function that was reserved for God in Isaiah and transfers it to Jesus in John's gospel, so that Jesus can say that those who do not believe 'that I am' will die in their sins. Isa 43:10 says: 'You are my witnesses ... so that you *know* and *believe* and *understand* that *I am*.' Jn 8:24 reflects the '*believe* that I am' and Jn 8:28 reflects the '*know* that I am' of the Isaian statement. D. M. Ball remarks:

> In John Jesus has been given this exclusive soteriological function that in Isaiah was reserved for God alone (cf Jn 3:17; 4:42; 10:9). Jesus can use the words *egô eimi* for himself in this way, because of his close identification with the Father. He does nothing on his own authority but speaks only as the Father has taught him (8:24) ... In other words 'he whom God has sent utters the words of God'(3:34) to such an extent that he can use words reserved for God and apply them to himself. Again the phrase which contains *egô eimi* speaks of an intimate identification of Jesus with the exclusive God of Isaiah.[237]

'*To know that I am YHWH*' is another biblical expression that has influenced the use of *egô eimi*. It occurs in historical circumstances such as the Exodus, where both the Israelites and the

236. Isa 43:13.
237. D. M. Ball, *op. cit.*, 190f.

Egyptians, including Pharaoh himself, come *'to know that I am YHWH'* – the Israelites because of their being liberated from slavery, the Egyptians and Pharaoh himself because of the punishment inflicted upon them.[238] Ezekiel also uses the expression, as W. Zimmerli points out in his study: 'Such a knowledge always takes place within the context of a very concrete history, a history embodied in concrete emissaries and coming to resolution in them.'[239] Isaiah makes a similar statement: 'Then all flesh shall know that I am *YHWH*, your Saviour, and your Redeemer, the Mighty one of Jacob'[240] and the Isaian 'I am he' is synonymous with the 'I am *YHWH*' of Ezekiel. The concrete historical circumstance of Jesus' 'being lifted up' is for John the saving event, and the threat is that they will die in their sins if they do not believe. The opposite is also suggested, that if they believe their sins will be forgiven. Again Isaiah is called to mind: *'I am, I am* (the one who is) blotting out your iniquities for my sake, and your sins, and I shall not remember (them).'[241]

In the Targum of Isaiah there are also interesting parallels. The difficulty of dating the Targum makes it impossible to say whether John knew the *targum* itself or a related tradition. It contains a striking relationship to the passage in John. It refers to the eternity and uniqueness of God and the foreshowing of the future to Abraham, also called 'your father' as in John where he is described as rejoicing to see, that is to foresee, 'my day', the day of Jesus.

> I am he that is from the beginning, yea the everlasting ages are mine, and beside me there is no god. I, even I, am the Lord; and beside me there is no saviour. I declared to Abraham your father what was about to come; I delivered you from Egypt ... Yea from everlasting I am he, and there is none that delivereth from my hand.[242]

In response to his highly significant challenge and claim: 'Unless you believe that I am...', the Jews responded with the question: 'Who are you?' Again Jesus responds in terms of the reality and truthfulness of the one who sent him and how he announces to

---

238. Ex 6:7; 10:2; 16:12; 29:46; 31:13; 7:5; 14:4; 7:17; 8:22.

239. W. Zimmerli, *I am Yahweh*, 3.

240. Isa 49:26.

241. *egô eimi, egô eimi ho exaleiphôn tas anomias sou heneken emou, kai tas hamartias sou kai ou mê mnêsthêsomai.*

242. *Tg. Isa.* 43:10-13. Ball, *op. cit.*, 196f, quoting J. F. Stenning, *The Targum of Isaiah*, 144, 146.

the world what he heard from him. He has much to say and much to judge about them. They did not know that he spoke to them about the Father. He reaffirms, in words reminiscent of his defence after the cure at the Pool of Bethesda, that he does nothing of himself, only what he learned from the Father, these are the things he says. The one who sent him is with him. He has not left him alone, because he always does what pleases him. As for the critical listeners who do not understand these things, when they have lifted up the Son of Man, then will they know that *I am*. Having said these things many came to believe in him.

Children of Abraham: Truth, Freedom, Slavery (Jn 8:31-59)
Abraham is described in Jubilees as the first to celebrate the Feast of Tabernacles, in its pre-Mosaic and pre-Solomonic phase. 'And he built booths for himself and for his servants on that festival and he first observed the feast of booths on earth.'[243] His introduction into a discussion during the feast is therefore no great surprise. He was seen as the Father of all the children of Israel and descent from him was regarded as automatically guaranteeing salvation. The challenge to this over-confident attitude found here in John's gospel is widespread in the New Testament and early Christian writing. It is found on the lips of John the Baptist and Jesus in the synoptics and in the writings of Paul and early Christians like Justin.[244] John the Baptist reminded his audience that God could raise up children to Abraham from the very stones.[245] Jesus' parable of the rich man and Lazarus shows the futility of appealing to father Abraham if one does not live a good life as a child of Abraham should.[246] Abraham was the model of hospitality and generosity in the biblical story of his entertaining the strangers.[247] The rich man is the total opposite leaving the needy one outside his gate. Paul paid great attention to Abraham and his real significance in the story of salvation. In Galatians and Romans the faith of Abraham is praised and he is seen as the father of all believers, Jew and Gentile, because through his seed all nations will inherit the blessing of salvation.[248] Paul sees the 'seed' of Abraham as Jesus through whom

243. Jub 16:30.
244. Justin, *Trypho*, 140. cxl; P. G. 6:797.
245. Lk 3:8.
246. Lk 16:19-31.
247. Gen 18:1-15.
248. Gal 3:1-14; Rom 4:1-25.

[handwritten note at top: Jews believed because of Abraham, they had an automatic right to salv—]

the blessing of salvation will be given to the nations.[249] He challenges the interpretation of the Sarah/Isaac and Hagar/Ishmael story which sees the children descended from Abraham and Sarah through Isaac as free and the children descended from Abraham and Hagar through Ishmael as slaves.[250] In this context Paul presents a treatise on the real meaning of freedom and slavery.[251] This early Christian debate about freedom and slavery, children of Abraham and children of enslavement, is reflected here in the discussion between Jesus and his critics. It was still an issue of serious debate when Justin wrote the *Dialogue with Trypho* and criticised the Jews because they expected to receive the kingdom no matter what their personal lives had been.[252]

Jesus said to the Jews who had come to believe in him: 'If you abide (remain) in my word, you will truly be my disciples, and you will know the truth, and the truth will set you free.'[253] 'Abiding in the word' and 'having the word abide in you' are in practical terms the same. Five key concepts are packed into this statement. They are abide/remain (*menein*), word (*logos*), truth/truly (*alêtheia/ôs*), disciple (*mathêtês*) and set free (*eleutherôsei*). The instruction to those Jews who believed in Jesus and are about to become disciples, is to abide in his word. 'Abide' (*menein*) is the word used for dwelling and indwelling. It is in the first question put to Jesus in the gospel: 'Rabbi where do you dwell? (*rabbi pou meneis*)'. This is reflected in the Second Letter of John where the followers are told that the one who does not abide in the teaching of Christ does not have God.[254] Abiding in the word signifies drawing one's life from the word, the revelation of Christ, which is Christ himself. He embodies the Father's saving love. He is the truth, the incarnation of the *Logos*, the transcendent revealer of God. His revelation is the liberating truth because it gives liberty through knowledge of the Father's love and saving purpose. It removes those who accept it from the subjection to the *sarx*, the *kosmos*, *ta kata* and from sin, and everyone who sins is a slave.[255] Believing this makes one free. This revelation is the truth, guaranteed by God, and accepting

---

249. Gal 3:16.
250. Gal 4:21-27.
251. Gal 5:1-26.
252. Justin,*Trypho* 140. cxl; P. G. 6:797.
253. Jn 8:31f.
254. 2 Jn 9.
255. Jn 8:32, 34.

this truth and abiding in it binds one to Christ as a disciple. Being thus bound to Christ one is free from the slavery of being bound to the world and its sinfulness.

Those who refuse the truth of Jesus' revelation of the Father who sent him have chosen slavery. This is an argument parallel to that made by Paul in Galatians. In choosing slavery they have chosen another master. He is the opposite to God the Father of truth. He is the father of lies, the devil who speaks *the lie* (*to pseudos*), the final denial of ultimate reality, for the truth is not in him, that is, there is nothing in him that corresponds to the eternal divine reality revealed in Jesus, the Word.

In speaking of freedom through the truth the reader is also aware of how the rabbis spoke of the study of the Law as a liberating experience, freeing one from worldly care. The reader remembers also that in Qumran there was an emphasis on the polarity between the spirit of truth and the spirit of lies and here too the spirit of truth is seen as liberating one from the influence of the spirit of lies: 'And then God will purge by his truth all the deeds of men ... and will sprinkle on him a spirit of truth like water that cleanses from every lying abomination.'[256] This is very close to the polarity between the God of truth and the father of lies and their 'children' in Jn 8:42-47.

Focusing again on Abraham, Jesus proclaims: 'Your father Abraham rejoiced that he would see my day. He saw it and was glad.' Scholars have made many suggestions about what this verse means. In keeping with the approach of this gospel, it is very likely an allusion to something in the Abraham narratives in Genesis.[257] As a counter argument to his opponents' claim to be children of Abraham and their implication that he may not be, Jesus claims that he is in fact the very fulfilment of the prophetic vision of Abraham. Looking at Genesis one sees the double reference to laughing or rejoicing on the occasion of the announcing of the forthcoming birth of Isaac and the joy of the event itself. The birth of Isaac ensured the continuity of the promise until its fulfilment and thereby defeated the old age and impending death of the parents. Subsequently the sparing of Isaac from sacrificial death further secured the promise.

---

256. 1QS iv 20f.
257. This is more in keeping with John's gospel than some other vision such as his heavenly vision of Christ or Christ's post crucifixion visit to Hades to those who had died before him, both of which have been suggested.

Through the descendants thus made possible through Isaac all nations would be blessed, a blessing now fulfilled in the one who would draw all to himself and die not only for the nation but to gather together in unity the scattered children of God.[258] Paul had suggested in Galatians that the birth of Isaac was prophetic of the birth of Christ when he wrote: 'The promises were addressed to Abraham and his posterity. It does not say descendants as if there were several, but one, which is Christ.'[259] Abraham rejoiced greatly at the promise and was glad to see the prophetic vision of its fulfilment.

Again perceiving only on the physical level, the critics responded that Jesus was not yet fifty and how could he have seen Abraham? Then Jesus uses the great contrast of the gospel between finite and infinite existence, with which the Word was introduced in the prologue, and which has been used a number of times in discussion of his identity and origins. With the solemn proclamatory 'Amen, amen …' formula he declares: 'Before Abraham *came to be, I am.*' Perceiving this as blasphemy they picked up stones to throw at him but he hid himself and went out of the Temple.

The contrast between the verbs is striking. Not only is there a difference in meaning 'come to be' and 'be', but also the aorist and the present stand in stark contrast. The discussion so far has dealt with Jesus' identity. He was asked was he greater than Abraham and who exactly he claimed to be. Seeing the interconnectedness between the various *ego eimi* statements in the chapter, and the common background in Isa 42-43, the reader remembers a corresponding use of verbs and tenses in the contrast between YHWH and the false gods. YHWH states 'Be my witnesses and I am a witness says the Lord God, and the servant whom I have chosen, so that you may know and believe and understand that *I am*, no other god *came to be* before me …'[260]

The opposition are quick to see the implications of Jesus' statement as an identification of himself with the nature and prerogatives of God. They now become extremely vocal and strident, accusing him of being a Samaritan (i.e. a heretic) and a demoniac. The division has now passed beyond the point of reconciliation and so they become intent on killing him.

---

258. Jn 11:50-52.

259. Gal 3:16. My own translation.

260. Isa 43:10. *genesthai moi martyres … hina gnôte kai pistusête kai synête hoti egô eimi, emprosthen mou ouk egeneto allos theos kai met' emou ouk estai.*

At the Pool of Siloam (Jn 9:1-10:42)

1. THE PLOT: BLINDNESS AND SIGHT

The Feast of Tabernacles with its emphasis on water and light provides the backdrop for the thematic development of Jesus' promise of living water and his proclamation of himself as the Light of the World. The one who has declared himself Light of the World now gives sight to a man born in darkness. The imagery becomes reality in the physical and spiritual sight of the recipient of Jesus' gift. The miracle of the granting of sight to a blind man is a 'sign' through which Jesus reveals, with authority, that he is the Light of the World.

> In giving physical sight, Jesus shows that by his teaching, life and personal presence he was the source of the spiritual vision we call believing. The whole account reads like a picturesque, symbolic presentation of the manner in which one comes to believe in Jesus as 'Lord'.[261]

This is the only story in the ministry where Jesus is not the main character. The blind man takes centre stage. He becomes the lightning conductor for the pent up opposition to Jesus and in the process he becomes a full-blown believer. The event foreshadows in story, and reflects in fact, the plight of the early Christians who suffered harassment and exclusion in the days of the early church and its struggle with the Pharisees. It probably also reflects various reactions to the early Christian ministry of healing.

2. THE MAN BORN BLIND

The reader meets the blind man as an outsider, a marginalised person, reduced to begging because of his blindness. People talk *about* him. The disciples discuss his possible sinful condition, his neighbours discuss his identity, his parents avoid involvement in a possible dispute about him, the authorities discuss his cure, harass him and consign him not only back to the margins, but expel him altogether from the community. Jesus talks *to* him and leads him from darkness to light, from darkness on the margins to the centre stage where the spotlight of his new found sight highlights the blindness of the sighted authorities. In one of the extraordinary stories of the gospel, it is not Jesus but the man born blind who comes centre stage as he bears witness to the 'sighted' people.

---

261. W. J. Harrington, *John: Spiritual Theologian*, 56.

Whereas the man healed at the Pool of Bethesda in chapter five showed by his response that miracles do not necessarily lead to faith, the man cured of his blindness in chapter nine shows that given the right dispositions miracles can lead to faith and a relationship with Jesus which develops and endures even in the face of hostility and sustained opposition. The drama surrounding the healing of the blind man shows up in clear light the scepticism of the neighbours, the fear of the parents, the hostility of the authorities and the faith of the healed man. The hostile reaction of the authorities leads on to Jesus' teaching on good and bad leadership in the following chapter dealing with the Good/Ideal Shepherd and the Door of the Sheepfold.

Like the dialogue with the Samaritan woman, this story of the blind man is an exposition of the stages of growth in faith. Here, however, the growth takes place in the context of hostility and exclusion. The blind man is thereby shown up in great contrast to the paralytic healed earlier at the pool of Bethesda and whose healing does not seem to have produced any real faith on his part. On the contrary he reported (or naïvely identified) Jesus to the authorities and exposed his benefactor to their hostility. The formerly blind man here, however, rises to the challenge posed by hostile authority, at first identified as 'the Pharisees' and then as 'the Jews'. His faith develops from a feeling of gratitude for the man whom initially he does not know, through a series of hostile interrogations by the authorities, to a faith expressing itself in an act of worship of his benefactor. While his neighbours discussed if he were the same person who was formerly blind, his parents ungratefully gave into cowardice before the hostile authorities to prevent their expulsion from the synagogue, and a division arose among the authorities, the positive and determined reaction of the healed man himself showed clearly that a disease of the eyes does not prevent a deeper sense of seeing. Blind eyes are not the worst form of blindness, as is evident from the reactions of his parents, neighbours and the authorities. As the man grows in insight and faith, those claiming spiritual sight and leadership grow more blind and spiritually obtuse.

There are nine references to 'opening eyes', seven in the passage itself and two in subsequent passages.[262] Those who defend Jesus from the charge of having a demon, after they hear him

---

262. Jn 9:10, 14, 17, 21, 26, 30, 32 and 10:21; 11:37.

speaking about the Good Shepherd, say in his defence: 'These
are not the words of a demon. Can a demon open the eyes of a
man born blind?' Following the death of Lazarus some of the
Jews present at the tomb remark: 'Could not he who opened the
eyes of the man born blind have kept this man from dying?'[263]
Again the reader is reminded of the Isaian Servant by the reference to 'opening the eyes of the blind' to give physical and
spiritual sight. The reactions of the authorities to the healing recall the Isaian reference to seeing and not seeing because the
heart is gross, the ears dull and the eyes shut.[264]

The healing takes place in the waters of the pool from which
the water for the festal rituals was drawn, and whose name,
Siloam, is interpreted as 'sent', highlighting the divine mission
of Jesus as 'the one sent'. Bathing in the water has overtones of
the life-giving water which Jesus promised, and in the community of early Christians from which this gospel emerged, the
baptismal imagery of water and light were closely linked. The
First Letter of John associates the light with the baptismal teaching and faith which initiates one into the community.[265]

The healing is a sign that Jesus is continuing the work he was
given to do, and through which he reveals who he is, whom he
represents and what he is endeavouring to achieve. The healing
sets the discussion arising from the accusation of Sabbath viol-
ation in the context of light and darkness, belief and unbelief,
good and bad leadership. As the blind man comes to sight the
blindness of the Pharisees is exposed. The leaders are shown up
in very poor light. This in turn leads on to a discussion on the
role of the shepherd in the community and Jesus' role as the
model shepherd who lays down his life for his sheep.

3. THE HEALING

At the beginning of the episode Jesus 'sees' the blind man. As
often in such a case 'seeing' on the part of Jesus, who needs no
testimony about anyone since he can see what is in them, points
to Jesus' assessment of the person. Such was the case with
Nathanael and Peter, to both of whom he gave a name in keeping with what he saw in them.[266] The disciples on the other hand

---

263. Jn 10:21; 11:37.
264. Isa 42:7; 6:9f.
265. 1 Jn 5-10.
266. Jn 1:42,47.

saw in the man born blind the sign of a possible punishment for
his own or his parents' sin. The collective responsibility and
guilt of a family was a belief in earlier times. An unborn child
could, for example, be seen to have shared in the sin of a mother
who took part in pagan worship, though it was still in the
womb.[267] This kind of thinking was challenged by Jeremiah and
Ezekiel: 'In those days people will no longer say: "The parents
have eaten sour grapes, and the children's teeth are set on
edge".'[268] The teaching about physical punishment for sin, even
unintentional sin, was challenged by Job when offered by his ad-
visers as a reason for his misfortune. It is here challenged by
Jesus.[269] He responds to the disciples' question about the cause
of the man's blindness with a statement about God's work, reminiscent of his defence after the healing at Bethesda, when he
identified his own *work* with the *work* of the Father and later at
Tabernacles when he remarked: 'I performed one *work* and all of
you are astonished.'[270] Here Jesus says that the blindness makes
possible the manifestation of the *works* of God in the blind man
and goes on to say: 'I must *work* the *works* of him who sent me,
while it is still day; night comes when no one can *work*.'[271] Then
he reiterates his claim to be the Light of the World: 'As long as I
am in the world I am the light of the world.'[272] The Jews, revert
to the old way of thinking about physical sickness and sin and
when their interrogation reaches a point of bitterness because
they are unable to browbeat the healed man, they dismiss him as
having been born utterly steeped in sin.

4. The Drama

In this case, unlike the former healing where the man carried his
bed (mat) and was thus observed breaking the Sabbath, it is
Jesus himself who now appears to break the Sabbath by kneading the clay and spittle and healing the man who was not seen to
be in immediate danger of death. Maybe the kneading of clay
and its application to the man was an allusion to the creation of
man and a pointer to the ongoing action of God in sustaining
creation even on the Sabbath.

267. J. Mc Polin, *op. cit.*, 100.
268. Jer 31:29; Ezek 18:2.
269. Deut 5:9; Job 3:3-4; Jer: 31:29f; Ezek 18:2.
270. Jn 5:17; 7:21.
271. Jn 9:4f. *var* 'we must work'.
272. Jn 9:5.

In this case it is the healed man who presents the case for Jesus' defence and in the process focuses and develops his own faith. The development of insight, faith and commitment on the part of the man who was healed is revealed through the names he uses for Jesus. Beginning with 'the man', 'the one who opened my eyes', he goes on during his interrogation to call him 'a prophet', and finally when Jesus 'finds' him and asks him if he believes in the Son of Man, he replies that he does and he worships him. Just as Jesus had 'seen' him at he beginning, now he 'finds' him. The initiative is again with Jesus. The reader will hear him reminding the disciples at the Last Supper that they have not chosen him, but he has chosen them.[273]

The narrative, in seven scenes, is one of the most vivid and dramatic in the gospel. As it traces the development of faith on the part of the healed man, it shows up the faith levels and consequent divisions among the various groups encountered in the story. First of all the neighbours and casual acquaintances are divided as to the identity of the man and the truth of the miracle. The man responds with a positive identification of self and verification of the actual miracle. Having described the healing, he responds to their question about the whereabouts of Jesus with a statement that he does not know.

They brought him to the Pharisees. On hearing what Jesus had done some of the Pharisees said he could not be from God because he does not keep the Sabbath. Others said that a sinner could not produce such signs. Dissension broke out and to obviate the dilemma the Pharisees asked the man about his own opinion of Jesus, to which he responded: 'He is a prophet.'

The 'Pharisees' are now replaced by the 'Jews' as interrogators, possibly a reflection of later controversy between Christians and Jews, involving expulsions from the synagogue. They try to deny the miracle by denying that he had ever been blind. They summon the parents. The same questions are put to the parents as were put to the man himself by the neighbours and acquaintances. They question them about his identity and the reality of his blindness and how he was healed. The first question they answer affirmatively, acknowledging that he was their son and had been born blind. The second question they avoid answering because of fear of being expelled from the syn-

273. Jn 15:16.

agogue if they professed belief in Jesus as the Christ. They stated that their son was of age and could answer for himself.

Then they try, unsuccessfully, to bully the man into denying the miracle or condemning Jesus. They fail to do so and in the process show up their own blindness. They order him to give glory to God, a formula for confessing one's sinfulness (maybe intimidating him with the implication that his blindness was caused by his own or his parents' sins). As they grow more blind the man sees more and more. He states clearly in regard to himself that he had been blind and now he sees. In regard to Jesus he first states that he does not know that he is a sinner – responding to their accusation that he must be a sinner for breaking the Sabbath and implying that the man himself must know it. When they ask him again about how Jesus opened his eyes, he asks them if they want to become his disciples. There is typical Johannine irony here. Jesus had opened his eyes physically and spiritually. Now he proclaims this and asks if they want to become his disciples (and have their eyes opened too). Reacting furiously they proclaim that they are disciples of Moses and cynically tell the man that he can be Jesus' disciple. Then they go on to use the phrase by now well established in discussion about Jesus. *We know* is heard again in: '*We know* that God does not listen to sinners', '*We know* this man is a sinner' and '*We know* that God has spoken to Moses', but the very claim to know, with the full force of Johannine irony is turned round to reveal their ignorance: '*We do not know* where this man comes from'. In reply the man makes a devastating remark about their lack of religious discernment: 'He opened my eyes and *you don't know* where he comes from. *We know* that God does not listen to sinners. Ever since the beginning of the world it is unheard of for anyone to open the eyes of a man who was born blind. If this man were not from God he could do nothing.' Again *where from* is a key word in discussion about Jesus. In spite of repeated telling, they have to keep asking: 'How did he open your eyes?' If they knew where he came from they would not have to ask. Resorting to the defeated man's tactic they then stoop to personal abuse and assert that his blind condition resulted from sin, branding him 'steeped in sin', and expel him from the synagogue.

Hearing this Jesus seeks him out and puts the question to him: 'Do you believe in the Son of Man?' He responds to Jesus

with the address *kyrie*, Lord, which shows a deepening faith,
and asks: 'Who is he?' Jesus responds 'You have seen him and
he is the one talking to you'. This self revelation of Jesus, this
time in terms of the Son of Man, parallels Jesus' self revelation to
the Samaritan woman and evokes an equally positive response.
In his new found sight the man truly sees, confesses his faith,
and worships Jesus as Son of Man.

The references to expulsion from the synagogue, here and
elsewhere, reflect the experience of early Christians. The synagogue was not just a building for worship and scripture study. It
was a community with all the social networking and mutual dependence of a closely knit community. Expulsion would have
serious religious, social, cultural and economic consequences.

Jesus' comments on the blindness of the Pharisees are over-
heard by them and they take offence. Jesus responds by reminding them that since they boast of seeing when in fact they are
blind, their sin remains. This is an exact reversal of the opening
question about the sin that caused the man to be born blind.
'Who has sinned … that this man was born blind?' The 'sighted'
leaders are told: 'If you were blind you would have no sin.'

The outline of the stories in chapter five (at the Pool of
Bethesda) and nine (at the pool of Siloam) are very similar,
maybe pointing to a common origin at an earlier stage in transmission. In both cases the healing is at a pool, the 'medical history'
is given, Jesus takes the initiative, on the Sabbath, and accusations of breaking the Sabbath follow. Officials question the
healed person who at first does not know the healer. Jesus finds
the healed person and invites him to faith. In both cases there is
a reference to some connection between sin and suffering. Jesus'
defence is that he does the work of his Father or of the One who
sent him. However, the Johannine theology and dramatic technique has used both stories very skilfully to portray two opposite reactions on the part of the healed.

5. THE MODEL SHEPHERD AND THE DOOR OF THE SHEEPFOLD
(Jn 10:1-21)

Jesus continues his commentary on leadership with a solemn
'Amen, amen, I say to you …' declaration about the nature of
leadership and how it should be acquired and exercised. The
Pharisees have claimed that they see, but they are blind. Soon
the listeners (the Pharisees) will hear Jesus' words but remain

deaf to them, because they do not belong to his sheep, who alone hear his voice.[274] Being thus blind to the light and deaf to the voice of the revealer, they can neither believe in him nor in the works the Father does through him.

Keeping in mind the fact that the chapter and verse divisions are not part of the original text, one can see here an artificial chapter division. Not only does the division cut the discourse off from its setting in the dispute with the authorities about good and bad leadership, it places the 'Amen, amen ...' declaration at the beginning, whereas such declaratory statements usually come in the middle of a passage. The division was obviously made because of an apparent change of topic and an obvious change in narrative genre. Scholars have noticed and reacted differently to this change. Some have suggested a 'rearrangement' of the text, putting verses 1-18 after verse 28, others have seen verses 1-18 and verse 16 as insertions into the text by a later editor.

These and other suggestions reflect a sensitivity to text, topic, style and genre and an awareness of the history of the development of the traditions and stages of textual composition. However, there can be a tendency to overlook or underestimate the fact that the text as it now stands is integrated into the overall gospel and reflects what has gone before and is in turn reflected in what follows. Ulrich Busse puts the case against insertions and rearrangements succinctly, quoting as support Haenchen and Jülicher:

> ...the close interlacing of all parts of the text of chapter 10 with the wider context renders any version of rearrangement unlikely. It is not just Haenchen who thinks that the time for 'rearrangement hypotheses' is over. Already Jülicher suggested that: 'Critics all too often use as criteria their own sense of logic, their attention to detail and their desire for a correct flow of thought. In short, they call for a gospel written the way they would have written it.'[275]

The genre of 10:1-18 has also been the subject of a good deal of attention. It has been variously understood as allegory, simili-

---

274. There has not been any indication of a change of audience since they were last mentioned.
275. U. Busse, 'Open Questions on John 10', *The Shepherd Discourse of John 10 and its Context*, 9, quoting Haenchen, *Johannesevangelium*, 57, et al.

tude, parable, proverb, riddle, concept and image.[276] It is called
a *paroimia* in the text, a term used again three times in chapter
sixteen.[277] This reflects the Hebrew use of the *mashal* or the
Aramaic *matla*, capturing the more enigmatic element of *mashal/
matla*. It covers various forms of speech, figurative discourse,
parables, riddles, aphorisms and so forth, a form of speech that
both conceals the truth from the spiritually obtuse and reveals it
to the spiritually open on the way to fuller enlightenment, as it
does when translated in the synoptics as *parabolê* in the broad
sense of a 'figure of speech'.

The sense of Jesus' speech, at first hidden and obscure (10:6),
becomes in a second moment more transparent as the parable is
explained (10:7-16); it attains its greatest clarity at the moment of
his glorification when Jesus will speak openly – *parrêsia laleo* –
John 16:25, 29 – when the Counsellor, the Holy Spirit will be
sent, all things will be taught, all that he has said will be brought
to remembrance (14:26). Not only the term itself but above all
the way it is used, as opposed to speaking openly, shows some
close similarity to the use of *parabolê* in the synoptics.[278]

The apparent lack of clear definition of genre in Jn 10:1-18
points to the individuality of the author who really is introducing an image field which can be approached from many angles
and applied to many aspects of the reality under review. This
enables the author to connect Jesus a number of times with the
various metaphors of keeping sheep and so to use them for the
purpose of identifying who Jesus really is. In contrast to his
counterparts, variously described as thief, stranger and hireling,
Jesus really is who he claims to be.[279] The imagery is shared with
the synoptics, but the genre is clearly not that of a synoptic parable of the kingdom which would contain some or all of the ele-

---

276. The Greek word *paroimia*, parable, figure, or image is often used to translate
the Hebrew *mashal* which can mean a proverb or riddle. The LXX tends to translate *mashal* as *parabolê*, like a parable in the synoptics, but *paroimia* becomes more
common in the later Greek Old Testament. *Paroimia* tends to capture the more
enigmatic element of *mashal*. It is used in Prov 1:1; 25:1 and five times in Sirach.
However, Sir 47:17 uses *paroimia* and *parabolê* synonymously.
277. Jn 16:25 (twice), 29.
278. M. Sabbe, 'John 10 and its Relationship to the Synoptic Gospels' in *The
Shepherd Discourse of John 10 and its Context*, 91. cf Mk 4:10-11//Mt 13:10-11//Lk
8:9-10.
279. cf U. Busse, *op. cit.*, 11.

ments of seeking, finding, discovery, surprise, mystery, suspense, and reversal of established values and perceptions.[280]

U. Busse elaborates on the integration of chapter ten into the dynamic at work in this part of the gospel.

> ... the confrontation with Jesus' deeds (compare the Sabbath healing, chapter 5, with the healing of the blind man, chapter 9), which issues in either salvation or judgement, extends over a number of chapters ... Verbally (*rhêma*) the peak of the argument is reached in the chapter about the shepherd and after the Lazarus miracle (*ergon*) his death is decided in principle by the people's leaders. Thus in chapter ten the confrontation between Jesus and the leaders of the people, which started in chapter five, moves towards its first climax. This takes place after Jesus' refutation as illegitimate and wrong of the seemingly legitimate claim of the Pharisees to lead Israel. The basis for this is found in 9:40, where Jesus' deeds result in a separation of the ways leading to salvation on the one hand and to disaster on the other.[281]

The images/metaphors of shepherd and door are employed to illustrate the theme of good and bad leadership, legitimate and illegitimate authority. They are prompted by the reaction of the authorities to the healing of the blind man. The blindness of the Pharisees is reflected in the listeners' inability to hear.[282] The dialectic between pairs of opposites furthers the ongoing dialectic of the gospel. The contrasting patterns of activity illustrate the dialectic. On the one hand there is secrecy, violence and cowardice and on the other openness, caring and courage. The robber, bandit and hireling, summed up as 'the stranger', stands out against the good/model shepherd, selflessly laying down his life, no stranger but someone on intimate terms with the sheep. They know him and identify his voice and he knows them by name.

The exchanges with the Pharisees, the Jews, and the crowd punctuate the discourse, as was the case in chapter six with the discourse on the Bread of Life, and the discourses on light and water at the feast of Tabernacles. The 'interventions' are part of the overall rhythm/dialectic of the gospel, not editorial inser-

---

280. J. D. Turner, 'The History of Religions Background to John 10', in *The Shepherd Discourse of John 10*, 33-52, 43, following the argument of J. D. Crossan, *In Parables: The Challenge of the Historical Jesus*, New York, 1963.
281. U. Busse, *op. cit.*, 8.
282. Jn 9:41; 10:6.

tions, as sometimes alleged. This is particularly the case in chapters five to eleven where they highlight the growing tension, division and hostility among the listeners. The use of *palin*, ('again') in Jn 10:19 illustrates the fact of the ongoing nature of the reactions.

The Shepherd (Jn 10:1-6, 8, 10-16)

The image field is approached through a negative assessment of shepherds who climb over walls in the dark to steal sheep. The rabbis had a very poor regard for shepherds. They excluded them from being judges or giving evidence on the grounds of being dishonest and pasturing their flocks on other shepherds' land.[283] They classed them with the marginalised and sinful people. This assessment is not unlike that of the Greek world in which the mythological figure of Hermes was presented as the former stealer of cattle from Apollo, but now gatekeeper of the fold to prevent other shepherds who were thieves and rogues from entering – a poacher turned gamekeeper scenario.[284] Jesus enters the image field through this negative view which he is now applying to the current leadership. Against this he will develop the positive aspects of shepherding.

First of all the assumption of leadership should be, to use contemporary language, 'up front' and transparent, without selfish or ill-inspired motives. This is the significance of the shepherd entering by the door or gate, not climbing over the wall. The question immediately rises in the mind of the reader: 'To whom is Jesus referring when he speaks of those who climb over the wall as the robbers and bandits?' The word *kleptês* simply means 'robber' but *lêstês* has a broader meaning. It is used by Mark to describe a robber in the expression 'a robbers' den' but Luke uses it to describe Barabbas who was a bandit/outlaw and a political agitator.[285] The *kleptês* comes to steal, slaughter and destroy, a good description of the dishonest, life-negating work of the sheep-stealer.[286] But the commentary opens onto a broader canvas. Using the term *lêstês* in addition to the straightforward

---

283. *b. Sanhedrin*, 25b.
284. J. D. Turner, *op. cit.*, 33-52; J. Jeremias, *poimên*, *TDNT*, 6, 1968, 487-8.
285. Mk 11:17; Lk 23:13, 19.
286. R. E. Brown, *John*, Vol I, 386, n. 10 points out that the verb used for 'slaughter', *thuein* is not the usual verb for 'kill' which is *apokteinein*. *Thuein* is the verb used for slaughtering in the context of sacrifice, so there may be a reference/allusion here to the priests and their ritual activity of slaughtering.

kleptês may make one think of the false messiahs and political agitators past, present and future. Or it may be a general comment on the 'climbing over the wall' of the puppet religious and political system to which the people were subjected since Antiochus Epiphanes displaced the legitimate High Priest Onias III and sold the office to his brother Joshua who exchanged his Hebrew name for the Greek Jason.[287] Perhaps all of these considerations are in the background and it is demanding too much of the text to press it into meaning one group rather than another. The comments are probably meant to be generic and interpreted and applied as hearer or reader sees a relevance to one's own situation.

On the positive side, 'shepherd' was a long established metaphor for gods and leaders in the Greek and Ancient Near Eastern World. The shepherd's crook was used widely as a symbol of royal authority. In Greek literature Apollo, Hermes and Hermes' son Pan are featured as shepherds. Hermes, son of the Father God, Zeus, is also the guardian of doors and access ways, gatekeeper/doorkeeper of temples and sanctuaries and the *psychopompos*, the one who accompanied souls from their bodies to celestial bliss or unbreakable bonds. Apollo, as seen from the epithet *Agyieis*, was also regarded as a gatekeeper preventing evil from entering the city. In Egypt the Pharaoh carried the shepherd's crook as symbol of authority, together with the *ankh*, the key to eternal life (later adopted by Coptic Christians as their form of the cross). The Egyptian god of the underworld Osiris is described as a shepherd. The king in ancient Mesopotamia was frequently so described and in the hymn to Enlil, the All Beneficent, Enlil is called shepherd (in line 84).[288] Ancient representations of the birth of Mithra show a man with a shepherd's staff standing looking on or a group of shepherds watching from behind a rock.[289]

Philo idealised the shepherd image seeing the human faculty *nous* as the shepherd of the irrational powers of the soul, and the divine *logos* as the nourisher of the world.[290] In the Gnostic tradi-

---

287. This action caused the Essenes to depart totally from the Jerusalem-Temple sphere of influence and set up the Qumran community in the desert near the Dead Sea, seeing themselves as the legitimate inheritors of the promises and the messianic community in waiting.

288. J. D. Turner, *op. cit.*, 38.

289. R. E. Brown, *The Birth of the Messiah*, Anchor Bible Reference Library, 420.

290. J. Jeremias, *poimên*, *TDNT*, 6, 1968, 487-8.

tion the shepherd/redeemer is the door to the world of light. 'The soul learns about her light ... and runs into her fold, while her shepherd stands at the door.'[291] This broad mythological background provided images and language for many strands of thought and philosophical and religious teaching. No specific dependence on any document is necessary to explain its use either in Christian or Gnostic circles, nor is it possible to pronounce on the exact nature and direction of mutual influences. However, if one sees a gnostic influence, or just compares the Johannine and Hermetic approaches, an interesting scenario emerges. It is summed up very well by J. D. Turner.

> If the shepherd discourse were written with a Hermes figure in view, then certain points would be scored over Hermes, since Jesus was more than Hermes: not only a divine shepherd, but *the* true shepherd who gives his life for the sheep; not only a guardian and shower of ways, but *the* very way, truth and life themselves; not only the keeper of sacred doors, but *the* very door itself; not only the leader of souls to their post-mortem destination, but *the* grantor of eternal life; not only a son of god, but *the* Son of God.[292]

This broader experience of shepherds and shepherding had in part its origin in the experience of shepherds in the areas surrounding cities in the ancient world. They had a quasi urban existence, living on the margins of organised urban society. The Israelites on the other hand had a certain concept of the city as a place of luxury and paganism. They idealised their experience in the desert and saw it in terms of the nomadic lifestyle of the shepherds who accompanied their flocks into the heart of the mountains and uninhabited places. The nomadic experience of the people during the wandering in the desert lent itself very readily to the idealisation of this imagery. Whereas some influence of the broader world experience of shepherding may be in the background of Jn 10, the main influence is from the Israelite experience.

The understanding of God as shepherd of Israel is deeply rooted in biblical and apocryphal tradition. Jacob blessed the sons of Joseph: 'May God who has been my shepherd from my birth until this day ... bless these boys.'[293] Moses prayed: 'Let the

---

291. Nag Hammadi Codices, VI 32.
292. J. D. Turner, *op. cit.*, 51f.
293. Gen 48:15 (JB).

Lord ... appoint someone over the congregation who shall go out before them and come in before them, who shall lead them out and bring them in, so that the congregation of the Lord may not be like sheep without a shepherd.'[294] Ps 22 (23) opens with: 'The Lord is my shepherd there is nothing I shall want' and goes on to describe God as a shepherd leading the flock to pasture and as a host preparing a feast. Ps 79 (80) begins with the plea: 'O shepherd of Israel, hear us, you who lead Joseph's flock' and Ps 99 (100) proclaims: 'We are his people, the sheep of his pasture, enter his gates with thanksgiving.'

The king was designated shepherd of the people. David, a former shepherd himself, was told 'You are the man who shall be shepherd of my people Israel, you shall be the leader of Israel.'[295] The judges too were called shepherds of the people.[296] From this the image of the shepherd-king was to emerge. Even the pagan king Cyrus was spoken of as a shepherd for the people because he liberated them from the exile and facilitated the restoration of Jerusalem and the Temple. 'I am he who says of Cyrus, my shepherd – he will fulfil my whole purpose, saying of Jerusalem, "Let her be rebuilt" and of the Temple, "Let your foundation be laid".'[297]

The prophets condemned severely the leaders who failed to exercise a competent and caring shepherding role over the flock of God. Ezechiel condemned their failure as he castigated them for feeding themselves rather than the sheep, for not looking after the stray, bandaging the wounded, or making the weak strong, but leaving them as prey to the wild animals.[298] In response to their failure God promised to undertake the shepherding, and to raise up a new David who would be a good shepherd. 'I myself will pasture my sheep, I myself will show them where to rest – It is the *Lord YHWH* who speaks. I shall look for the lost one, bring back the stray, bandage the wounded and make the weak strong ... I shall be a true shepherd to them ... I mean to raise up one shepherd, my servant David, and put him in charge of them and he will pasture them.'[299] Jeremiah also proclaimed God's condemnation of the shepherds 'who allow

294. Num 27:16f.
295. 2 Sam 5:2.
296. 2 Sam 7:7.
297. Isa 44:28.
298. Ezek 34.
299. Ezek 34:15, 16, 23 (JB).

246   THE GOSPEL OF JOHN

the flock of my pasture to be destroyed and scattered'. The condemnation is followed by God's promise to provide shepherds
for the flock. 'Woe to the shepherds who destroy and scatter the
sheep of my pasture! ... I myself will gather the remnant of my
flock ... I will bring them back to their fold ... I will raise up
shepherds over them who will shepherd them, and they shall
not fear any longer, or be dismayed, nor shall any be missing,
says the Lord.'[300] Micah and Zechariah also spoke of a future
Davidic figure who would shepherd the people, and keep them
together under one shepherd.[301] This imagery plays a part also
in non-canonical books such as Psalms of Solomon, 2 Baruch
and the Damascus Document.[302]

The sentiment of Moses' prayer is recalled in the synoptic
tradition when Jesus had compassion on the crowd who followed him out in the countryside, because they were harassed
and dejected like sheep without a shepherd.[303] The comparison
of the crowd to 'sheep without a shepherd' is a powerful evoc-
ation of the scattered and uncared for flock.[304] Luke portrays
Jesus' comforting words: 'There is no need to be afraid, little
flock, for it has pleased your Father to give you the kingdom', a
saying that evokes the image of a shepherd-king.[305] The Lucan
parable of the shepherd seeking the lost sheep emphasises the
care of the shepherd for maintaining the integrity of the flock,
shown in the concern for the straying individual.[306] Matthew
portrays Jesus' warning to the disciples about the effect of his
coming death in terms of the scattering of the flock: 'I shall strike
the shepherd and the sheep of the flock will be scattered.'[307] The
Matthean description of false prophets as 'wolves in sheep's
clothing' evokes the tradition of seeing the threat to the flock in
terms of wolves or other wild animals. The imagery of bad shepherds consigning the sheep to the wolves as described by
Jeremiah, Ezekiel, Zephaniah and Zechariah is recalled in Paul's
address at Miletus to the elders of Ephesus where he expresses
his concern that after his departure 'wolves will invade you and

---

300. Jer 23:1,4.
301. Mic 5:3; Zech 13:7-9; cf Jer 3:15,23:4-6; Ezek 3423f; 37:24.
302. Ps Sol 17:24,40; 2 Bar 77:13-17; CD 13:7-9.
303. Mt 9:36; Mk 6:34.
304. Mk 6:34.
305. Lk 12:32.
306. Lk 15:3-7.
307. Mt 26:31.

have no mercy on the flock'.[308] A similar concern is expressed two centuries later in the Jewish apocalyptic writing: 'Desert us not as a shepherd (deserts) his flock in the power of harmful wolves.'[309] Reflecting on the loss of Jerusalem and the Temple the author of 2 Baruch wrote more or less at the same time as the fourth gospel:

> For the shepherds of Israel have perished, and the lamps which gave light are extinguished, and the fountains from which we used to drink have withheld their streams. Now we have been left in the darkness and in the thick forest and in the aridness of the desert … Shepherds and lanterns and fountains came from the law and when we go away, the law will abide. If you, therefore, look upon the law and are intent upon wisdom, then the lamp will not be wanting and the shepherd will not give way and the fountain will not dry up.[310]

These readings emphasise protection, caring, feeding, gathering together, seeking the lost and not losing any of the flock. They show how widespread the imagery of shepherding was in the ancient world, and in the New Testament itself. Already in St John's gospel Jesus has been presented as one who provides life-giving food and drink – the wine of the kingdom, the water of life and the bread from heaven. He has sought out the lost, made the weak strong and bandaged the wounded, as seen from his encounter with the Samaritan woman and her fellow towns-people, his healing of the 'weak' man at Bethesda and the blind man at Siloam. He has expressed concern about not losing any part of what was given into his care. This will be a major concern in his final prayer at the Last Supper when he will speak of not losing any, except the one who chose to be lost.[311] All this is summed up in the work of the *model* or *ideal* or *good* shepherd, *ho poimên ho kalos*.

Here now the care for gathering the flock and protecting them comes to the fore. Jesus defines the essence of the sheep-shepherd relationship as following the shepherd because of recognising his voice as he calls them by name. This emphasises familiarity of knowledge, love, care and commitment in contrast to self interest and dishonesty. 'Leading out' (*exagein*) appears in

---

308. Mt 7:15; Jer 23:1-8; Ezek 22:27; 34:7,25; Zeph 3:3; Zech 10:2f; 11:4-17; Acts 26:29.
309. 4 Ezra 5:18.
310. 2 Bar 77:11,13-16.
311. Jn 17:12.

the important shepherding texts of the Old Testament for 'lead-ing out to pasture'. Leading the flock out to pasture was a very significant event in a nomadic culture. It meant leading the flock into the mountains with all the hazards of wild animals, bandits, and possible danger from weather extremes. One of the earliest feasts, eventually incorporated in the Passover festival, was the preparation for the leading out to pasture of the flocks. It entailed the sacrifice of a lamb or goat and the sprinkling of the blood on the tent for protection. Moses prayed that God would 'appoint a leader for this community, to be at their head in all they do, a man who will lead them out and bring them in, so that the com-munity of YHWH may not be like sheep without a shepherd'.[312]

Recognising the voice of the shepherd when he *calls* one by name emphasises the shared knowledge of Jesus and his own. They know each other intimately. They have a relationship based on interpersonal knowledge, trust and love. He knows them by name, and they recognise his voice. This shared knowl-edge will figure significantly when Martha goes to Mary and says 'the Master is here and is *calling* you', and when he *calls* Lazarus by name from the tomb. When he addresses her by name, Mary Magdalene identifies him as the Risen Lord on Easter morning.

The Door (Gate) of the Sheepfold (Jn 10:7, 9)
The hearers did not understand the parable/imagery of the shepherd. Jesus returns to the image of the gate of the sheepfold, but changes its meaning, using another solemn 'Amen, Amen' declaration in which he proclaims himself the door or gate (*thura*) of the sheepfold.[313] Having described himself as the shepherd who enters through the gate, he now describes his role in terms of the gate. He is the gate to the pasture, that is to life, so

---

312. Num 27:17.
313. The Sahidic version, two Coptic mss and P45 read 'the shepherd' rather than 'the door/gate' in verse 7. This may be due to a copyist's attempt to align the image with the 'shepherd' in preceding verses. It is less likely that an original Aramaic word for shepherd was mistakenly translated as door/gate or that a copyist was aligning the image with a subsequent reference to door/gate in verse 9, especially since there is a difference in significance between both uses of the door/gate imagery, one being the door *to* the sheep, and the other the door *for* the sheep. Door/gate is the 'more difficult' reading and as such more likely to be original, the easier reading being always more likely to be a mistake or an at-tempt to harmonise or align a difficult one. cf R. E. Brown, *The Gospel According to John*, Vol I, 386; R. Schnackenburg, *op.cit.*, Vol II, 288.

that those who enter through him will have life to the full, a sentiment found in his farewell discourse: 'No one comes to the Father except through me.'[314] The expression 'go in and out' like 'opening and closing' is a Semitic parallelism signifying authority and the security of possession established in a relationship. Examples already quoted showed the widespread connection between the images of shepherd, doorkeeper (gatekeeper) and door (gate). The synoptic and Johannine traditions seem to draw from the same general tradition of imagery. The vocabulary is strikingly similar in the synoptic and Johannine sayings.[315] In the synoptic tradition Jesus speaks of the 'narrow gate' (*thura/pulê*) and the 'hard road' (*hodos*) that lead to life (salvation), and in the Johannine tradition he says, 'I am the door (gate)' and 'I am the way.'[316] Furthermore, the saying about entering the door and following the way to salvation in Matthew, is followed by a warning about false prophets who come in sheep's clothing but inwardly are ravening wolves. This is very close in sentiment and vocabulary both to John's evil shepherds who climb over the wall and to the hireling who runs away and abandons the sheep when he sees the wolf coming.[317]

The opening and closing of the door is an image that figures quite prominently in Jesus' teaching, especially in the parables of the kingdom. Entering through the door symbolises entering the kingdom and the role of the doorkeeper in opening or closing of the door is therefore very important. Peter is given the keys of the kingdom.[318] The foolish virgins knock on the locked door only to be told 'I do not know you.'[319] The wicked whom the householder *does not know*, (the shepherd *knows* his sheep!) appeal to their former friendship with the master of the house who has just locked the door. He responds saying, 'I do not know where you come from' and they find themselves locked out.[320] The servant who watches the door for his master's return is praised.[321] The unwilling master of the house when the friend

---

314. Jn 14:6.
315. entering, door/gate, being saved ; *eiserchomai, thura/pulê, sôzomenoi/sôthêsetai*.
316. Mt 7:13f; Lk 13:24. Luke, like John, uses *thura*, Mt uses *pulê* for gate, but the imagery is the same. Jn 10:7, 9; 14:6.
317. Mt 7:15; Jn 10:12f.
318. Mt 16:19.
319. Mt 25:11-13.
320. Lk 13:25-27.
321. Lk 12:36.

called at night does not want to open the door.[322] In his teaching on prayer Jesus says the door will be opened for the one who knocks.[323]

Laying down and taking up his life (Jn 10:17, 18)

Jesus returns to the imagery of the shepherd in order to spell out the price of shepherding, the commitment that knows no limits. The good shepherd lays down his life for his sheep. In this there is the great contrast with the hireling who runs away from danger. After five chapters of hostility and division Jesus is now clearly speaking of laying down his life for his sheep. Jesus, the pre-existent *Logos* made flesh, who has identified himself as 'I am', now declares: 'For this reason the Father loves me, because I lay down my life that I may take it up again. No one takes it from me but I lay it down of my own accord. I have power to lay it down, and I have power to take it up again; this charge I have received from my Father.'[324] In the following chapter Jesus will demonstrate in positive action how he lays down his life for his friend Lazarus by coming to restore his life in a situation where he will certainly face death. In that circumstance he proclaims himself the resurrection and the life. 'Laying down one's life' is seen in Mark's gospel as the purpose of the coming of the Son of Man: 'For the Son of Man did not come to be served but to serve and to give his life as a ransom for many' and in the farewell discourse in John Jesus states in the context of his commandment to 'love one another as I have loved you' that there is 'no greater love than to lay down one's life for one's friends'.[325] On Easter morning he will show how he has taken up again the life he laid down for the friend whom he loved and had called by name from the tomb.

The outcome. Division (Schisma) (Jn 10:19-21)

Again there follows another division (*schisma*) among the Jews, some saying he was possessed by a devil, some that he was out of his mind. Others, however, were saying that these were not the words of a demented person and that surely a devil could not open the eyes of a man born blind. This remark further ties the Good Shepherd discourse to the preceding chapter.

---

322. Lk 11:5-8.
323. Lk 11:9f.
324. Jn 10:17f.
325. Mk 10:45; Jn 15:12f.

The Feast of Dedication (Jn 10:22-39)

1. THE PLOT

The themes of Tabernacles and shepherding continue in the passage dealing with the Feast of Hanukkah. Sometimes called the Feast of Dedication or the Feast of Lights, *Hanukkah* was also called at times the Feast of Tabernacles of the Month of Chislev, a designation that brought out its close association with the Temple.[326] The terms *Hanukkah* (Hebrew) and *Enkainia* (Greek) are used for the dedication or consecration of the altar in the Tabernacle of the Exodus days, in the Temple of Solomon and in the Second Temple,[327] so the term is evocative of the consecration of all the houses of God in Israel's history. In this there is a bond between the feasts of Tabernacles and *Hanukkah*, and hence the term 'Tabernacles of the Month of Chislev'.[328]

Whereas Jn 10:1-21 looks back on the events of Jn 9 and the failure in leadership, Jn 10:22-39 looks ahead to the Feast of Dedication/*Hanukkah*. Sheep and shepherding which had been the subject of Jesus' teaching at Tabernacles played a part also in the Feast of Dedication, as the *haphtarah* or prophetic readings were about sheep and shepherds on the Sabbath nearest the feast, and Ezekiel 34, the flagship of shepherding texts in the Old Testament, was the reading for the second year of the cycle. In this way the image of the shepherd binds closely together the teaching on leadership arising from the healing and controversy at Tabernacles and the teaching at the forthcoming Feast of Dedication.

2. BACKGROUND TO THE FEAST

The feast recalls the building of a new altar and the rededication of the Temple when the Maccabees ended the Syrian occupation and destroyed the 'abomination of desolation'.[329] The Syrian ruler, Antiochus IV, Epiphanes, a title meaning, 'God made manifest', on assuming the Seleucid throne in Antioch in 175 BC, planned to extend his rule right down to Egypt. Consolidation of power, based on uniformity of culture and religion imposed by force, was his way of achieving his goal. He imposed

---

326. In Hebrew *Hanukkah*, dedication; in Greek *enkainia*, renewal. It is celebrated close to the Christian feast of Christmas.
327. Num 7:10f; 1 Kings 8:63; 2 Chr 7:5; Ezra 6:16.
328. 2 Macc 1:9.
329. Dan 9:27; cf Mt 24:15.

Hellenistic practices on the Jews. A corrupt element in the priesthood and aristocracy facilitated his venture. He built a gymnasium in Jerusalem, where Jews through mutilation of their genitals to hide their circumcision, expressed contempt for the mark on their bodies which set them apart as the people of the covenant. He deposed the legitimate High Priest, Onias III and sold the office to his brother Joshua, who took the Greek name Jason.[330] The Temple having been profaned by the placing of an idol of Ba'al Shamem, an oriental version of Olympian Zeus, on the altar of holocausts, the critical point was reached on 15th Chislev 167 BC when sacrifice was offered by a Jew in Modein to Olympian Zeus. Mattathias, followed by his son, Judas Maccabaeus, led the revolt that drove out the Syrians. The 'desolating sacrilege' was ended and a new altar built. The Temple was rededicated on 25th Chislev 164 BC, three years after the erection of the pagan altar.[331]

> They kept eight festal days with rejoicing, in the manner of the feast of Tabernacles, remembering how, not long before, at the time of the feast of Tabernacles, they had been living in the mountains and caverns like wild beasts. Then carrying branches, leafy boughs and palms, they offered hymns to him who had brought the cleansing of his own Holy Place to a happy outcome. They also decreed by public edict, ratified by vote, that the whole Jewish nation should celebrate those same days every year.[332]

The celebrations took on the rituals of Tabernacles, lasting eight days, chanting the Hallel and waving branches and palms in joyous processions. The continuity of this rededicated Second Temple and its altar with the Solomonic Temple and Moses' altar is stressed.

> Then the Lord will bring these things once more to light, and the glory of the Lord will be seen and so will the cloud, as it was revealed in the time of Moses and when Solomon prayed that the Holy Place might be gloriously hallowed ... As Moses had prayed to the Lord and fire had come down from

---

330. Some Jews co-operated, concealing their circumcision. Reactions against this 'paganisation' are seen in the abandoning of Jerusalem and the Temple by the Qumran community, the writing of the Book of Daniel, the emergence of the Hasidim, and the revolt of the Maccabees.
331. 1 Macc 1: 54; 4:41-46; 2 Macc 1:9; 6:1-7.
332. 2 Macc 10: 6-8.

heaven and burned up the sacrifice, so Solomon also prayed, and the fire from above burned up the holocausts.[333]

The feast celebrated the victory of the Jewish people over the pagan foreign oppressor, and also over the renegade element in their midst, the Hellenising priests and aristocracy. That Hellenising element provoked a series of reactions represented by the Essene rejection of Jerusalem and its temple cult, the movement of the Hasidim, the armed revolt of the Maccabees and the apocalyptic Book of Daniel. The very identity of the people and their religious way of life was at stake in the crisis.

The name of the feast, Dedication, or 'consecration', signifies an anointing and setting aside for exclusive worship and service of God. Just as 'Siloam' was taken to refer to 'the one sent', so here, though not so explicitly stated, as Jesus immerses himself in the celebration of 'Dedication', there are messianic overtones as the crowd wonder if he is possibly 'the anointed one', the Messiah.

As Jesus is walking in the Portico of Solomon during the Feast an exchange takes place in two parts between himself and the Jews. The first arises from their request that he take them out of suspense and tell them plainly if he is the Messiah, the second is a violent reaction to his response. He points out that the *works* he has done in the Father's name bear witness to him. They have not believed because they are not his sheep. Up to this point in the gospel, when Jesus criticised his audience for not accepting him, he says that it is because they do not know the Father who sent him, or they do not love the Father, or the word is not in them, or they are afraid to come into the light lest they be exposed because their deeds are evil, and no one can come to him unless drawn the Father. The reason he now gives for their unbelief sums up all the aforementioned reasons in the language of shepherding, 'because you are not my sheep'.

The qualities of Jesus' flock and their reward are now put in terms of shepherd and sheep. The flock has been given to him by the Father, no one can snatch them away. They hear his voice, he knows them and they follow him. He promises them eternal life. His promise has been made throughout the gospel. It will be dramatically illustrated in the raising of Lazarus when Jesus proclaims himself the resurrection and the life and promises those who believe in him that even if they die they shall live.

---

333. 2 Macc 2:8-12; cf Lev 9:24; 2 Chr 7:1.

Throughout the gospel the unity of Father and Son has been emphasised. The union in divinity was revealed in the prologue in
the statements that 'the Word was with God and the Word was
God' and that the Son is 'ever in the bosom of the Father'. The
many references to doing the Father's will, carrying out the *work*
he was given to do, doing what he has seen the Father doing and
saying what he has heard from the Father emphasise the union
of wills between Father and Son. The statements that rejecting
the Son implies rejecting the Father who sent him, and honouring the Son implies honouring the Father, further illustrate the
union in divinity and identity of purpose between Father and
Son. Jesus sums up this relationship in the words: 'The Father
and I are one.' 'Their oneness is such that ... the words and
works of the one are the words and works of the other.
Nevertheless, the evangelist always safguards the distinction
between the persons. "However close and indissoluble the
union of the Father and the Son (and of the Son and believers), it
is never a fusion but a communion".'[334]

After his healing work at the pool of Bethesda when he said
'My Father *works* till now and I *work*', the listeners accused him
of blasphemy for making himself equal to God. Here when he
proclaims: 'The Father and I are one', they again accuse him of
blasphemy and take up stones to throw at him. He speaks of the
good (noble, *kalos*) *work* he has done and asks them for which of
his works do they wish to stone him. The term 'good/noble' re-
echoes the '*good* or *noble*' shepherd for which the term *kalos* was
also used. For which of his shepherding actions or duties are
they going to stone him?

His response repeats the same basic claim. He does his
Father's *works*, and if they do not find it possible to believe him,
they should believe the *works* because they show that 'The
Father is in me and I am in the Father.'[335]

If those to whom the word was addressed are called gods,
what about the one who was *consecrated* and *sent* into the world.
This is another argument from the smaller to the greater example, like the argument about circumcision on the Sabbath. It
could be paraphrased: 'If the ones who were only addressed by
God are called 'gods', how much more fitting it is to call the one
who was consecrated and sent into the word by that same title.'

---

334. G. Rossé, *op. cit.*, 27, and quoting X. Leon-Dufour, *Lettura del Vangelo secondo Giovanni*, Vol I, 507.
335. Jn 10:34-38.

'Here the christological confession that Jesus is Son of God from eternity finds its subsequent legitimation because the shepherd's caring attitude, which leads to his giving up himself, is seen to have revealed God's love for the world.'[336] Here the entire content of the gospel to date is summed up. The Word became flesh and dwelt among us. God so loved the world that he sent his only son that those who believe in him might not perish but have eternal life. On him the Father has set his seal. He does and says everything he learned from his Father. He is the Revealer *par excellence*. He is the only Son ever at the Father's side who has made him known.[337]

Again their efforts to arrest him failed. This time the narrator does not state that his *hour* had not yet come, perhaps because it is about to come, (particularly in an earlier stage of the formation of the gospel, when the account of the public ministry may have concluded at the end of chapter ten).

3. JOHN (THE BAPTIST): FINAL REPORT (10:40-42)

The departure of Jesus from the Temple and his withdrawal across the Jordan seem to mark the closure of his public ministry. This sense of closure is further emphasised by the reference to John the Baptist which forms an inclusion with the opening of the ministry. It shows the increasing following of Jesus and the fulfilment of the prophecy of John in his regard. For these reasons some scholars believe that this marked the end of the public ministry of Jesus in an earlier stage of the composition of the gospel and that the story moved from here to the Sanhedrin meeting at which the High Priest proclaimed that it is better for one man to die for the people than that the whole nation should perish. This is a fulfilment of what Jesus said about the shepherd laying down his life for his sheep and a comment on the salvific nature of his death, displaying the brilliance of Johannine irony on both counts.[338] It may have been even more obvious if the meeting took place at this point in an earlier stage of the gospel formation.

Furthermore the noticeable softening of attitude to the ordinary Jews in the next two chapters up to the Sanhedrin trial would seem to favour the view that these chapters come from

---

336. U. Busse, *op. cit.*, 16.
337. Jn 1:18.
338. Jn 11:47ff.

another stage in the formation of the gospel.[339] However, they are now integrated into the gospel text as it stands. This can be seen, for example, from the reference back to the opening of the eyes of the blind man when the friends of the bereaved family of Lazarus surmised that the one who opened the eyes of the blind man could have saved him from dying[340] and from the *calling* to Mary and Lazarus in the manner of the Good Shepherd. They hear his voice and come to him, Mary from her house, Lazarus from his tomb. (There is a play on the words *voice* and *calling* both made from the same root of the Greek word *phônê*).[341] The opening words of chapter eleven referring to an invalid/sick/ weak person, *tis asthenôn*, call to mind Jesus' healing of one of the 'crowd of sick', *plêthos tôn asthenountôn*, at the Pool of Bethesda, and the sequel to it when his critics first desired to kill him. This time they will succeed.

---

339. Jn 11:19, 31, 33, 36, 45; 12:9, 11.
340. Jn 11:37.
341. Jn 11: 28, 43. *ho didaskalos phônei se; phônê megalê ekraugasen.*

The Raising of Lazarus (Jn 11:1-54)

1. THE PLOT: JESUS THE RESURRECTION AND THE LIFE

The sense of foreboding and the threats to Jesus' life which came to a climax when he 'escaped' from the Temple and went over the Jordan, set the scene for the raising of Lazarus, a life-giving act which resulted in Jesus' own death. Thomas spelled out the mortal danger for Jesus and his disciples from the Jews who wanted to stone him if they returned to Judaea. However, Jesus put himself in the situation of laying down his life for his friend. When he announced his intention of going up to Judaea again, Thomas called the Twin, on hearing his reason for going, said prophetically: 'Let us also go that we may die with him.'[342] However, Jesus did not see the death of Lazarus or the threat to himself as the end of the story but looked beyond it to its real purpose, the glory of God, the glorification of the Son of God and the faith of the disciples.[343]

The story is linked into the narrative plot of the gospel through the reactions on the one hand of those who report the event to the authorities and bring about the trial and sentencing of Jesus, and on the other hand through the enthusiasm of the various elements of the crowd that made up the triumphal entry into Jerusalem, some being witnesses to the raising of Lazarus, others coming to see the one who had been raised.[344] Thematically it brings together and highlights the christological claims and titles of Jesus at the climax of his ministry and on the eve of his *hour* of glorification. The titles 'Lord' and 'Son of God' emphasise the high christology of the story, while his affection for Martha, Mary and Lazarus, and the comment of the by-standers at the tomb when they saw him weep 'see how much he loved him', emphasise his humanity, evident in his warm affection in a network of relationships.[345]

The theme of 'life' permeates the gospel and here in the story of the raising of Lazarus it stands in stark contrast to death. Both are manifest in the raising of Lazarus and the resulting recommendation of the High Priest that Jesus must die for the people.

342. Jn 11:16.
343. Jn 11:4, 15.
344. Jn 12:9, 17.
345. The references to Jesus' affection for Lazarus have led some scholars to speculate that Lazarus was the 'beloved disciple'. The term *philein* means to love in the sense of having affection for someone.

In the monologue following the discussion with Nicodemus Jesus had said: 'God loved the world so much that he gave his only Son that those who believe in him may not perish but may have eternal life.'[346] In his defence following the healing of the cripple at the Pool of Bethesda he said: 'As the Father raises the dead and gives them life, so also the Son gives life to whomever he wishes.'[347] On the same occasion he proclaimed: 'An (the) *hour* is coming when all who are in their graves will hear his voice and will come forth – those who have done right unto the resurrection of life.'[348] Following the cure of the blind man at the Pool of Siloam and the hostile reaction of the authorities, Jesus said 'the good shepherd lays down his life for his sheep ... I lay down my life for my sheep ... For this reason the Father loves me, because I lay down my life in order to take it up again. No one takes it from me, but I lay it down of my own accord. I have power to lay it down, and I have power to take it up again.'[349] The call back to Judaea to the dying Lazarus and his family puts these words and claims of Jesus to the test. Now at the death of Lazarus he proclaims: 'I am the Resurrection and the Life, the one who believes in me even though he dies will live.'[350]

The themes of light and darkness which permeate the gospel provide context and mood in this story. Light and life, and their opposites, darkness and death, have been evident throughout the gospel beginning in the prologue where the motif was introduced: 'In him was life and the life was the light of humanity. The light shines in the darkness and the darkness did not overpower it.'[351] At the pool of Siloam Jesus showed himself to be truly the light of the world through the powerful sign of opening the eyes of the man born into darkness, a feat never achieved since the beginning of the world. Jesus the Light of the World brings light to the darkness and so those who walk with him walk in the light of day. Now, having reminded the disciples that those who walk during the day do not stumble because they see the light of the world, in contrast to those who walk at night

346. Jn 3:16.
347. Jn 5:21.
348. Jn 5:28f; cf Jn 4:21, 23. Note the use of the term '*hour*' in ' *an* hour is coming in which' (*erchetai hôra en hê*). It could be translated '*the* hour in which', if one sees the phrase as an idiom in which the relative pronoun gives the value of a definite article retrospectively to the antecedent noun.
349. Jn 10:11, 15, 17f.
350. Jn 11:25.
351. Jn 1:4.

and stumble because the light is not in them, he sets out for the tomb of Lazarus where he will show himself to be the resurrection and the life. The friends of the bereaved family remark that the one who opened the eyes of the man born blind could have saved this man from death, linking the themes of light and life and setting the scene for Jesus' gift of life to the one laid in the tomb, following his gift of light to the one born in darkness.[352]

As happened in the case of the opening of the eyes of the blind man, the scene, or rather series of scenes, surrounding the raising of Lazarus, leads on the one hand to belief, recognition and discipleship and on the other to unbelief, rejection and condemnation. This 'schism' has its result – the condemnation of the Good Shepherd whose task was to gather together the scattered sheep and to lay down his life for them. Ironically, however, he will declare that when he has been lifted up, a reference both to crucifixion and his return to the Father in glory, he will draw all to himself. By dying for them the shepherd will gather all the sheep into the fold.[353]

The raising of Lazarus is the climax of the public ministry, the sign *par excellence*. It replaces the synoptic account of the cleansing of the Temple as Jesus' final challenge, the catalyst bringing about his trial *in absentia* by the Sanhedrin, which led in turn to his arrest, Roman trial and crucifixion. It is both the prologue to Jesus' passion and the foreshadowing of his resurrection. It brings his ministry to a climax and precipitates his *hour*.

2. The Literary Form

The story in its early stage of development probably resembled the synoptic stories of the raising of the widow's son at Naim[354] and the raising of the daughter of Jairus.[355] The skeleton of these stories consists of an appeal to Jesus, the grief of the mourners with an emphasis on their tears, the moving of Jesus to pity, sometimes also to annoyance or anger, the raising of the dead and the reaction of the witnesses.[356] These same elements are present in the Johannine account of the raising of Lazarus, but the skeleton is fleshed out quite differently and the interpretation is thoroughly Johannine in style and theology. In the synop-

---

352. Jn 11:37.
353. Jn 12:32.
354. Lk 7:11-16.
355. Mt 9:18-19, 23-26; Mk 5:22-24, 35-43.
356. G. Rochais, *Les récits de résurrection des morts dans le Nouveau Testament*, 15.

tic gospels Jesus' 'miraculous' activity is largely interpreted in the light of prophetic expectation, particularly that of Isaiah. This is particularly evident from such passages as Jesus' response to the messengers of John the Baptist who asked him if he was truly the one to come, and his programmatic sermon in Nazareth.[357] In his response to the messengers of the Baptist, for example, Jesus replied with a mixture of quotations from Isaiah: 'Go and tell John what you have heard and seen. The blind see, the lame walk, the lepers are cleansed, the deaf hear, *the dead are raised*, and the poor have the good news preached to them.'[358] In the gospel of John, on the other hand, the skeleton is fleshed out in a very dramatic style and presented in Johannine theological, christological and soteriological language which is articulated by the narrator and the characters in the story. In the words of R. E. Brown: 'The miracle has been made to serve the purpose of Johannine theology.'[359] Instead of a sign followed by an explanatory discourse or debate, the raising of Lazarus is interpreted beforehand in the introduction, conversations and prayer of Jesus that precede the sign.

Some commentators have suggested that the raising of Lazarus is a theological statement formulated in the light of Jesus' own resurrection and put together from Luke's accounts of Martha and Mary,[60] the rich man and Lazarus,[61] the widow's son at Naim,[62] and the synoptic accounts of the daughter of Jairus.[63] If one were to embark on this line of argument, would it not be equally, or even more plausible, to argue that a synoptic-style account of the raising of Lazarus could have given rise both to the parable of the rich man and Lazarus in Luke and the raising of Lazarus in John? However, such discussion is hypothetical and can distract from, or altogether avoid, the radical call to faith in the actual Johannine account as it stands. Sandra Schneiders wisely warns that, 'the fusion of the history of the earthly Jesus with the history of the Johannine community is so complete that it is virtually impossible to distinguish, much less,

357. Mt 11:5; Lk 4:16-22.
358. Mt 11:5; cf Isa 26:19; 29:18ff; 35:5f; 61:1.
359. R. E. Brown, *The Gospel According to John*, Vol I, 430.
360. Lk 10:38-42.
361. Lk 16:19-31.
362. Lk 7:11-17.
363. Mt 9:18-19, 23-26; Mk 5:21-24, 35-43; Lk 8:40-42, 49-56.

separate them.'[364] The Lazarus story is more than a 'post resurrection' story, seeing Lazarus as 'exhibit A' of the resurrection,
to quote B. Witherington.[365] Lazarus is not raised to 'glorified
life' but restored to 'this' life, emphasising the value of this life,
lived in faith. Jesus is the resurrection (of the dead) but also the
life (of the living). The raising of Lazarus emphasises the value
of 'here and now' faith-filled living, as a preliminary to resurrection when death comes. This is graphically illustrated by the fact
that Lazarus rose still bound with the wrappings of the tomb
from which he had to be released by the command of Jesus and
the service of others. M. Harris states: 'Before Jesus' resurrection, it could be said that "the dead are restored to life…"'. After
his resurrection it can be said "the dead will be raised immor-
tal".'[366]

Distance, location and movement from place to place enhance the narrative. Distance from the sick man and the distraught sisters, coming a journey into mortal danger, Martha's
going from the house to the place where she met Jesus, and subsequently Mary's running from the house and the company to
the same place to meet him; their approach to the tomb, and finally Jesus' withdrawal with the disciples to Ephraim in the
wilderness, give life, colour and dramatic effect to the narrative
as it builds up the dramatic tension.

3. THE READER

Raising the dead poses for the reader the most fundamental and
radical question of faith and challenges theological, philosophical and scientific presuppositions. There is always the danger of
reading the story through the spectacles one finds most comfort-
able, be they theological, philosophical or scientific, and finding
one's own presuppositions reflected in the text. The raising of
Lazarus, however, forces the reader to pause and reflect together
with Martha, Mary and their friends and to face the tomb and
listen as Jesus prays to the Father. Unlike the shorter synoptic
accounts of the widow's son at Naim and the daughter of Jairus
which do not force the reader to stop and think along with the

---

364. S. M. Schneiders, *Written that You May Believe, Encountering Jesus in the
Fourth Gospel*, 152.
365. B. Witherington, *John's Wisdom*, 210.
366. M. Harris, 'The Dead are restored to life: Miracles of Revivification in the
Gospels', in *Gospel Perspectives*, ed D. Wehnam, 310-317; 320.

participants, John's account involves the reader in the doubts, faith, and reactions of the witnesses, and supplies a privileged insight into the prayer of Jesus.

4. THE STORY: INTRODUCTION OF CHARACTERS/URGENT MESSAGE (Jn 11:1-16)

The story of Lazarus begins by introducing *tis asthenôn*, a certain infirm, sick or weak person, Lazarus of Bethany, and his infirm condition is mentioned twice more in the opening verses. The expectation is immediately created in the reader's mind: 'What will Jesus, the good or model shepherd, do now and how will the official shepherds react?' One of the main criticisms of the bad shepherds, according to Ezekiel, was their failure to make the weak/infirm strong.[367] Jesus' healing of one of the *plêthos tôn asthenountôn* (crowd of infirm people) at the Pool of Bethesda and his cure of the blind man at the Pool of Siloam resulted in hostile reactions from these official shepherds. Their hostile reaction to this 'miracle' in Bethany will precipitate Jesus' *hour* of death and glorification.

Mary and Martha are also introduced at the beginning of the story. These friends and disciples of Jesus were obviously wealthy people. They could provide hospitality, organise a banquet, obtain expensive ointment and own a tomb. Mary seems to have been the more well known of the two because Bethany is said to be the village of Mary, and Martha is introduced as her sister. Then she is described as the one who anointed Jesus with ointment and wiped his feet with her hair. This is surprising because the story of the anointing has not yet been told in this gospel. The incident was probably so well known in the community that it could be mentioned before it was described. The humanity of Jesus and his capacity for friendship are patently obvious in the statement: 'Lord, he whom you love is ill' and it is further emphasised by the statement 'Jesus loved Martha and her sister and Lazarus.' Maybe mentioning Martha first in this list points to a prior acquaintance with Martha through whom he got to know her sister and brother. The address, 'Lord' is the usual post-resurrection title and address for Jesus. Interestingly it is used as an address throughout the story of the raising of Lazarus.

The dialogues with Martha and Mary highlight the difficult

---

367. Ezek 34:4. LXX *to êsthenêkos ouk enischusate.*

steps to full faith in Jesus, showing at the same time the personality traits of the two sisters who are known also from Luke's account of them. In the Lucan story Martha was the busy one, up and doing, responding to the practical details of hospitality but perhaps in her eagerness and anxiety to have everything in readiness missing the essentials of what was going on. Mary was the quiet, reflective one, 'sitting at the Lord's feet (a symbol of the pupil or disciple) and listening to him'.[368] For this reason she may have been quicker to perceive the real meaning of what was taking place. They are similarly portrayed in St John's gospel. On hearing of the approach of Jesus, Martha rushed out to meet him and got on with what she had to say: 'Lord, if you had been here my brother would not have died.' Mary stayed quietly at home until she heard the teacher had come and was calling her. Then she 'rose quickly and came to him', she saw him, and fell at his feet. Then she spoke. *Seeing* him and *falling at his feet* speak volumes about her perception and faith and set the context and tone for her comment: 'Lord, if you had been here my brother would not have died.'

Martha comes across in the story in two capacities. She is the sister of Lazarus, the individual struggling with the death of her brother and her own growing faith in Jesus. She also functions in the narrative as a representative figure articulating the resurrection faith of the Johannine community in the face of the death of its members. There is a certain tension between the roles and this seems to account for the full profession of faith in Jesus as Christ, Son of God, the One coming into the world on the one hand, and, on the other, the very understandable hesitations of the dead man's sister about the opening of the tomb.

On hearing the news Jesus states that the purpose of the *astheneia*, the weakness or illness of Lazarus is not the death that threatens but something far greater. The glory of God and the glorification of the Son of God will be achieved or manifested through it (*dia autês*). The Lazarus episode sets in motion the process of glorification of the Son of God because it precipitates the hour when the shepherd lays down his life for the sheep, and gathers all into the flock of God.

The 'strange' hesitation of Jesus for two days before coming to Bethany reminds one of his enigmatic reply to his mother at Cana, of his critical remark to the royal official about seeking

---

368. Lk 10:38-42.

signs and wonders and his rejection of the brothers' suggestion
that he go to Jerusalem at the Feast of Tabernacles to perform a
sign. His remark about the purpose of the illness is particularly
reminiscent of his remark that the blindness of the man whose
eyes he opened was for 'the works of God to be made manifest
in him'.[369] Now he says that the illness of Lazarus, and the delay
in going to him until after his death, was for the glory of God,
and the faith of the disciples.[370] Jesus responds to God's design,
not to human prompting. In letting Lazarus die, Jesus was able
to manifest his gift of life to all believers. Ironically the raising of
Lazarus would lead to Jesus' own death and glorification.[371]
After the cure of the invalid at Bethesda, Jesus in his defence
proclaimed: 'Amen, amen, I say to you, the hour is coming, and
now is, when the dead will hear the voice of the Son of God, and
those who hear it will live.'[372] Using the same title 'Son of God'
for himself Jesus now announces 'This illness is not unto death;
it is for the glory of God, so that the Son of God may be glorified
by means of it' (di' autês, referring to the illness).[373] Staying two
more days where he was may well imply that Jesus then went to
Bethany *on the third day*, the day traditionally associated with the
manifestation of God's glory[374] and the day when '(*YHWH*) will
bring us back to life, on the third day he will raise us and we will
live in his presence'.[375] Glory is not just 'praise' earned by God
and given by the people to God. It is the revelation of God, and
the Son of God, as the author and giver of life.

> The glory of Jesus revealed during his lifetime by means of
> his works is his communion of being, life, and action with his
> Father; but his glorification on the cross, the *doxa* that will be
> given him when he is raised up from the earth, is his union
> with believers.[376]

The death and raising of Lazarus set the divine plan in motion.

Return to Judaea: Two Understandings (Jn 11:7-16)
The interplay of life and death, light and darkness are now the
driving force of the story. Presence and absence also figure.

369. Jn 9:3.
370. Jn 11:4, 14.
371. cf Jn 12:23f; 17:1.
372. Jn 5:25.
373. Jn 11:4.
374. Ex 19:16-20; 24:16f.
375. Hos 6:2f.
376. S. Schneiders, *Written that you may believe*, 155f.

Though Jesus was at a distance from the scene in Bethany, he knew Lazarus had died. This may be an emphasis in the Johannine community on the presence of the apparently absent Jesus, particularly in the face of the death of a member. Sandra Schneiders puts it very well: 'The death of Lazarus and Jesus' physical absence, both of which are real and yet not definitive of Christian experience, are the symbolic catechesis of the mutual indwelling of Jesus and his disciples, which gives them, even now and within the experience of death and absence, eternal life.'[377]

When Jesus announced, 'Let us go to Judaea again', Thomas saw the journey ending only in Jesus' death because of the recent attempts of the Jews to stone him. The imagery of light and darkness is again brought into play, as Jesus tells them that those who walk during the day do not stumble because they have the light of the world, but those who walk at night stumble because the light is not in them. The night of his passion is already casting its shadow. Judas will go out into the night, and the arresting party will have to come with artificial lights to arrest the Light of the World. Jesus tells the disciples: 'Lazarus has fallen asleep but I am going to awaken him.' He is using a biblical concept that one sleeps in God and one is never dead to God. They think of physical sleep and its healing power and respond accordingly to Jesus. Here again Johannine irony is at play and the narrator draws the reader's attention to its effect. Jesus then tells them plainly that Lazarus is dead and he is glad because it will be the opportunity for them to believe. Death is not the end of Lazarus' story. It is for God's glory so that the Son of God may be glorified through it. Thomas called the Twin on hearing his reason for going said, prophetically, 'Let us also go that we may die with him'. Jesus now goes to give life to Lazarus and pays for it with his own death. But, as has become increasingly obvious, his death will also be his glorification.

Martha (Jn 11:17-27)
When Jesus came to Bethany, Lazarus was already four days in the tomb, a fact mentioned by the narrator and repeated by Martha.[378] This detail may be emphasised because of the belief that the spirit hovered round the body for three days after death,

---

377. *Ibid*.
378. Jn 11:17, 39.

and so four days emphasises that all hope is gone.[379] Lazarus is beyond all doubt, dead and decomposition has set in. This is further emphasised by the remark that the odour of putrefaction would be present. This detail heightens the dramatic tension as it paints the stark reality and creates a new level of suspense.

The conversation between Martha and Jesus is heavily laden with christological titles, eschatology and soteriology. Her address to Jesus has something of a reproach in it. She confronts him with the statement: 'Lord, if you had been here my brother would not have died.' Her follow up statement is somewhat enigmatic. 'But even now I know that whatever you ask from God, God will give you.' Is it an indirect request for a miracle, for the impossible? Perhaps it is a statement that in spite of Jesus' failure to respond immediately to the summons to the dying Lazarus, that God is still with him and Martha still regards him as God's special agent who can do something to alleviate their grief and sense of loss. This understanding of Jesus as a miracle worker, a rabbi blessed by God who does marvellous things because God is with him, is presented as a mark of 'underdeveloped' faith throughout the gospel.[380] As in the case of the first disciples Jesus reacts with a challenge by way of a promise of something greater to come. Whatever Martha meant, Jesus responded with the assurance: 'Your brother will rise again.' Martha hears this with the understanding of a believing Jewess of her time, and replied that she knew he would rise again on the Last Day. She is uttering what she considered the religiously correct response. She is giving him a little lesson on resurrection! But in the circumstances she may have regarded Jesus' affirmation as a platitude, a covering statement or lame excuse for his non-attendance when needed. Jesus reacts strongly and clearly. He addresses the substance of the remark, which reflects the belief in the resurrection of the dead on the last day. This belief was current in Judaism since the late second century BC, as witnessed in the Book of Daniel.[381] It was the doctrine of the Pharisees and it was widely accepted among the ordinary people. The Sadducees did not accept this doctrine,[382] but it continued to be held by the Pharisees and the ordinary people, and in the first century AD found its way into the Eighteen

---

379. *Gen Rabbah* 100 (64a).
380. Jn 2:23-25; 1:49-51; 3:1-11; 4:25f; 6:25-27; 7:31.
381. Dan 12:2.
382. Mt 22:23//Mk 12:18//Lk 20:27; Acts 23:8.

Benedictions in the prayer: 'You, O Lord are mighty forever, for you give life to the dead'.

This belief in the resurrection of the dead is now taken up and reinterpreted by Jesus in relation to his own person and mission. 'I am the Resurrection and the Life.' In all such cases where he uses 'I am' with a predicate he is defining who he is in terms of his life-giving relationship with the community. He is not only pointing forward to the fact that he himself will rise from the dead, but he is stating also that his resurrection has implications for the believers. There are two predicates, resurrection and life. Elaborating first on the meaning of 'I am the Resurrection' Jesus says: 'The one who believes in me, though he die, yet shall he live', and then on 'I am the Life' he says, 'Whoever lives and believes in me shall never die.' C. H. Dodd comments:

> This may be taken as a confirmation of the popular eschatology as enunciated by Martha: faith in Christ gives the assurance that the believer will rise again after death. But the second statement is not the simple equivalent of this. 'Everyone who is alive and has faith in me will never die.' The implication is that the believer is already 'living' in a pregnant sense which excluded the possibility of ceasing to live. In other words, the 'resurrection' of which Jesus has spoken is something which may take place before bodily death, and has for its result the possession of eternal life here and now.[383]

Jesus now challenges Martha to say if she believes this. She says, 'Yes, Lord', and utters a confession of faith which is a summary of Christian belief in Jesus, expressed in the titles Christ, Son of God, the One coming into the world. This is the life-giving confession of faith that is called for at the end of the gospel: 'These are written so that you may come to believe that Jesus is the Christ, the Son of God and that believing you may have life in his name.'[384] This profession of faith is very close to the language and high christology of Peter's profession of faith in St Matthew's gospel, which also came in response to a direct question from Jesus about faith in him.[385] However, Martha's subsequent reaction to the opening of the tomb betrays the fact that, though she has uttered the correct formula, she has still not

---

383. C. H. Dodd, op. cit., 147f.
384. Jn 20:31.
385. Mt 16:13-20.

reached full faith in Jesus as the resurrection and the life. Her personal faith has yet to match her developed formula, which in fact reflects the faith confession of the early Christian community, hence the tension between her personal and representative roles in the story. In this Martha reflects the steps to personal faith and the representative roles of the first disciples, Nicodemus, the Samaritan woman and elements of the crowd. They too had traditional expectations and used traditional titles but had to be challenged to see beyond them. Jesus had responded to the confessions of the first disciples with the promise of greater things to come, and surpassed the expectations of the Samaritan woman with the title bearing the divine name, 'I am'. He had surpassed the expectation of the crowd and supplied a new bread from heaven and refused to be king according to their expectation of the role. Martha is having a similar experience, but she is on a steep learning curve. Her profession of faith is a response to the word of Jesus, before any sign is given, like that of the royal official. For the moment she leaves Jesus where she met him. Why has she not invited him to her house? Is this symbolic of her not having advanced in her understanding/faith? Or has she gone to fetch her sister at the call of Jesus like the Samaritan woman leaving Jesus at the well, to call 'her husband'/ the Samaritans?

Mary (Jn 11:28-32)

Martha now goes to call her sister. Why did Jesus not accompany her to the house? The secretive way in which the message was conveyed, and the fact that the friends did not know where Mary was going, lead one to ask if it was a security measure because of the possible threat to his life or the lives of the disciples, because, as the narrator points out, Bethany was close to Jesusalem. For this reason many Jews had come out to sympathise with the sisters, but it also meant that Jesus was close to the place from which he had recently escaped with his life. Or did he want to meet Mary away from the gaze of the friends who had come to the house to be with the family in their grieving? Or was he exhausted from his journey and needed space and quietness to rest away from the crowd?

Martha calls Mary with the words 'The teacher is here and is calling you.' Although referring to Jesus in these circumstances as 'teacher' could be interpreted as a pointer to Martha's as yet underdeveloped understanding and faith in Jesus, the verb used for calling (*phônei*) is very significant. In Greek the verb *phônein* (to call) and the noun *phônê* (voice/sound) are from the same root. Already in the gospel the *sound* of the wind has been used to describe the presence and work of the Spirit;[386] the friend of the bridegroom rejoices at hearing the *voice* of the bridegroom;[387] the dead will hear the *voice* of the Son of God and live;[388] the dead will leave their graves when they hear his *voice*.[389] The Jews are criticised for not having heard the *voice* of the one who sent him.[390] In the context of the Good Shepherd Jesus refers to his own 'speaking' in terms of *phônein*/calling. The sheep hear the *voice* of the shepherd, he *calls* them by name, they know his *voice*; other sheep will listen to the shepherd's *voice* and the sheep that belong to the shepherd listen to his *voice*.[391] Coming after the discourse on the Good Shepherd with its concentration on 'voice' and 'calling', one immediately senses the presence of the Good Shepherd calling Mary. She responded to the voice of the shepherd as she rose quickly and went to him, meeting him at the place where Martha had left him.[392]

The Jews who were consoling her saw her hasty exit and followed, thinking she was going to weep at the tomb. This sets up a stark contrast in the movements. Mary is going in haste and hope to the presence of Jesus and his promise of life and resurrection, the Jews are heading to the tomb, the place of death and bereavement. The movement brings the Jews into the narrative, some of whom will later take part in the triumphal entry of Jesus into Jerusalem, others of whom, reminiscent of the man healed at Bethesda and the neighbours and acquaintances of the man born blind, will report the incident to the authorities.

Martha *went out* to meet Jesus. Mary *was called* out to meet him. There is quite a difference between their reactions on meeting him. When Martha heard that he was approaching she *went out*, *met him* and *spoke*, that is, she got straight on with what she had to say. Mary on the other hand *was called* and *rose quickly*

---

386. Jn 3:8.
387. Jn 3:29.
388. Jn 5:25.
389. Jn 5:28.
390. Jn 5:37.
391. Jn 10:3, 4, 16, 27.
392. Is this 'place' meant to be symbolic of the level of Martha's faith at this moment, a level from which Mary starts and progresses? 'Place' usually has symbolic meaning in St John's gospel as it regularly has throughout the Bible.

and *went* to him. She *saw* him, *fell at his feet* and then spoke. Keeping in mind the emphasis St John's gospel places on the importance of *seeing*, one immediately senses the effect *seeing* Jesus had on Mary. She *fell at his feet*. *Falling at his feet* is the reaction of people like the only one of the ten healed lepers who returned to give thanks to Jesus and praise to God in Luke's gospel. So too the arresting party will fall to the ground in awe when they come to arrest him in the garden.

The same words spoken by both sisters on encountering Jesus sound very different. 'Lord, if you had been here, my brother would not have died' on the lips of Martha seemed to say: 'You should have been here!' and on the lips of Mary: 'If only you were here!' Mary's remark seems to be a real confession of faith in Jesus as life-saver/life-giver, Martha's a rebuke for the late arrival of the miracle worker. Shortly the reader will see Mary's extraordinary understanding and affection in his regard when she anoints his feet with costly ointment and wipes them with her hair.[393] The contrast between Martha and Mary parallels the contrast between Peter and the Beloved Disciple. Martha, like Peter, articulates a confession of belief, on being challenged by Jesus to do so. Mary, like the Beloved Disciple, manifests belief and discipleship spontaneously in 'intimate' body gestures. She sees him, falls at his feet, anoints his feet and wipes them with her hair, proleptically preparing him for burial. The Beloved Disciple reclines on his bosom at the Last Supper, stands at the foot of the cross and witnesses the blood and water pour from his side.

Approaching the Tomb (Jn 11:33-37)
When Jesus saw Mary weeping and the Jews who were with her weeping, 'He was deeply moved in spirit and troubled.' Mary's weeping triggers this emotion in Jesus. Many scholars view this weeping of Mary and the Jews as a sign of failure to believe in Jesus as the resurrection and the life and have seen Jesus' distress and anger primarily as a result of their lack of, or lapse in, faith. This misses the point of the human story of the immediate family and friends and the situation of the first Christians who experience the death of their loved ones. Mary draws Jesus into the human drama. Grieving was not a private but a public affair, where the process of lamentation was facilitated by the hiring of

---

393. Jn 12:1-8.

two flute players and 'keening' women to weep at the grave. It was the communal acknowledgement of the loss endured by death and the trauma it occasioned for the bereaved. Jesus is truly made flesh and experiences with his friends their human sense of separation and loss. People suffering loss who give vent to their feelings in a demonstration of grief do not necessarily lack faith. The beatitude in Matthew, 'Blessed are those who mourn, they shall be comforted' (i.e. God will comfort them) fits well the scenario at the tomb of Lazarus. Faith can be eminently present in grief. The rich legacy of the psalms of communal and individual lamentation bear ample witness to the faith of those who make loud lamentation to God who alone can support them in their loss and suffering. Jesus, however, brings a whole new dimension to that grief-based faith.

His reaction goes much deeper than the expected grief of be-reavement. The Greek expressions *embrimrasthai tô pneumati* (to be deeply moved) and *tarassein heauton* (to shudder) seem to be two Greek expressions aiming to translate an Aramaic expres-sion for being 'strongly moved'.[394] On its own *embrimbrasthai* has the basic meaning of expressing anger, 'snorting with anger', and combining it with *tô pneumati* 'in spirit' points to great internal emotion. Anger is a common reaction of Jesus in the synoptics in the face of sickness and distress which are seen as a sign of the presence and power of Satan's kingdom. The equivalent scenario here in John is the presence of death.[395] The same verb will be used in chapter twelve to describe this deep, inner reaction in the face of death and all it stands for by way of apparent destruction of life causing such anguish, as Jesus con-templates his own forthcoming death, the Johannine equivalent of the Gethsemane 'agony'.[396] In the biblical mindset there is a broad association of sickness and death with sin and the power of Satan.[397] Here Jesus is confronting these powers in the human context of bereavement and the realisation of his own approach-ing death. *Tarassein*, signifies 'being troubled' and used with the reflexive *heauton*, signifies 'shuddered'. *Tarassein* will also be used in the Last Supper account to describe both the troubled state of the disciples in the face of the imminent departure and

---

394. Brown, *John*, Vol I, 425, n. 33.
395. Jn 12:27.
396. *Ibid*.
397. Gen 3:19; Jub 4:1ff; Mk 2:5; Jn 5:14; 9:2f.

death of their master and the distress of Jesus himself at the betrayal by Judas into whose heart Satan has entered.[398]

When Jesus asked: 'Where have you laid him?' he was to
hear re-echoed words reminiscent of the initial conversation
with his first disciples in the gospel when he invited them to,
'Come and see!' When he spoke those words he was inviting his
first disciples to see where he dwells and the reader already
knew he dwells ever at the Father's side. The disciples were invited to see the dwelling place of the one in whom is life and
light. Now the One who is the light of the world and the resurrection and the life is invited to 'come and see' the dwelling
place of death and darkness.

Jesus wept (*edakrusen*). The verb *dakruein* is unique in the
New Testament. The verb used of Mary and the Jews in their
grieving is *klaiein*. The verb used of mourning generally, of the
official funeral lamentation, and in the beatitude 'Blessed are
they who mourn' is *thrênein*. *Dakruein* therefore appears to point
to the *dakrua*, the tears, and is probably best translated as 'he
burst into tears'.[399] The Jews responded to this by commenting
on how much he had loved his friend. Some commented on how
the one who opened the eyes of the man born blind could have
saved him from death. In so doing they draw together, yet
again, the motifs of light and life, so often coupled together in
the gospel.

At the Tomb (Jn 38-44)
As Jesus approached the tomb he was again 'deeply moved'.
The stone, symbol of the barrier between life and death, lay
across it. On his command to remove the stone, Martha, in spite
of her earlier statement of faith, protested that he was already
four days dead and there would be an odour. This time it is
Jesus who gives the reprimand: 'Did I not tell you that if you
would believe you would see the glory of God?'[400] The Lazarus
story began with the statement that his death was for the glory
of God. Now Jesus reminds Martha and the bystanders of the
glory of God that is to be made manifest. This is the final sign
that will inaugurate the glory.

---

398. Jn 14:1, 27; 13:21.
399. cf Heb 5:7. The author of Hebrews describes Jesus 'pleading with tears' with
the one who could have saved him from death. The tearful pleading with the
Father which Hebrews portrays is part of the role of the perfect High Priest.
400. Jn 11:40.

They took away the stone and Jesus looked upwards, the typical gesture for prayer, and gave thanks, like a classical Jewish prayer. Here we experience the words of Jesus' prayer. The Johannine writings state that Jesus does nothing on his own, everything he does he has learned from his Father. He says only what he has heard from the Father. His food is to do the will of his Father. He knows that the Father always hears him. He does what is pleasing to the Father and what he asks is in accordance with the Father's will and is therefore granted. He summed it up: 'I and the Father are one.' He expects his followers to have the same confidence in prayer. Now at the tomb of Lazarus all this is put to the test as Jesus prays to the Father in the hearing of those present. He is not praying 'to the gallery' or simply for the benefit of the bystanders, but illustrating how he is always in union with the Father and his prayer puts the initiative in the hands of the Father. He rejoices that his prayer leads people to faith, like Elijah who prayed 'that this people may know that you, O Lord, are God.'[401]

As in all cases in the New Testament the miracle itself is told with brevity and discretion. Its significance lies in the fact that Jesus gives life to the dead Lazarus as a sign of his power to give eternal life, which already begins for the believer in this earthly life and not just on the last day. Here is the combination of realised and final eschatology. The argument of Jesus in his defence after the healing at Bethesda is so vividly recalled that some commentators wonder if chapter five was the original location of the Lazarus story during an earlier stage in the formation of the gospel. There Jesus proclaimed: 'An hour is coming in which all those in the tombs will hear his voice and will come forth – those who have done right unto the resurrection of life.'[402] Here Lazarus is in the tomb, and Jesus who proclaims himself to be the resurrection and the life, shouts in a loud voice (*phônê megalê*) 'Lazarus, come forth.' The Shepherd has called his name 'in a loud (great) voice'. Lazarus responds by emerging from the tomb, still bound, however, with the wrappings of death. Others have to unbind him. This highlights the fact that he has returned to 'this' life and so he will die again in the natural course of events. Jesus, on the other hand, will leave his own cloths that bound him in death in the tomb as he rises glori-

---

401. 1 Kings 18:37.
402. Jn 5:28f.

fied.[403] The raising of Lazarus points forward to the resurrection of Jesus and at the same time emphasises the difference between the two events.

Lazarus will die again, but his raising by Jesus shows that death is conquered even if it still remains a universal experience. In raising Lazarus Jesus shows himself to be the resurrection and the life. Lazarus is raised as one whom Jesus loves, one of a community whom he loves and who believe in him. Present and future eschatology are present in the 'revived' Lazarus. The raising of Lazarus is a pointer to the life that Jesus offers. 'Eternal life is this, to know you the only true God and Jesus Christ whom you have sent.'[404] His 'restored' life is a sign that those who believe will never die and those who die believing in him will live.

The theme of Jesus' *doxa* was introduced at Cana. At the Feast of Tabernacles the narrator drew attention to the coming glorification, by pointing out how the Spirit was not yet given because Jesus had not yet been glorified[405] and Jesus himself told the Jews that the Father would glorify him.[406] The *hour* was also introduced at Cana and has been referred to (together with its equivalent *kairos*) on an ongoing basis as the opposition to Jesus increased.[407] His references to the 'lifting up of the Son of Man', like the serpent in the desert 'so that everyone who believes in him will have eternal life' and his reference to the raising up of the Son of Man so that 'you will know that *I am*' during his discourse at Tabernacles when he claimed to act and speak in the Father's name, also look forward to the crucifixion/glorification.[408] It is now becoming obvious from the unfolding circumstances of his ministry that Jesus' *hour* and *doxa* will be revealed in his death. The blow is about to fall.

5. THE SANHEDRIN MEETING (Jn 11:45-54)

The calling of the Sanhedrin shows two levels of reaction to the fact that Jesus is working many signs and winning over the people. There is the religious concern 'everyone will come to belief in him', and the political concern 'the Romans will come and de-

---

403. Jn 20:6-10.
404. Jn 17:3.
405. Jn 7:39.
406. Jn 8:52-54.
407. Jn 2:4; (*kairos* 7:7f); 7:30; 8:20.
408. Jn 3:14; 8:28.

stroy both our holy place and our nation'.[409] There is great Johannine irony in the pronouncement of the High Priest, Caiaphas, that it is good for one man to die for the people. On the lips of the High Priest this meant salvation from Roman reactions to a perceived political threat. In the comment of the narrator it is a prophetic utterance about salvation of a totally different kind through the vicarious death of Jesus on behalf of Jew and Gentile, unwittingly uttered by the High Priest. For the reader it is the perfect example of the Good Shepherd who lays down his life for his flock. In so doing he will gather into one the dispersed children of God. As the writer of 1 John states: 'He is the atonement for our sins, and not for ours only, but for those of the whole world.'[410] In gathering them 'into one' (*eis hen*), Jesus is gathering them into one communion with himself and thereby with his Father. 'Gathering' (*synagein*) is reminiscent of the symbolic gathering of the *klasmata* after feeding the multitude, so that none would be lost.

Johannine irony, even biting sarcasm, is evident in the remark that Caiaphas was High Priest 'that year'. In fact he was High priest from 18 to 36 AD. In Jewish tradition the office was for life, but they had become so dependent on the Romans that they sat very precariously in office and could be unseated for the slightest reason. 'Those who sit so uneasily place political expediency above the word of God. He was not God's man; he was Rome's man.'[411]

Departure (Jn 11:53-54)
Because of their determination to put him to death, Jesus withdrew to the wilderness near a town called Ephraim with his disciples and no longer went about openly.

409. Jn 11:48.
410. 1 Jn 2:22.
411. F. B. Craddock, *John*, 89.

The Final Passover (Jn 11:55-20:31)

1. THE PLOT

The focus on the family of Bethany links chapter twelve to the preceding chapter. The anointing of Jesus' feet and the focus on Judas foreshadow what is to come in Jesus' betrayal, death and burial in the following chapters.

The Passover of the Jews was near and many went up from the country to Jerusalem before the Passover to purify themselves.[412] The final Passover of Jesus' life has arrived. The crowds come from the country, anxious to see him, but doubt that he will arrive. They are obviously conscious of the danger to his life. The authorities are resolved to capture him and are happy to enlist anyone who will assist in his arrest. In the midst of this foreboding Jesus comes to Bethany, where Lazarus was, whom he had raised from the dead. There he was guest at a dinner with Mary, Martha and Lazarus.[413] The two sisters again reflect the Lucan picture. Martha is serving and Mary is at Jesus' feet, the typical posture of a disciple.

It was six days before the Passover. The mention of six days alerts the reader to the idea of a final week of work leading to the seventh day, the great Sabbath day of rest after Jesus proclaimed that the Father's work was completed,[414] and to the eighth day, the first day of the week, the day of resurrection, the *kyriakê*.[415] This final week leading to the glorification forms an inclusion with the opening week of the ministry with its climax at Cana, introducing and prefiguring the 'hour' and the 'glory' of Jesus.[416]

---

412. Jn 11:55.

413. This meal, the last with his loved ones in Bethany, has striking similarities with the Last Supper, the last meal with his disciples. There is washing or anointing of feet, followed by protests, sharing with loved ones and the emphasis on the presence of Lazarus whom he loved, the presence of Judas and remarks on his betrayal and talk of Jesus' departure and death. The two sisters again reflect the Lucan picture. Martha is serving and Mary is at Jesus' feet, the typical posture of a disciple.

414. Jn 19:30.

415. The *kyriakê* or Lord's Day, as the Christians came to call the first day of the week, the day of the resurrection.

416. Sandra Schneiders, *Written That You May Believe*, 107, counts the six days back and concludes that the meal took place on the previous Sunday, reflecting the practice of the first Christians who met for their Eucharist on Sunday evening. Others count back from the beginning of the Sabbath on Friday evening and see the meal taking place on the previous Sabbath evening.

2. THE ANOINTING (Jn 12:1-11)

The ministry is drawing to a close and the shadow of death looms large. The anointing of his feet and the references to betrayal are writ large. His triumphal entry into Jerusalem introduces the idea of 'King' which dominates the passion and sets the tone for his execution as King of the Jews. His prayer on realising that his death is imminent is one of acceptance because it will glorify the Father, overcome the ruler of this world and 'raise him up' from the earth, a phrase emphasising the means and the meaning of his death. The ministry ends with a closing soliloquy about the consequences of accepting or rejecting the light that has come into the world.

The anointing of Jesus by Mary of Bethany is sandwiched between the order of the authorities that Jesus be handed over for arrest and their decision to kill Lazarus as well as Jesus. Judas is introduced into the scene with his criticism of the anointing and the remark that he was the one who was to betray Jesus. In Mark's gospel the anointing takes place between the authorities' seeking an opportunity to arrest Jesus and the offer of Judas to arrange it. Sandwiched between the scheming of the authorities and the betrayal by a disciple, the noble action of the woman stands out as a gesture of love and discipleship. The Marcan and Johannine settings of the anointing seem to reflect an early tradition in which the noble action is highlighted by its dark frame.[417]

Two similar stories have survived in the New Testament which reflect each other in detail, and popular telling often confuses both. First of all there is the story told only by Luke of the sinful woman who entered the house of Simon the Pharisee in Galilee, wept at Jesus' feet and dried them with her hair. She is not named. In response to the indignant reaction of those at table Jesus commended her love and faith and said many sins were forgiven her because she had loved much.[418] There is another

---

417. Scholars refer to this 'sandwiching' of material in which the picture and its frame highlight and mutually interpret each other as an intercalation.

418. Lk 7:36-50. Later tradition identifies her as Mary Magdalene, probably because she is named, immediately after the story of the woman of bad reputation, as one of the women who accompanied him, whom he healed of ailments and in her case, from whom he had driven out seven evil spirits (Lk 8:2). The statement that Jesus cast seven evil spirits from her could mean that she was mentally, physically or emotionally ill, or 'possessed'. It has been interpreted, without justification, as signifying an immoral life, possibly due to a misidentification of her with the woman of bad reputation in the preceding story and maybe also due in part to a confusion arising from the fact that the name of the woman in the other

story of a woman, who anointed Jesus in Bethany shortly before his death and in response to those who pointed out that it was a 'waste' of expensive ointment which 'should have been sold and the money given to the poor' he responded by interpreting her action as an anointing for his burial. She is identified in John's gospel as Mary, sister of Martha and Lazarus.

There are differences in detail between the various accounts of this anointing in Bethany. Matthew and Mark do not name the woman, but say the anointing took place in the house of Simon the Leper. John names the woman as Mary (of Bethany) but does not mention the name of the householder (Simon the Leper). In fact he never mentions any leper in his gospel. Matthew and Mark describe how she poured the precious ointment on his head, resembling a 'messianic/royal' anointing and how Jesus in turn interpreted the action in terms of preparation for his burial.[419] Unlike these accounts which mention the anointing of Jesus' head, John emphasises the fact that Mary anointed his feet and wiped them with her hair. Anointing the feet was an action particularly associated with preparation for burial. This is very significant in a context where the High Priest has already pronounced the death sentence on Jesus and the word had gone out that anyone who knew his whereabouts should hand him over for arrest. In a prophetic gesture prompted by love and hospitality this devoted disciple now prepares him for burial.

The variations on the story of the anointing in Bethany pose some questions. Could Simon the Leper have been the owner of the house in which Lazarus' family lived, or could he have been one of the family? Is it just a coincidence that the householder in Galilee where the sinful woman wept at Jesus feet was also called Simon or was there a fusion of detail between two similar stories in the tradition?[420] Matthew and Mark speak of anointing Jesus' head, John speaks of anointing his feet. Is this another fusion of details or is it not possible that both took place in one great act of anointing, with tradition seeing significance in different de-

---

anointing story in Bethany was also Mary. Since the time of Gregory the Great the sinful Woman of Lk 7 (whom Luke was charitable enough to leave unnamed), Mary of Bethany and Mary of Magdala have been regarded – wrongly – as the same person and honoured as one saint. Preaching, art, literature, stage and cinema have perpetuated the unfounded destruction of her reputation.
419. Mt 26:6-13; Mk 14:3-9.
420. Lk 7:36-50.

tails? The three accounts of the Bethany anointing emphasise the costly nature of the ointment, the indignation of the disciples (Mt) or of 'some who were there' (Mk) and the reference to the poor. John's gospel focuses the indignation and the reference to the poor on the person of Judas and this affords the narrator the opening to identify Judas as the betrayer and the opportunity to comment further on his dishonesty in managing the common fund. Luke and John both describe how the woman dried Jesus' feet with her hair. This may in some way reflect a custom in the Greco-Roman world, as seen in Petronius' *Satyricon*, where a diner wiped excess oil or potable substances from the hands onto the hair of servants.[421]

The similarities in detail between these three accounts of the anointing in Bethany and the account of the repentant woman in Galilee have led to a certain confusion and overlapping in detail. A 'cross over' in details may well be evident in the fact that Luke, Matthew and Mark, but not John, mention that it was an alabaster jar. Significantly too, Luke mentions the anointing of the feet, both in the initial account itself and in Jesus' rebuff to his host when defending the woman from criticism and malign judgement of her character (and motives?). Later tradition identifies the woman in Galilee as Mary Magdalene, probably a confusion arising from the fact that the woman in Bethany is called Mary, and Mary Magdalene is named in a summary statement as one of the women from Galilee who were with Jesus and whom he healed of ailments, specifying Mary Magdalene as one from whom he had driven out evil spirits. The summary follows closely on the story of the sinful woman but does not follow from it.[422] The unwarranted assumption that it does has wrongly given rise to the belief that Mary Magdalene was a person of immoral life. The statement that Jesus cast seven devils from her could mean that she was mentally, physically or emotionally sick, or 'possessed'. Since the time of Gregory the Great the repentant sinner, Mary of Bethany and Mary Magdalene have been regarded – incorrectly – as the same person and celebrated as one saint.

In a dry, dusty climate, with its resultant mud in a rainy season, one's feet needed regular washing. It was customary to supply water to a guest to wash his own feet. Loosening the straps

421. Petronius, *Satyricon*, 27.
422. Lk 8:2.

of the sandals, removing them and washing the feet was the job of a slave. However, it was not required of a Jewish slave to perform such service. There was a rabbinic axiom which stated that a disciple might perform any act of service for the master except that of unfastening his sandals, even though it was customary for disciples to render to their master many kinds of service. *Midrash Mekilta* on Ex 21:2 states that the washing of a master's feet could not be required of a Jewish slave.[423] However, washing the feet of an honoured guest was performed on occasions as a gesture of recognition and outstanding hospitality. Furthermore, the intimate nature of footwashing and its significance within a relationship are borne out in an Alexandrian Jewish work, *Joseph and Asenath*. It tells how Joseph's bride-to-be offered to wash his feet. Joseph protested, saying that such a service was the task of a servant girl, but Asenath replied: 'Your feet are my feet … another shall not wash your feet.'[424]

Here in St John's gospel there is not an actual footwashing but rather an analagous and far more striking action, the anointing of the feet of Jesus with pure nard, an extremely expensive perfume, made from a plant grown in northern India, and costing in this case three hundred denarii, a year's wages.[425] (Women sometimes wore small flasks of nard around their necks with which to freshen up.) For Mary of Bethany it was the sacrificing of something very precious, the action of a devoted disciple demonstrating her faith in, and love for, Christ. The narrator points out that the aroma filled the house. The reference to the aroma may reflect the same tradition as that in Midrash Rabbah on Eccl 7:1 which says: 'The fragrance of a good perfume spreads from the bedroom to the dining room; so does a good name spread from one end of the world to the other.' Mark reflects a similar understanding: 'Wherever the gospel is preached in the whole world, what she has done will be told in memory of her.'[426] This assessment stands in stark contrast to the damning character report on Judas. The fragrance also stands in stark contrast to the stench of death feared by Martha

423. R. E. Brown, *The Gospel According to John*, Vol I, 44, quoting Bernard, *A Critical and Exegetical Commentary on the Gospel According to St John*, I, 41.
424. *Joseph and Asenath*, XX, 1-5.
425. A denarius a day was the usual pay at the time. Taking sabbath days and holy days into account there were approximately three hundred working days in the year. Nard was made from a plant grown in Northern India.
426. Mk 14:9.

before the opening of the tomb of Lazarus. Not long ago there was concern for the stench of Lazarus' dead body in the tomb. Now the aroma of Jesus' body, prepared for burial, fills the house.[427] Jesus' death presents a complete contrast to the decay of the tomb.

In responding to Judas' criticism of Mary's action, Jesus points out how she was taking responsibility beforehand for his burial. The reader can see here the action of a disciple for the master, a prophetic action in proleptically anointing his body for burial. The faith and generosity of Mary stands in stark contrast to the dishonesty and avarice of Judas. Anticipating the burial of Jesus, she becomes the first disciple to understand the significance of his death.[428]

Judas saw it as a waste, and covered his avarice with false concern for the poor, a bluff called immediately by Jesus who reminded him that the poor were always present and in need of help, a remark very likely charged with the implied question and reprimand: 'What have you done for them before, and what will you do for them in the future? Don't be using them as an excuse!' The narrator adds to Jesus' reprimand the information that Judas was a thief, helping himself to the common fund of which he had charge. Matthew and Mark also describe Jesus' reprimand and state in addition that Jesus said the woman had done *a good work*. The Jews divided *good works* into almsgiving and charitable deeds, the latter including among other pious works the fitting burial of the dead. Then he explained that she had prepared him for burial. He said that they will always have the poor present, but will not always have him. These sentiments are very similar to those in the Johannine account.

The mind and motives of Judas have been a subject of discussion throughout history. Luke and John see the Prince of Evil at the root of Judas' actions. Both say that Satan entered into Judas, and John also says that Judas was a devil. This 'religious/philosophical' interpretation is translated into terms of what is often seen as the root of all evil, love of money. Mark and Luke show the chief priests tempting Judas with the offer of money.

427. Mark (14:9) states that 'Wherever the gospel is preached in the whole world, what she has done will be told in memory of her.' This may be reflected in the statement about the aroma filling the house as the *Midrash Rabbah* on Eccl 7:1 says: 'The fragrance of a good perfume spreads from the bedroom to the dining room; so does a good name spread from one end of the world to the other.'
428. W. J. Harrington, *op. cit.*, 64.

Matthew shows him demanding the money. John further develops this money loving weakness in terms of stealing from the common fund in his charge.[429] Since New Testament times historians, priests, poets, playwrights and many others have continued to speculate on his motives.

The two sisters again reflect the Lucan picture. Martha is said to 'serve' (*diakonein*) as Mary performs the action of a devoted disciple, like the pupil of a rabbi, preparing to follow him in the service of the word. It is not a relegating of Martha to a 'menial' kitchen sink role but an elevation of her to an established and highly prized and important role in the hospitality ministry of the community. It should be kept in mind that very early on there was a debate in the Jerusalem church about the neglect of hospitality, in overlooking the Hellenist widows. In reply to the criticism the argument was made by 'the twelve': 'It would not be right for us to neglect the word to serve at tables'(*diakonein*). Following this seven were chosen for this service of hospitality. The apostles prayed over them and laid hands on them. Some communities already had an established order of deacon by the time of the writing of John's gospel.[430] Hospitality was seen as very important in early Christian communities, as evidenced by the criteria for enrolment as a widow in the First Letter to Timothy. 'She must be a woman known for her good works and for the way in which she brought up her children, shown hospitality to strangers and washed the feet of the saints.'[431] The account may well foreshadow in story and reflect in fact the practice of the early Johannine tradition in its Eucharistic assembly. It may be possible that footwashing was part of the service of hospitality at the Eucharistic assembly in the community.

3. ROYAL ACCLAMATION (Jn 12:12-19)

The meal and anointing, like a royal banquet, are followed by the acclamation of the crowd and the procession to greet the royal visitor to the city. When the great crowd of the Jews heard that Jesus was there they came (to Bethany) not only to see Jesus but Lazarus also whom he had raised from the dead. On account of the response of people like these the authorities were determined to kill Lazarus as well as Jesus.[432] This linking of the death

---

429. Mk 14:11; Lk 22:5; Mt 26:15; Jn 12:4-6.
430. Acts 6:1-6; Phil 1:1; 1 Tim 3:8, 12, 13; Rom 16:1.
431. 1 Tim 5:10.
432. Jn 12:9f.

of Lazarus to the enthusiasm of the crowd and the decision of
the authorities to put him to death as well as Jesus, is a specifically Johannine contribution to the account of the triumphal
entry of Jesus into Jerusalem and the motives for the trial and execution of Jesus. It sets the tone for what follows.

Together with the synoptics, John has the crowd coming out
from the city to welcome him. This group would have been
made up of inhabitants and visitors on the occasion of the festival. John has already mentioned the visitors and their discussions about Jesus and whether or not he would come to the festival. They were aware of the authorities' determination to arrest
him.[433] John mentions in addition those who 'went on' testifying
about the raising of Lazarus. The imperfect tense *emarturei* signifies that it was an ongoing or repeated activity on their part.[434]

There are a number of points of contact between the story as
told in John and in the three synoptics. All four gospels record
the enthusiasm of the crowd, the entry on a beast of burden, the
royal overtones, the citation of scripture and the reaction of the
authorities. Matthew, Mark and John prefix Hosanna to the citation from Psalm 117 (118), 'Blessed is he who comes in the name
of the Lord' and John adds the suffix 'even the King of Israel'.[435]
This royal dimension is reflected in Matthew's reference to 'Son
of David' and Mark's 'Blessed is the kingdom of our father
David that is coming.'[436]

There are several distinctive elements in John's account. In
the synoptics the crowd mentioned consists only of the crowd
coming out from the city. John emphasises the crowd associated
with the Lazarus story in order to connect closely the raising of
Lazarus with the excitement and homage of the crowd and the
determination of the authorities to kill not only Jesus, but
Lazarus as well. Distinctively Johannine also is the reference to
the disciples' subsequent understanding of 'what had been done

---

433. Jn 11:55-57.
434. There are two readings of verse 17. Some mss have *hote ton Lazaron ephônêsen*
and others have *hoti ton Lazaron ephônêsen*. If one reads *hote* then the whole sentence can be translated: 'The crowd who were with him when he called Lazarus
from the tomb and raised him from the dead were testifying.' If one reads *hoti*,
then it can be translated: 'The crowd that was with him were testifying that he
called Lazarus from the tomb and raised him from the dead.' The difference is
academic and does not affect the substance of the story.
435. Ps 117 (118):25f.
436. Mt 21:9; Mk 11:10.

to him'. The narrator's comment about the disciples' subsequent understanding of what had been done to Jesus, why he reacted as he did and the significance of the biblical references on the lips of the crowd is a repetition of the comment about their understanding of Jesus' action, biblical quotation and *logion* at the 'cleansing' of the Temple. Both stories may have been formed together in an earlier period of the gospel tradition. The reference to palm branches is found only in John's gospel.[437]

Because of the acclamation of the crowd who came to see Jesus and Lazarus whom he had raised from the dead, the authorities decided to put Lazarus to death as well because on account of him many were deserting and believing in Jesus. The idea of 'deserting' betrays an attitude of partisanship, probably reinforced subsequently by the growing tension between the early church and the Jews.

The scene initiates the royal inauguration of Jesus which continues throughout his trial, execution and death until his royal burial. Meeting a royal visitor, a king or emperor, outside the gates and escorting him into the city was a custom in the Greco-Roman world. The usual term used for a pilgrim bound for Jerusalem is 'going up' to Jerusalem but here Jesus is said to 'come' to the city. This emphasises the royal and messianic nature of the visit. The 'edited' quotation from Zechariah 'do not be afraid, daughter of Sion, see your king is coming ...' (simultaneously recalling Zepheniah's call to shout for joy because God, the king of Israel, 'is in your midst') has the very significant change from 'Rejoice heart and soul' to 'Do not be afraid', the exhortation-cum-assurance of the typical biblical epiphany, as seen already in the scene when Jesus came to the disciples in their distress on the sea.[438] More than an earthly king is coming to the city! The shouts of the crowd and the waving of palm fronds embellish the royal occasion. 'Hosanna! Blessed is the one who comes in the name of the Lord – the King of Israel.' Hosanna, literally means 'Save us, we pray', but had become an acclamation or greeting and shout of homage and praise. It was associated with the enthusiastic waving of the palm fronds and

---

437. Palms are believed not to have grown in the Jerusalem area, but to have been brought to the city from the region of Jericho for occasions such as the feast of Tabernacles. This has led to some speculation about the actual timing of Jesus' triumphal entry into the city.
438. Zech 9:9f; Zeph 3:14; cf comment on Jn 6:20.

sheafs of foliage at the festivals and so they were often called a
'hosanna'.[439] The quotation, 'He who comes in the Lord's name'
is from Psalm 117 (118), one of the Hallel Psalms associated with
the entry to the Temple at Passover and Tabernacles. Here it emphasises the messianic significance of 'the one who comes'.[440]
The significance of the royal occasion is now clearly stated in the
Johannine addition to the psalm: 'and (blessed is) the King of
Israel'. Meeting him with palm fronds had a very special significance. Palms were associated especially with Temple feasts like
Tabernacles and Dedication, and historically the palms were associated with national liberation. In the days of the Maccabees
the Jews carried palm fronds to the Temple following its purification and rededication after the expulsion of Antiochus
Epiphanes' troops and 'the abomination of desolation'. Later
again when Simon captured the Jerusalem citadel the Jews, carrying palm fronds, took possession of it.[441] In *The Testament of
Naphtali* the palm fronds are given to Levi as a sign of power
over Israel.[442] The palm fronds in John carry therefore the connotation of hailing Jesus as a national liberator. The Jerusalem
crowd now reflect the initial reaction of the Galileans after the
multiplication of the loaves when they wanted to carry him off
and make him king.[443]

Jesus responds to their messianic expectations, acknowledging his royal status but with a gesture that interprets it in line
with biblical expectations different to those uppermost in the
mind of the enthusiastic crowd and the jaundiced eye of the authorities. In royal fashion he enters the city seated on a young
donkey, symbol of the king coming in peace. The donkey had
associations with the house of David. The blessing of Jacob proclaimed concerning the ruler from the House of Judah: 'Binding
his foal to the vine and his donkey's colt to the choice vine, he
washes his garments in wine and his robe in the blood of
grapes.'[444] The narrator interprets the gesture in terms of
prophecy and adds that the disciples did not understand its

---

439. *Sukka* 37b. At Tabernacles as the psalm 117 (118) was chanted the males present waved the lulab at the words 'Blessed is he who comes in the name of the
lord' (verses 25, 26).
440. Ps 118:26
441. 2 Macc 10:7; 1 Macc 13:51.
442. Testament of Naphtali 5:4.
443. Jn 6:15.
444. Gen 49:10f.

meaning until Jesus was glorified.[445] Typical of Johannine style the quotation combines passages from Zechariah and Zephaniah. Also typical of John's gospel is the fact that the key phrases are quoted but they are intended to convey the overall ideas of the context from which they are borrowed. Zechariah proclaimed: *Rejoice heart and soul, daughter of Sion! Shout with gladness, daughter of Jerusalem! See now your king comes to you: he is victorious, he is triumphant, humble and riding on a donkey. He will banish chariots from Ephraim and horses from Jerusalem; the bow of war will be banished. He will proclaim peace for the nations. His empire shall stretch from sea to sea, from the river to the ends of the earth.*[446] John replaces the opening words of the Zechariah quotation with a verse from Zephaniah, *'Zion, have no fear, do not let your hands fall limp. Yahweh your God is in your midst a victorious warrior.'* He thus combines the impact of both texts. Zephaniah prophesied: *Shout for joy, daughter of Zion. Israel, shout aloud … Yahweh the King of Israel is in your midst … When that day comes, word will come to Jerusalem: Zion have no fear, do not let your hands fall limp. Yahweh your God is in your midst, a victorious warrior.*[447] In changing the exhortation to rejoice to an exhortation to have no fear, John raises the level of the event to that of an epiphany of which ' have no fear' is an established element.

The backgrounds to the composite quotation emphasise the peaceful nature of the coming of the king. This is a far cry from the national liberator in the tradition of the Maccabees, and the one expected by many of Jesus' contemporaries, against whom the Jerusalem authorities and the Roman occupiers were constantly on guard, especially on the occasion of Passover and the other major pilgrimage feasts. Jesus acknowledges but significantly reinterprets his kingship as he later does in his trial before Pilate when he says: 'My kingdom is not of this world.'[448] R. Schnackenburg sums up the significance of the scene.

> The evangelist sees in the event a testimony to the true kingship of Jesus, which has nothing to do with political claims or force, but is the revelation of truth and the releasing of divine salvation. In this sense Jesus is the expected Messiah, and more, the Son of God (Jn 1:49; 11:27; 20:31). This is made visible in the entry, as Jesus fulfills the prophecy of Zechariah

---

445. cf Jn 3:22 in connection with the cleansing of the Temple.
446. Zech 9:9f (JB).
447. Zeph 3:14,16f (JB).
448. Jn 18:36f.

and is greeted by the crowd, which represents Israel as the people of salvation (cf 1:31).[449]

Throughout the scene the crowd act almost like the chorus in a Greek play voicing the background issues, providing a stimulus and acting as dialogue partner.

4. THE GREEKS (Jn 12:20-22)

When the Pharisees saw the crowds, inhabitants of the city and pilgrims from the country, coming to Jesus, they proclaimed in a great moment of irony, 'You see, you can do nothing, the whole world has gone after him!'[450] – prophetic words, soon to be symbolically fulfilled in the coming of the Greeks, asking to see Jesus.[451] With the arrival of the Greeks, representatives of the wider non-Jewish world, the 'whole world' is seen to be going after him. These are *Hellênes*, Greeks by birth, not *Hellênistai*, Greek-speaking Jews. Since they have come to Jerusalem during the feast they appear to be God-fearers, Gentiles who believe in the God of the Jews, observe the moral law, pray and do charitable works, inspired by the Jewish religion and way of life.[452] These Greeks who come to Jerusalem and ask to see Jesus serve the function in John's gospel that the Magi serve in the gospel of Matthew.[453] The Magi were Gentiles who religiously observed the signs of the times and had knowledge of the Jewish expectation of a Messiah. And just as their arrival in Jerusalem, seeking 'the one who has been born king of the Jews', provoked suspicion, hostility and the intent to kill the new born king, so now the Greeks arrive just as the authorities are planning to put to death the one whom the crowd have hailed as king. The promise of the Good Shepherd and the unwitting prophecy of the High Priest are being fulfilled. Jesus promised : 'I lay down my life for my sheep. There are other sheep I have that are not of this fold, and these I have to lead as well.'[454] Caiaphas 'prophesised': 'It is

449. Schnackenburg, *op. cit.*, II, 376.

450. Jn 12:19.

451. This reaction parallels the indignant reaction of the authorities to the children's enthusiastic cry 'Hosanna to the Son of David' and their request to Jesus to control his disciples, in the gospels of Matthew and Luke respectively. cf Mt 21:15f; Lk 19:39f.

452. Josephus, *Jewish War*, 6:422-7, states that 2.7 million pilgrims came to the feast, a number not including foreigners, or the ritually impure. Even if exaggerated, the figure shows the popularity of the feast. Godfearers came, but did not eat the Passover Lamb, etc.

453. Jn 12:21; Mt 2:1-12.

454. Jn 10:15f.

good for one man to die for the people' and the narrator pointed
out how this was a prophecy that Jesus would die for the nation
– 'and not for the nation only, but to gather together in unity the
scattered children of God'.[455] The arrival of the Greeks at this
critical moment highlights the universal scope of Jesus' mission
and saving death.

Their arrival shows how the news of Jesus' mission has
reached the nations. This would prove a good missionary text,
reinforced by the fact that Philip himself who figures in the
story, became a missionary to the Gentiles in Asia Minor, at
Hierapolis in the Lycus Valley, not much more than a hundred
miles along the Lycus and Meander Valleys from Ephesus, a
thriving centre of Christianity since the time of Paul, and a city
associated with the Johannine tradition.[456]

The Greeks approach Philip. He approaches Andrew and
they both approach Jesus. These two disciples are regularly seen
working together as a team. Their names are always given in the
Greek form, and they come from Bethsaida, near the Greek-
speaking pagan cities of the Decapolis. They were therefore the
obvious persons to approach. But there are unanswered questions. Why did Philip approach Andrew before approaching
Jesus? Did Jesus receive the Greeks? The details are lost most
likely because the significance of the event, rather than the historical details, becomes the focus of attention. The request to
'see' Jesus is more than a casual tourist photographic opportunity.
'Seeing' is a theologically laden term in John's gospel. 'Seeing' or
'not seeing' signify the acceptance of Jesus' claims concerning
his identity and mission, leading to personal commitment or rejection. The *coming* of the Gentiles and their desire *to see* Jesus is
so theologically important that the writer never tells us about a
meeting with Jesus. Rather he highlights the fact that Jesus' response was to proclaim the arrival of his *hour*. R. E. Brown
suggests that the lack of detail points to a poorly remembered
incident from early tradition that has been used as the basis for
theological adaptation because of its significance.[457]

Jesus' Hour (Jn 12:23-26)
When Jesus is told that the Greeks wish to see him he proclaims:

455. Jn 11:50-52. These statements probably represent also the rapid expansion of
the church at its beginnings.
456. Eusebius, *HE*, 3:31.3; 5:24.2-3.
457. R. E. Brown, *op.cit.*, I, 470.

'Now the *hour* has come so that the Son of Man may be glorified.'[458] This declaration of the arrival of the *hour*, first anticipated
at Cana and then regularly referred to throughout the ministry,
is followed by a discourse on its meaning in the context of Jesus'
impending death and glorification.

His declaration that the *hour* has arrived is followed by a
commentary on the theme of death and life. The fundamental
importance of the commentary is underlined by introducing it
with the familiar Johannine oracular formula: 'Amen, amen, I
say to you'. Jesus compares his death to the seed falling to the
ground to produce more fruit.[459] The contrast here is between a
death that produces fruit and a life that does not produce fruit,
that is, a life that remains 'alone'. The point of the contrast,
therefore, is not between the living grain above ground and the
dead grain in the ground, but between the 'alone' and the 'much
fruit'. The fruit here refers to the followers of Christ, and in this
context it refers particularly to the Gentiles who are coming to
him. As in many other cases in the gospel, the story of Jesus reflects the experience of the early church. In the nearest synoptic
parallels, the grain of mustard seed produces a tree in whose
branches the birds of the air can nest, an image drawn from
Daniel,[460] and the seed sown by the sower on good ground produces a harvest way and beyond anything expected.[461] Jesus
used a related image at the well in Samaria when he told the disciples that the fields were ripe for the harvest, referring to the
mission to the Samaritans.[462]

Having spoken of dying in order to bring others to life, Jesus
points out that his followers cannot escape death any more than
their master and they too must pass through death to eternal
life. Drawing a sharp contrast between life that is bounded by
time and space (*phychê*) and life that opens onto eternity (*zôê*),
Jesus now focuses on the fundamental attitude required in the
face of this understanding of life and death. The required attitude is underlined by sharp contrast with its opposite in a typical biblical antithetical parallel. The double contrast is emphas-

---

458. Jn 12:23.
459. Ignatius of Antioch used this imagery of his martyrdom, speaking of himself as the grain of wheat. *Letter to the Romans*, 4:1.
460. Mk 4:30-32; Dan 14:12 (LXX).
461. Mk 4:26-29 and //s.
462. Jn 4:36.

ised by the use of *love* and *hate* and *destroy (lose)* and *preserve.*[463] Love and hate, destroy and preserve, are stark opposites in speech and the contrast sounds extreme to our ears. However, the meaning of the contrast is well illustrated by two synoptic sayings which can be used to interpret one another. Luke's version of Jesus' *logion* about hating father and mother, and one's own self, as a necessary condition for being his follower, often causes raised eyebrows, if not real shock. However, the parallel statement in Matthew's gospel makes the point in a more straightforward way and thereby highlights the semitic style of the Lucan version of the saying. Matthew simply says, 'The one who loves father or mother more than me is not worthy of me.'[464] Similarly here in St John's gospel the 'hating' signifies rejecting worldly attachment that impedes one's entry into the kingdom.

There are similar statements in the synoptics dealing with saving, finding and seeking to gain one's life, and ending up destroying it. As here in John's gospel they are enunciated in the context of Jesus' forthcoming death, and his call to a discipleship of suffering and service. In the synoptic accounts the passion predictions are followed by the injunction to take up one's cross and follow Jesus. 'If anyone wants to be a follower of mine, let him renounce himself and take up his cross and follow me. For anyone who wants to save his life will lose it; but anyone who loses his life for my sake, and for the sake of the gospel, will save it. What gain, then, is it for a man to win the whole world and ruin his life?'[465] Whereas the synoptics speak of 'following' or 'coming after' Jesus, John speaks of 'serving', *diakonein*. Jesus in John's gospel has a similar message as he proceeds to condemn love of life in this world, love of darkness more than light and love of human glory (*doxa*).[466] Worldly attachments that diminish love for Christ are to be abandoned.

Crisis (Jn 12:27-30)

The comments on death are followed by the moment of crisis, the agony of accepting death. This crisis is described in the synoptics and in Hebrews. In the synoptics Jesus' crisis and prayer are in Gethsemane: 'And a sudden fear came over him, and a

---

463. *philein / misein* and *apollynai / phylaxein*.
464. Lk 14:26; Mt 10:37.
465. Jn 12:24f; cf Mk 8:35f; 16:25; Lk 9:23-25; cf Mt 10:38f.
466. Jn 12:25; 3:19; 12:43

great distress. And he said to them, "My soul is sorrowful to the point of death ..." and going on a little further he threw himself on the ground and prayed that, if it were possible, this hour might pass him by. "Abba (Father)!" he said "everything is possible for you. Take this cup away from me. But let it be as you, not I, would have it".[467] The author of Hebrews states: 'During his life on earth, he offered up prayer and entreaty, aloud and in silent tears, to the one who had the power to save him out of death, and he submitted so humbly that his prayer was heard. Although he was Son, he learned to obey through suffering...'.[468] The crisis is depicted here at the end of the public ministry in John's gospel. He accepts death as it will glorify the Father, overthrow the ruler of this world and when he is lifted up, he will draw all to himself. His prayer resembles the prayer at the tomb of Lazarus. 'Jesus' reliance on his Father to raise Lazarus is partly echoed in his reliance on the Father when faced with the prospect of his own death and burial.'[469] The temptation to pray to the Father to 'save me from this hour' is dismissed in the realisation that *this hour* is the purpose for which he was sent. The Letter to the Hebrews speaks of his 'submitting humbly' and the synoptics speak of his obedience in accepting the cup that the Father gives him to drink, 'not my will but yours be done'. Here in John's gospel the emphasis is on the *hour* and the *glorification*. R. E. Brown points out that when Jesus says 'Glorify your name' he is praying

> ... that God's plan be carried out; for the name that the Father has entrusted to Jesus (17:11, 12) can only be glorified when its bearer is glorified through death, resurrection, and ascension. Only then will men come to realise what the divine name 'I AM' means when applied to Jesus (8:28).[470]

Brown goes on to point out that 'Glorify your name' is the Johannine equivalent of the first and third petitions of the Lord's Prayer.[471] 'Hallowed be your name', not in the sense of the people's praise of God but of God's sanctifying his own name. The petition 'Your will be done' is in fact synonymous with 'glorify you name/hallowed be your name'. The parallel for John's

---

467. Mk 14:32ff and //s.
468. Heb 5:7ff.
469. T. Brodie, *op. cit.*, 402.
470. R. E. Brown, *op. cit.*, I, 475f.
471. Mt 6:9f.

'Glorify your name' in the synoptic 'agony' is 'Your will be done'.[472]

In Hebrews, Jesus' prayer 'was heard' and in Luke's account a comforting angel came from heaven.[473] The prayer of submission is answered in John's gospel by a theophany. In this gospel there has been no account of the baptism of Jesus with the voice from heaven acknowledging the beloved son, neither has there been a transfiguration scene with the Father assuring the disciples that this is his beloved Son in whom he is well pleased and to whom they ought to listen. Now at the end of Jesus' ministry there is a theophany reminiscent of the synoptic baptism and transfiguration scenes.[474] Like the transfiguration it comes in close proximity to predictions of Jesus' rejection and death and foreshadows his resurrection and glorification. The assurance given to the disciples at the transfiguration is paralled here with the assurance to the crowd. 'That voice did not come for my sake but for yours', a statement reminiscent also of Jesus' prayer at the tomb of Lazarus which he uttered 'because of the crowd standing around, that they may believe that you sent me'.[475] The aorist 'I glorified' (*edoxaza*) refers to the works of Jesus through which the Father's name was glorified, and may also refer to the hour of glorification already initiated. The future 'I shall glorify it' (*doxazô*) seems to refer to the 'raising up' of the Son in glory when he will draw all to himself. This is borne out at the Last Supper when Jesus remarks: 'Now has the Son of Man been glorified, and God has been glorified in him. God will, in turn, glorify him in himself and will glorify him immediately.'[476] 'The death of Jesus would be his most eloquent sermon: the ultimate revelation of the Father.'[477]

Victory (12:31-36)

The hour of the glorification of Jesus entails the judgement on the ruler of this world (*ho archôn tou kosmou toutou*), a Johannine designation for Satan, but reflecting also the *archontes*, the rulers who have been so opposed to Jesus throughout his mission. The ruler will be cast out. Some manuscripts say 'he will be cast

472. Mt 26:42.
473. Lk 22:43.
474. Mk 1:11 and 9:2ff and //s.
475. Jn 11:42; 12:29f.
476. Jn 13:31f.
477. W. J. Harrington, *op. cit.*, 65.

down'. This second reading forms an interesting contrast with the *lifting up* in the next verse as Jesus proclaims 'When I am lifted up, shall draw all to myself.' The narrator informs the reader that he said this signifying by what kind of death he was to die. The 'drawing' of the Father is accomplished when the Son 'draws' all to himself. In drawing all to himself Jesus is drawing them into the relationship he has with the Father. This has been facilitated unknowingly by Caiaphas who decided on Jesus' death for the people. On that occasion the narrator pointed out that not only the people but all the scattered children of God are thereby gathered into one (*eis hen*), that is, into one in union with Christ, and consequently in union with the Father. Entering such a communion they enter the new Temple.

This is the third *lifting up* statement in the gospel. The combined lifting up in glory and lifting up in death draws much of its imagery from the Suffering Servant (Isa 52:13-53:12). The other two 'lifting up' statements mention the Son of Man explicitly. Though not mentioned here, the crowd seems to conclude that the Son of Man is implied. 'We have heard from the law that the Messiah remains forever, and how do you say that it is necessary for the Son of Man to be lifted up? Who is this Son of Man?' The Messiah and Son of Man are thus mentioned together by the crowd.

The triumphal entry with the waving of palms and the royal overtones brings the Davidic Messiah to mind, but the hidden Messiah, like a hidden Son of Man of the Book of Enoch may also be in the mind of the crowd.[478] The discussion about a hidden Messiah continues between Jews and Christians even into Justin's time.[479]

In reply, Jesus returns to a favourite theme, the light and walking in the light, choosing the light while there is still time, while he is still with them. The darkness must not overtake them. They are to be children of the light.[480] These remarks are reminiscent of the remarks made on the occasion of the healing of the blind man and the raising of Lazarus. Accepting or rejecting the light is a motif providing the major dynamic of the gospel, just like accepting or rejecting the invitation of Wisdom

---

478. Enoch 7:27; 1:26.

479. Justin, *Trypho*, 32:1 (PG 6:541, 544).

480. 'Children of the light' becomes one of the major themes in the New Testament, especially in regard to behaving as children of the light. cf M. Mullins, *Called to be Saints*, 181, 308-10.

or keeping or not keeping the law in the Old Testament. Those who reject the light pronounce their own condemnation. The reasons for their rejection are explored throughout the gospel. They are afraid of the light lest their deeds be exposed.[481] They do not know the Father, not ever having heard his voice or seen his shape and his words find no home in them.[482] They do not have the love of God in their hearts.[483] They do not believe the witnesses.[484] They seek glory from one another and do not seek the glory that comes only from God.[485]

Jesus said these things and departing, hid himself.

5. CONCLUSION OF THE PUBLIC MINISTRY (Jn 12:37-50)

The conclusion of the public ministry is summed up in two parts. In the first part (12:37-43) the reactions to Jesus are compared to the reactions to Moses and Isaiah, implicitly, by way of allusion, to Moses and explicitly, by way of quotation, to Isaiah. In the second part (12:44-50), Jesus draws together the central themes of his ministry.

Jesus, Moses and Isaiah (Jn 12:37-43)

The public ministry was introduced by John the Baptist with a quotation from Isaiah about preparing a way for the Lord. It is now drawn to a conclusion by the narrator of the gospel with a double quotation from the same prophet: 'Lord, who has believed our message, and to whom has the arm of the Lord been revealed?'[486] and 'He has blinded their eyes and hardened their heart, so that they might not look with their eyes, and understand with their heart and turn – and I would heal them.'[487] The form of the latter quotation does not follow exactly either that of MT or LXX, leaving one to look for Johannine editing. The reference to 'ears' is dropped and God is described as the one who does the hardening of heart (reminiscent of the story of Moses where God hardens the heart of Pharaoh). This is not a statement of 'predetermination' by God of the response of the people

---

481. Jn 3:20.
482. Jn 5:37f.
483. Jn 5:42.
484. Jn 5:19-47.
485. Jn 5:44.
486. Jn 12:38; Is 53:1.
487. Jn 12:40; Is 6:9f. cf the reaction to Jesus' parables (Mt 13:14; Mk 4:12; Lk 8:10) and the reaction to Paul's preaching in Rome (Acts 28:26).

but a Semitic way of expressing an appeal to believe. It also shows how refusal to respond fits into God's plan.

Dropping the reference to 'ears' in the quotation from Isaiah and emphasising 'eyes' is in keeping with the importance of *seeing* in the gospel of John, for to *see* the wisdom of God, the word of God, or the glory of God is to *see* them in the words and works and also in the very person of Jesus.[488] His works bear witness to him and to his Father. They show the unity of Father and Son. To reject one is to reject the other.

As one reads: 'Although he had performed so many signs in their presence, they did not believe in him',[489] one is struck by the parallel with the rejection of Moses. 'Moses called all Israel together and said to them: "You have seen everything that Yahweh did before your eyes in Egypt, to Pharaoh, to his servants and to his whole country – the great ordeals which you yourselves witnessed, those signs and the great wonders. But until today God has not given you a heart to understand, eyes to see or ears to hear".'[490] One is also reminded of the divine ordinance: 'I shall raise up a prophet like yourself. I shall put my words into his mouth ... anyone who refuses to listen to my words, spoken by him in my name, will have to render an account to me.'[491] Moses wrote a song as a witness against the Israelites if they violated the covenant. 'Write down this song to use ... a witness on my behalf against the Israelites.'[492] The whole Mosaic Book of the Law was to be a witness. 'Take this Book of the Law and put it beside the Ark of the Covenant of Yahweh your God. Let it lie there as evidence against you.'[493]

Many believed but through fear of the Pharisees would not confess their belief, lest they be put out of the synagogue. They preferred the praise of people, the human glory to the glory of God. This, by way of contrast, is reminiscent of Moses who sought the glory of God and was in turn glorified by God.[494] This fear of being put out of the synagogue became a real experience on the part of followers of Jesus later in the first century, and so it is a prominent theme here in the gospel.

---

488. M. M. Thompson, *op. cit.*, 142.
489. Jn 12:37.
490. Deut 29:2-4.
491. Deut 18:18f.
492. Deut 31:19.
493. Deut 31:26.
494. Ex 34:29.

Summary of Message (Jn 12:44-50)

'Jesus cried out and said …'[495] These words introduce the final public assessment by Jesus of the response to him during his ministry. There is neither time, place nor context given. The assessment stands on its own as a timeless comment for all generations. It is a summary of the central themes of his preaching.

1. (a) the one who believes in me, believes not in me but in the one who sent me, (b) the one who sees me sees the one who sent me.
2. I have come as light into the world so that everyone who believes in me should not remain in darkness.
3. If anyone hears my words and does not keep them, I do not judge him, for I did not come to judge the world, but to save the world. The one who rejects me and does not receive my word has a judge; on the last day the word that I have spoken will serve as a judge.
4. I have not spoken on my own, but the Father who sent me has himself given me a commandment about what to say and what to speak. And I know that his commandment is eternal life. What I speak therefore, I speak just as the Father has told me.

Accepting Jesus as the one sent from God empowers the believer to see God, to enter the light and embark on eternal life. This is another way of stating the promise made in the prologue: 'To those who received him he gave power to become children of God.' But the prologue also recalls that 'He came unto his own and his own received him not.' In rejecting him and his word, one rejects the Father who sent him and commanded him what word to speak. That word will be judge on the last day.

---

495. Jn 12:44.

Farewell to the Disciples (Jn 13:1-17:26)

The Farewell Meal

1. THE PLOT

The public ministry of Jesus is complete and now the narrative focuses on his final hours, his last meal with his disciples, his trial, death, and post-resurrection appearances. Scholars refer to these chapters of the gospel of John as *The Book of Glory*. It opens with a reference to the approaching feast of Passover, and to the fact that the *hour* has come for Jesus to pass from this world to the Father. With these words the *hour* is now explicitly interpreted in terms of Jesus' death and glorification. Mentioning the approach of Passover draws the reader's attention to the feast which provides an interpretative backdrop against which the final drama unfolds. Jesus now speaks of an imminent exodus from this world, and a return to bring his followers with him. This is the new Passover, effected in the death of the definitive Paschal Lamb, the Lamb of God who takes away the sin of the world.[1]

Like the proverbial flashback of one's life at the point of death, Jesus' life is summed up in terms of the love he had for the disciples. 'Having loved those who were his own in the world, he loved them to the end (*eis telos*)', that is, to the perfection of that love which reaches its goal in Jesus' death for those who believe in him. Following the dialogue with Nicodemus Jesus proclaimed: 'God so loved the world that he gave his only Son so that those who believe in him may not perish but have eternal life.'[2] Jesus is both the revealer of that gift of love and the gift itself. In practical terms this means that the love of God reaches out to the disciples 'to the very end' in spite of their confusion, ignorance, failure, denial and even betrayal. This is the practical dimension of love 'to the end', *eis to telos*. Jesus himself is the example to be followed in carrying out the 'new commandment': 'Love one another as I have loved you ... Greater love than this no one has than to lay down one's life for one's friend.'[3]

---

1. Jn 1:29, 36.
2. Jn 3:16.
3. Jn 13:34; 15:9-14.

The footwashing is closely linked to Jesus' death, being introduced with the statement that Jesus knew that the Father had
given all things into his hands and that he had come from God
and was returning to God. The link with his death is further illustrated by the references to Judas which permeate the passage.
The sharing of the morsel from the dish, an act of special recognition for a guest, is the moment of Judas' final rejection of Jesus.
'The footwashing as an action symbolic of Jesus' death is performed because he knows that he has the power to save others
and the power to lay down his own life for this purpose.'[4]

2. THE MEAL

Now at this banquet, a farewell meal among friends, love will be
the keynote of the celebration. The dark shadow of betrayal
throws Jesus' love into high relief as 'the devil put it into the
heart of Judas to betray him' and on being handed the morsel by
Jesus, he rejected his master as 'Satan entered him'. The control
of Satan and the darkness into which it leads Judas also highlight the victory of Jesus who loves to the end and sees victory in
his death because he knows that the Father has given all things
into his hands, and he is returning to the Father. The ideas of
love and victory are henceforth intertwined as a *leitmotif*
throughout the action and discourse of the Last Supper. Judas,
on the other hand, departs from Jesus, the light of the world, and
enters into the darkness of night, in which those who do not
walk in the light of day, will stumble.[5]

The 'Last Supper' which Jesus shared with his disciples is the
setting for the institution of the Eucharist in the three synoptic
gospels. In John's gospel, however, the eucharistic teaching is
contained in chapter six and the Last Supper is the setting for
Jesus' final symbolic actions, the washing of the feet of the disciples, the sharing with the betrayer of the morsel from the dish,
the farewell discourse(s) and the priestly prayer. In this gospel
the death of Jesus and consequently the final meal take place a
day earlier in the festal calendar than in the other gospels and
the sequence of events moves towards the death of Jesus in the
afternoon of the Eve of the Passover. In the other gospels Jesus
dies on the feast. This has resulted in a debate about whether or
not historically the Last Supper was the Passover meal itself.

---

4. R. E. Brown, *op. cit.*, II, 564.
5. Jn 11:9ff.

Following John's chronology it was not, a fact reinforced by the reference to its taking place in the period 'before the festival of the Passover', by the disciples' belief that Judas had left the table to buy something for the feast and also by the absence of any reference to the elements of the meal and their interpretation, an essential aspect of the Passover ritual. However, it took place in the overall context of the Passover feast and the gospel emphasises the Passover dimension by focusing on the fact that Jesus dies at the hour when the paschal lambs are being slaughtered on the eve of the feast. This is the Johannine way of emphasising what the other gospels imply, that Jesus did not *eat* the Paschal Lamb, he *is* the Paschal Lamb.

However, as it is now presented in the gospel of John this meal corresponds to the Last Supper in the other gospels in its portrayal of the betrayal by Judas, the prediction of Peter's denials, and the immediate sequel in the garden where Jesus was arrested. In other respects it appears to draw on different traditions of his farewell discourse or possibly reminiscences of other meals during that final week, all of which are now edited together and told in the context of the final meal. It is evident also from the 'Synoptic Apocalypse' that Jesus was speaking in 'farewell discourse' mode throughout his final visit to Jerusalem. The remark 'Rise, let us be going', seems to bring the discourse in Jn 13:31-14:31 to an end and 16:4b-33 which has similar themes is often seen as another version of the same discourse, both of which are here edited together in the final edition of the gospel. It may in fact be the case that the former speech was made at a meal earlier in the week, and the latter is a deepening of the themes at a subsequent meal, after the manner of a sage, teaching and further expounding later.

The meal also displays aspects of a Greco-Roman banquet at which the guest of honour, a philosopher, teacher or religious figure, would lead a symposium after the meal proper. Following a transition in which a libation was poured to a god, a hymn or prayer recited, and the women withdrew to pursue their own company and interests, the men drank and discussed. In New Testament times many Jews had adopted and adapted this kind of meal for special occasions. Jesus' meal with Simon the Pharisee where he 'reclined' at table and a woman 'invaded' the male space, only to be defended by Jesus' pointing to her love and Simon's failure in hospitality and etiquette, is a case in point.[6] The tradition associated with the Passover festival would have accustomed them to seeing the festive meal as an occasion for historical and religious instruction. Aspects of Greco-Roman practice, such as reclining for the meal, mentioned twice with reference to the Beloved Disciple, are in evidence here at the Last Supper. Knitting these traditions together Jesus speaks as a Jewish Wisdom teacher, and his disciples function very much like the interlocutors in a symposium. In Greco-Roman society the symposium was the opportunity for establishing reputation and showing off social status. In this context, however, Jesus' washing of the feet of the disciples and emphasis on unity and love are countersigns to the 'status' game.[7]

In ancient literature, biblical and secular, the farewell discourse or valedictory played a very significant part. It acquired a particular weight and poignancy from the situation in which it was delivered and it was the final trump card in the hand of the departing prophet, teacher, leader or head of tribe or family. Gathering together the central insights and primary motivation of his life, the departing person entrusts them to the guardians of his legacy. The farewell discourse is often accompanied by a memorable gesture such as a last meal together, a blessing or, as in this case, a footwashing. The emotional state of the hearers and the reinforcement of the advice with a blessing or curse, promise or warning, reinforce the message. The discourse often includes a prophetic statement about the future of certain courses of action.[8] The final days of Jesus' ministry follow this tradition with the apocalyptic discourses in the synoptics and the farewell discourse(s) at the final meal in St John's gospel.[9] Jesus once more before his rejection and departure calls his disciples to hear and heed the voice of Wisdom. Unlike all other examples, however, Jesus speaks not only of his departure but also of his

---

6. Lk 7:36-50.
7. Paul has to counter such attitudes in 1 Cor 11-14.
8. The Old Testament contains the farewell discourses of Jacob, Joshua, Samuel and David. Some books, such as Deuteronomy, The Testimony of the Twelve Patriarchs, The Assumption of Moses and Jubilees are structured as farewell discourses. In the New Testament Paul's speech at Miletus to the elders of Ephesus summed up his ministry and issued warnings for the future about false teachers. The Second Letter of Peter and the Second Letter to Timothy are both valedictories. In secular literature, for example, Oedipus spoke of the future of the city, in Sophocles' *Oedipus at Colonus*, 1518-55. Cambyses reinforced his message to the Persians with a blessing and a curse.
9. Mk 13:1-37; Mt 24:1-25:46; Lk 21:5-36.

return. His absence, though keenly felt, will facilitate a new presence and a depth of intimacy with himself, the Father and the Holy Spirit-Paraclete. This presence and intimacy are made possible only by his departure. Like the pain of childbirth, the sorrow at his departure will be replaced by the joy that new life has come into the world.[10]

St John's gospel, with its substantial farewell discourse(s), would have been a very good missionary document in the Greco-Roman world, being easy to understand and emphasising the ongoing missionary task of Jesus' followers. Furthermore, Jesus is portrayed as a Jewish sage and functions like personified Wisdom in Proverbs who built her house and then called her disciples, including the simple and immature, to a feast saying, 'Come, eat of *my* bread and drink of *my* wine, live and walk in the way of insight.'[11] The discourse highlights the more universal aspects of Jesus' character, ministry, and mission, the traits that would appeal to Gentiles as well as to some diaspora Jews among the potential converts. In other words, Jesus is portrayed as offering teaching and sharing fellowship in a setting with which anyone in the Greco-Roman world could identify.[12]

3. LITERARY CRITIQUE

The Last Supper scene contains three distinct literary genres. Chapter thirteen is a narrative dealing with the washing of the disciples' feet and the handing of the morsel to Judas, together with the predictions of Judas' betrayal and Peter's denials. Chapters fourteen to sixteen are a farewell discourse (valedictory) and chapter seventeen is a prayer.

The discourse was not recorded by a stenographer but was the product of the remembered occasion, full of closure, meaning, foreboding and promise. It was later articulated in full rational speech by the writer drawing on available knowledge of the departed one.[13] 'Various elements from the recorded memories of the community are laid side by side to form 13:1-17:26 as the

---

10. Jn 16:21.
11. Prov 9:5f.
12. B. Witherington, *John's Wisdom*, 233f.
13. Though articulated in totally different genres the apocalyptic discourses in the synoptics and the Johannine final discourse of Jesus cover many of the same points and elucidate very clearly the message of Jesus for his disciples as he approached the end of his life.

text now stands ... Consequently the canonical form of the last discourse is "an artistic and strategic whole with a highly unified and coherent literary structure and development, unified and coherent strategic concerns and aims, and a distinctive rhetorical situation".'[14]

The discourse proper runs from Jn 14:1 to 16:33, that is between the symbolic narrative and the final prayer. Some scholars have suggested that Jn 13:31-38 should be considered an introduction to the discourse proper in chapter fourteen rather than an integral part of chapter thirteen. However, being in narrative form it seems more like an integral part of 13:1-38 where it serves as the conclusion to the narrative. Furthermore it contains two of the 'Amen, amen ...' statements which are used to introduce and conclude the betrayal and denial prophecies. It concludes the references to the failure of Judas and Peter, both of whom dominate the narrative and make no appearance in the discourse. At the same time, however, it does set the scene for the discourse proper with its emphasis on the departure of Jesus and the glorification of the Son of Man, so it serves a dual purpose.

There are a number of seams or joinings (Jn 13:31; 14:31; 17:1) pointing to the fact that it is a composite discourse. Two large sections, Jn 14:1-31 and 16:4b-33, are like two versions of the same speech, in slightly different language but making similar points about Jesus' departure, its significance and consequences. C. K. Barrett stresses the parallels between Jn 14 and Jn 15-17, pointing out the 'repeating' themes – Jesus' relation to the Father; his departure to the Father; his coming again; his revelation of the Father; prayer in his name; keeping his commandments; the Paraclete; the peace Jesus gives; and judgement of the world and/or the devil. He suggests that these repetitions point to alternate versions of the same discourse.[15] B. Witherington is of the opinion that a 'better explanation is that we are dealing with successive discourses given in a short span of time on related themes'. He sees such repetition as an integral element of Wisdom teaching, and adds: 'It is clear enough, however, that the first discourse is the most unified and reveals the clearest logical progression.'[16] At Jn 14:31 the discourse seems to be fin-

14. F. J. Moloney, *John*, 370 quoting F.F. Segovia, *The Farewell of the Word. The Johannine Call to Abide*. Minneapolis: Fortress, 1991, 284.

15. C. K. Barrett, *The Gospel according to St John*, 2nd ed., 1978, 449ff.

16. B. Witherington, *op. cit.*, 248.

ished when one reads: 'Arise. Let us go forth', but then it goes on for two more chapters and is followed by the final prayer, before they actually leave the supper room. Furthermore Jn 15:1-17, dealing with the vine and the branches and 15:18-16a dealing with hostility and persecution, though now forming one discourse, seem to have originated as two independent discourses. The discourse concludes, not with a blessing or curse as in the farewell discourses of Jacob or Moses, but with an extended prayer of Jesus for his followers (Jn 17:1-26), rather like the prayer of Sirach.[17]

4. THE WASHING OF THE DISCIPLES' FEET (Jn 13:1-11)

The farewell discourse in St John's gospel is placed in a special setting marked by a number of distinctive actions and exchanges. The introductory narrative in chapter thirteen begins with the prophecy about the betrayal by Judas and concludes with the prophecy of the denial by Peter. Between these prophecies Jesus performs two prophetic, symbolic actions.

Laying aside his outer/festal garment and guest of honour/teacher/master status, he dresses as a servant and performs the menial task of washing the feet of the disciples. As mentioned already, both in connection with John the Baptist's remark about not being fit to untie the strap of Jesus' sandal and the anointing of Jesus' feet by Mary of Bethany, a disciple was expected to do for the teacher what a servant does for his master except wash his feet, as this was regarded as too demeaning. A Jewish slave was not expected to wash his master's feet. It could, however, be done as a gesture of hospitality for a very honoured guest. Herein lies the significance of Jesus' action. He assumed the condition of a slave and washed his disciples' feet. He would not call them servants any more, but friends, for he too is a servant. Here the Son of God is also Servant of God, having taken the human condition on himself and as Servant, in the tradition of the Servant Songs of Isaiah, he will represent his followers as he is lifted up, taking their sins on himself, praying all the time for sinners, as he is raised to great heights, glorified by the Father.[18] However, washing their feet also casts him in the role of host as he shows them the honour reserved for very special guests. He is the host who will welcome/receive them into his Father's house whither he is going to prepare a place for them.

17. Sir 51.
18. Isa 52:13-53:12.

Accepting Jesus' Salvific Death (Jn 13:6-11)

By dying for his followers Jesus will receive them into his Father's house and the footwashing symbolically portrays this redeeming, welcoming and cleansing nature of his forthcoming death. This service from him they must accept if they are to be part of him. Peter misses the point and protests, just as he does following the prediction of the passion in the synoptics.[19] He protests at having to accept the servant model of salvation by Jesus. As in the case of the cleansing of the Temple and the entry into Jerusalem, the disciples did not understand the significance of what was taking place, but they would understand 'later'.[20] This delay in understanding highlights the fact that the foot-washing is not simply an act of humility, a ritual of hospitality or a 'penitential' or 'purificatory' rite like those practised by John the Baptist or the Qumran community. The disciples would have been familiar with these 'rituals' and not have needed any explanation. It is, however, a salvific act, an action that can only be understood when they have experienced Jesus' hour of death and glorification, that is, his death, resurrection and sending of the Paraclete. The narrative focuses on Peter and his objection. The salvific and cleansing nature of Jesus' action is particularly apt in his case in the light of Peter's forthcoming denials and his subsequent realisation of his need for cleansing and restoration. This will be well portrayed in his triple confession of love for Jesus and Jesus' confirmation of him in his shepherding role in Jn 21:15-19.

In response to Peter's objection Jesus not only speaks of the necessity of the footwashing itself, but emphasises that he him-self must perform it. 'If *I* do not wash you, you will have no her-itage (*meros*) *with me.*' 'Having or sharing a heritage' has a well established history in the Bible. The LXX uses *meros* to translate the Hebrew *hêleq*, heritage. Originally it referred to the God-given heritage of Israel, where each of the tribes except Levi re-ceived a heritage or share in the promised land.[21] Later it came to signify a share in the afterlife and it is used in this context in Revelation.[22] The 'heritage' is described in John specifically as a heritage *with him*, and this is subsequently spelled out in the

---

19. Mk 8:31-33; Mt16:21-23.
20. Jn 2:22 'after he was raised'; and 12:16 'after he was glorified'.
21. Num 18:20; Deut 12:12; 14:27.
22. Rev 20:6; 21:8; 22:19.

farewell discourse as 'where I am you also may be'.[23] This is reminiscent of the question put by the first disciples to Jesus, a question which was really asking for an invitation: 'Where do you live?' and Jesus' answer, containing the invitation: 'Come and see.' The reader, enlightened by the prologue, realises the profundity of the response because it is an invitation to join him where he is. As the Word he is 'with God' and as the unique Son he is 'ever at the Father's side'.[24] He is now returning to the Father and promises to prepare a place for the disciples. To share this 'dwelling' entails accepting Jesus' death on their behalf, his laying down of his life for his friends so that they will share in his death/resurrection. Peter therefore has to accept this service from Jesus if he is to have 'a heritage/share with him'. Only in this way can Jesus receive him into his Father's house. The simplest explanation of the footwashing, then, is that Jesus performed this servile task to prophesy symbolically that he was about to be humiliated in death. Peter's questioning, provoked by the action, enabled Jesus to explain the salvific necessity of his death and how it would bring believers their heritage with him as it cleansed them of sin and brought them new life.[25]

In the case of Peter himself there may also be a parallel with the patriarchal blessing for the firstborn, the one specially chosen to lead the family or tribe, with patriarchal authority over his brothers and sisters, receiving the special blessing and seen as the link in the chain of the promises. The blessing did not always fall to the 'natural' firstborn, sometimes the plan of God was otherwise. Jacob superseded Esau by stealth, Ephraim and Manasseh had their order reversed by Jacob, Judah the 'fourth born' was given rank as firstborn because of the incest of Reuben and the crimes of Simeon and Levi against the men of Shechem.[26] Peter may not appear to be the best candidate, but he will be restored by Jesus and reconfirmed in his commission when he has repented of his denials and confirmed his commitment in his love for the master.

Jesus tells Peter: 'The one who has bathed (*leloumenos/louein*) does not need to wash (*nipsasthai/niptein*)'. The former verb refers to bathing the whole body, the latter to washing a part.

23. Jn 14:3.
24. Jn 1:1:1, 18.
25. cf R. E. Brown, *op. cit*, II, 568
26. Gen 27; 48:17-20; 49; cf 35:22; 34.

Later on in the discourse he clarifies his meaning when he tells them: 'You are already made clean by the word I have spoken to you.'[27] Being washed by the word they are clean all over. They have received the Father's revelation in Jesus. This image of the bath of the word is a theme also in Ephesians.[28] His followers must accept this saving death on their behalf, symbolised in the washing of the feet. This acceptance comes to be expressed in baptism and so baptism is seen early on among the believers as a dying with Christ, a being baptised into his death. In Mark's gospel Jesus, referring to his approaching death, asks James and John: 'Can you drink the cup that I must drink, or be baptised with the baptism with which I must be baptised?'[29] They answer in the affirmative. Accepting Jesus' death and entering into it is the basis for the development of Paul's theology of Christian baptism as baptism into Christ's death. Here in John's gospel Peter accepts the challenge after his initial reaction, but Judas does not accept, nor has he been affected by, the 'washing'. The christological and soteriological meaning of the action is kept alive in the sacramental celebration of baptism as the church appropriates these dimensions in ritual. However, it must be emphasised that the primary purpose of the action was not to 'institute a new rite' but to insist on the practice of what the act symbolises. As Jesus speaks of 'what I have done for you' his emphasis is on the love which the disciples receive 'to the end', *eis to telos*.

The remark that the one who has bathed has no need to wash, has the words *except for the feet* added in some manuscripts. This is generally seen by scholars as an interpolation in the light of later penitential practices related to forgiveness of sin after baptism.[30]

Jesus' further remark, 'Not all of you are clean' is the occasion for the narrator's intervention to enlighten the reader that Jesus knew who his betrayer was, and to protect the reader from the possibility of thinking that Jesus did not know! The narrator had entered a similar cautionary remark after Jesus asked Philip: 'Where can we buy bread for these people to eat?'[31]

27. Jn 15:3.
28. Eph 5:26. *loutron*, bath, not the vessel but the water of the bath; cognate of *louô*, bathe.
29. Mk 10:38.
30. P. Grelot, 'L'Interpretation pénitentielle du lavement des pieds' in *L'homme devant Dieu: Mélanges H.de Lubac.* 2 vols. Paris: Aubier, 1963, 1: 75-91.
31. Jn 6:5.

Leaving an Example/Hypodeigma (Jn 13:12-17)

A second interpretation of the footwashing follows. It can be seen as a moral example of service to be followed by the disciples in serving one another. If the 'teacher and Lord' has acted in a particular way, the disciples should follow his example. It is a challenging reversal of roles and status. If he has done a menial service for them, they should not consider themselves 'above' doing the same service for one another. This is reinforced by the statement 'No disciple is more important than his master; no messenger (*apostolos*) is more important than the one who sent him.'[32] There are a number of synoptic parallels to the Johannine text. Matthew, Luke and John have similar statements where Jesus points out that the disciple is not more important than the teacher and the apostle is not more important the one who sent him. In Mark's gospel Jesus tells the disciples that 'Anyone who wants to become great among you must be your servant, and anyone who wants to be first among you must be slave to all. For the Son of Man did not come to be served but to serve and to give his life as a ransom for many.'[33] This vicarious death is very close to the Johannine picture of the Good Shepherd who lays down his life for his sheep and the description of love in the farewell discourse: 'Greater love than this no one has than to lay down one's life for one's friends.'[34]

Vicarious death is the ultimate implication and deepest expression of service. On closer examination, 'leaving an example' (*hypodeigma*), in relation to the footwashing, is seen to be rich in biblical allusions relating to saintly and noble death. Sirach says of Enoch and his death that 'he pleased God and was taken up, an example (*hypodeigma*) for the conversion of all generations'.[35] In Second Maccabees the martyrdom of Eleazer is destined to 'leave the young a noble example (*hypodeigma*) of a good death'.[36] Jesus is asking his disciples to follow his example in doing for one another as he has done for them, to repeat in their own lives the loving gesture of footwashing which symbolised laying down one's life for one's friend. In the discourse proper Jesus will spell this out as the supreme expression of love. 'Love one

---

32. Similar *logia* are found in Mt10:24f; Lk 6:40, where in both cases it is stated in addition that the disciple should be like the teacher.
33. Mk 10:43-45.
34. Jn 15:12f.
35. Sir 44:16.
36. 2 Macc (LXX) 6:28; cf 4 Macc 17:22f.

another as I have loved you. Greater love than this no one has than to lay down one's life for one's friends.'[37] Jesus adds a makarism/beatitude about those who do these things. 'If you know these things you are *blessed* if you do them.'

This is the first of only two beatitudes in this gospel. It is found here in the context of love and the second is found later on in the words of the Risen Lord when he responds to the confession of faith by Thomas, who has seen him, with the words: '*Blessed* are those who have *not* seen and have believed.'[38] 'Blessed' in this sense (*'ashrê/makarioi/beati*) refers to an eschatological state made possible by the presence of the Risen Christ and the coming of the kingdom. It is much more than the ordinary feeling of happiness that comes and goes with changing circumstances. It is an inner state of peace and contentment that endures even when one mourns and suffers in this world. 'Happy' therefore is too weak a translation, and at times seems quite out of place, as for example when one reads the apparently contradictory statements in some translations of the Sermon on the Mount, 'Happy are those who mourn.'[39] In spite of this, 'happy' is regularly used nowadays instead of the long established 'blessed', with its established associations of faith, redemption, and hope, even in the face of unhappiness and misery. This is largely because of the possible confusion with the other set of words usually translated as 'blessed' (*barûk, eulogêtos, benedictus*) which refer either to God as the receiver of human worship and praise or to a human being blessed by God in some special way, as in the phrases, 'Blessed be the Lord, the God of Israel' and 'You are blessed among women and blessed is the fruit of your womb.'[40]

Betrayal/I am/My Messenger (Jn 13:18-20)
Following the makarism, 'If you know these things you are blessed if you do them', Jesus states that not all are thus blessed. He knows whom he has chosen. He chose the betrayer, knowing

---

37. Jn 15:12f.
38. Jn 13:17; 20:29.
39. Mt 5:5. 'Happy those who mourn' is truly contradictory and an inappropriate translation unless one denies the terrible pain of bereavement, suffering and personal loss. Better by far is the apparent benign confusion of terms than the risk of appearing to deny the human experience of suffering. 'Blessed are those who mourn.' They are very *un*happy but God will comfort them.
40. Lk 1:68, 42.

full well his disposition. His remark is a prophecy that will be
fulfilled together with the fulfilment of the scripture: 'The one
who eats my bread lifted his heel against me.'[41] There is an interesting set of allusions to the Eucharist in the adaptation of this
quotation from Ps 40 (41) and the subsequent offer of the morsel
to Judas. In the LXX version of the text, the verb *esthien* is used
for eating. *Esthien* and *phagein* are the two verbs usually used
for the human action of eating. However, John uses the rather
surprising verb *trôgein* here, the verb used four times in the eucharistic section of the discourse on the Bread of Life.[42] John (or
his source?) obviously chose this verb deliberately when speaking of the Eucharist. One can only speculate about why he did
so. Perhaps it gave special emphasis to the deliberate act of eating. For this reason some scholars think that Jn 6:51-58 may originally have formed part of the Last Supper narrative. This argument is strengthened by the references following closely on the
eucharistic texts in chapter six to the fact that Jesus knew from
the outset those who did not believe and who it was who would
betray him, since the references to betrayal are an integral part
of the institution narratives.[43] Further eucharistic allusions are
found in the adaptation of the quotation from Ps 40 (41) to read
'loaf/bread' in the singular, instead of the original plural
'loaves', as *ho trôgôn mou ton arton* replaces *ho esthiôn artous mou*.
The eucharistic allusions will be further extended in the handing
of the morsel to Judas. Just as Baptism is a sub-theme in the footwashing, Eucharist is a sub-theme in the sharing of the morsel.

Jesus predicts the betrayal so that, 'When it does happen you
will believe that *I am*.'[44] This *I am (egô eimi)* statement of Jn 13:19,
like that in Jn 8:28, is a prediction of a future event. In the circumstances of Jesus' betrayal, leading to his trial, passion and
death by crucifixion, the sovereignty of God and Jesus' true
identity will be revealed when Jesus is identified as *I am*, the divine name applied to the Lord of the Old Testament in texts such
as Isa 43:10 which states: 'You are my witnesses and my servant
whom I chose that you may ... believe that *I am*', and Ezekiel

41. Jn 13:18f; Ps 40 (41):9f.
42. Jn 6:51-58. In classical Greek this verb is generally translated as 'munching,
crunching', like munching hay, and usually used of animals. It eventually came
into use as a description of human eating.
43. Jn 6:64; cf Mt 26:20-25; Mk 14:17-21; Lk 22:21-23; Jn 13:21-30.
44. Jn 13:19.

24:24 which states: 'When this comes about, then you will know that I am the Lord.'

Jesus, in a solemn 'Amen, amen' statement, points out that those who welcome his disciples, welcome him, and those who welcome him welcome the one who sent him. This is a *leitmotif* throughout the gospel, and there are corresponding sayings in the synoptics.[45] The solemn 'Amen, amen' statements (verses 16 and 20) give a sense of closure to the scene of the footwashing, enclosing in its final part the beatitude (makarism), the themes of Jesus' choice and Judas' betrayal, and the 'I am' prophetic declaration.

5. THE MORSEL (*PSOMION*) AND THE BETRAYAL (Jn 13:21-30)

This section opens and closes with 'Amen, amen' statements, the first prophesying Judas' betrayal, the second prophesying Peter's denial.

Jesus is troubled in spirit. This trouble is related to his vision of the presence and power of Satan who is associated with the powers of darkness and death, and who has already taken possession of Judas. Jesus had been similarly troubled before the tomb of Lazarus and following the arrival of the Greeks when he realised that his *hour* had come.[46] He solemnly announces the forthcoming betrayal. 'Amen, amen, I tell you, one of you will betray me.' This parallels a similar announcement at the Last Supper in Matthew's gospel, except that Matthew's text has a single 'amen' at the beginning of the sentence.[47] John's gospel strongly emphasises Jesus' awareness of the arrival of his *hour*, his foreknowledge of his betrayal, the identity of the betrayer, and his control of the whole unfolding drama. He takes control as he commands Judas to do his treacherous deed quickly, just as he will do in the garden when he presents himself to the awe-struck arresting party and when he will remind the wavering and perplexed Pilate that he would have no authority over him were it not given to him from above.

The hospitality of Jesus shown in the footwashing when, in spite of objections, he insisted on washing the feet of the one who would deny him, is now followed by his extraordinary gesture of hospitality to the one about to betray him. The guests at

---

45. Mt 10:40; Mk 9:37; Lk 10:16. Variations on the same theme.
46. Jn 11:33; 12:27.
47. Mt 26:21.

the banquet appear to have been arranged in such a way that Jesus had the Beloved Disciple on his right. On Jesus' left was Judas, and to the right of the Beloved Disciple was Peter. This arrangement would fit the description of the Beloved Disciple's reclining on Jesus' breast, Peter's speaking to him, and Jesus' handing of the morsel to Judas. The betrayer is therefore occupying a place of honour near Jesus at the table and, in keeping with the oriental hospitality custom of inviting the guest of honour to dip together with the host in the dish or offering the guest a choice morsel from it, Jesus hands Judas the morsel. In so doing he illustrates the fact that the one about to betray him is one whom he is treating as a guest of honour. This highlights the depth of betrayal and illustrates why Jesus quoted the psalm: 'He who eats my bread raised his heel against me.'[48] This is the breaking of a sacred code of behaviour whereby the guest does not break the bond of fellowship with the host while sharing his table. Jesus' hospitality is reciprocated with Judas' definitive decision and action of betrayal.

In sharp contrast to the betrayer is the Beloved Disciple, who reclined on the breast of Jesus at the supper, a position recalling Jesus' relationship to the Father, 'in the bosom of the Father' (*eis ton kolpon tou Iêsou* // *eis ton kolpon tou Patros*), a closeness further illustrated by his leaning back 'onto the breast of Jesus' (*epi to stêthos tou Iêsou*).[49] The Beloved Disciple enters the narrative here and figures prominently from here on.[50] The disciples are unaware of what is going on. Peter asked the Beloved Disciple to inquire of Jesus who would betray him. When Judas had gone out they thought he was gone to buy something for the feast or to give something to the poor, as was customary at the time of the feast. Furthermore, the Beloved Disciple is seen to be 'closer' to Jesus, more of a confidant than Peter. This 'competition' between them will be reinforced again in the post-resurrection narratives, and may be a reflection of perceptions, misunderstandings or even tensions, between believers in the Johannine tradition and those in the wider Petrine tradition at the time of the writing of the gospel.

---

48. Ps 40(41):9f.

49. Jn 1:18.

50. It is quite possible that he was a Judaean, probably a Jerusalemite, or someone with family or connections there, as he was known to the High Priest and his staff, and his privileged position at table may well reflect his being the householder.

Just as Baptism is a sub-theme in the footwashing, so Eucharist is a sub-theme in the sharing of the morsel. Jesus dipped the morsel (*psômion*), *took and gave* it to Judas. Here again the eucharistic allusions are in evidence as they were in the adapted quotation from Ps 40 (41). The formula *took and gave* (*lambanei kai didôsin*) reflects the eucharistic formula. In the three accounts in the gospels of the institution of the Eucharist, all three have the verbs '*took, said a blessing* (or *gave thanks*), *broke*, and *gave*'. The account in 1 Corinthians has '*took* and *gave thanks*'.[51] In the six accounts of the multiplication, all of which reflect the eucharistic formula, the five synoptic accounts have the verbs '*took, said a blessing* or *gave thanks, broke* and *gave*'. John has '*took, gave thanks* and *gave*'. 'Take', *lambanein*, is used in all the accounts of the institution of the Eucharist and the reflection of the formula is found in all the multiplication narratives.[52] Here in this text, the verb *take* serves no necessary function other than that of an allusion to the formula. Otherwise it would be superfluous.[53] It is in this moment of rejection of the morsel that 'Satan enters' into Judas. Jesus, however, is in control and gives the instruction to Judas to go and do quickly what he has to do. Judas leaves the light and enters the darkness. As he left the supper room he went out into the darkness of the night. When he had gone Jesus proclaimed the imminent arrival of the final triumph: 'Now the Son of Man has been glorified and God is glorified in him.'

Jesus has washed the feet and shared the table with those who denied and betrayed him. He later reminds them: 'You have not chosen me, I have chosen you', that is, I have chosen you, and love you to the end, in spite of knowing all about your possible failure, denial and betrayal. Following the footwashing Jesus issued the commandment to follow his example. Now after the sharing of the morsel, he issues the 'new commandment' to 'love one another as I have loved you'. This is very

---

51. Mt 26:26; Mk 14:22; Lk 22:19; 1 Cor 11:24.
52. Mt 14:19; 15:36; Mk 6:4f; 8:6; Lk 9:16; Jn 6:11. Textual scholars pose the question as to why some mss do not have *lambanei* in Jn 13:26. Is it dropped to avoid allusion to the eucharistic formula because of sensitivities about Judas sharing the Eucharist, or is it a Johannine harmonisation with the synoptics in the texts where it is included?
53. The sharing of the morsel (*psômion*) may have been part of the Johannine Eucharistic practice. In Greek Christianity the term *psômion* is used for the Eucharistic Host.

striking in the light of his command to do for one another what he has done for them. He loved them to the point of laying down his life for them.

6. TRANSITION (Jn 13:31-38)

Several themes are brought together in these verses which serve both as a conclusion to the narrative section and as an introduction to the body of Jesus' discourse. They include the arrival of the *hour*, the *glorification* of Father and Son, the imminent *departure* of Jesus and the *new commandment of love* by which all people will know his disciples. They include also Peter's enthusiasm to follow Jesus and to die for him, though in fact he is not yet ready to do so, and Jesus' prediction of his triple denial before the cock crows. B. Witherington comments:

> Although the betrayal of Judas means that night and darkness have come, it also means that the bright light of the Son's glorification is about to shine forth in the crucifixion, which reveals both evil at its worst and God in God's most loving mode at one and the same time.[54]

The announcement of Jesus' impending departure and the conversation with Peter, who inquires where he is going and protests his desire to lay down his life for him, form a bridge between the events at the beginning of the supper and the dialogue that follows.

Jesus attempts to allay the fears and misgivings of the disciples at his departure, which are understandable because they have not yet received the Holy Spirit. He points out that his going will be to their long-term advantage. This is an overarching theme or *leitmotif* of the entire discourse that follows. In an excellent summary F. J. Moloney states:

> Many themes adumbrated during the ministry have now come to the fore: the frailty of the disciples,[55] the betrayal of Judas,[56] the denials of Peter,[57] the departure of Jesus,[58] the impossibility of following him to the Father 'now' into an 'afterward' when disciples will know and will follow,[59] the

---

54. B. Witherington, *John's Wisdom*, 247.
55. cf 1:35-49; 4:27-38; 6:1-15, 60-71; 9:1-5; 11:5-16.
56. cf 6:70-71; 12:4-6.
57. cf 1:40-42; 6:67-69.
58. cf 7:33-34; 8:21.
59. cf 2:22; 12:16.

knowledge of Jesus,[60] his love for his own,[61] the cross as the moment of Jesus' glorification[62] and the revelation of God in and through the event of the cross.[63] Puzzles produced by the story of Jesus' public ministry converge, and in this sense 13:1-38 introduces the reader to 14:1-20:31.[64]

---

60. cf 2:24-25; 4:1; 5:42; 6:15; 10:14-15.
61. cf 3:16-17, 34-35.
62. cf 1:51; 11:4; 12:23, 33.
63. 3:13-14; 8:28; 12:23, 32, 33.
64. F. J. Moloney, *John*, 387.

The Farewell Discourse: I (Jn (13:31-38);14:1-31)

1. INTRODUCTION: CONSOLATION AND PROMISE

There is a striking paradox between the two main lines of thought running in opposite directions through chapter fourteen. Jesus is about to depart and to return, to be absent and yet present in his absence. His departure is necessary for his return in a new mode of presence. The disciples will experience the sadness of his departure and the joy of his return. For his departure there are words of consolation and reassurance, for his return words of joy and promise. Significantly, words of comfort open the discourse that will introduce the Paraclete/Comforter. The words which begin the discourse 'Let not your hearts be troubled', are followed quickly by similarly comforting words, 'Do not let your hearts be troubled or afraid', which appear in close association with the equally comforting promise 'My peace I leave with you, my peace I give you.'[65] The disciples are confused and anxious. Their sentiments are articulated by Thomas, Philip and Judas (not Judas Iscariot), who struggle with Jesus' words and promises. Like dialogue partners, their questions punctuate the discourse as they provide the opportunity for Jesus to explain further the significance of his departure and the promise of his return.

Three sets of imperatives or exhortations punctuate the chapter, creating the sense of three major sections. They are the imperatives to believe, to love and to 'keep my word'.[66] Closely related to the various commands and exhortations are the promises that Jesus will return, and that he, the Father and the Spirit-Paraclete will come to dwell with the believer. The chapter is like a tapestry woven round a number of central themes which run through it like colour threads appearing and then reappearing in heavier concentration. Repetition of themes is a rhetorical device in which a theme is mentioned, brought to an initial level of perception and articulation, and then subsequently developed and reinforced.

The 'return' of Jesus is to be understood in a sense different from that of popular eschatology. When he said, 'I will come again and take you to myself, that where I am you too may be',

---

65. Jn 14:27.
66. The imperative form of the verb is not used in each case, but the meaning is imperative.

he meant that after his death, and because of it, his followers would enter into union with him as their living Lord, and through him into union with the Father, and so enter into eternal life.[67] J. McPolin explains this new situation:

> Jesus' passing to the Father leads to a new situation that is characterised by 'keeping my commandments,' i.e. by living according to his word (cf 15:10). This relationship between Jesus and the disciples has already been explained in terms of faith (v 12), but now Jesus speaks of a loving relationship based on active docility to his word. This desire of Jesus to be loved is perfectly at home in the covenant atmosphere of the Last Discourse and Supper (cf 13:34-35). Just as the covenant God of Sinai desired to be loved exclusively by his people (Deut 6:5), Jesus now calls for exclusive love because he is God's visible presence among disciples, establishing a new covenant of friendship with them.[68]

2. BELIEVE (TRUST) (Jn 14:1-14)

The dominant note struck in this section of the discourse, emphasised at the opening and again at the close of the section, is the imperative to *believe*, *(pisteuein eis)*, a verb that could be equally well translated here as to *trust*. This imperative: 'Believe (trust) in God, believe (trust) also in me' is followed by the question: 'Do you not believe that I am in the Father and the Father is in me?' and the further imperative, reinforced with an appeal to Jesus' works: 'Believe me that I am in the Father and the Father is in me; but if you do not, then believe me because of the works themselves.' The promise of greater works brings to a climax the exhortation to believe. 'Amen, amen, I tell you, the one who believes in me will also do the works that I do and, in fact, will do greater works than these because I am going to the Father.'[69] Going to the Father, shedding the limitations of the *sarx*, he will be omnipresent like Wisdom, and with the Father he will be everywhere at once. Within this context of belief, a number of themes are explored.

Preparing a Place (Jn 14:1-6)

Opening with: 'Let not your hearts be troubled', Jesus urges his disciples to believe in God and in himself. This is striking as it is

---

67. C. H. Dodd, *Interpretation*, 405.
68. J. Mc Polin, *op.cit.*, 160.
69. Jn 14:12.

poignant – asking them to believe in an obviously doomed man about to die. Then he tells them that he is going to prepare a place for them, and that he will return to take them with him, 'so that where I am you will be also'. 'Being with him' reminds the reader of the approach of the first disciples when they asked: 'Rabbi, where do you dwell (*pou meneis*)?' and Jesus' reply: 'Come and see.' 'Dwelling' both as verb (*menein*) and corresponding noun (*monê*) has profound significance in the gospel. When John the Baptist bore witness to the Spirit coming upon Jesus he said the Spirit came from heaven and remained/ resided/dwelt upon him (*emeinen ep'auton*).[70] This describes a permanent relationship or communion with the Spirit. These two examples at the outset describe important relationships and are an interpretative key for the many uses of *menein/monê* in the gospel. 'Where', 'whence' and 'whither' have been recurring throughout the gospel as disciples and people wonder where Jesus dwells, where he has come from and where he is planning to go. This questioning helps to set the scene for the development of the theme of 'dwelling' throughout the gospel and is very much in evidence here in the farewell discourse(s).

Jesus tells the disciples that he is going to prepare a place for them. The terms *preparing* and *place*, both individually and combined in the phrase *preparing a place*, have significant biblical overtones, usually, but not exclusively, cultic.[71] The Bible speaks of *preparing* the land and *preparing* the people to be God's people and to act accordingly.[72] David *prepared a place* for the Ark of God and pitched a tent for it.[73] The work of building the Temple is described in terms of *preparing* the Temple. 'Now all the work had been *prepared* from the day when the foundation was laid, until Solomon finished the house of the Lord.'[74] Similarly the Book of Wisdom speaks of *preparing* the holy tent.[75]

The term *place* also has significant biblical overtones. It usually refers to 'the Holy Place', the *place* of worship and sacrifice. Jacob's dream at Bethel also revealed the holiness of *the place* and caused him to exclaim: 'Surely God is in this *place* ... it is the

---

70. Jn 1:32f. *katabainon kai emeinen* (1:32); *katabainon kai menon* (1:33).
71. M. Coloe, *op. cit.*, 164.
72. Ex 23:20; 2 Sam 7:24; 2 Chr 29:36.
73. 1 Chr 15:1, 3, 12; 2 Chr 1:4; and LXX 2 Chr 3:1.
74. 2 Chr 8:16.
75. Wis 9:8.

House of God'.[76] Regularly the Temple is called 'the Holy
Place'.[77] or the *place* where God will set his name[78] and God's
dwelling *place*.[79] It is prominent in the Abraham - Isaac story in
Genesis. The story of the binding and sacrificing of Isaac emphasises the *place* pointed out by God for the intended sacrifice.
There are four references to *the place* in the story as the reader ac-
companies the loving father and the only, beloved son whom he
is preparing to sacrifice, to *the place* of intended sacrifice. The
Second Book of Chronicles associates that place, Moriah, in the
Genesis story with Mount Moriah in Jerusalem, the *place* David
chose for the Temple, and henceforth the Holy Place associated
with the Temple became identified with *the place* of the
Abraham-Isaac sacrifice.[80] The story of the binding of Isaac and
leading him to *the place* of sacrifice is recalled as Jesus is bound,
loaded with the cross and led to *the place* called the skull, in
Hebrew, Golgotha.[81] From these biblical antecedents one can
appreciate the significance of the phrase 'going to *prepare a place*
for you'. Jesus now goes on to speak of the *place* in terms of his
Father's House.

My Father's House
At first glance the reference to 'many rooms/mansions' makes
one think of the 'many rooms' in a house, palace, temple or, in a
transferred sense, in heaven itself whither Jesus is returning to
the Father to prepare a place for the disciples. This heavenly
home is the ultimate eschatological goal of salvation. Here, however, the dominant theme in the text is not where the believer
will abide, but where God, Father, Son and Spirit-Paraclete,
abide. Jesus will take, that is, he will receive and welcome, his
disciples into his Father's house. This raises the question,
'Where, then, is his Father's house?' The reader looks back to the
first use of the term 'My Father's house' in the gospel, (which is
also its first use in the Bible). At the 'cleansing of the Temple'
Jesus spoke of 'my Father's house' and in the confrontation that
followed his action, the *logion*, 'Destroy this Temple and in three
days I will build it up', shifted the centre of divine dwelling to

---

76. Gen 28:11-19.
77. Ex 26:33; Lev 16; 1 Kings 8:6, 8, 10.
78. Ex 20:24; Deut 12: 5, 11, 21.
79. Pss 74:7; 76:2; 132:7; Ezek 37:27.
80. Gen 22:1-19.
81. Jn 19:17.

himself, in his risen glorified state, according to the interpretation supplied by the narrator. The reader therefore knows that 'my Father's House' is the dwelling place of God. For Jesus it is the New Temple, the Bethel of the Son of Man, the 'place' of worship in spirit and in truth which is neither in Jerusalem nor in Gerizim, but is now being relocated in himself and through his glorification, in the believing and redeemed community. This community enjoys the interpersonal relationships made possible by Jesus' going to the Father and returning to establish the indwelling of Father, Son and Spirit-Paraclete in the believers. In being 'lifted up' Jesus draws all to himself so that they will be 'with me where *I am*'. The Father's love and life, present in Jesus, are so great that there is room for all disciples in that communion which he offers. All the expressions, 'place', 'dwelling places', 'my Father's house' (cf 2:16), refer to Jesus himself, who is the new temple because in him and through him believers enjoy communion with God.[82] As seen already, 'place' for John refers not only to a physical space or location, but at a much deeper level it refers to a relationship. Jesus is now going to prepare 'the universal and permanent possibility of an abiding communion with the Father'.[83]

The Way, the Truth and the Life (hê hodos, hê alêtheia, hê zôê)
In the dialogue with Thomas about the *way* to *the place* where he is going, Jesus proclaims: 'I am the way, the truth and the life.' The assertion, 'I am the way', is in response to Thomas' comment about not knowing either *where* he is going or the *way*. In this Thomas is like the Jews who wonder where he is going.[84] Typical of the gospel, Thomas' misunderstanding on the physical level is the opportunity for Jesus to respond on the spiritual level. 'I am the *way*' is another *I am* statement with a predicate, signifying Jesus' life-giving relationship with the community of believers. He is the way to the Father, to the rooms in the Father's House. Not only the place but also the way to the place is explained in terms of relationship.

In proclaiming 'I am the way' Jesus conjures up the imagery of God leading the people through the wilderness as described in Deuteronomy: '*YHWH* your God who has gone in front of

---

82. Jn 2:19; 4:21-24; 7:38, 39; 14:23. cf J. McPolin, *op. cit.*, 156.
83. F. J. Moloney, *John*, 394.
84. Jn 7:35f; 8:22.

you on the journey to find you a camping ground, by night in the fire to light your path, by day in the cloud.'[85] This divine accompaniment was celebrated in the metaphor of God as Shepherd of Israel in texts like Ps 22 (23) where the shepherd leads the flock to pastures green, through the valley of darkness (death). God accompanied the people on the way through the wilderness en route to the promised land. (Deutero) Isaiah called on the people to prepare the way of the Lord as the new Exodus, this time from Babylon, was about to take place.[86] The way to the promised land became a metaphor for life's journey with its religious and ethical obligations, choices and values. These are called the way of *YHWH*, the ways which *YHWH* commanded, the ways which the righteous keep.[87] In the wisdom tradition they are called the way of wisdom, the way where wisdom can be found, the way of the righteous 'which *YHWH* knows', the ways which please *YHWH* and the way from which the wicked depart.[88] *YHWH* leads Israel in the way it should go and shows them the good way they ought to follow.[89] Speaking of the true way from which the wicked departed, the author of Wisdom lamented: 'Clearly we have strayed from the way of truth; the light of justice has not shone for us, the sun never rose on us.'[90] Not only 'the way' but its final goal is stressed. 'The way of the virtuous … leads to life', is highlighted in turn by the contrast: 'The way of the wicked leads to doom.'[91]

'The way' figures prominently in the New Testament. Among the opening words of the gospel were those of John the Baptist calling out: 'Prepare the way of the Lord.' 'Preparing the way' strikes many a biblical chord. Relating to his mission and the challenge it issues, Jesus in Matthew's Sermon on the Mount urges the listeners to 'enter by the narrow gate, since *the way* that leads to perdition is wide and spacious, and many take it; but it is a narrow gate and *a hard way* that leads to life, and only a few find it.'[92] Here in a typical synoptic style *logion*, are two images together, the *way* and the *door*. Both appear in John's gospel

85. Deut 1:33.
86. Isa 40:1ff.
87. Deut 5:23; Ex 32:8; Jer 5:4ff; 7:23; 1 Sam 12:23; 2 Sam 22:22; Prov 16:7.
88. Job 28:13, 23; Prov 16:7; Wis 5:6.
89. Ps 24 (25):9; Is 2:3; 48:17; 1 Kings 8:36; Prov 4:11.
90. Wis 5:6.
91. Ps 15 (16):11; Ps 1:6.
92. Mt 7:13f.

where they are set in specific contexts and elaborated on at greater length. Jesus proclaimed himself to be the door to the pasture, that is, to salvation, whither the shepherd would lead the flock.[93] He now makes the same claim in relation to the *way*, this time in the language of the Father–Son relationship: 'Nobody comes to the Father except through me.'[94] In the Letter to the Hebrews Jesus is portrayed as the way into the sanctuary which is not available to the levitical priesthood. He is seen there as the way in so far as he is the priest offering effective redeeming sacrifice.[95] In Mark and Luke-Acts the term 'the way' is used for the following of Jesus, for discipleship in Mark's gospel and for membership of the community, the church, in the Acts of the Apostles. In Mark's gospel, for example, the formerly blind man followed Jesus 'on the way', and in the Acts of the Apostles Paul's Damascus Road experience took place when he was going to arrest, and bring to Jerusalem, any men or women he could find who were ' followers of the way'.[96]

Here in St John's gospel, Jesus not only leads the believers along the way, or teaches them a way of wisdom and righteousness, but he himself *is* the way. He is the way because he is the revelation of God and reveals that 'the ways of *YHWH* are love and fidelity/truth'.[97] He reveals the thoughts and ways of God 'whose thoughts and ways are as far above human thoughts and ways as the heavens are above the earth'.[98] He is the way by being the truth and the life, the source of revelation and regeneration.[99] He is the way soteriologically by his saving death.[100] He is the way ecclesially by his drawing to himself (*helkuein*) and gathering together (*synagein*) the believing community and his return to make it the place of indwelling for Father, Son and Spirit-Paraclete.[101]

---

93. Jn 10:7f.
94. Jn 14:6.
95. Heb 9:8; 10:9f.
96. Mk 10:52; Acts 9:2; cf 19:9, 23; 22:4; 24:14, 22.
97. Ps 24 (25):10.
98. Isa 55:8f.
99. Since the three nouns, way, truth and life, are grammatically co-ordinates, their inter-relationship has to be gleaned from the context and the gospel as a whole. The way to the Father is the subject of the question posed and so should be the referent for the other two points in the answer.
100. J. L. McKenzie, *Dictionary of the Bible*, 'Way', ad loc.
101. Jn 12:32; 11:51f. In the Letter to the Hebrews he is seen as the way into the sanctuary which is not available to the levitical priesthood. He is seen as the way there in so far as he is the priest offering effective redeeming sacrifice. cf Heb 9:8; 10:9f.

Jesus' claim to be the way is not simply eschatological. Bultmann emphasises the revealer-revelation aspect of 'the way'. He points out that the question about 'the way', is very quickly deflected into a question about the present fellowship with the Revealer, so that 'the anxiety in which the believer is placed is not anxiety about the promised otherworldly future, but about the believing existence in the world'.[102] He understands *Egô eimi hê hodos* (I am the way) as 'pure expression of the idea of revelation' and explains that the Revealer is the access to God which man is looking for, an explanation further clarified in the statement 'nobody can come to the Father except through me'. The Son is the only access to the Father. 'The believer finds God only in *him*, i.e. God is not directly accessible; faith is not mystical experience, but rather historical existence that is subject to the revelation.'[103]

Jesus is the way because he is the truth and life (*hê alêtheia kai hê zôê*). The truth is the revealed reality of God and God's dealings with humanity, and the life is the divine gift which bestows life on the believer, here and hereafter, through the Father's gift of the Son, as Jesus asserts in his prayer at the end of the supper: 'Eternal life is this: to know you the only true God and Jesus Christ whom you have sent.'[104] Jesus is both the revealer and the revelation of God and as such he is the way and the goal of the way, being himself the truth and the life. Like bright threads in a tapestry, truth and life have been dominant themes throughout the gospel.[105] Here they are brought together, summed up as the way, and predicated of Jesus in the one *ego eimi* assertion: ' I am the way, the truth and the life.'

Seeing the Father (Jn 14:7-14)
Philip's request 'Show us the Father' facilitates Jesus' explanation of himself as the revealer and the revelation of the Father. Philip is reminiscent of Moses and his request to see the glory.[106] Maybe he was hoping for some kind of theophany, because he saw Jesus and the Father as two totally distinct realities. Jesus' answer emphasised the fact that one should not be looking for

---

102. R. Bultmann, *op.cit.*, 602.
103. R. Bultmann, *op. cit.*, 606.
104. Jn 17:3.
105. Truth: 1:14, 17; 5:33; 8:32, 40, 44-46; Life: 1:4; 6:33, 35, 48, 63, 68; 8:12; 10:10; 11:25.
106. Ex 33:18.

visionary experiences, but should put one's belief in Jesus and his revelation of the Father in his person, words and works. In the words of Bultmann just quoted, 'God is not directly accessible; faith is not mystical experience, but rather historical existence that is subject to the revelation.' Jesus is that revelation and so he responds to Philip: 'If you had known me you would have known the Father ... henceforth you know him and have seen him ... He who has seen me has seen the Father.'[107] Jesus explains again, as he has done repeatedly throughout the gospel, that he has been speaking and working on behalf of the Father, and so the works witness to the love, salvific plan and authority of the Father. They are therefore a call to faith: 'Believe me for the sake of the works themselves.'[108] He made the same point when he referred to his works as a witness to the Father's authority for his ministry of word and deed after he was accused of breaking the Sabbath and blaspheming at the Pool of Bethesda.[109]

3. LOVE (Jn 14:15-24)

Just before the final exchange between Jesus and Peter at the supper, before Jesus began the discourse proper, he gave the disciples 'a new commandment', the one and only commandment he gave them: 'Love one another as I have loved you.' He added: 'By this will everyone know that you are my disciples, if you love one another.'[110] Here in the discourse proper the imperative to love is described in terms of 'keeping my commandments' and 'keeping my words'. 'If you love me you will keep my commandments', and 'The one who has my commandments and keeps them is the one who loves me.'[111] This is repeated in reference to 'the words' of Jesus: 'The one who loves me keeps my words and my Father will love him', and 'The one who does not love me does not keep my words.'[112] In this context of the imperative to love, a number of themes are explored, notably that of the sending of the Paraclete.

Now that he is returning to the Father and shedding the *sarx* with its limitations of earthly existence, Jesus will be ever present to the believing and praying community, and will do even

---

107. Jn 14:7-9.
108. Jn 14:11.
109. Jn 5:15-20.
110. Jn 13:35.
111. Jn 14:15, 21.
112. Jn 14:23f.

greater works, having shed his earthly limitations. He will be omnipresent like the Father, and like Wisdom will take up his abode among God's people. The community will pray 'in his name', that is, in communion with him as he was with the Father. As they speak and act in his name the Father will respond to them as to Jesus. They will say and do what they learned from him in his time with them. St Paul explained the same disposition in terms of putting on, and acting in accordance with, the mind of Christ.[113] Remembering, in the face of a hostile world, what Jesus said and did, will be made possible by the gift of the other Paraclete, the Advocate-Counsellor who will enable them to remember and lead them to an understanding of all that Jesus said and did.

Paraclete/Comforter/Advocate (Paraklêtos)

When Jesus promised to send a Paraclete or Advocate/Counsellor he spoke in terms of 'another' Paraclete. What does the term mean and the role involve? Why speak of 'another' Paraclete? The expression 'another Paraclete' implies similarity of function and agenda with a 'former Paraclete'. Who was that former Paraclete? A Paraclete is the agent of *paraclêsis*, which has different meanings in the Hebrew and Greco-Roman traditions. The Johannine presentation draws on both. First of all there is the Hebrew, biblical tradition in which God is the comforter of Israel, and is therefore by implication the Paraclete, as is seen in the LXX translation of Deutero-Isaiah, '*I am, I am*, the one consoling/comforting you, (*ego eimi, ego eimi, ho parakalôn se*).'[114] This comforting action of God is announced by the prophet with the words 'console my people, console them, says your God' at the beginning of what has been often called 'the Book of Consolation' (Isaiah chapters 40-55), but the comforting action is found in other chapters of Isaiah as well. The verb *parakalô*, is used to translate the Hebrew verb *nhm*, which means to *console*, or offer comforting words or perform comforting actions. The nouns for comforting and comforter, *paraclêsis* and *paraklêtos*, come from the same root. Simeon was awaiting the 'consolation/comforting of Israel'[115] and Jesus introduced himself with some of these comforting words of Isaiah: 'The Spirit of the Lord

---

113. 1 Cor 2:16; Phil 2:5 et al.
114. Isa 51:12 (LXX).
115. Lk 2:25.

is upon me, he has anointed me and sent me to bring good news to the poor, to bind up hearts that are broken ...'[116] The comforting action of *paraclêsis* is spelled out in this passage as it is in Jesus' response to the messengers of the Baptist: 'Go and tell John what you have heard and seen, the blind see, the lame walk, the lepers are cleansed.'[117]

Jesus' followers continued his ministry of comforting words and actions. Paul was invited to address 'words of consolation' to the community in Pisidia, and in writing to the Corinthians he said that 'the one who prophesies talks to other people, to their improvement, their encouragement and their consolation.'[118] The Antioch community 'took comfort' from the apostolic letter from Jerusalem. Perhaps one of the most striking examples is what Paul wrote to the Corinthians after one of his reconciliations with the troublesome community: 'Blessed be the God and Father of our Lord Jesus Christ, a gentle Father and the God of all consolation, who comforts us in all our sorrows, so that we can offer others, in their sorrows, the consolation that we have received from God ourselves. Indeed, as the sufferings of Christ overflow to us, so, through Christ, does our consolation overflow ...'[119] Several more references to consolation follow immediately in the letter.

Paraclêsis is therefore comforting action, words or writing. God is the first Paraclete, comforting the people through word and deed. Jesus is, by implication, a paraclete in his acting and speaking on behalf of the Father. New Testament preachers and letter writers were seen as agents of God's comforting action. The 'other' Paraclete promised by Jesus will continue the *paraclêsis* of Jesus. The promise is made in circumstances calling for comfort and the promise of ongoing consolation and support in the absence of Jesus. The 'succession' role of the Paraclete, following Jesus, recalls also the pairs of successor figures like Moses-Joshua and Elijah-Elisha, the second coming after the first departs and continuing his work.

There is another, forensic, meaning to the word Paraclete, a meaning more dominant in the Greco-Roman world, where a *paraclete* is seen in terms of a legal adviser, helper or advocate in

---

116. Lk 4:18ff; Is 61: 2ff.
117. Mt 11:4f; Is 26:19; 29:18; 35:5; 61:1.
118. Acts 13:15; 1 Cor 14:3.
119. 2 Cor 1:3-7.

court. Throughout the ministry of Jesus one observes the ongoing trial to which he was subjected. He called witnesses to his
defense – the Father, the Baptist, the scriptures, the works the
Father authorised and empowered. Now his followers face an
ongoing trial in a hostile world. They too will need witnesses to
assist them in this trial and to make the case for their defense.
They will have their Advocate, the other Paraclete, who will
prove the case against an evil, condemning world and show
who was in the right and who was in the wrong. In the synoptic
apocalypse the disciples are forewarned about the difficulties
they will face in the world after Jesus' departure, and are given
the same assurance, but in different language. Mark presents
Jesus' warning and consolation as follows: 'As for yourselves,
beware; for they will hand you over to councils; and you will be
beaten in synagogues; and you will stand before governors and
kings because of me … do not worry beforehand about what
you are to say; but say whatever is given you at that time, for it is
not you who speak, but the Holy Spirit'.[120] Luke has a similar
statement, finishing with 'the Holy Spirit will teach you what
you must say'.

The Paraclete in this context, though not exactly the professional defence council designated by the Latin title *Advocatus*, is
one who is 'called alongside' (*ho parakeklêmenos*) and comes to
the aid of the accused, the attacked or the condemned person.
The Paraclete speaks on behalf of the friend in trouble, and gives
favourable witness, refuting the accuser. In the First Letter of
John Jesus is portrayed as a *paraclete*/advocate pleading with the
Father for those who have sinned after their conversion to
Jesus.[121] A. E. Harvey states:

> The standard and most comprehensive activity of any advo-
> cate (is) to bear witness, or give evidence. But instead of giv-
> ing favourable evidence about the followers of Jesus in the
> heavenly court (which is the function of the *paraclete* in 1 John
> 2:1) this *paraclete* will give evidence about Jesus in the earthly
> court …[122]

The two titles *Paraclete* and *Spirit of Truth* appear in the gospel
only within Jesus' farewell discourse(s) in the five so-called
'promises of the Paraclete'.[123] These promises are made to the

120. Mk 13:9-11; Lk 12:11f.
121. 1 Jn 2:1.
122. A. E. Harvey, *op. cit.*, 112.
123. Jn 14:16-17; 14:26; 15:26; 16:7-11; 16:13-15.

disciples not only to comfort them in the absence of Jesus but also to prepare and instruct them for their role as disciples and witnesses after Jesus' lifetime. Two of the five references are here in chapter fourteen.[124] The first refers to the Paraclete as the Spirit of Truth whom the Father gives in answer to Jesus' prayer and who will be with them forever. The second describes the Paraclete as the one 'whom the Father will send in my name, he will teach you all things, and bring to your remembrance all that I have said to you'. The second reference in fact spells out the meaning of the first. The Paraclete is a Spirit of Truth who helps disciples to grow in 'truth', that is, to grasp more deeply the self revelation of Jesus in his person, words and works and to appropriate the meaning and message of Jesus for their lives. The Spirit accomplishes this work within them in characteristically inward action on mind and heart.

The Paraclete is seen here in the farewell discourse(s) as a distinct figure, an independent agent with markedly different functions to those of the Spirit in the narrative sections of the gospel. Only here is it stated that the Spirit indwells the believer, conveys the divine presence of Father, Son and Spirit and communicates *shalom*, the divine gift of peace which endures in spite of persecution and rejection. Only in the farewell discourse(s) is it stated that the Spirit teaches the disciples and leads them into all truth, reminds them of Jesus' words, testifies, and enables the believers to testify, on Jesus' behalf, accuses or convicts the world, speaks what he has learned, declares what is to come and glorifies Jesus.[125]

The Spirit-Paraclete is described as *another* Paraclete who, like Jesus, is *sent* by God. Jesus speaks of him as the one 'whom the Father will send in my name, the Spirit of Truth who issues from the Father'. He emphasises his own role in the sending of the Spirit when he speaks of 'the one whom I shall send from the Father', and when he promises that 'I will send him to you.'[126] The language of agency is patently evident in the case of the Spirit-Paraclete as it was throughout the ministry of Jesus. Just as Jesus did and taught what he learned from the Father, so too the Spirit-Paraclete 'will not speak on his own, he will speak whatever he hears ... he will take what is mine and declare it to

124. Jn 14:16-17, 26.
125. Jn 14:26; cf 1 Jn 2:27; 14:26; 15:26; 16:8-11, 13.
126. Jn14:26; 15:26; 16:7.

you'.[127] This is language reminiscent of the sending of the prophets, the Baptist and Jesus himself. The Spirit *comes* from God like the prophets or angels as a divine messenger, and functions as God's agent to reveal, accompany and chastise.[128] Believers can receive, welcome, know and recognise the Spirit.

Unlike the narrative sections of the gospel where the life-giving power of the Spirit is portrayed with the imagery of water and wind/breath, the portrait of the Paraclete here resembles that of Michael and the Spirit of Truth in the Qumran literature. It resembles also the interpreting angel of apocalyptic tradition where the apocalyptic seer embarks on a heavenly journey and returns to teach the 'things to come', revealing 'all things'. Unlike the evil angels of some apocalyptic traditions who reveal without permission, Jesus and the Paraclete have been sent/commanded to do so, and reveal in accordance with the command they have received when they were sent.

4. KEEP MY WORD (Jn 14:25-31)

In the context of the imperative or exhortation to 'keep my word' the final verses of this section of the discourse summarise much of what has been said. After the second promise of the Spirit-Paraclete Jesus assures the disciples that he leaves them the gift of his peace, a peace the world cannot give. Then he encourages them again not to be troubled or afraid. His going and his return are reiterated in one sentence. Then he speaks of love. If they loved him they would rejoice because he is going to the Father. The ruler of the world is coming but he has no power over Jesus. Again the context and mood of the arrest and death of Jesus are being prepared beforehand. In the garden he will present himself for arrest to those who have fallen down in awe before him, and he will remind Pilate that he would have no power over him had it not been given to him from above.[129] All this will happen because the Father commanded it and Jesus carries it out. Because of this the world will know that he loves the Father.

He is going to the Father so they should rejoice because 'The Father is greater than I.' This assertion has been the subject of christological debate but to discuss it on the level of later christo-

---

127. Jn 16:13-15.
128. Jn 15:26; 16:7, 13
129. Jn 18:4-14; 19:11.

logical controversies is to miss the point of what is actually being said in the discourse, the main thrust of which is the return of the one sent to the one who sent him. The relationship of sender and sent was already spelled out for the disciples after the footwashing, when Jesus affirmed that 'no servant is more important than his master; no messenger is more important than the one who sent him'.[130] This observation made in regard to Jesus and his disciples is now made in relation to Jesus and his Father. These are expressions relating to the *Logos* become *sarx* rather than the '*Logos* with God', or the only Son 'ever at the Father's side'. It is the Father who brings everything to fulfilment. It is he who sent the Son because he loved the world so much. It is he who has determined the hour and the time, the *hôra* and the *kairos*. It was from him that the Son learned everything that he said and did. The emphasis on the Son as agent, as the one sent, focuses attention on the role of the Father who sent him. The Son's 'obedience' to the Father is seen as a harmony of wills rather than ' obedience' in the sense of a servile submission of will, and so the words and works of Jesus are by definition the words and works of the Father. This is *functional* subordination of Son to Father and of Spirit to Father and Son. Now the Son returns to the Father, to the one who sent him. The Father will send the Spirit-Paraclete, the Spirit of Truth who issues from the Father, in Jesus' name.[131] C. K. Barrett points out how the beginnings of Trinitarian theology are found here in the gospel – Father, Son and Spirit are seen as divine, described in personal terms, act with divine power and are experienced as divine presence.[132]

The final sentence of the chapter, however, 'Rise, let us go forth' seems to signal the end of the farewell discourse but to the surprise of the unsuspecting reader it goes on for another two chapters, (chapter sixteen being almost a doublet of chapter fourteen), and then it is followed by the priestly prayer in chapter seventeen. The most likely explanation for this is that various independent versions of the discourse, or versions of more than one discourse during that final period in Jerusalem, circulated in the period of formation of the gospel and they have been included here in an overall framework with different emphases which together contribute to the overall effect.

---

130. Jn 13:16. cf Mt 10:24; Lk 6:40.
131. Significantly, the term Paraclete is personal, not impersonal and neuter like *pneuma*.
132. C. K. Barrett, *op. cit.*, 456ff.

The Farewell Discourse II (Jn 15:1-16-4)

1. COMMUNITY OF LOVE: THE VINE AND THE BRANCHES

'I am the true vine, my Father is the vinedresser.' 'I am the vine, you are the branches.' These two *I am* statements introduce the next section of the discourse. One describes Jesus' relationship with the Father, the other his relationship with his disciples. He has already spoken of his love for the Father, and for the disciples and he has instructed the disciples to love one another.[133] Now all this is summed up in the metaphor or image of the vine and the branches. Under the care of the Father, Jesus as vine is the source of life and life-giving sustenance for the branches, his disciples. The verb *menein*, to abide or remain, is used ten times in verses four to six, emphasising the relationship of Jesus to his disciples. But this relationship is not static. It must bear fruit. The fruit borne by vine and branches is love. Bearing fruit keeps the relationship alive, a relationship arising from obedience to the command to love, and patterned on Jesus' relationship with the Father. There was a great emphasis on faith, light and life in the first half of the gospel. In the second half the emphasis is on love, *agapê*. This love is the product of faith in Jesus which enables those who accept him to become children of God, sharing in a communion of love with God and one another. This love is set in stark contrast to the hatred of the world, a threatening scenario equivalent to that portrayed in the synoptic tradition, most vividly by Matthew, where the disciples will be brought before hostile authorities and tribunals.[134]

The christology and soteriology throughout the gospel have been presented against the background of the history of Israel as it is recalled and celebrated in the established institutions, festivals and religious language of the Jews. Now two related metaphors or images, traditionally used to describe the relationship of God and the people, are taken up and reapplied in the light of Jesus' claims and promises. The vine and the vineyard were established in the Old Testament as symbols of the people and the land of Israel. Isaiah wrote: 'Let me sing for my beloved my love-song concerning his vineyard: My beloved had a vine-

---

133. He has already emphasised 'indwelling', union with him, doing his work and even greater works, and being with him where he is, all aspects of this life-giving relationship.
134. Mt 24:9-13.

yard on a very fertile hill. He dug it and cleared it of stones, and planted it with choice vines; ... The vineyard of the Lord of hosts is the House of Israel, and the people of Judah are his pleasant planting'.[135] He also wrote: 'A pleasant vineyard, sing about it! I, the Lord, am its keeper; every moment I water it. I guard it night and day so that no one can harm it.'[136] The psalmist proclaims: 'There was a vine: you uprooted it from Egypt; to plant it you drove out the nations, you cleared a space where it could grow, it took root and filled the whole country ...'[137]

In these readings from the Old Testament the emphasis is clearly on God the vinedresser who plants, cares for and expects healthy fruit from the vineyard. If the vineyard does not perform to required standards corrective measures, such as severe pruning, are applied. The imagery of bearing fruit emphasises the covenant obligation to act with justice, integrity and love. Not bearing fruit, or producing sour grapes, points to failure in this regard, and calls for corrective punitive action on God's part. Isaiah laments: 'He expected it to yield grapes, but sour grapes were all it gave ... He expected justice but found bloodshed, integrity, but only a cry of distress.'[138] Jeremiah offers a similar criticism: 'I had planted you, a choice vine, a shoot of soundest stock, how is it you have become a degenerate plant?'[139]

Sirach applies the metaphor of the vine to Wisdom which he describes as a fruit-bearing vine that has taken root in the midst of God's people. 'Like the vine I bud forth delights, and my blossoms become glorious and abundant fruit. Come to me you who desire me and eat your fill of my fruits.' Sirach goes on to identify Wisdom and Torah, seeing Torah as the repository of Wisdom.[140]

Underpinning all this imagery was the fact that God had chosen Israel as the covenant people, not because they were great or important but out of love for them. Hosea pointed to this love when he wrote: 'When Israel was a child I loved him and out of Egypt I called my son.' The covenant bond called for love of God

---

135. Isa 5:1,2,7.
136. Isa 27:2, 3.
137. Ps 79 (80):8-16.
138. Isa 5:2, 7 (JB).
139. Jer 2:21 (JB); cf Deut 32:32; Jer 8:13; Mic 7:1-6; Ezek 15:11-8; 1:5ff; 19:10-14.
140. Sir 24:17-23.

and mutual love between the people which would reflect the loving kindness of God. The heart of the deuteronomic and levitical teaching is recalled in the double injunction, designated by Jesus as the greatest commandment of the Law: 'You shall love the Lord your God with your whole heart and your whole soul, with all your strength and all your mind and your neighbour as yourself.'[141]

In the farewell discourse Jesus uses this well established imagery and applies it to his own situation. The Father is the vine-dresser, expecting the fruits and taking corrective/punitive measures where necessary. Jesus is the vine and the believers are the branches, united to Jesus as the life-giver. Life flows from the vine to the branches. The disciples were pruned by the word Jesus spoke to them.[142] In viticultural terms pruning is an action leading to healthier life and growth. The fruit of that healthy life and growth is love. The vine joins the Bread of Life and the giver of living water as another striking metaphor for Jesus in his role as the giver and sustainer of life.

As with the covenant love of the Old Testament, so here also there is a *koinônia* – a communion of love between the disciples, Jesus and the Father.[143] The *koinônia* has its commandment: 'As the Father has loved me, so have I loved you; abide in my love. If you keep my commandments you will abide in my love, just as I kept my Father's commandments and abide in his love ... This is my commandment that you love one another as I have loved you. No one has greater love than this, to lay down one's life for one's friends. You are my friends if you do what I command you ... I am giving you these commandments so that you may love one another.'[144] The Father is glorified by the fruit they bear, that is by the love they have which shows them to be disciples. It is also how the world will know his disciples. Jesus describes the greatest love in terms already used to describe the dedication of the Good Shepherd who lays down his life for his sheep. This

---

141. Lk 10:25-28; Deut 6:5; Lev 19:18. cf Mt 22:34-40; Mk 12:28-31.
142. It extends the image already used in chapter 13 of being 'bathed in' 'puri-fied' or 'washed clean' by the word. The pruning, ritual washing and prepara-tion of the believers for 'consecration' in the truth has been taking place all through the ministry.
143. This is a parallel concept to the Pauline Body of Christ, where the believers are united as the parts of one body under the one head, Jesus Christ. cf 1 Cor 12:12-30, cf Rom 12:4f.
144. Jn 15:9, 10, 12, 13, 17.

Jesus himself is about to do and Peter has professed his willingness to do likewise, but was reminded of his forthcoming loss of courage in the immediate future. However, eventually he will 'be led where he would rather not go', as he lays down his life for the flock in his charge.[145]

Leon-Dufour points out that, 'while the fraternal love of believers can demand a supreme gift, it is first of all a state, namely, their way of life in union with the Son.'[146] It is 'a gift received, rather than a moral requirement; it is the sign that the life of believers is in continuity with the divine communion in which they share.'[147] G. Rossé is of the opinion that the translation 'Love one another as I have loved you' (Jn 13:34) is too weak because it conveys the idea that Jesus is simply a model to be imitated and says that it would be better translated as 'Love one another with the love with which I have loved you.' Jesus describes this love for his disciples in Jn 15:9: 'With the love with which the Father has loved me, so have I loved you.'[148] This is a whole new way to love, and so it is a 'new commandment' and at the same time a sign to all that they are the disciples of the one who is so loved by the Father.

Describing himself as the true vine, Jesus, like Wisdom and Torah, is also presenting himself as the authentic source of life, light, nourishment, instruction and empowerment. This is reminiscent of the Wisdom tradition with its questions, such as: 'Where does Wisdom come from, where is understanding to be found?'[149] Jesus is the source of Wisdom, being the Bread of Life, the revealer and the revelation and the Word made flesh.

In the 'high priestly prayer' with which Jesus will bring the Last Supper to a climax and a conclusion, he prays to the Father for the disciples: 'Sanctify them in truth. Your word is truth.'[150] In saying this he further clarifies what he said after the washing of the feet: 'The one who has bathed does not need to wash for he is clean all over.' His comment that they were already made clean by the word he had spoken to them, is reminiscent of the description of the 'bath of the word' in Ephesians.[151] The word

---

145. Jn 21:15-19.
146. X. Leon-Dufour, *op. cit.*, Vol 3:107, translated in G. Rossé, *op. cit.*, 72.
147. *Ibid.*
148. *Ibid.*
149. Job 28:12.
150. Jn 17:17.
151. Eph 5:26.

by which God calls, instructs and sanctifies the people is essential to the new birth and central to the ongoing covenant relationship. This emphasis on the power and function of the word
is found in all traditions in the New Testament. Speaking of the
'new birth' the First Letter of Peter, for example, describes it as
'not of perishable seed but of imperishable, through the living
and abiding word of God.'[152] Paul speaks of having begotten his
converts through his preaching of the good news to them.[153]
James has a similar statement: 'He brought us forth by the word
of truth.'[154]

This communion with Jesus ensures oneness of outlook with
him, and thereby with the Father. This oneness of mind with
Jesus is the true context and deepest meaning of prayer. 'If you
abide in me, and my words abide in you, ask whatever you will
and it shall be done for you.' The prayer of Jesus and the prayer
of his followers are one. The Father will respond to their prayer
as to the prayer of Jesus.

Jesus acknowledges that there are those who do not belong
to the community of believers. That is 'because they do not
know him who sent me'. Here is the Christian parallel to the
Jew-Gentile division in the former covenant. No longer determined in ethnic terms, the unbelievers 'who do not know God',
in Johannine terms, 'who do not know the one who sent me', are
designated the unbelieving, hostile world (*kosmos*) and they
have their false god, their equivalent of Ba'al, in the Prince of
this World.

2. HATRED AND PERSECUTION (Jn 15:18-16:4A)

The emphasis on love in the community is followed by emphasis
on the hostility, and threat of persecution and death from an unbelieving world. The separation of the believers from the world
is described in terms of their being 'chosen out of' the world,
and 'not belonging to the world'. This is a new 'chosen, holy
people' approach, no longer defined along ethnic or racial lines,
but determined by knowing or not knowing God and the One
God has sent. Not knowing God and the One God has sent is the

---

152. 1 Pet 1:23; *dia logou zôntos theou kai menontos*.
153. 1 Cor 4:16.
154. Jas 1:18. The Letter to the Colossians is very close to the First Letter of Peter
when it speaks of 'the word' (*logos*) of the truth, the good news that has come to
you' and the Letter to the Ephesians is also very similar: 'You who have heard
the word (*logos*) of truth, the good news of your salvation.' Col 1:5f; Eph 1:13.

antithesis of the formula for eternal life: 'Eternal life is this, to know you the one true God and Jesus Christ whom you have sent.'[155] In biblical language knowing and loving are closely related terms, in fact in places they are almost interchangeable. Thus 'not knowing' is equivalent to 'not loving', and therefore, in Semitic idiom 'hating'. It is a sentiment expressed in the quotation which reflects Ps 68 (69):4: 'They hated me without cause.' The believers, on the other hand form a *koinônia*, a community of love.

This community shares the marks of the covenant people. They too are *chosen, called, loved* and *holy*. Jesus now emphasises the chosen/election theme: 'You have not chosen me I have *chosen* you'. Earlier he had spoken about how the Good Shepherd *calls* the sheep. The whole tenor of the speech is about *love* and the divine indwelling will ensure the *holiness* of the people. The revelation they have received becomes, under the guidance of the Paraclete, the basis of their witness to the world. But the world will treat the disciples as it treated Jesus. The servant will receive the same treatment as the master.'They do not know him who sent me.' They have rejected the word. 'If I had not come and spoken to them, they would not have sin … If I had not done the works among them that no one else did, they would not have sin; but now they have seen and hated both me and my Father.'

The Paraclete

The Paraclete, the Spirit of Truth, is again promised. This time the Paraclete's function is described in terms of bearing witness, and the disciples are associated with bearing witness because they have been with Jesus from the beginning. The witness is borne to all Jesus has said and done and the function of the Paraclete is to enable the disciples to remember these things. Then they can bear witness. The remembering also involves what Jesus told them about the hostility they will endure at the hands of those who 'have not known the Father, nor me'.

Whereas in the first part of the discourse, in chapter fourteen, Jesus warns that the world does not receive the Paraclete because it neither sees nor knows him, here the rejection is not just by way of unbelief or indifference, but outright hostility, resulting in trials, persecution and possibly the death of the followers,

---

155. Jn 17:3.

just as happened in the case of Jesus.[156] They will be put out of the synagogues and even those who kill them will consider themselves offering service to God. This foreshadows in story and reflects in fact both Jewish and Gentile hostility experienced by the early Christians.

By the time of the final writing of the gospel, some believers had been excluded from the synagogue. The gospel shows sensitivity to this exclusion in Jn 16:2, as it had in Jn 9:22. The exact date and extent of such exclusion is not known. The persecution by Paul, of which he can say subsequently in his letter to the Galatians that he was acting from intense religious conviction, points to the beginning of such troubles.[157] What is well known, however, is that the Roman emperor Nero had launched a savage persecution of Christians in Rome and Clement of Rome wrote later of a huge number (*poly plêthos*) dying in the savagery. This act of barbarism was condemned even by the anti-Jewish and anti-Christian Tacitus using the equivalent phrase in Latin for a huge number (*multitudo ingens*) to describe those who perished, and going on to say that even the hostile Roman mob were moved to pity that any group should be so subjected to the whim of one man.[158] Domitian had subsequently targeted the Christians in Asia Minor, an area traditionally associated with the Johannine tradition. These attacks were probably the catalyst for the Book of Revelation with its references to Rome as the scarlet whore drunk on the blood of the saints and of the martyrs of Jesus.[159] Jesus had warned his followers beforehand so that when 'their hour' came they would remember that he told them, and because he had already told them they would not stumble or give way to despair. They would die for one another as they witnessed in a hostile world to bring other disciples to Christ.

---

156. Jn 14:16, 17.
157. Gal 1:13f; cf Acts 9; 22; 26.
158. 1 Clement, 6:1; Tacitus, *Annals*, XV, xliv.
159. Rev 17:6.

The Farewell Discourse III (Jn 16:4-33)

1. JESUS' DEPARTURE: I WILL SEND THE PARACLETE (Jn 16:4-15)

Now that Jesus is departing he addresses issues that were not pressing when he was with the disciples. Already in chapter fourteen the reader has heard Thomas and Philip asking Jesus about his departure, and the way to the Father, and heard also Peter's profession of his willingness to go with him and die with him. It is surprising therefore to hear Jesus remark: 'None of you asks me where I am going.' This obviously points to the fact that this is either another discourse or an independent version of the former one that has been edited into the overall material. It runs parallel to chapter fourteen, but like two waves breaking on the shore, the second resembles but comes at a different angle and may bring a larger or smaller volume of water than the first. Though it treats some of the same topics, it is no mere duplicate as it has its own special emphasis. It focuses on the meaning and consequences of Jesus' departure, stressing the positive effects that will follow for the disciples, with reference to the Paraclete (Comforter/Advocate)[160] and with reference to Jesus himself.[161] There is also an increased emphasis on the *hour* Jesus has to face and the immediate effect it will have on the disciples, that is, prior to the resurrection and coming of the Paraclete. The disciples speak more in this discourse, and Jesus himself speaks more plainly and less figuratively.

Commenting on their sorrow at his departure Jesus tells the disciples that it is for their advantage that he is going, because if he does not go the Paraclete cannot come, but if he goes he will send him. In chapter fourteen he said it was good that he was going, that is, it was good for Jesus himself, and by implication for the disciples, because he was going to the Father. Here the emphasis is directly on the fact that it is good for the disciples, because it is the glorified Christ who will send the Spirit-Paraclete and 'only through the internal presence of the Paraclete do the disciples come to understand Jesus fully ... only the communication of the Spirit begets men as God's children (3:5; 1:12-13); and in God's plan it is the Spirit that is the principle of life from above.'[162]

---

160. Jn 16:4-15.
161. Jn 16:16-33.
162. R. E. Brown, *The Gospel According to John*, vol II, 711.

The entire gospel to date has come across largely as a trial of Jesus and ironically at the same time as a judgement by Jesus on his own judges. Sin in St John's gospel is primarily 'the sin of the world', that is sin of disbelief in the One sent, and thereby the rejection of the One who sent him. The roots of this disbelief lie in not knowing, loving or honouring the Father and not seeking the Father's glory, but one's own. This resulted in the rejection of the One sent, the only Son sent as the Father's gift for the salvation of the world. Judgement in this context here refers to God's justice, manifest in the glorification and exaltation of the one they had rejected and condemned in their worldly justice. It is the judgement of God on the sin of the world and the Prince of this world whose powers seemed momentarily to have gained the victory over Jesus in his death.

The trial of Jesus continues in his followers. It is a re-run of that trial in so far as the same factors are at work. Now, however, the reader is presented with another dimension to that trial, as the role of the Advocate is here clearly stated in forensic or legal terms. The action of the Spirit is to convince/convict (*elenchein*) the world about sin, righteousness and judgement. The verb *elenchein* has legal overtones and has a range of meanings, especially in classical Greek, including convict, accuse, cross-examine, and put to shame, depending on who is the recipient of the proof or the object of the conviction. If the recipient of the proof is the world itself, then 'convince' is but part of the process, since the problem is not 'that the world simply holds wrong opinions about Jesus and sin and the like ... (but) the sense is that the Advocate, through the disciples, will convict the world concerning sin, because the world does not believe in Jesus'.[163] If the meaning is to bring the all-illuminating and inescapable light to bear on the unbelief of the world, then 'convict' is the appropriate translation, and it includes 'convince', as the guilty party may well see the light.

What kind of trial is the reader to imagine when reading of this 'convicting or convincing' role of the Paraclete? It is the trial that takes place in the courtroom of the minds and hearts of the disciples, then and now by the internal action of the Spirit-Paraclete. This results time and again in the outward witness borne to the internal verdict, in the courtroom of world opinion. Though the trial, at one level, looks ahead to the final conviction

163. B. Witherington, *op. cit.*, 264.

in the eschatological reckoning, the emphasis throughout the gospel is, however, on the realised eschatology, experienced in the lives of disciples of Jesus, then and now. Though not ruling out a future eschatological event, the dominant sense is that of the here and now judgement in the world.

Jesus speaks about another function of the Paraclete. Being the Spirit of Truth he will guide them along the way of all truth. Again a parallel with Jesus' ministry is seen here in the activity of the Paraclete. The verb *hodêgein* means 'to lead along the way' and is related to *hodos*, way, one of the self designations of Jesus. *Spirit, way* and *truth* figure in the spirit theology of the Old Testament and here they are taken up and developed in Johannine perspectives. In the Psalms the Spirit is mentioned as guide: 'Your good *spirit* will guide me on *ways* that are level and smooth', and 'O, Lord teach me your *paths*; guide me in your *truth.'*[164] Just as Wisdom is seen as a guide and teacher, on which the *Logos*/Word is patterned, so too the Spirit-Paraclete, is Spirit of Truth fulfilling a similar role.

Jesus has just said to the disciples: 'I have much more to tell you but you cannot bear it now', and now he goes on to say that the Spirit-Paraclete will declare to them the things to come. The reader asks: 'What things are being referred to?' Typical of this gospel the reader is left with a few options and probably they are related. The bringing to light of sin, justice and judgement, which has just been mentioned, will be a factor in the disciples' ongoing 'formation'. The experience of Jesus' trial and death, which he subsequently refers to in his remark about their being scattered each to his own home, is also something they will have to experience when the moment comes. So too the joy on seeing the Risen Lord, combined with the gift of peace and the transmission of the Holy Spirit, cannot be experienced until afterwards. The ongoing effect of the death, resurrection and glorification of Jesus will have to be experienced in the life long experience of the believers then and now. The Spirit-Paraclete will aid each new generation in the understanding and interpretation of the once-for-all revelation in Jesus and support them when they are on trial for such witness before the world.

M. M. Thompson sounds a very necessary note of caution about seeing the Paraclete almost exclusively in christological terms and thereby collapsing the distinction between the Risen

---

164. Pss 142 (143):10; 24 (25):4-5.

Jesus and the Paraclete. The Paraclete does not 'replace' Jesus, but makes his presence real, being sent at Jesus' request and in Jesus' name. He functions in a manner modelled on Jesus himself and testifies to his life-giving word and work. They share overlapping functions such as teaching, testifying, revealing, judging and speaking about what they have seen and heard.

The glorification of the Son and his departure from the world do not mean the absence of the Father's glory, life, word, wisdom and presence from the world. The Spirit-Paraclete carries on the work of the Father and of the Son. 'Because Jesus has now returned to the Father, the Spirit is portrayed in terms that show not only how the Spirit bears witness to, and carries on, the work of the Son but also how the Father, the source of all life, continues to give life into the world when the one who is bread of life and life itself is no longer in the world.'[165]

The Spirit not only *testifies* to Jesus but also *glorifies* him and causes his followers to *remember* what he said and did. The Father and the Spirit testify to, and glorify, the Son. They will accompany/be with the disciples, as will the Son. 'Although the Son has now returned to the Father, he continues to be the means through which the Father gives life to the world, and the Spirit both bears witness to Jesus' life-giving work and makes the presence of Jesus real and known to his followers.'[166]

2. A LITTLE WHILE (Jn 16:16-22)

Jesus here has another conversation with the assembled disciples about his departure, reminiscent of the conversations with the Jews, Peter, Thomas, Philip and Judas (not Iscariot). This time he says: 'A little while and you will not see me, and again a little while and you will see me.' The transitory joy of the world at the apparent victory over Jesus is contrasted with the lasting joy of the disciples following his victory. Their present tribulation is compared to a woman in labour whose moment of distress is forgotten in the joy of the new life born into the world.[167]

---

165. M. M. Thompson, *op. cit.*, 184f.
166. *Ibid.*
167. This imagery was used in the LXX version of Isaiah: 'Like a woman with child who cries out in her pangs in her time of labour, so were we … We have brought forth the spirit of your salvation'. It is followed by an appeal to those who lie in the dust to rejoice because the anger of the Lord lasts only a little while (*mikron*) (Isa 26:16). (Trito-) Isaiah calls on all who love Zion to rejoice with her after describing her labour pains in bringing forth her children (Isa 66:7-14).

'A little while', *mikron*, is twice mentioned. The first mention seems to refer to the short time left before his death. The second refers to the momentary loss due to his departure, before his return as risen Lord, not only in his resurrection appearances, but also in his enduring presence in absence through the working of the Spirit-Paraclete among the believers. His return also has overtones of his final return in glory, as portrayed in the synoptic sayings about coming on the clouds and all his angels with him.[168] However, in keeping with the consistent trend of this gospel, the dominant meaning is the 'realised eschatology' of his ongoing presence among the believers.

3. ON THAT DAY (Jn16:23-33)

In the final section of the discourse Jesus points out how he had been accustomed to speaking figuratively, typical of a wisdom teacher who used figures of speech such as metaphors, riddles, parables, aphorisms, allegory and so forth. Now he will speak plainly.

'That day' refers to the new era inaugurated through the death and resurrection of Jesus, a time when the grief and pain of loss at his going gives way to the lasting joy born of faith, which arises from the awareness of his risen presence among the believers. The influence of the Spirit-Paraclete enables this awareness to grow in them. Jesus' death does not deprive him of his life as he returns to the Father and to the life he always had with God, in the bosom of the Father.

When Jesus sees them again joy will have replaced the present sorrow, and that joy no one will take from them. The reader will notice that Jesus does not say here '*you* will see *me*' but rather '*I* will see *you*'. His new presence will entail an absence to the senses. The communion of prayer will have been established. They will be able to ask the Father in Jesus' name, because under the influence of the Spirit-Paraclete they will be in communion with him and act according to his will. To use the Pauline terms, they will have put on the mind of Christ.[169] Until his departure and glorification this was not possible, and so

---

In Revelation 12 the woman clothed with the sun, having cried out in the pangs of labour, gives birth to a male child who is to rule all the nations. In Mark's presentation of the synoptic apocalypse, the tribulations heralding the end of the world are described as the beginning of birthpangs. cf Isa 26:16; Mk 13:8.
168. Mt 24:30f; 26; 64; Mk 13:26f, 14:62; Lk 21:27f.
169. 1 Cor 2:16; Phil 2:5; et al.

Jesus could say: 'Hitherto you have asked nothing in my name.' This new communion in prayer will complete their joy: 'Ask and you will receive, that your joy may be full.' This communion is now described in terms of a bond of belief and love with Jesus, for which the Father loves them, and which gives them immediate access to the Father in prayer.

Jesus now restates that he has come from and returns to the Father and this evokes a final statement of faith from them. They acknowledge that he came from God. Jesus tells them that the Father loves them because they have loved him. They know his origin and destination. However, their faith is not yet complete as they have not yet seen Jesus glorified, nor have they received the Spirit-Paraclete. For this reason Jesus finally forewarns them that they will be scattered leaving him alone. Again the mood is being set for the passion narrative as he proclaims that he is not alone as the Father is with him.

He concludes the discourse with his promise of peace and a call to be of good cheer, even in the midst of tribulation in the world, because he has overcome the world. There will be a time of answered prayer, a time of peace and joy, an age when the prince of this world is judged and all because Jesus has already overcome the world. These promises are directed to the disciples and the subsequent generations of disciples they will win with their witness.

The Farewell Prayer of Jesus (Jn 17:1-26)

1. INTRODUCTION

There are several references to Jesus praying in the New Testament. Some of his prayers are private, some public; some are personal, some communal. Many times in the synoptic accounts of the ministry Jesus is said to be at prayer and his prayer is usually a private conversation between himself and the Father. He withdraws to be alone for his prayer.[170] His prayer in Gethsemane and on the cross are exceptions in so far as the gospels give the substance of the prayer. Some prayers are public such as: 'I bless you, Father, Lord of heaven and of earth for hiding these things from the learned and the clever and revealing them to mere children. Yes, Father, for that is what it pleased you to do.'[171] The synoptic accounts refer also to communal prayers such as the psalm singing at the end of the Last Supper.[172] Sometimes Jesus is seen to follow an established ritual, as in raising his eyes to heaven and saying the blessing or giving thanks before eating. Such is the case in the accounts of the multiplication of the loaves. 'He took the five loaves and the two fish, *raised his eyes to heaven and said the blessing.*'[173]

The Letter to the Hebrews speaks of Jesus pleading with the one who could save him from death.[174] Seeing him at prayer the disciples asked Jesus to teach them to pray.[175]

St John's gospel contains three pivotal examples of Jesus' prayer to the Father, spoken out loud for the benefit of the listeners. At the tomb of Lazarus he prays for the faith of those witnessing the event, after the arrival of the Greeks he prays the Johannine equivalent of the synoptic Gethsemane prayer,[176] and now at the Last Supper he makes his all-embracing prayer, the longest in the gospels. It reflects the content and thrust of the whole gospel of John. It is a theological and christological synthesis, but above all it is a prayer, and by far the longest section in it is the prayer for the disciples.

It is not just a private prayer of Jesus, but a public, didactic

---

170. Mt 14:23; Mk 1:35; Lk 3:21.
171. Mt 11:25.
172. Mt 26:30; Mk 14:26.
173. Mt 14:19; Mk 6:41; Lk 9:16.
174. Heb 5:7.
175. Lk 11:1-4; cf Mt 6:7-13.
176. Jn 11:41f; 12:28.

one, from which the hearers are to learn and deepen their faith, as in the case of his prayer at the tomb of Lazarus. In its context it resembles the prayer of the Wisdom teacher or sage after the *symposium*, like the prayer at the conclusion of the Book of Sirach, in which Sirach, the Wisdom teacher, gives thanks to God for supporting him through life: 'I will give thanks to you, Lord and King … for you have been protector and support to me.' He then goes on to conclude his prayer with an appeal to the disciples: 'May your souls rejoice in the mercy of the Lord, may you never be ashamed of praising him. Do your work before the appointed time and he in his time will give you your reward.'[177] Similarly Jesus' prayer flows naturally from the farewell discourse(s), reiterating and summing up its themes – the hour and the glorification of Jesus, his departure from the disciples, the joy they will experience, the hatred of the world, the division between the disciples and the world, their consecration in truth and the divine indwelling in the believers. As a prayer it reflects the ability of the Johannine writer to produce a unique blend of genres and a comprehensive statement of themes.

The prayer has been likened also to the prayer of the high priest for the people, a parallel further emphasised by the emphasis on 'making God's name known', a function of the high priest who pronounced *the Name* on the Day of Atonement. It also resembles the prayer of dedication or consecration which sets a person, place or thing aside for exclusive service of God. In this regard it is Jesus' prayer of dedication of himself to his final missionary act, that is, his death and glorification. At the same time it is a prayer of dedication or consecration of the disciples in truth, for their own lives and their missionary activity. It is the comforting prayer of the departing Jesus for his disciples to support them in their forthcoming distress at his departure, but it is also the triumphant prayer of the already risen and glorified Lord to support them in their subsequent lives of faith and mission.

Looking at the prayer from the point of view of formal structure, one sees formal indications of prayer in his raising his eyes to heaven, his address 'Father', spoken six times,[178] and his use six times of the verb *erôtaô*, to ask in prayer. The significance and

---

177. Sir 51:1, 2, 37, 38.
178. This includes one 'Holy Father' and one 'Righteous Father' address.

results of Jesus' coming into the world as revealer of the Father form the basis of the prayer in 17:1-12, and his departure from the world and its significance for the believers form the basis for 17:13-26. Four main themes or concerns emerge as Jesus prays for himself (17:1-5), for his disciples (17:6-19), for their converts (17:20-23) and for the perfection of all who believe in him (17:24-26).

There are striking similarities between this prayer at the Last Supper and the instruction Jesus gave to his disciples and believers when he taught them the prayer, conventionally known as the Lord's Prayer.[179] Jesus prays for the glorification of the Father and the edification and strengthening of the faith of present and future disciples. This reflects closely the opening aspiration of the Lord's Prayer: 'May your name be held holy, your kingdom come, your will be done on earth as in heaven' and it fits well into the Johannine concept of glory.[180] Jesus prays that the Father save the disciples from the evil one, in a world where they will be put severely to the test, as he has just warned them in the discourse. This is a petition echoing the final petition of the Lord's Prayer, 'do not put us to the test but deliver us from evil.'

2. Glorify (Jn 17:1-5)

Jesus' prayerful gesture in 'looking up to heaven' reflects established ritual, and sets the tone at the opening of the prayer. The address 'Father', six times in this prayer (once using the title, 'Holy Father', and once 'Righteous Father') resembles the manner of Jesus' address in the synoptic portrayal of his prayer in Gethsemane.[181] Prayer ultimately is a relationship, a communion with God and here is a privileged moment of intimacy between the Son and the Father which is shared with his disciples. This intimacy of prayer heightens the Son's awareness of the love of the Father.[182] That love expressed itself in 'gift'. The Father *gave* the Son his mission, his words, his name, his glory,

179. Lk 11:2-4; Mt 6:9-15. Perhaps the 'Lord's Prayer' should more accurately be called 'The Disciples'/Believers Prayer' and this prayer at the Last Supper called 'The Lord's Prayer'.
180. 'Glory' in the context of the believers' response to God is acknowledging God for who God is and responding to the invitation of God to the relationship of faith (trust) and love offered in Jesus.
181. Jn 17:1, 5, 11, 21, 24, 25; Mt 26:39; Mk 14:36; Lk 22:42. Matthew has 'My Father', Mark, 'abba, Father', and Luke 'Father' in Jesus' prayer in Gethsemane.
182. Jn 17:23f, 26.

his life-giving power, his disciples and his power over all flesh, empowering him to give eternal life to all whom he had given him. Now the Son prays for the fulfilment of that mission of life-giving love. He announces that his *hour* has come wherein the power of God will be finally manifested as he fully reveals the Father when he lays down his life in love for his friends. His death is the full disclosure of the love of the Father who 'loved the world so much that he gave his only Son that those who believe in him may not perish but may have eternal life'. The revelation of this gift of love in the death of Jesus marks the completion of his mission and the perfection of the work the Father gave him to do. In this the Son is glorified and the Father is glorified in the Son.

Having completed the task entrusted to him, he will return to the glory of the Father's presence. That task was to offer eternal life to the believers. It is now accomplished for 'eternal life is this, to know you the one true God, and Jesus Christ whom you have sent.' In biblical terms, 'to know' is to enter into a relationship, a community of love, a *koinônia*. The First Letter of John states it simply: 'Our fellowship is with the Father and with his Son Jesus Christ.'[183] The relationship between Father and Son is the divine and divine-human reality of Jesus in which the believers participate. Herein they find life, dwell and pray in Jesus' name and live in a communion of love.

3. REVEALING THE NAME (Jn 17:6-8)

When Jesus says twice: 'I have made your name known',[184] the reader is confronted with the most profound truth about Jesus. He has revealed the name of God. In biblical language a person's name sums up that person's identity, function, rights, and demands. Here in the prayer of Jesus, the name of God signifies who God is and the life and love the Father communicates to the Son and through the Son to those who believe in him. In giving his name to the Son the Father has communicated his whole self to him. In turn the Son has revealed the name to those whom the Father took from the world to give him. This revelation has opened up a whole new scenario and possibility of relationship with God: 'I have made your name known ... now they know that everything you have given me is from you, for I have given

---

183. 1 Jn 1:3.
184. Jn 17:6, 26.

them the words that you gave me.' For their part they have *received the words*, they *know* I came from you and they *have believed* that you sent me.'[185] Jesus has already stated in the discourse: 'No one comes to the Father except through me', and 'The one who has seen me has seen the Father.'[186] Now in his prayer he says: 'Eternal life is this, to know you the one true God and Jesus Christ whom you have sent.'[187] He sums up this extraordinary revelation in the words: 'I have made your name known', that is, he has revealed the inner life of God and in so doing has invited the believers to participate in it.

God had revealed the divine name to Moses at the burning bush. As the name was seen to contain in itself all the holiness and transcendence of God, its sacred character was protected by circumlocution, avoidance and substitution. The written Tetragrammaton *YHWH* was read as *Adonai*, (LXX *Kyrios*), *Lord*. In Jesus' time only the high priest pronounced the divine name on the Day of Atonement. In Second Temple Judaism, Samaritan texts and many rabbinic writings, 'the name' is used as a surrogate for God. Contemporary with the New Testament the historian Josephus speaks of 'the name I am forbidden to speak' and the 'the hair-raising name'.[188] Among the Qumran documents there is a clear avoidance of pronouncing the name and the stark warning is given: 'Whoever enunciates the name (which is) honoured above all ... shall not go back to the Community Council.'[189] Not only has Jesus revealed in his person, words and deeds the power and authority of God and God's love for humanity and gift of salvation, but in revealing the love of Father and Son he has made manifest the glory of the inner life of God, a glory that has been concealed or protected throughout the history of salvation.

4. GIFT OF COMMUNITY (Jn 17:9-11A)

Jesus now turns his attention to his disciples and their mission in the world. His intercession for present disciples, and those who would become disciples through their word, forms the central part of his prayer. He prays for them because they are a gift from

---

185. Jn 17:6-8.
186. Jn 14:6, 9.
187. Jn 17:3.
188. Josephus, *Ant.*, 2.275f; *Jewish War*, 5.438.
189. IQS 6:27-7:2.

the Father, because he is glorified in them and also because he is
concerned for them after his departure. First of all, they are a gift
from the Father. Everything Jesus has is a gift from the Father.
His mission which resulted in the gathering of the disciples is
such a gift. So too are his words and deeds through which the
disciples came to believe. They belong to the Father, as the
gospel has already made clear, because they know the Father,
they have the love of the Father in them, and seek not their own
glory, or praise from one another, but the glory of the Father.
They came to Jesus because the Father drew them to him. Jesus
can therefore say they are the Father's gift to him, which he now
returns to the Father. The glory achieved through the completion of his mission is their sharing through faith in the life and
love of Jesus and the Father, for this is to the glory of the Father.
Now that his own mission is complete, Jesus prays for them as
they continue his mission in the world, often in hostile circumstances. He asks the Father to keep them in his name. Keeping
the disciples in the Father's name signifies keeping them in the
vital relationship in which Father and Son share with them their
life and love. Jesus' request is therefore that they keep union
with one another through their communion with God. W.
Harrington puts it in a nutshell:

> The disciples are being sent as Jesus was sent, to challenge
> the world, so that people might at last turn from darkness to
> light. He prays for those whom he leaves behind to carry on
> his work. He commits them to the Father's care and prays es-
> pecially that they may experience among themselves the
> warm communion of Father and Son.[190]

5. HOLY FATHER, PROTECT THEM (Jn 17:11b-19)

The address 'Holy Father' calls to mind the biblical awareness of
the holiness of God. Rudolf Otto's classical study of holiness defines it in terms of the numinous, that mysterious quality of the
divine which he describes as 'wholly other' and which strikes
the human being in the presence of the divine as the essential
difference between creature and creator.[191] The holiness of God
is the source of all life, love and power.

Persons, places and things can be described as holy because
of association with the divine. A person or a group can be de-

---

190. W. J. Harrington, *op. cit.*, 79.
191. R. Otto, *The Idea of the Holy*, 9ff, 20ff, 49ff, 88ff.

scribed as holy because of a special favour, designation, experience or power given by God.[192] A place may be so described because of an association with the divine presence or cult, an object because it has been set aside for the exclusive service of God.[193] Through emancipation, election and covenant God made Israel holy, consecrated and set apart from the 'unholy' nations.[194] Thus they were designated the *Immanuel* people, the people among whom God was pleased to dwell. They maintained their holiness by means of exclusive cultic allegiance to YHWH, and living according to the prescriptions enshrined in the covenant. In the case of chosen individuals or groups a special preparation in holiness often precedes a demonstration of the presence and power of YHWH.[195] Such a preparation may involve cultic action such as ritual washing and purifying sacrifice.

It is very significant then that Jesus addresses his Father as 'Holy' (*hagios*) as he begins the section of the prayer in which he speaks about setting the believers apart from the unbelieving world. He prays that the Father will make the disciples holy by consecrating them (*hagiazein*) in truth. They are consecrated by the Father's word, which is the truth revealed in Jesus. Carrying out the mission entrusted to him by the Father, being himself both the truth and the revealer of the truth, Jesus manifested in himself the holiness of God and through his revelation of the truth the disciples are brought into the realm of the holy. Those who follow him are 'consecrated', 'set apart' in communion with him and the Father. The bond thus established is an invitation to eternal life and love in communion with God. This brings the disciples into the sphere of God's life, into the realm of the holy, and thus consecrates them and makes them holy.[196]

Prayer is regularly accompanied by a vow, a sacrifice, a fast or a good work. Jesus' prayer for the consecration of his followers is here accompanied by an act of consecration of himself. In this he is referring to his forthcoming death and exaltation as his act of consecration, a 'setting apart' of all things, especially his

192. Ex 28:41ff; 29:37; Lev 6:11ff; 16:4; 30:29; Isa 65:5; Hag 2:12.
193. Gen 28:16; Ex 3:5; 28:43ff; Deut 26:15ff; Josh 5:15; Pss 5:8ff, 45 (46):5; 77 (78):54; Zech 2:16; Isa 27:13; Jer 31:22ff, 42:8; 52:1ff. The great example of 'consecration' or 'setting aside for God' is the act of sacrifice in which an animal is put completely beyond human use.
194. cf The Holiness Code: Lev 17-26.
195. Ex 19:10; Josh 3:5; 7:13.
196. In the parable of the vine, the word that Jesus has spoken is seen as the instrument of pruning (Jn 15:3).

own life, into the hand of God. In the language of worship it could be seen as a purifying sacrifice preparing the people for consecration to God, and in the language of moral response it could be seen as the ultimate obedience to God, manifested in the vicarious suffering of the Servant, leading to his exaltation and its saving effects on the followers.[197] In the language of St John's gospel, Jesus' death and exaltation are the supreme example of a consecration or 'setting apart' for the glory of God. It is the supreme example of giving glory to God and being glorified in return. It is not a seeking of 'selfish' reciprocal glorification, but a supreme moment of revelation through which the followers are touched by the glory of the Father, manifest in the Son's exaltation.

The people of Israel were holy, with God dwelling in their midst. They were constituted a holy people by emancipation, election and covenant. They preserved their holiness by remaining cut off from the unclean nations. The disciples of Jesus are emancipated from the prince of this world and his influence in the world. They are elected by Jesus. He told them: 'You have not chosen me, I have chosen you.' God has gifted them in Jesus with grace and truth, the *hesed* and *emet* foundations of the covenant bond. They have received the new commandment of love. They are the new Temple with Father, Son and Spirit-Paraclete dwelling in their midst in a whole new way as they share communion of life and love with God. Now the disciples of Jesus are 'separated' from the unbelieving world, the *kosmos* and the repetition of the words 'protect', 'guard', 'not lose', 'not belonging to the world' in Jesus' prayer emphasise the holiness, consecration and separation of the believers in the face of an unbelieving, hostile world which is ready to contaminate and steal the disciples. Jesus prays to the Father to protect them, recalling how he himself protected them when he was with them and not one was lost except *ho huios tês apôleias*, 'the son of perdition/destruction'.

Who is this 'son of perdition (or destruction)'? The reference is usually taken as referring to Judas. F. J. Moloney, however, points out that though it is often regarded as a reference to Judas, this expression must be given the meaning it has in the only other place it appears in the New Testament, that is, in the Second Letter to the Thessalonians where it refers to a Satanic

---

197. Deut 15:19, 21; Isa 52:13-53:12; Jn 1:29, 36.

figure.[198] The gospel of John twice refers to the action of Satan in taking over Judas. 'The devil had already put it into the heart of Judas son of Simon Iscariot to betray him', and 'Satan entered him.'[199] He explains further that the only person in the story Jesus could not 'care for' is Satan who planned the betrayal. He kept and cared for all the disciples entrusted to him by the Father, including Judas. As his gestures indicate when he washed the feet and shared the morsel with Judas despite Satan's designs, not even Judas can be judged as lost.[200] As W. J. Harrington wisely remarks, judgement is best left to a loving and forgiving God.[201]

6. PRAYER FOR COMMUNITY/THAT THEY MAY BE ONE (Jn 17:20-23)

Jesus prays especially for one special gift for his disciples, a life of intimacy with God, a communion with himself and his Father. Three times he repeats his prayer for this 'oneness'. He is praying not only for those who are at table with him, but also for all subsequent generations who through their word will come to believe. Through his revelation to them, and through their revelation to others, Jesus opens up the possibility of sharing in the oneness or communion of love that exists between him and the Father. 'It is not a matter, then, of a simple union of a moral kind, but a unity at the level of being, a unity that has as its model and permanent source ... the oneness of the Father and the Son ... The unity of which he speaks is that which shapes the Christian community on the model of the life of the Trinity.'[202] This 'oneness' is not only an end in itself, it is also a witness to the world so that the world will believe that Jesus was sent by the Father.

7. GLORY (Jn 17:24-26)

The prayer comes to a climax in a cluster of the theological insights of the gospel. Jesus prays that those 'whom you have given me', may be 'with me where I am', to 'see my glory', because 'you have loved me before the foundation of the world'. The disciples are seen as the Father's gift, drawn by him to Jesus.

198. 2 Thess 2:3, 8-9.
199. Jn 13:2, 27.
200. Jn 13:1-17; 21-38. cf F. J. Moloney, *The Gospel of John*, 467f.
201. W. J. Harrington, *op. cit.*, 80, commenting on this issue states that people can trivialise the wondrous mercy and forgiveness of God, 'an attitude that finds unsavoury expression in the demonisation of Judas. In Jn 12:6 he had become a petty thief. It was assumed that he would have to come to a sticky end – hence two, wholly contradictory, versions of his death. cf Mt 27:3-10; Acts 1:18-20.'
202. G. Rossé, *op. cit.*, 82.

They are with Jesus in fulfilment of the initial invitation of the gospel to come and see where he dwells. The glory of the unique Son who addresses God as Father, and the recalling of his pre-existence with the Father, enhance this final plea. And then, the final address to the Father, addressing him as *dikaios* (just/right-eous) sums up the 'covenant' theology of the 'people set apart' protected by God who is 'just (righteous)', that is 'faithful' to the relationship originally established in the Old Testament and now fulfilled in the communion of love between Father and Son into which the believers are drawn. The 'righteousness' of God is the quality of faithfulness of God to the covenant partner, whether that entails saving the innocent, protecting the weak and vulner-able, punishing the wicked or forgiving the repentant.

R. E. Brown sums up the grandeur of the prayer:

It is fitting that this beautiful prayer, which is the majestic conclusion of the last discourse, is itself terminated on the note of the indwelling of Jesus in the believers – a theme bol-stered by Jesus' claim to have given glory to the believers and to have made known to them God's name … the motif of the New Covenant runs through the Johannine account of the Last Supper even though there is no explicit mention of the eucharistic body and blood of Christ … the commandment of love, mentioned in the first lines of the last discourse (13:34), is 'new' because it is the essential stipulation of the new covenant. So also the closing note of indwelling is an echo of covenant theology. After the Sinai covenant the glory of God that dwelt on the mountain (Ex 24:16) came to dwell in the tabernacle in the midst of Israel (Ex 40:34). In Johannine thought Jesus during his lifetime was the tabernacle of God embodying the divine glory (Jn 1:14), and now in a covenan-tal setting he promises to give to his followers the glory that God gave to him. In the language of Deuteronomy the Tabernacle (or the site that housed the Ark) was the place where the God of the covenant had set his name. So now the name of God given to Jesus has been entrusted to his follow-ers. The Lord God who spoke on Sinai assured his people that he was in their midst (Ex 29:45; Num 11;20; Deut 7:21; 23:14). Jesus, who will be acclaimed by his followers as Lord and God (Jn 20:28), in the last words that he speaks to them during his mortal life prays that after death he *may be in them*.[203]

---

203. R. E. Brown, *op. cit.*, II, 781.

The Passion Narrative

Introduction to the Passion Narrative

1. THE PLOT

The *hour* has come. Jesus himself has announced its arrival. The Father wills it, the enemies of Jesus plot it, the gospel story prepares for it, and the reader expects it.[1] It is the Father's will and so Jesus takes charge of the situation. Political and religious interests have joined forces against him but their destructive scheming is the enabling of his triumph. The ruler of this world has no power over him.[2] He has overcome the world.[3] He had already foreseen and predicted the betrayal.[4] In fact he had ordered Judas to do his evil deed quickly.[5] In the garden the armed forces, awe-struck in his presence, hesitate to arrest him but having negotiated the safety of his disciples, he presents himself for the taking. In similar vein he will later remind Pilate that he would have no power over him had it not been given to him from above.[6] He knows where he has come from and where he is going. In his going he will be lifted up from the earth and draw all to himself.[7] Here is the supreme irony of the gospel – his death 'will not be, as in the synoptics, an hour of darkness – the Saviour delivered into the hands of sinners – but the hour of his elevation on the cross, his return to the Father, and his glorification'.[8]

The plot is enabled and enhanced by the literary structure and technique, the characterisation, the themes, the imagery and the biblical allusions. The whole story is set in the world of Johannine theology.

2. THE JOHANNINE THEOLOGY

Revelation is the central theological theme of Jesus' life and ministry in John's gospel and it reaches its high point in the passion narrative. His coming into the world and the manner of his

---

1. Jn 12:27f.
2. Jn 14:30.
3. Jn 16 :33.
4. Jn 6:70f; 13:21.
5. Jn 13:27-30.
6. Jn 19:11.
7. Jn 12:32.
8. I. de la Potterie, *The Hour of Jesus*, 3.

death are a declaration that 'God so loved the world that he gave his only Son that those who believe in him might not perish but have eternal life.'[9] Jesus' whole life has been a revelation of the Father and of his love. 'The one who has seen me has seen the Father.'[10] 'The Son who is close to the Father's heart ... has made him known.'[11] 'The Son can do nothing by himself; he can do only what he sees the Father doing; and whatever the Father does the Son does too. The Father loves the Son and shows him everything he does himself.'[12] The Father has entrusted all judgement to the Son and has appointed him supreme judge.[13] The Father has made him the source of life.[14] For this reason Jesus could proclaim that he lays down his life of his own free will and it is in his power to take it up of his own free will. Nobody can take his life from him.[15] 'He who sees the man Jesus and does not confine his gaze to the outward appearance, to the body only, but can contemplate the mystery beyond it and recognise in the man Jesus the Son of God – such a one will see the Father in the Son.'[16]

All through the passion narrative the gospel is functioning on two levels, the visible, and the invisible which is revealed through the visible. The richness of St John's gospel, especially in its biblical allusions, lies in the fact that it has an open ended approach which introduces the reader to rich fields of imagery through generalising quotations which often defy exact or exclusive location in the Old Testament. By way of such allusions it stimulates the imagination and draws the reader's attention to several passages or traditions. The detailed imagery and embedded allusions, together with the irony in the account, serve as pointers to the invisible, as windows on the divine.

The circumstances of Jesus' death motivated the first Christians to search the scriptures for new insight into the plan of God. They found help towards understanding and accepting God's 'scandalous' and 'foolish' plan[17] in the Songs of the

---

9. Jn 3:16.
10. Jn 14:9.
11. Jn 1:18.
12. Jn 5:19f.
13. Jn 5:22, 27.
14. Jn 5:26.
15. Jn 10:17f.
16. I. de la Potterie, *The Hour of Jesus*, xii.
17. 1 Cor 1:23ff.

Suffering Servant, especially the Fourth Song (Isa 52:13-53:12) and in the Psalms of Lamentation, especially Pss 21 (22) and 68 (69). They reflected on the death of Jesus also in the light of the texts and prayers that highlighted the spirituality of the just ones who trusted in God in spite of their sense of unjust suffering and of apparent abandonment by God and humanity. This is the spirituality of the just ones, the poor people of *YHWH*, the *annouim*, marginalised and persecuted but loyal and placing total confidence in God while making loud and confident lament. The close parallel with scripture and the canonised tradition of the Suffering Just One, the poor man who cried and the Lord heard,[18] enabled the first Christians to see here the accomplishment of God's plan in the fate of Jesus. Far from seeing his death as a tragic derailing of his life and mission, they came to see the death of Jesus as central to the divine plan, and illustrative of the divine compassion for innocent suffering. This insight was so widespread in the early tradition that it turns up in all four gospels. In St John's gospel the Word made flesh dwells among us at the very heart of humanity's experience of suffering and betrayal, of the powers of Satan and darkness. Here at the heart of human experience the Son glorifies the Father and is in turn glorified by him.

3. History, Sources and Tradition

The purpose of the passion narrative is not the preservation of detailed historical information for its own sake. Its purpose is primarily religious, and secondarily apologetic. It explores the significance of the passion as the final hour of the Father's revelation in Jesus and its implications for salvation. It is carefully composed to make it quite clear to the Romans that Jesus and his followers were not political revolutionaries, a false portrayal perpetrated in Roman circles even as late as eighty years or so after Jesus' death when Tacitus wrote his Annals.[19] Pilate is carefully presented as declaring Jesus' innocence of any political crime, a declaration which by implication declares the innocence of his followers. John's gospel fixes the blame for Jesus' death on a miscarriage of Roman justice by an indecisive and incompetent official, long since dismissed from his post. In so doing it exonerates the Roman justice system, explaining its failure in

---

18. Ps 21 (22):24f.
19. Tacitus, *Annals* XIV. xliv.

terms of a high official under severe pressure, and threat, from a powerful lobby mostly of priestly cast, and associated with the house of Annas and Caiaphas. The narrator's comment that Caiaphas 'was high priest that year' is a brilliantly cynical reflection on the powerless state of the office. It was meant to be an office held for life. Saying he was high priest 'that year' implies that he may be replaced if he did not please the occupying power. Annas had been high priest from 6AD to 15AD and was followed in office by four of his sons and his son-in-law. This creates a situation in which the high priest is powerless before Pilate and could be made or unmade at will, and, as the story will show, Pilate in turn is powerless before the emperor. However, Pilate probably needed the local support and had to keep Annas and his faction sweetened. In the eyes of the Jews a deposed high priest was still high priest for life, and it seems that Annas still wielded serious power and influence. All either party could do was issue threats and scheme to unnerve each other with their apparent power. The house of Annas with its influence was important to the Romans for keeping their finger on the pulse of the Jewish people, and the Roman backing was in turn very important for keeping in power the highly political family of Annas. Authority was tenuous on all sides. Jesus leans on this weakness throughout the passion narrative as he manifests total control and talks to Pilate about power, authority, control and truth. The account also carefully addresses the situation of the Jewish believers who are coming under pressure from the Jewish authorities and members of synagogue and/or family. It illustrates the fact that Jesus himself had similarly suffered and had predicted such suffering for his followers after him.

Unlike the synoptics, John mentions (Roman) soldiers at the arrest of Jesus and this is an indication that the Romans had prior knowledge of, and given consent to, the arrest of Jesus. This argues against the idea that Pilate and the Romans were taken by surprise when Jesus was presented to them for trial on the following day. It also challenges over-simplistic views of Jewish responsibility for the judicial murder of Jesus that ignore the broader picture of universal human failure represented by the Roman involvement.

The focus on religious significance and apologetic considerations rather than historical detail in the tradition and in the written gospels has left us without the kind of detail for which a modern historian or interested reader looks. This is true of the four gospel accounts. Scholars are therefore left to debate the detail of events, the nature of the 'trials', the existence or non existence of a formal condemnation of Jesus by the Jewish authorities, the relative guilt of the Jews or Romans for the judicial murder of the one publicly and legally declared innocent. The nature and substance of the orally transmitted laws at the time of Jesus, prior to their codification in the Mishnah, can only be conjectured. The possibly overriding influence in the Sanhedrin of the priests and scribes, mostly of the Sadducee party who did not acknowledge the oral tradition but followed the letter of the Old Testament, are sources of debate. So too are the practice of the Passover amnesty and the Sanhedrin's power or lack of it to carry out capital punishment. All this strikes a clear warning about oversimplified attitudes, some of which have led in the past to anti-Semitism with its disastrous consequences.

Pilate was appointed Prefect (not Procurator) of Judaea in 26 AD, a position he held until he was removed, following complaints, in 37AD.[20] His appointment may have owed a good deal to the recommendation of his friend Seianus, the regional Roman official, a known anti-Semite. Pilate himself also pursued policies which offended Jewish sensibilities. He wanted to place Roman standards with the image of the emperor Tiberius in Jerusalem in spite of serious objections and only stopped when he realised that people were ready to die rather than have the Holy City so profaned. He took Corban money (funds dedicated to Temple use) to build an aqueduct and clubbed to death those who protested at his action.[21] Lk 13:1 speaks of his murder of Galileans while they were sacrificing in Jerusalem. Eventually he was removed after his mishandling of religiously motivated trouble between Jews and Samaritans.[22] His fall may have been facilitated by the fact that he no longer had a powerful ally in Seianus, whose removal from office in 31AD had left him vulnerable in a changed, or changing, relationship with the authorities, and in particular with the emperor himself in Rome.[23]

---

20. A contemporary inscription in Caesarea, the seat of his administration, calls him Prefect.
21. Josephus, *Ant.*, 18.3.1; *Jewish war* 2.9.2-3.
22. There was trouble at a Samaritan religious procession in 35AD.
23. Tacitus, *Annals*, 6, 8. Tacitus states that anyone who was a close friend of Seianus was a friend of Caesar (Tiberius).

On being presented with Jesus for trial, Pilate's initial reaction may have been aggravation at being dragged into a religious squabble among the Jews, a fact highlighted by his remark to the Jewish authorities that they take him themselves and try him by their own law. This aggravation expressed itself again in the notice he hung on the cross and his refusal to change it. Furthermore, the narrator informs the reader of St John's gospel that Pilate knew they handed Jesus over out of envy. For these reasons he may have begun the process hoping to release Jesus in order to 'gall' them for using him in an internal Jewish squabble. However, his attitude changed when he was threatened with a complaint to Caesar, the emperor Tiberius. Now he was caught between his disdain for the Jews and their squabbles and his fear of losing his status as *amicus Caesaris*, friend of Caesar. As Prefect he had the *imperium*, that is, complete control in the name of the emperor, in criminal, jurisdictional, military and taxation affairs. In capital cases he could not delegate his authority. However, he did everything to avoid making a decision, and ended up making, or having forced upon him, one of the great historical examples of a decision made in moral cowardice.

It is worth noting that details such as the name of the servant whose ear (lobe) Peter cut off, the fact of 'the other disciple' being known to the high priest, knowledge of local place names and designations such as Lithostrotos, Gabbatha, Golgotha, the mention of the garden and the fact that Jesus and his disciples used to meet there, all contribute to the overall impression that underlying its theological and literary traditions the fourth gospel reflects an historically accurate knowledge of Jerusalem at the time of Jesus. Furthermore the reference to Roman troops (*speiran*) at the arrest, to their carrying of lanterns and torches, and the mention of the fact that it was to the house of Annas that they led Jesus, before taking him to the house of Caiaphas, further indicate the likelihood that underpinning the story is the eyewitness testimony of the Beloved Disciple who is most probably the same person as 'the other disciple' who was known to the high priest. However, here the gospel story itself and not the reconstructed historical facts is our main focus of interest.[24]

24. The classic study of these issues surrounding the trial of Jesus is that of J. Blinzer, *The Trial of Jesus*, Westminster, Md., Newman Press, 1959. Another comprehensive study is R. E. Brown,*The Death of the Messiah, From Gethsemane to the Grave. A Commentary on the Passion Narratives in the Four Gospels.* 2 Vols., Doubleday, Garden City, New York, 1994.

4. THE CHARACTERS

Jesus is the central figure in the entire passion narrative just as he is throughout the entire gospel. Unlike the protagonist in a novel or drama his character does not develop or change. It remains as it has been throughout the story. He suffers no crisis. He is all-knowing and in total control. On the other hand, some of the other characters are profoundly affected by the crisis. Peter first tries to defend Jesus by violent action against the powerful people in the garden, but then denies ever knowing Jesus or having been his disciple when challenged in the courtyard by the inconsequential people, the maid, the slaves and the guard. Pilate changes chameleon like in the presence of the crowd but appears clear and focused as a foil to Jesus when they are closeted together. He gives the force of Roman law not only to his declaration of Jesus' innocence but also, in one of the great ironies of the gospel, to his description of Jesus as King of the Jews on his official public execution notice. Other characters such as the Mother of Jesus and the Beloved Disciple have highly symbolic and representative roles, representing the infant church at its birth. So too have Nicodemus and Joseph of Arimathea as they represent those good and upright Jews who are secret admirers or disciples, both in Jesus' own time and in the time of writing the gospel, who have hesitated to declare their allegiance in public because of fear of the Jews.

5. THE READER

The religious, social, cultural and political background of the readers for whom the gospel was originally intended would have influenced the formation of the narrative. Once written the text took on a life of its own and generations of readers, from New Testament times to the present day, bring different backgrounds and perspectives to the reading of the text. The original readers may well have heard the stories of the arrest, trial and execution of Jesus circulating in the oral tradition of the community prior to reading this gospel. They may also have read one or more of the synoptic accounts in their final or an earlier form. John's gospel gives a whole new perspective. It interprets, in the light of its own theological insights, the events, which may have been already familiar to the originally intended readership. It also sets the implied readers' own experience of Jewish and Roman hostility in a framework rooted in the experience of

Jesus and his contemporaries. Pilate and the Jewish authorities are prototypes of these forces hostile to the first readers.

Readers of all generations bring to the text their own richness of understanding of the story of Jesus and see how it resonates with the broader story of God's people as it reveals the divine plan of salvation. For present day readers, Pilate and the Jewish authorities can function in the narrative as prototypes of contemporary influential forces working against the believer.

6. THE LITERARY STRUCTURE

Literary structure or arrangement serves to highlight and interpret a text. In contemporary western society a storyteller, preacher or speechmaker tends to build up to a climactic finale and the punch line comes at the end. Even if the main point has already been introduced and repeated we expect a climactic moment of emphasis to conclude the story or discourse. In biblical literature, on the other hand, the emphasis is regularly placed at the central point of a discourse, allowing for a step by step approach to the central point and a parallel series of steps departing from it, like mirror images reflecting and interpreting each other.[25] Therefore the modern reader has to adjust to the fact that the biblical writers use different techniques for emphasis.

The passion account in St John's gospel falls into this concentric or chiastic arrangement. It begins and ends in a garden and the central part is the trial before Pilate, set between the scenes in the house of Annas and the scenes on Golgotha. Just as the trial before Pilate is the centrepiece of the passion narrative, so too this trial is itself a concentric arrangement of scenes, having as its centrepiece the mock coronation of Jesus. In this way the structure of the whole account highlights the kingship of Jesus as it is portrayed in ironic contrast with earthly kingship and power.

    A. The Garden: Epiphany and Arrest (18:1-11)
       B. The House of Annas: (18:12-27):
          C. **Trial before Pilate** (18:28-19:16a)
       B Golgotha (19:16b-37).
    A The Garden: Royal Burial.(19:38-42)

The questioning of Jesus in the house of Annas provides an-

---

25. This procedure is technically known as a chiasm, chiastic structure or concentric passage.

other example of literary structure. It is arranged in such a way that the story of Peter's interrogation and denials is divided into two parts with the questioning of Jesus sandwiched in the middle. This arrangement highlights the contrast between the characters of Jesus and Peter and the outcome of their respective interrogations.[26]

The gospel as a whole displays another literary technique. As it approaches its climax various scenes recall parallel scenes at the beginning of the gospel. The opening and closing scenes of the ministry function like a frame, or a set of bookends, holding the story tightly together from opposite ends.[27] In this way the passion account in many respects forms an *inclusion* with earlier passages in the gospel, as for example, the public presentation of Jesus to the Jewish people by Pilate with the words: 'Behold the Man'[28] and 'Behold your king'[29] on the last day of his life, at the hour when the paschal lambs are being sacrificed in the Temple, reminds the reader of the beginning of the ministry when John twice presented him as the Lamb of God.[30] Another example is the presence of the *mother/woman* on Golgotha at the hour of glorification which recalls the *mother/woman* of Cana and the first introduction of the *hour* and the *glory* now brought to fulfilment. Jesus' handing over of the Spirit just before he died is another example, as it recalls the coming of the Spirit upon Jesus at the beginning of the ministry, and the particular witness of the Beloved Disciple to the blood and water from Jesus' pierced side recalls the witness of the Baptist to the divine revelation concerning the identity of Jesus and his baptising in the Holy Spirit.[31]

---

26. This procedure is known as intercalation, a shorter and more concentrated version of the chiasm.
27. This procedure is known as Semitic inclusion.
28. Jn 19:5.
29. Jn 19:15.
30. Jn 1:29, 36. Note the use of the revelatory formula 'Behold ...' which introduces a solemn revelation where witness is borne by one person about another to a third party or parties, announcing that person's identity and role in the salvific events about to be recounted.
31. Jn 1:33f; 19:33ff. Water symbolises the life-giving power of the Spirit in the imagery of St John's gospel.

The Arrest, Trial and Crucifixion of Jesus
(Jn 18:1-19:16)

1. IN THE GARDEN (Jn 18:1-12)

The scene in the garden in St John's gospel is a far cry from that in the synoptic accounts. Here there is no prayer for deliverance, no sweat like blood, no comforting angel, no disappointment with the sleeping companions, no kiss of Judas, no fleeing disciples, no temptation on Jesus' part to plead for an escape from drinking the cup, no healing of the servant's ear. In sharp contrast to Mark's picture of Jesus prostrate on the ground, John has him standing tall, knowing everything that was to happen beforehand, and the arresting party falling prostrate before him. Far from being abandoned by the disciples Jesus negotiates their freedom in fulfilment of his word: 'I did not lose a single one of those whom you gave me.'[32] Jesus' own words, spoken at the supper are here quoted with the solemnity of a verse from the Old Testament. Peter's violent impetuosity is countermanded by Jesus' calm and authoritative statement about fulfilling the will of his Father, by drinking the cup he had given him to drink.

The garden is not named. Maybe it is deliberately meant to transcend the individual garden and recall that garden where the original trial took place when humanity failed the test and rebelled against the will of God. Similarly the reference to crossing the Kidron creates a mood as it recalls the story of the flight of David after his betrayal at the hands of his son Absalom, and how he crossed the Kidron weeping and approached the Mount of Olives only to learn of his further betrayal at the hands of his close adviser Ahitophel.[33] The irony in the story is at its finest where it describes the arresting party coming with artificial lights to arrest the one whom the gospel clearly portrays as the Light of the World. Judas both leads and stands in the midst of those who operate in the dark. He had already chosen the darkness, as the narrator pointed out, when he entered into the night on leaving the supper table.[34] The reader is conscious of Jesus' warning: 'They prefer darkness to light because their deeds are evil. And indeed, everyone who does evil hates the light and avoids it, for fear his actions should be exposed.'[35]

32. Jn 18:9; cf 17:12.
33. 2 Sam 15:13-31; 17:23; Ahitophel subsequently hanged himself.
34. Jn 13:30.
35. Jn 3:19f.

The story now scales the heights of Johannine theology when it presents the universal power of God, the source of all life, in Jesus who lays down his life and takes it up of his own accord. With absolute confidence, therefore, Jesus can confront those intent on his death. The triple use of the now familiar divine formula *ego eimi*, 'I am/I am he', *ego eimi*, in the context of Jesus' self identification establishes both the earthly and heavenly identity of Jesus and provokes a reaction of powerlessness and awe on the part of the prostrate arresting party. However, he presents himself for arrest and they take him away. The earthly story, possibly well known already to the first intended readers from the oral tradition, and maybe also from one or more of the synoptics, is being retold from the perspective of the ultimate divine reality and purpose at work in the situation.

2. At the House of Annas (Jn 18:12-27)

Taking Jesus to Annas during the night, before taking him to the reigning high priest, points to the fact that this was not a formal trial but an interrogation with a view to presenting a case to a subsequent trial.[36] The presence of the Roman soldiers points to the likelihood of an already agreed strategy between Annas and the Roman authorities, but not necessarily Pilate himself. At the meeting of the Sanhedrin following the raising of Lazarus, Caiaphas, the ruling high priest, son-in-law of Annas, had shifted the accusation against Jesus from religious to political concerns, from the danger of the whole world 'following' Jesus to the danger of the Romans destroying the holy place and the nation.[37] The reference to sending Jesus to Caiaphas at the end of the interrogation reminds the reader of Caiaphas' earlier murderous judgement and unwitting prophecy.

The questioning of Jesus in the house of Annas about his disciples and his teaching provokes the response from Jesus: 'I have spoken openly to the world; I have always taught in synagogues and in the Temple, where all the Jews come together. I have said nothing in secret.' This remark is directed at Annas and the interrogators in the time-frame of Jesus' ministry, but it is equally

---

36. A formal trial should have taken place in the presence of the ruling High Priest and it should not have taken place during the night. Mt and Mk convey the impression of a night trial taking place. John's description of an interrogation for the purpose of preparing a case seems to be more historically correct. Luke has a Jewish trial in the morning.
37. Jn 11:47-50.

directed at the Roman authorities at the time when the gospel was written. Many believed the Christians were a secret society known to be opposed to the religion of the empire and especially to the cult of the emperor. They were therefore suspected of being politically hostile to the state. It was a period of political unrest and official suspicion. R. McMullen describes the political climate very well:

> Over the first hundred years of the Principate, people lumped together as the 'opposition' shared the same kind of background in any one generation ... They were alert to the same ideas, under the same dark skies, a close group ... It was their reception and banquets that emperors feared, where after the slaves had left the room, voices got lower and zeal hotter for revolution ...[38]

The Christians came under this umbrella of suspect groups. Already the victims of Nero and Domitian made up a huge number. The gospel is speaking directly to their situation. It is an *apologia* directed to the authorities.[39]

The questioning of Jesus in the house of Annas about his disciples and his teaching and the questioning of Peter in the courtyard about his discipleship cast each other in high relief. The story of Peter is divided into two parts with the questioning of Jesus sandwiched in the middle. Jesus holds his ground before the powerful and influential members of the interrogating body, while Peter loses courage before the powerless, inconsequential people, the maid, the slaves and the guards. Jesus' prophecy is fulfilled and the crowing cock rings out the fulfilment.

Unlike the other gospels, John does not describe any formal Jewish trial by the Sanhedrin between the arrest of Jesus and his being taken to Pilate. This is emphasised by Pilate's remark: 'Take him yourselves and judge him according to your law.'[40] Without prejudice to the historical facts, it is true to say that the dynamic of the gospel narrative does not really need a formal trial at this point to highlight the Jewish case against Jesus. The entire gospel has been such a trial of Jesus by the people and the officials. They were already intent on killing him.[41]

When he healed the cripple at the Pool of Bethesda and defended his action by saying: 'My Father works until now and I

---

38. R. McMullen, *Enemies of the Roman Order*, 40f.
39. It is also a *logos paraclêseôs* or word of comfort for their victims.
40. Jn 18:31.
41. Jn 7:20, 25; 8:59; 11:49f.

work', the Jews had then accused him of breaking the Sabbath and making himself equal to God.[42] To this he responded by making a solid defence in terms of his relationship with, and commission from, the Father. On that occasion he called as witnesses to his defence, his Father, the works he does, John (the Baptist), Moses and the scriptures. Here we have a *ribh*, a trial scene between Jesus and the Jews. On a subsequent occasion when the police failed to arrest him in Jerusalem and defended themselves to the chief priests and the Pharisees saying, 'Never has anyone spoken like this,'[43] Nicodemus protested against their condemnation of Jesus without any due process. 'But surely the Law doe not permit us to pass judgement on a man without first giving him a hearing and discovering what he is about.'[44] The charge of blasphemy was levelled against him by the Jerusalem crowd during the Feast of Tabernacles when they took up stones to throw at him.[45] On that occasion after the raising of Lazarus, the chief priests and the Pharisees met and, shifting the ground from a religious concern to a political one, stirred fear of Roman reaction to a possible messianic pretender. On that occasion Caiaphas became the unwitting prophet of Jesus' death and the interpreter of its salvific significance: 'It is good for one man to die for the people.'[46] Because of this ongoing judgement and condemnation of Jesus throughout the gospel, there was really no need to have a trial at this point. And so now they bring him to Pilate. They present him as one already judged and found guilty.

W. Harrington sums up Pilate's attitude:

We are to see Pilate's attitude in the light of the rest of the fourth gospel. He provides an example of an attitude to Jesus which purports to be neither faith nor rejection: the typical attitude of those who try to maintain a middle position in an all or nothing situation. Pilate's reluctance to make a decision for or against the light leads to disaster. Because Pilate will not face the challenge of deciding for the truth in Jesus and against the Jews, he thinks he can persuade the Jews to accept a solution that will make it unnecessary for him to declare for Jesus. This is the Johannine view of the episodes of Barabbas,

---

42. Jn 5:18.
43. Jn 7:46.
44. Jn 7:51.
45. Jn 8:59.
46. Jn 11:50.

the scourging, and the delivery of Jesus to the Jews as 'your king'. For John this is our own tragic history of temporising and indecision.[47]

3. AT THE PRAETORIUM: THE ROMAN TRIAL (Jn 18:28-19:16)

The Roman trial where Jesus is brought before Pilate (for judgement or sentence?) is one of the highly dramatic episodes or, more accurately, series of episodes, in the gospel. It is made up of seven scenes set alternately outside and inside the governor's residence, the Praetorium. The changing location sees Pilate move between attitudes and emotions as he ducks and weaves with the demands of the crowd outside and returns inside to the stark, glaring truth of Jesus' innocence, character and obvious moral power. His desire to free Jesus, placate and/or rile the Jewish authorities, and satisfy the mob fails each time and he has to come back face to face with Jesus, until he finally succumbs to the pressure from outside and hands Jesus over for execution. The concentric or chiastic arrangement of the scenes has the mock coronation of Jesus as its centrepiece and this highlights the important issue of Jesus' kingship, as the surrounding scenes bear out its significance. The initial political charge fails, only to expose the real issue, the accusation of blasphemy. The origin, role and power of Jesus are the real bone of contention.

A. Outside (18:28-32). Jews demand death sentence. Jesus handed over.
   B. Inside (18:33-38a). Pilate + Jesus: Kingship.
      C. Outside (18:38b-40).Not Guilty. Barabbas.
         D. Inside (19:1-3). **King of the Jews**
      C. Outside (19:4-8). Not Guilty. The Man.
   B. Inside (19:9-11). Pilate + Jesus: Power.
A. Outside (19:12-16a). Judgement. Death Sentence. Jesus handed back.

Scene one: Outside (Jn 18:28-32)
Scene one shows Jesus being transferred from Jewish to Roman jurisdiction and two powers, Jewish and Gentile, are now enlisted in the judgement. In scene seven, which parallels scene one in the concentric pattern, Jesus is condemned and handed back to the Jews for execution, to be carried out, however, by Roman authority and in Roman fashion. This fulfills what Jesus had prophesied about his death, that it would be 'a lifting up from

---

47. W. J. Harrington, *op. cit.*, 84f.

the earth', that is crucifixion, the Roman form of capital punishment for slaves and non-citizens.

The Jews reply to Pilate's statement that they should try him themselves by their own law evokes the response: 'We are not allowed to put anyone to death.'[48] Generally this has been taken to refer to the Roman restrictions on the Sanherdin's power of capital punishment. Some scholars have asked if the statement 'it is not lawful for us to put a man to death' could refer to the Mosaic law which prohibits killing and if this historically points to the failure of the anti-Jesus lobby to have him convicted by a lawful Jewish court. It is known that the Romans removed the Sanhedrin's power of capital punishment about forty years before the fall of Jerusalem, but the exact date is not known.[49] Or could it be that taking Jesus to Pilate points to an attempt by his powerful enemies to utterly reject him and his claims, and to highlight their rejection by handing him over to the Romans, the foreign occupiers of their land, for the most demeaning of executions? The gospel does not focus on this historical issue but rather turns its attention to the significance of Roman execution by death on a cross, and sees this as fulfilling both Jesus' prophecy about being 'lifted up' and the unwitting prophecy of Caiaphas that he would die for the people.[50]

The refusal of the anti-Jesus lobby among the Jewish authorities to enter the Pretorium lest they be defiled and unable to eat the Passover, highlights the irony of the scene, typical of this gospel. Ritual purity is a serious concern for them. Judicial murder is not.

Scene two: Inside (Jn 18:33-38a)
Scene two presents two great powers in face to face confrontation, Pilate sent by the emperor, representing the epitome of earthly power with its attendant jurisdiction and military might, and Jesus sent by the Father representing the heavenly power, the kingdom not of this world, the spiritual power summed up in terms of truth. As in all four gospels Pilate opens the interrogation by asking Jesus: 'Are you the king of the Jews?' Three views of kingship are involved. If this question arises in Pilate's

---

48. Jn 18:31.
49. It is not lawful for us, *ouk exestin hémin*, elsewhere in the New Testament refers to the Mosaic Law.
50. Jn 3:13f; 8:28; 12:32; 11:50.

own mind, it means 'are you an earthly king in opposition to Caesar's rule?' If, however, the question is put into his mouth by the Jews, it means, 'Are you the messiah-king expected by the Jews, anointed by God and empowered to initiate social and political revolution, the 'man', the *gibor*, the warrior king?' To neither of these understandings can Jesus give an affirmative answer. He turns the tables on Pilate and asks him if this is his own question or has someone been talking to him. Pilate is immediately put on the defensive and responds with: 'Am I a Jew?', a remark designed to distance himself from these troublesome Jews, but showing at the same time how the interrogator can so easily become the interrogated in the presence of truth itself. He is probably also showing a certain disdain for the Jews in asking such a rhetorical question, as if to emphasise that he is not part of that troublesome, superstitious crowd who provoked this scenario. Jesus now shifts the ground and redefines kingship in terms of the 'unworldly' kingdom where witness is borne to the truth. He does not say his kingdom is not 'in' this world, but that it is not 'of' this world.[51] As B Witheringtom points out:

> ... he is speaking about the source and thus about the nature of his kingdom. It is not a worldly political kingdom in origin or character. That it is 'not of this *kosmos*' means it has not been dreamed up or built up by humanity, and since *kosmos* in this gospel generally means fallen humanity organised against God, the meaning is likely to be that Jesus' kingdom and movement are not another political scheme of fallen human beings to establish their own sovereignty in the world.[52]

Jesus' interest is not in the title 'king' as a designation for someone who controls an earthly kingdom that has armies to defend and promote its power, but in the fact that he is the agent of God, the one sent by the Father, to bear witness to the truth. From now on Pilate will be seen to represent a power which does not witness to the truth. When Pilate asks him, 'What have you done?' the reader knows that Jesus' whole life and ministry have been a revelation of, and witness to, the truth, a revelation of the Father and of his *charis kai alêtheia*, his grace (faithful loving kindness) and truth.[53]

---

51. Here too, the Roman authorities are being seen as a possible audience.
52. B. Witherington, *John's Wisdom*, 291.
53. Jn 1:14, 17.

Scene three: Outside (Jn 18:38b-40)
Pilate is no witness to the truth and the justice that springs from it. He proclaims the innocence of Jesus and immediately under-mines his own judgement. The weakness of supreme human power without principle and moral courage is exposed. The governor is governed by aggravation and fear of the governed. The truth he has spoken with his lips is denied by his actions. He allows those whom he knows to have already spoken untruth-fully to do so again. In his weakness he feels compelled to placate those speaking untruths and pursuing injustice. He is unable to commit himself to the truth. The offer of a choice between Jesus and Barabbas is a ploy to avoid standing by his own better judgement and therefore a refusal to commit himself to the truth.

All four gospels speak of the custom of freeing a prisoner at Passover. Therefore the custom cannot be easily dismissed though it has come under scrutiny from historians. It is pointed out that outside the New Testament no other record of such a custom at Passover has been found. However, similar customs are recorded. It may have been an application of the Jewish prac-tice of buying the freedom of a prisoner on the occasion of Passover as a practical way to commemorate their liberation from the slavery of Egypt.[54] It could equally have been an application to this specific time and place of the broader custom of offering an amnesty on Roman festivals and special occasions such as the emperor's birthday. If so it was probably one of those half-official local customs that are often used to bring about a compromise with a nod and a wink, and probably not officially recorded for posterity. Whatever the historical reality, John's gospel uses the offer of an amnesty to great effect. The choice is between Jesus and Barabbas. Jesus has been described throughout the gospel as Son, Son of God and Son of Man. In his discourses, he has contrasted his paternity with that of his crit-ics. He is now accused of blasphemy for calling himself God's Son. He is put up beside Barabbas, a name which means in Aramaic, 'Son of the Father'. The reader naturally asks, 'who is his father and what does he stand for?' The narrator tells us that he was a bandit. Jesus' repeated warning that rejecting him, they rejected his Father who sent him is poignantly evident here. In

---

54. E. Bammel, 'The Trial before Pilate', in *Jesus and the Politics of His Day*, ed. E. Bammel and C. F. D. Moule. 427, reflecting the practice in *m. Pesah*, 8.6.

accepting Barabbas they accept his father, and what he stands for, and align themselves with him. The choice of Barabbas robs Jesus of his life, the Jews of their heritage and Pilate of his authority.

Scene four: The central scene
Although there is no reference to place in this scene, the reader can infer from the next scene where Pilate is said to go out again, that the flogging had taken place inside the Praetorium. However, no mention of place is made in the scene itself and this conveys the sense of the universal, timeless, symbolic character of the event.[55]

The governor yields to the governed by flogging the one whom he has just declared innocent. John places this flogging and mockery at the centre of his chiastic structure to highlight his ironic approach to kingship and also to facilitate the subsequent presentation of Jesus as mock king to the crowd outside. The scene also highlights Pilate's cruelty. Whether his purpose in scourging a man he believed innocent was to move the accusers to compassion or to cover himself in case of a complaint to the emperor, in either case it shows how his lack of commitment to truth and his cowardice before the accusers and their possible influence with higher Roman authority result in an act of cruelty to an innocent victim.[56]

The physical abuse is followed by what the Bible portrays as the greatest personal abuse, mockery, which aims to destroy the person's self worth and identity and, in the religious context, to ridicule the person's faith and hope in the God who saves. The passion narratives all pick up on this theme so dominant in the psalms of the *annouim*. In his response to the mockery, the nature of Jesus' kingship is highlighted in the calm dignity he displays

---

55. I. de la Potterie, *The Hour of Jesus*, 60.
56. The flogging and mockery in the gospels of Matthew and Mark take place at the end of the trial as a preliminary to execution. This would reflect the more usual practice. Flogging was seen either as a punishment in itself after a trial and conviction, or as a preliminary to execution. In the latter case it was used to begin the weakening and bleeding process and to hasten the end. Otherwise a crucifixion could drag on for days. The flogging was done with a 'cat o' nine tails' whip often with hooks attached to rip the flesh and cause loss of blood and weakening of the condemned person before execution. In Luke the flogging is threatened but an actual flogging is not reported. Flogging in the midst of a trial is most unusual. Pilate may have considered, or at least hoped, that the trial would finish at this point.

in the face of the mock coronation, robing, royal salute and acts of obeisance. He thus turns the trappings of earthly power and kingship back on themselves in the countersigns of a crown of thorns, a purple robe stained with blood, a jeering salutation and a slap in the face. The irony is striking. The reader knows that the divine source of all power is revealed through Jesus and the apparently all powerful mocker is ultimately powerless, as Jesus will shortly point out to Pilate when he tells him he would have no power over him were it not given to him from above. The striking of his face places Jesus in the company of all those represented by the Songs of the Suffering Servant of (Deutero) Isaiah.[57] The unjust torture of the one already declared innocent places Jesus at the epicentre of human suffering and the mockery makes him king among the suffering servants of God. In the synoptics Jesus is stripped of his 'kingly' attire after the mock ceremony, but in John's gospel he goes to his death robed and crowned as a king.

Scene five: Outside (Jn 19:4-8)
The mock coronation is over and now there is a further 'ceremony' as the mock king is presented to the crowd like a new monarch presented for the acclamation of his subjects. As the Roman governor presents the tortured victim of prejudice, cowardice and injustice to the hateful gaze of his own who have rejected him, the ultimate consequences of the Word becoming flesh are proclaimed in the sentence, 'Behold the man.' For this God had given his only Son because he loved the world so much, but 'he came unto his own and his own received him not'.[58]

Pilate is probably hoping that this is the end of a ridiculous charade but it goes seriously wrong. He is mocking both Jesus and the Jews. It is as much as to say: 'Look at this miserable specimen you people have for a king. You might take him seriously, but I don't'. However, as usual in the fourth gospel, the speaker is saying and doing much more than he/she realises. In the theology of the gospel the presentation takes on a theological significance with the use of a solemn revelatory formula. 'Behold the man' is a revelation formula where witness is borne by one person about another to a third party, usually highlighting that person's salvific role. Like Caiaphas earlier, Pilate is now the unwitting prophet of Jesus' salvific role.

57. Isa 42:1-9; 49:1-6; 50:4-9; 52:13-53:12.
58. Jn 1:11.

Pilate's presentation of Jesus to the crowd at the end of his ministry recalls, and forms an inclusion with, John the Baptist's presentation of him at its beginning. Presenting Jesus to the crowd as 'the man', Pilate through the medium of the gospel presents the piteous spectacle to the gaze of every reader of the story. Whatever the implied motives of Pilate or the mindset of the author and narrator, the spectacle stands powerfully before the reader and resonates throughout one's religious understanding and human experience. Writers and artists have contemplated and represented this scene which has become one of the most frequently reproduced scenes in the history of art. Theologians and biblical scholars have searched the scriptures for understanding and words to express its significance. In the typical style of St John's gospel, the reader is led into an image field to reflect in the richness of biblical pastures.

'Behold the man' conjures up the image of 'the Son of Man'. The reader is well aware, as perhaps the original readers were, that the early Christian tradition, as witnessed especially by Mark's gospel, associated the title 'Son of Man' with the rejection and suffering of Jesus, as is evident from the passion predictions.[59] The 'lifting up' of the Son of Man in John's gospel puts this suffering in the context of the return to the Father, the glorification, and the gift of life. According to John's gospel he is the one who descended from heaven and in returning to the Father must be 'lifted up' so that whoever believes in him may have eternal life.[60] The 'Son of Man' is the one who has power to judge and to give life.[61] The 'lifting up' texts remind the reader also of the Fourth Song of the Suffering Servant who was 'so disfigured that he seemed no longer human' but before whom kings will stand speechless in awe when he is 'lifted up, exalted, raised to great heights'.[62] 'The man' also resonates with the messianic expectation of 'the Gibor', the great man who is the warrior king. Again in this allusion the Johannine irony is in evidence. This man, a spiritual/moral warrior is standing single-handed against the forces of evil, more powerful even than the military might of Rome itself.

As the pretensions of earthly monarchy are removed the real issue emerges. Pilate's declaration of 'no case against him' pro-

---

59. Mk 8:31; 9:31; 10:33f.
60. Jn 3:13f; cf 6:62.
61. e.g. Jn 3:15-21; 5:19-30, inter alia.
62. Isa 52:13.

vokes the reaction in which the real issue emerges. He claimed to be Son of God. This is a most profound claim in Jewish ears. Even though the anointed king was seen in a special way to be a son of God, Jesus was seen to make a much more profound claim to divine sonship and this constituted blasphemy in the eyes of his enemies.[63] Several times during the story of the ministry Jesus was accused of this blasphemy. He not only broke the Sabbath and claimed to be performing his Father's work as he did so, he claimed equality with God. He spoke of God as his own Father. He said 'Before Abraham came to be, I am.'[64] All this comes to the surface now as the sham political charge gives way to the real issue, the religious one, which drives the Jews to desperate measures and leaves Pilate in a state of fear. For a religious Roman the title 'Son of God' signified a divine status achieved by exceptionally blessed people after death or signified a relationship with a departed person who had joined the gods. Sometimes it referred to a special messenger of the gods.[65] The emperor Augustus, for example, was styled 'Son of the divine Julius', a title underpinning his extraordinary authority in pulling the Roman Empire together in the wake of the civil wars and establishing the *Pax Deorum*, the peace granted by the gods.[66] Whether a 'religious' man or not, Pilate was now confronted in Jewish and Roman terms with an extraordinary scenario with which he had neither the religious competence nor the political acumen to handle. His fear therefore grew in the face of these religious and political realities. The angry cry of the governed to 'crucify him' is matched by the growing fear of the governor.

Again he displays moral cowardice. Having declared Jesus innocent for the second and third time he is again shouted down with a barrage of hostility. Against such prejudice the mighty

---

63. This is also the heart of the accusations in the Synoptics, and is later reflected in the Talmud, *b. Sanh.* 43a. It continues to be the theological stumbling block between Jews and Christians.

64. Jn 8:58.

65. Julius Caesar had carefully crafted a divine lineage for himself to show his descent from Venus and Mars, and was followed in this by Augustus (Octavian), who enlisted poets like Virgil and Horace for his PR work.

66. Julius Caesar had created a divine pedigree for himself as descendant of Venus and Mars, deities he promoted at the expense of the traditional gods of the Roman Republic. Augustus in turn shifted the centre of religious life from the public arenas of the Capitol Hill and the Forum to the Palatine Hill, making the religion of the imperial family the religion of the empire, which in turn came to be seen as the extended imperial household.

writ of Roman law is powerless in its declaration of innocence. He becomes even more afraid. Earlier he had asked, 'What is truth?' when Jesus spoke to him of the truth in scene two above. He was bemused then and his state turned to fear. Earlier in the gospel, at the Feast of Tabernacles, Jesus had declared 'The truth will set you free.'[67] It is blatantly obvious now that Pilate is not free. He is enslaved to the Jews, the crowd, the emperor and his own fear of earthly and, possibly, supernatural powers.

Scene six: Inside (Jn 19:9-11)

Pilate is afraid and from here on is desperate to be shut of Jesus and the whole affair. He is trapped, powerless. He is tormented now by the question of Jesus' identity. He asks the pertinent question, so familiar to the reader from the many times it was addressed throughout the ministry: 'Where are you from?' Jesus' enemies throughout the gospel had no difficulty with the question. They were sure of the answer. He was from Galilee, where no prophet comes from.[68] They knew his family.[69] Some hinted at illegitimacy or Samaritan origins.[70] Good people however sensed that he was from God. In his farewell discourse to the disciples he told them that 'the Father himself loves you for loving me and believing that I came from God'.[71] Pilate's question parallels and further develops the issue at stake in scene two above when he asks Jesus if he is a king. This time Jesus remains silent, a demonstration of moral power that unnerves Pilate. Here the power of his kingship is manifested by his powerful silence. It reduces Pilate to powerlessness and to protesting his own power, only to be reminded by Jesus that he has no power but that allowed to him by God. Furthermore, the reader has seen Pilate's power already discredited and abused by him in the story so far. Against the power of God who will raise up his servant, Pilate now pits his powerless earthly authority, while Jesus by his silence is cast in the role of the Suffering Servant, dumb before his shearers, silent like the lamb led to the slaughter in the Servant Hymn. The reader remembers the Song of the Servant: 'Would nobody plead his cause? He was torn

---

67. Jn 8:32.
68. Jn 7:52.
69. Jn 6:42.
70. Jn 8:41, 48.
71. Jn 16:27.

from the land of the living and for our faults struck down in death.'[72]

Jesus' apparently transparent remark about the greater guilt of the one who handed him over to Pilate actually leaves the reader guessing as the question poses itself: 'Who handed him over? Judas? Annas? Caiaphas? The collective sinful opposition who rejected the one sent by the Father?'

Scene seven: Outside (Jn 19:12-16)

Fear, politics and self interest prevent Pilate from commiting himself to the truth and carrying out the just course of action. He has been reduced to a pawn in the game. He has claimed to have power to release or crucify Jesus but is shown to have no power as he leads him out to the judgement seat.[73] Again St John's gospel sparkles with irony. The sentence, usually translated as: 'He brought Jesus outside and he (Pilate) sat on the judge's bench' could also be translated as: 'He brought Jesus outside and seated him on the judge's bench.' It could also be translated as, 'He brought Jesus out and he (Jesus) sat on the judge's bench.'[74] Pilate himself pronounces no judgement at this point. He has already, three times, declared Jesus innocent of any crime. He hands Jesus over to the Jews for crucifixion without pronouncing sentence. This may point to his not sitting himself on the judge's bench. Seating Jesus on it would continue the 'mock' kingship charade, in which Pilate also co-operated as is evident from his presentation of Jesus to the crowd as the man and their king, followed by the inscription he had placed over Jesus' head on the cross, declaring him King of the Jews. One of

---

72. Isa 53:7, 8 (The 4th Song: Isa 52:13-53:12) JB.

73. Detailed knowledge of local names such as *The Stone pavement*, in Hebrew *Gabbatha*, is a pointer to the underlying Jerusalem based historical stratum in the gospel. In fact the form of the word, Gabbatha, is Aramaic.

74. *êgagen exô ton lêsoun kai ekathisen epi bêmatos. ekathisen* can be seen as transitive or intransitive. Scholars such as Von Harnack, Loisy, Macgregor, Bonsirven, de la Potterie, support the transitive use of the verb, i.e., Pilate put Jesus sitting in the judgement seat, or on the judges bench. The Gospel of Peter, 7, and Justin, Apology I, xxxv. 6, also have Jesus in the judgement seat, in the case of Justin it is the Jews who put him there as an act of mockery. cf R. E. Brown, John, II, 880f. I. de la Potterie points out that *bêma* has no article and as such is not the judge's bench but a more general reference to the raised platform on which the judge's bench was placed. The term *bêma* is used in the NT for the judgement seat of God or Christ (Rom 14:10; 2 Cor 5:10). Josephus, *Jewish War*, II, 301, describes an out-of-doors tribunal or platform, a *sella curilis*, erected in the courtyard to which the priests, nobles and eminent citizens brought their business.

the principal functions of a king is to judge. Whatever the original intention in the text, as it now stands it lends itself to different translations and a double meaning, one pointing to Pilate sitting in judgement, the others to Jesus. Without a word spoken,
the irony of the gospel sparkles as the Son of Man sits in judgement over the earthly judge.

Jesus' ministry began with John's proclamation to the crowd:
'This is the Lamb of God who takes away the sin of the world.'[75]
Now his ministry is brought to its completion, or perfection,
when he is condemned to die as the lambs are being slaughtered
for the Passover.[76] The day and the hour are carefully noted to
bring out the significance. It was 'the day of Preparation, about
noon'. Jesus dies as the definitive Paschal Lamb, the Lamb supplied by God the Father, and like the Suffering Servant he is both
led as a lamb to the slaughter and 'raised up' before the gaze of
those whom he will draw to himself. His earthly life and ministry ends with the pagan governor's proclamation to the crowd:
'Here is your King.' Unwittingly, Pilate has fulfilled the apocalyptic hope, and has proclaimed the Lamb both warrior and
king.

In rejecting the One sent, the crowd reject the one who sent
him, a fact brought out poignantly in the statement 'We have no
king but Caesar', a stark pronouncement for those whose identity
was grounded in the belief that God alone is king, and their only
king on earth was one chosen and anointed by God's power.
Now as many awaited such a messianic king, chosen, anointed
and empowered by God, in one remark they deny their history,
their identity and their messianic expectation. C. K. Barrett
points out that in Judg 8:23, 1 Sam 8:7 and many other passages
in the Old Testament, '… it is insisted that the only true king of
Israel is God himself, and that even a Jewish king can be tolerated
only on condition of his obedience to God and fidelity to the
national religion.'[77] In denying all claim to kingship save that of
the Roman Emperor those involved denied and abdicated their
own unique position under the immediate sovereignty of God.

---

75. Jn 1:29.
76. Noting the day and the hour points to the significance in relation to the
slaughter of the lambs. In the Jewish reckoning of the hours this would have
been noon, the hour for beginning the slaughter. However, if one insists on seeing it as the Roman hour, then it is early morning. It is still, however, the day of
the slaughter of the lambs.
77. C. K. Barrett, *The Gospel According to St John*, 454.

It must be noted that, as portrayed in the gospel, this abdication and denial by 'the Jews' of their special status refers only to that powerful element opposed to Jesus. Furthermore it reflects the subsequent heated theological debate and polemic of the Johannine Christians against 'the Jews' at the time the gospel was in formation.

In response to the call for crucifixion, Pilate hands Jesus over. Though he has not pronounced a death sentence, he authorises the Roman military to carry out the execution.

4. ON GOLGOTHA/CALVARY: THE CRUCIFIXION (Jn 19:17-42)

Unlike the synoptic accounts, John gives us no Simon of Cyrene, no weeping women of Jerusalem, no women from Galilee watching at a distance. The majestic figure of Jesus stands out alone without need of support. There is no cry of abandonment, no darkening of the heavens, no rending of the veil of the Temple. This is an hour of triumph, of glory. Far from being abandoned, the crucified Jesus, Son of God and Son of Man, is exalted, lifted up to draw all people to himself. A small group of family and friends, the nucleus of the nascent church, including the Mother and the Beloved Disciple, are drawn to the foot of the cross. The dying Jesus hands over the Spirit, and from his wounded side flow the blood and water, fountains of the sacramental life of the church.[78] The larger, representative crowd round about are drawn to 'look on the one they have pierced'.[79]

The first Christians found help towards understanding and accepting Jesus' terrible death in the Songs of the Suffering Servant and the Psalms of Lamentation, especially Pss 21 (22) and 68 (69). They reflected on the death of Jesus in the light of the experience of the Just One who trusted in God in spite of an overpowering sense of unjust suffering and apparent abandonment by God and humanity. This is the spirituality of the Just One of Israel, persecuted but loyal and placing total confidence in God while making loud lament. The close parallel with scripture and the canonised tradition of the Suffering Just One, the poor man who cried and the Lord heard,[80] enabled the first Christians to see here the working out of God's plan. Far from seeing the death of Jesus as a tragic derailing of his life and mis-

---

78. Preface of the Mass of the Sacred Heart.
79. Jn 19:37.
80. Ps 21 (22):24f.

sion, they see the hand of God in Jesus' own fulfilment of the role of the Just One of Israel and God's response. It is central to the divine plan, and illustrative of the divine compassion for the innocent suffering. This insight was so widespread in the early tradition that it turns up in all four gospels.

St John's gospel elevates this insight to the level of the Father-Son relationship and the details of the story are selected and pointed towards the ultimate significance of the event in the plan of God. The Word made Flesh dwells among us at the very heart of humanity's experience of suffering. That these events were seen to fulfil the scriptures was very important in a missionary document aimed at convincing Jew or Gentile of the divine plan in the horrific events surrounding the end of Jesus' life.

Throughout the passion narrative in John, but especially in the scenes on Golgotha (Calvary), what happens to Jesus is really pointing to what is being brought about for his followers, the church. St Thomas Aquinas has the evocative image of the 'pulpit of the cross' where every detail speaks the message of salvation. Like the trial before Pilate the crucifixion on Golgotha is composed of a number of concentric scenes, each very symbolic, opening onto the spiritual world of salvation. The central scene, or pivot of the chiasm, highlights the representative roles of the Mother and the Beloved Disciple in the nascent church.

The scenes/episodes on Golgotha (Calvary) are arranged in a concentric pattern.

A. (19:16b-18) Crucifixion/Elevation ('lifted up').

    B. (19:19-22) Inscription: Jesus of Nazareth, King of the Jews.

        C. (19:23-24) Soldiers' action. Seamless Robe.

            D. (19:25-27) **Mother/Son/Beloved Disciple.**

        C. (19:28-30) Soldiers' action. Wine/Hyssop. Spirit Given.

    B. (19:31-37) Not a bone broken. Blood and Water.

A. (19:38-42) Deposition. Royal Burial.

Scene one: King of the Jews (Jn 19:16b-22)

Like Isaac, the beloved son of Abraham, Jesus is loaded with the wood for his sacrifice and led to 'the place', called the skull, and crucified there between two others. Matthew and Mark tell us they were bandits, Luke says they were evildoers, John just mentions their presence and shows Jesus raised up in the midst of the crucified.[81] Jesus, already robed, crowned and saluted as king, is now proclaimed king in the three languages, Hebrew, Greek and Latin, which symbolised respectively the local Jewish tongue or their traditional religious language,[82] the widespread spoken language of the eastern part of the empire and the official government language of the entire Roman empire. These were the sacred and secular languages of the day, three languages symbolising all languages. Jesus' kingship is given the force of Roman law when it is written on the crucifixion notice which was the public, legal, proclamation of the crime, fixed to the cross. It is reinforced in the face of Jewish protests. Being raised on the cross he is publicly presented to the Jews and to the world like a new emperor or king after a coronation ceremony. He is enthroned before all the nations, proclaimed in all languages. He is *lifted up* and draws all people to himself as 'they look on the one they have pierced'.

The Jews protested about the inscription, saying he was a pretender, and an irritated Pilate, very likely feeling happy to have discomfited them, responded: 'What I have written I have written.' He may also have intended an extra bit of aggravation for his tormentors by adding 'Nazarene' to the inscription. The Jews/Judaeans looked down on the Galileans and believed prophets did not come from Galilee, and there was an attitude abroad that nothing good could come from Nazareth.[83] And here is a Nazarene 'pretender' publicly exhibited as 'King of the Jews/Judaeans'! Pilate had his revenge for the aggravation they caused him!

Being crucified with others he was 'reckoned with the unrighteous', and destined for 'a grave with the wicked'. Being thus reckoned with the unrighteous and destined for a grave with the wicked, Jesus is again seen in the context of the persecuted righteous one and the Suffering Servant, led like a lamb to

---

81. Mt 27:38; Mk 15:27; Lk 23:39-43.
82. If the local language is meant it may well have been Aramaic, a Semitic language spoken by the Jews at the time of Jesus and perhaps loosely referred to as Hebrew, in the sense of 'the language of the Hebrews'. However, it could also have been written in Hebrew, the formal religious language of those who charged Jesus with making himself king. Pilate may have been getting his own back for their truculence, a fact perhaps borne out by his refusing the change the superscription.
83. Jn 7:52; 1:46.
84. Isa 52, 53.

the slaughter.[84] The intervention of Joseph of Arimathea and Nicodemus 'gave him a tomb with the rich'. Ironically the Servant Song is doubly fulfilled: 'They gave him a grave with the wicked, a tomb with the rich, though he had done no wrong and there was no perjury in his mouth.'[85] He has been three times declared innocent, and remained silent when he could have denied his claims and thus perjured himself before the Father.

Scene two: The garments of Jesus (Jn 19:23-25)
Removing the last vestige of the dignity of the condemned man by leaving him to die naked emphasises the total loss of everything material and paves the way for a special detail in John. It was Roman practice for the executioner to take possession of the victim's personal effects. As usual, St John's gospel uses the tradition, but focuses on details to highlight special insight. Whereas the gospels of Matthew and Mark portray Jesus praying the opening line of Ps 21 (22), and all four gospels refer to the appropriation of his garments by the soldiers, an action in line with the division of the garments of the suffering just one in the psalm, John, however, emphasises the non-tearing of the seamless robe and the fulfilment of scripture. He quotes the verse 'They divided my garments among them, for my robe they cast lots.'[86] Ps 21 (22) uses this typical biblical parallel, where the same thing is said twice, using different words. 'They shared out (divided) my *garments* among them; for my *robe* they cast lots.' Unlike the original psalm, however, John's gospel uses the two words, garments (*himatia*) and robe (*chitôn*) for two different realities, and emphasises also the distinction between 'sharing out' and 'not tearing'.

There is a rich seam of Johannine symbolism in the verbs 'they shared out' (*diemerisanto*) and 'let us not tear' (*mê schisômen*). The personal garments of the executed person were regarded as the property of the executioners. On the symbolic level, at which John's gospel is telling the story of Golgotha, they represented the victim's legacy to the world. In this highly symbolic account of the episodes on Golgotha, the personal garments of Jesus represent, for those who receive them, their share in his 'inheritance' (*meros*). They share in the *meros*, as *diemerisan-*

85. Isa 53:9.
86. Ps 21 (22):18.

to means they shared an inheritance. The same vocabulary was used in Jesus' statement to Peter about sharing in his inheritance. Sharing his garments, symbolic of his person, life and work, points to the fact that the soldiers, his executioners, share in his inheritance. Ordinary garments and military clothing/armour are used consistently in the scriptures as metaphors for protection against the devil, for the essential qualities of the ideal Davidic ruler, and for virtues and vices which should be 'put on' or 'taken off', especially in the context of baptism. Isaiah says of the future Davidic prince: 'Integrity is the loin cloth round his waist, faithfulness the belt about his hips', and Paul speaks to the Thessalonians about putting on faith and love as a breastplate, and hope as a helmet.[87]

However, the subjunctive 'let us not tear' (*mê schisômen*) in contradistinction to 'sharing' highlights another very important aspect of Jesus' legacy. The word *schizein*, to 'divide' or 'tear', and especially 'to divide or tear a garment' figures in the Old Testament in the context of division among the people. The prophet Ahijah tore his new garment into twelve pieces to symbolise the forthcoming division of the kingdom of David and Solomon.[88] Several times in the gospel a 'division', *schisma*, is said to have occurred among the people.[89] All through Jesus' farewell discourse and final prayer he emphasised the importance of unity, building up to the climax at the end of the prayer, when he prayed for the unity of all who hear his word, and constitute the community of believers.[90] The seamless robe was not torn, unlike the other garments which were divided out in shares (*diemerisanto*, to each a *meros*, a share). The undivided robe stands for the unity of the community which Jesus left be-

87. Isa 11:5; 1 Thess 5:8.
88. 1 Kings 11:29-31.
89. Jn 7:43; 9:16; 10:19; 21:11. On many of these occasions the division occurred in the context of a charge of blasphemy. Such a charge was regularly accompanied by a tearing of garments, though this gospel does not mention such an action explicitly. One of the last things shouted by his enemies when Pilate brought him before the crowd was that he deserved to die because he claimed to be the Son of God. This is a clear implication of blasphemy, for which he dies, though his executioners refuse to tear his robe. There may be an element of refutation of the charge of blasphemy symbolically present in the text, or along the way during its formation.
90. Jn 17:11, 22-24. After the catch of one hundred and fifty three fish in the appearance on Lake Tiberias, a number probably signifying every type of fish known, and symbolically representing the universal mission of the disciples, the net is said not to 'tear' (*ouk eschisthê*).

hind. The Fathers of the church saw the symbolism in this light.

Some commentators, particularly since the time of the Renaissance, have focused their attention on the description of the robe (*chitôn*). In seeking its significance they have looked to the priestly garb described in Exodus as 'tunics of finely woven linen' and the high priest's garb described as follows by Josephus Flavius: 'this garment consists not of two parts ... but it is woven from a single length of thread.'[91] Following this interpretation the robe symbolises the (high) priesthood of Jesus, a priesthood remaining intact after his death as he continues his high priestly prayer on behalf of his disciples initiated at the Last Supper.[92]

Scene three: Mother and Beloved Disciple (Jn 19:25-27)
The reader who hastens to explore the deeper meaning of this scene and the representative roles of the persons mentioned could miss the poignant note of humanity that this episode introduces into the story. The great contrast with what has immediately preceded is brought out even in the grammar of the sentence. '*On the one hand* the soldiers did these things but *on the other* there stood by the cross of Jesus his mother, and his mother's sister, Mary of Clopas and Mary of Magdala.'[93] After the dark night and bitter morning of betrayal, accusations, flogging, mockery, despoliation and crucifixion, a mother, an aunt, a close friend and a beloved disciple appear on the scene. To this group Jesus hands over the Spirit in his last gesture before death. A new family of Jesus is created as his human family and his family of faith are brought together around the cross. In the midst of this loving group, a final caring gesture of a dying son for his widowed mother and an act of trust in his Beloved Disciple provide the context and the personnel for the birth of the church. Referring to the scene, O. Treanor writes about the Mother and the Beloved Disciple: 'Close to the heart of the crucified, they stand at the foot of the cross in mystical communion with the Word made flesh, caught up through suffering in the ineffable

---

91. Ex 39:27; Josephus, *Ant.*, 3.161.
92. Though many scholars see this as alien to the original intention of the text, the reader familiar with the broader New Testament tradition which includes texts such as the high priestly theology in Hebrews, is alive to a further meaning in the transparent reality which transcends the original intention of any one text. One's reading is further enriched thereby.
93. *hoi men oun stratiôtai...heistêkeisan de.*

love between Father and Son. They are the first fruits of Jesus' promise to draw all things to himself when he is lifted up from the earth; first fruits of his prayer that all might be one as he and the Father are one.'[94]

This scene is described at the climactic moment just before Jesus' death and forms the pivot or centre of the chiastic structural layout of the Golotha scenes. It forms an *inclusion* with the wedding in Cana, bringing to fulfilment the promise of that event. The revelatory formula 'Behold ...' is used to describe the establishment of the new relationships. 'In this formula the one who speaks is revealing the mystery of the special salvific mission that the one referred to will undertake ...'[95] Using this formula sets what would otherwise be a straightforward legal testimonial formula, 'Woman, behold your son/behold your mother', in the context of the broader theology and literary style of the gospel. Several interpretations of the deeper significance of the exchange suggest themselves.

The *hour* was introduced at Cana, and mentioned throughout the gospel. Now on Golgotha, as the Mother and the Beloved Disciple form the nucleus of the new community of faith, the reader is told that 'from that *hour*' the disciple took her into his home. It signifies both an hour in time, and the *hour* of Jesus' glorification. The personal names of the Mother of Jesus and the Beloved Disciple are never given in the gospel. Three representative terms are used, *woman, mother*, and *beloved disciple*. In this scene of just three verses the word *mother* is used five times. This indicates levels of meaning and deeper insights in the text than the immediate filial concern of Jesus as he gives the mother and the Beloved Disciple to each other.

In the broader New Testament tradition, Jesus' attitude to family ties were well known, judging by the synoptic texts. 'Who is my mother ? Who are my brothers?' 'My mother and brothers are those who hear the word of God and keep it.'[96] 'The one who does not hate father and mother is not worthy of me.'[97] It is quite clear from the discussion preceding the feast of Tabernacles that his brothers did not believe in him.[98] This is the

94. O. Treanor, *This is my Beloved Son*, 216.
95. R. E. Brown, *op. cit.*, II, 923.
96. Mt 12:48f; Mk 3:31ff.
97. Mt 10:37f; cf Lk 14:26.
98. Jn 7:5.

case also in Mark's gospel where his family thought he had gone mad and his own relations despised him.[99] The mother of Jesus is praised by Elizabeth, not for being the 'biological' mother of Jesus but for being 'the one who believed that the words spoken to her would be fulfilled.'[100] She is praised for being mother of Jesus in faith, and consequently in family relationship.

Here on Golgotha in John's gospel, however, we see a solemn endorsement of spiritual relationship of mother, son and brother, and by implication, mother, daughter and sister, since the Beloved Disciple represents all disciples. 'Because of the cross and from the moment of the cross a new family of Jesus has been created.'[101] 'The passage affirms the maternal role of the Mother of Jesus in the new family of Jesus established at the cross.'[102] Drawn to himself, sharing his *hour*, looking to the future as disciple and representative of the community of the Beloved Disciple, the woman becomes mother and the beloved disciple becomes her son, and thereby brother of Jesus, representing all disciples who are thus constituted his brothers and sisters. Now, lifted up from the earth, he draws to himself the nucleus of the new community of believers. They share his *hour* as they stand representatively at the cross.

In both the Cana and the Golgotha scenes, he addresses his mother as 'woman'. The reader probably finds this somewhat strange, but when he addresses her as 'woman' in the process of designating her 'mother' of the Beloved Disciple, the representative of all believers, then the Genesis story of Eden springs to mind with its imagery of a new Eve, the woman, mother of all the living.[103] Adam called the *woman* Eve, because she is 'mother of all the living'. The name 'Eve' in Hebrew is etymologically related to the word for life, and in the Greek of the LXX it is *Zôê*, life.[104] In this imagery of *woman, mother* and *life*, one sees a new Eve, the first disciple obedient to the word at Cana, now standing obediently at the cross, the new tree of life, and becoming the mother of all those living through the life-giving power of Jesus. As son of Jesus' mother the Beloved Disciple is now brother of Jesus and in turn represents all disciples who are thus constituted

99. Mk 3:21; 6:4.
100. Lk 1:45.
101. F. J. Moloney, *The Gospel of John*, 504.
102. *Ibid.*
103. As it did in the story of the wedding at Cana. Jn 2:1-10.
104. In the LXX it is *Zôê*, life.

his brothers and sisters. St Augustine wrote of her: 'She is clearly the mother of the members of Christ … since she has in her charity joined in bringing about the birth of believers in the church, who are members of its head.'[105] The changed relationship will be made clear in Jesus' instruction to Mary Magdalene to 'go and find the *adelphoi, brethren,* an inclusive term for brothers and sisters (no longer simply called the *disciples!*), and tell them: " I am ascending to my Father and your Father, to my God and your God".'[106]

R. E. Brown recalls another biblical allusion, that of the Lady Zion:

> In becoming the Mother of the Beloved Disciple (the Christian), Mary is symbolically evocative of Lady Zion, who after the birth pangs, brings forth a new people in joy.[107] Her natural son is the firstborn of the dead,[108] the one who has the keys of death;[109] and those who believe in him are born anew in his image. As his brothers, they have her as mother.[110]

Scholars also see a connection with the woman of Revelation 12, giving birth to the messianic child, and through him to the messianic community, destined for persecution, but saved by the action of the mother fleeing into the desert. This woman is also representative of the church where Christ is continually coming to birth and is another example of the mother taking action to ensure the future of the child and the promise of which he is the bearer, like the matriarchs discussed in relation to the first Cana story.

Many other interpretations, and 'spiritual applications' of this scene have been made over the centuries. R. E. Brown gives an overview of them in his commentary.[111] Church fathers such as Athanasius, Epiphanius and Hilary saw in the scene a proof of Mary's perpetual virginity, since she obviously had no other child to look after her. Ephraim the Syrian sees the instruction to the Beloved Disciple to take care of the Mother in the same vein as Moses' instruction to Joshua to take care of the people, so he clearly sees the Mother as representing the church. There is a

105. St Augustine, *De S. Virginitate*, 6; PL 40, 399.
106. Jn 20:17f.
107. Isa 49:20-22; 54:1; 64:7-11; cf Jn 16:21.
108. Col 1:18.
109. Rev 1:18.
110. R. E. Brown, *op. cit.*, II, 925f.
111. R. E. Brown, *op. cit.*, II, 942f.

long tradition, particularly in Catholic circles, of seeing this episode as the establishment of a spiritual relationship between the individual Christian and the Mother of Jesus.

The biblical, theological and liturgical traditions of the church emphasise the role of Mary, but always in relation to Christ and the church.[112] The Second Vatican Council emphasises the importance of this point by including Mary in the Dogmatic Constitution on the Church in which she is seen quite clearly in relation to Christ and the church.[113]

The importance of the scene for the genesis of the new believing community is emphasised by the narrator who can now affirm that Jesus knew that all was completed, its purpose achieved. The words that introduced the Last Supper scene are appropriate here to signify what has really taken place in the meantime. 'Having loved those who were his own in the world, he loved them *to the end.*'[114]

Historical Critical Considerations of the Scene
This scene of the Jesus, his Mother and his Beloved Disciple on Golgotha has been widely represented in Christian art and celebrated in liturgy, music, poetry and popular devotions. Some commentators, however, point to the fact that the Mother of Jesus and the Beloved Disciple are not mentioned in the synoptic accounts of the crucifixion. For this reason their presence in John's gospel is sometimes seen as unhistorical and simply symbolic with theological/ecclesiological significance. This opinion arises largely from seeing the synoptic gospels, especially Mark, as a more reliable basis for historical judgement and comparison. It must be kept in mind, however, that scholars now accept not only the fact that the synoptic gospels are also highly theological, not just straightforward uninterpreted eyewitness accounts, but that underlying the theology and literary features of John's gospel there is also an independent and equally ancient and historical tradition.

---

112. The loss of this perspective could lead to excessive Marian devotion of a purely pietistic and personal type, in which Mary is seen independently of Christ and the church, an approach which would diminish her role and encroach on the uniqueness of Jesus as mediator.
113. *Lumen Gentium*, §§ 60-65 deal with Mary in relation to Christ and the church and §§ 66-67 deal with devotion to Mary in the church. She is seen very clearly as Mother of the Church.
114. Jn 13:1.

It is necessary therefore to investigate the different traditions in an attempt to discover why they treat any particular passage as they do. Both traditions have their theological and apologetic agenda. The fact that the other gospels do not mention the Mother of Jesus or the Beloved Disciple can be explained by their having another focus of interest. A basic principle in law and in logic is that absence of evidence is not evidence of absence. To say that someone was absent because of not being mentioned in a particular tradition, especially since that tradition (even if it is reflected in three separate accounts) had its own specific agenda, is not logical. This is doubly the case when another tradition, with a different focus and agenda mentions the person's presence. Two independent traditions, the synoptic and the Johannine, are not in contention. They have focused on different moments.

In this case the three synoptic gospels are obviously following one tradition very closely. Take Mark's account, for example, as representative of the underlying synoptic tradition. He mentions Mary of Magdala, Mary the mother of James the Younger and Joset, Salome and other women from Galilee standing at a distance from the cross, and mentions them at the end of the crucifixion account.[115] After the account of the burial Mark states pointedly that two of them watched where he had been buried and took note of the place where he was laid. Matthew says Mary of Magdala and the other Mary were sitting opposite the sepulchre, and Luke says the women who had come from Galilee took note of the tomb and the position of the body.[116] In the next sentence Mark names the same women and tells how they went to the tomb as the sun was rising on the first day of the week. Mark's intention, like that of Matthew and Luke, is very clear. The women who saw him crucified were the same women who saw him buried and discovered the empty tomb. Their witness to the death, burial and resurrection is Mark's reason for referring to their presence at the crucifixion and the focus of his interest. The very close similarity of all three synoptic accounts seems very likely to point to an ancient, well rehearsed 'apologia' for the resurrection, emphasising the fact that the same people had witnessed him die, seen him placed in a clearly identifiable tomb and later found that the tomb was

---

115. Mk 15:40f. cf Mt 27:55; Lk 23:49.
116. Mk 15:47.

empty. The story of these women and their presence on Calvary/Golgotha focuses on them as witnesses to the truth of the underlying facts surrounding the resurrection.[117]

John's interest is entirely different and focuses on the gathering of the nascent church at the foot of the cross. E. Stauffer has shown that people being crucified could make a declaration of last will and testament from the cross.[118] In this case the declaration reflects Jewish family law where one person is legally entrusted to another. This was also in keeping with Roman practice of allowing the condemned person some last words to finalise affairs with family and friends, before capital punishment was carried out, usually immediately after sentencing. B. Witherington points out: 'Historically there is nothing improbable about a few grieving women, especially relatives, being allowed near the cross of a loved one, especially if it was guarded as was true in Jesus' case.'[119] The family and friends may then have been moved away to a distance. This may account for two different scenarios emerging in the traditions.

Furthermore, some argue for the unhistorical character of the Beloved Disciple's presence because the impression given by the synoptics is that all the disciples had left Jesus and fled from the garden, fulfilling his prophecy at the supper, in which Jesus quoted Zechariah: 'I shall strike the shepherd and the sheep will be scattered.'[120] The Johannine account has Jesus securing their safe passage from the garden, in fulfilment of his promise that not one of them would be lost.[121] In both cases there is an understandable 'generalising' tendency to fit the fulfilment, which 'overlooks' Peter's non-flight when he followed him to the high priest's courtyard, and possibly also explains the presence of the Beloved Disciple. The latter, however, appearing on the scene here may well point to his being a Jerusalem disciple, as mentioned earlier in relation to his possible hosting of the supper, who turned up on hearing of the arrest, or was contacted be-

117. The angelic formula/announcement differs in the accounts, highlighting the individual approaches of the synoptics, but also, by contrast, emphasising the uniformity of the underlying tradition of the fact of the women's witness.
118. E. Stauffer, *Jesus and His Story*, 136ff.
119. B. Witherington, *John's Wisdom*, 309.
120. Mk 14:27; Zech 13:7; Mk 14:50.
121. Jn 17:12; 18:8f; cf 6:39; 10:28.
122. Other factors such as the tradition of John and the Mother of Jesus in Ephesus, commemorated in the area of the modern town of Seljuk, at the hill of

cause of his local knowledge and influential connections.[122] These considerations serve to present a case against the arguments for an all too easy dismissal of the historical basis for his presence in the scene.

Scene four: Thirst, Wine, Hyssop, Spirit (Jn 19:28-30)
This scene has two references to completion, the first a remark of the narrator that Jesus knew that all was now completed, the second, Jesus' final words: 'It is finished/completed/perfected' (*tetelestai*). Highlighted between them is the cry of Jesus, 'I thirst.' The term *complete, finish* or *perfect* in this gospel has the meaning of bringing to conclusion or perfection and achieving the purpose of the work Jesus was sent to do. Many times in the story of the ministry Jesus looks ahead to this completion. 'My food is to do the will of him who sent me and to *complete* his work.'[123] 'The works that the Father has given me to *complete*, the very works that I am doing, testify on my behalf that the Father has sent me.'[124] 'I glorified you on earth by *completing* the work you gave me to do.'[125] 'Having loved his own who were in the world, he loved them *to the end/to the completion.*'[126] Jesus' final word *tetelestai*, it is finished/completed/perfected, refers therefore to the whole purpose of Jesus' coming from the Father into the world. Placing the *I thirst* between these two affirmations of completion gives it a very high profile and alerts the reader to a meaning deeper than the physical thirst, a meaning further highlighted by the statement that Jesus' cry, *I thirst,* was to fulfill the scriptures. The narrator does not specify the scripture passage and how it is fulfilled, probably because the intended readers were expected to understand without explanation. The reader today, however, is left to ask the question and to seek understanding from looking at the broader tradition in the New Testament and the specific approach of St John's gospel in related matters.

In the accounts of Mark and Matthew Jesus is offered wine mixed with myrrh or gall when he cries out the opening line of Ps (21) 22, 'My God, my God, why have you forsaken me?' The

Panaya Kapulu, and the magnificient ruins of the basilicas to both their memories in that area, are a pointer to an early Christian tradition of such an arrangement for Jesus' mother's future.
123. Jn 4:34.
124. Jn 5:36.
125. Jn 17:4.
126. Jn 13:1.

bystanders think he is calling on Elijah, and in the context of mocking skepticism about the possible arrival of the prophet to help him, one of them offers him the drink. In Luke's account, the offer of a drink is an act of mockery accompanying the taunt: 'If you are the King of the Jews, save yourself.' In the synoptic accounts the drink offering recalls the suffering and mockery of the just person in Ps 68 (69):22: 'For my thirst they gave me vinegar/sour wine to drink', though the text is not quoted. The focus is on the offering of the drink and on the accompanying mockery.

Only in St John's gospel does Jesus call out 'I thirst.' Here the focus is on the asking. Jesus takes the initiative. A jar of sour wine. a bowl of vinegar, was there for the asking. Jesus had accepted the cup the Father gave him to drink. 'Am I not to drink the cup the Father gave me?'[127] The final request of Jesus is for a drink. The bowl of vinegar, the cup of suffering, brought his work to completion. This symbolises the full measure of suffering which he accepts. In this he has carried out the work of the Father to its ultimate completion, achieved its purpose, and brought it to perfection. 'For *my thirst* they gave me sour wine.' Though the psalm refers to a hostile gesture in the offering of sour wine to the victim, and it is so interpreted in the synoptic tradition, here the Johannine approach is brought into play. Instead of having the hostile gesture forced on him, Jesus invites the gesture, just as he invited the arresting party to take him, and release his followers, in the garden. In that case, too, his action is followed by a statement that it fulfilled the scriptures. The offering of the drink is an action common to all three synoptics and in fact Matthew and Mark have Jesus die immediately after the drink is offered. Jesus in John's gospel is seen to 'order' or 'invite' the final action that heralds his death. Jesus himself thirsts for, and requests, the fulfilment. In the irony of the gospel the reader remembers the importance Jesus placed on *asking* for the gift of God. He told the Samaritan woman that if she asked for a drink he would give her living water, the water of life. The Galileans at his prompting asked for the bread of life. In proclaiming his thirst Jesus asks for the drink which heralds fulfilment of the scripture, and the completion of the work the Father gave him to do.[128]

---

127. Jn 18:11.
128. cf Jn 4:34; 6:34; 19:28.

Significantly the vinegar is offered on a hyssop stick, a fact mentioned only in John's gospel. The hyssop was used for sprinkling the blood of the Paschal Lamb on the doorposts of the Israelites in Egypt to save them from the destroying plague, and to mark them out as God's firstborn.[129] Jesus, the Lamb who takes away the sin of the world, dies as the lambs are being slaughtered for the Passover. His final request results in raising aloft the hyssop, a powerful symbol of the historic delivery of the people through the blood of the lamb.

And now, finally the Spirit is given. The Son has been glorified so the Spirit can be given. Leaning his head forward to look down on those assembled beneath, he communicates to them the Spirit. 'He handed over the Spirit', *paredôken to pneuma* does not mean 'he expired'. It is not a euphemism for death, unlike Mark and Luke who use the verb *exepneusen*, 'expire', and Matthew who uses *aphêken to pneuma*, 'give up/surrender the spirit'. The Johannine Jesus 'bowed his head and handed over/ delivered/entrusted the Spirit to the nascent church. The text does not say '*his* spirit' in the sense of 'his breath of life', but '*the* Spirit'. John's use of the active participle *klinas*, bowed, points to a deliberate action, not the falling down of the head of someone already dead but the leaning forward of someone still alive.[130] The image is of Jesus looking down on the assembled group and, now that the *hour* of his *glorification* has come, he gives the Spirit to his followers.

Scene five: Blood and Water (Jn 19:31-37)
The preparation for the Passover and the ensuing Sabbath necessitates the removal of the dead bodies from the place of crucifixion. The desire for ritual purity, evident since the reference to the people who came from the country to purify themselves for the feast, continues throughout the story with the Jews unwillingness to incur ritual impurity by entering the Praetorium, and their anxiety about the dead bodies of the crucified being on display during the festival. The Roman practice was to leave the bodies of the crucified on the cross as a warning to other malefactors. According to Philo, however, they some-

---

129. Ex 12:22f; cf Heb 9:18-20 – sprinkling with hyssop to seal the covenant.
130. The idea of the head falling forward in death is communicated by the use of the past participle passive *inclinato* in the Latin translation *inclinato capite*, since Latin has no past participle active.

times gave the bodies to the relatives, as for example on the occasion of feasts.[131] The Jewish sensitivities on this occasion reflect the Law of Deuteronomy and the Book of Joshua which stated that the bodies of hanged criminals should not remain overnight on a tree. Josephus points out that the Jews saw this ruling as covering the case of the crucified as well.[132] The crurifragium or breaking the legs (sometimes other bones as well) with a heavy mallet hastened death, and in the case of crucifixion could be seen as a mercy, as otherwise the slow suffocation endured by the victim could drag on for days.

When the soldiers came to Jesus and found him dead, why did they pierce his side? R. E. Brown states that the verb *nyssein* has the connotation of pricking or prodding, sometimes lightly (so as to awaken a sleeping man), sometimes deeply (so as to inflict a mortal wound). The sequence of the narrative suggests that the soldier gave an exploratory jab to see if the apparently dead body would react and thus be still alive.[133] However, the quotation in vs 37, 'They will look on the one they have pierced', uses the verb *ekkentein* which connotes a 'piercing through' of the victim. In the gospel of John the ensuing flow of blood and water take on a great significance in salvific and ecclesiological/sacramental terms.[134]

John's gospel highlights the significance of what has just taken place in the death of Jesus. Just before he died he handed over the Spirit, and now the gospel stresses the flow of blood and water from his side. Its importance is pointedly stressed by the narrator's comment that it is an eyewitness account by a truthful witness. The narrator stresses the truth of this witness in a manner more insistent than any other comment in the gospel, and says that the purpose of this witness is 'that you also may believe'. It is therefore to be seen as more than a simple description of a bodily function following a spear thrust into the side. It

---

131. Philo, *In Flaccum* 10: 83.

132. Deut 21:22f; Josh 8:29; Josephus, *Jewish War*, 1V.5.2.317.

133. R. E. Brown, *op. cit.*, II, 935. He points out that the common English translation 'pierce' more accurately represents the verb *ekkentein* of vs 37.

134. In the broader New Testament tradition the salvific, revelatory and life-giving power of Jesus' death is borne out in different ways. The rending of the veil of the Temple shows forth the mercy seat of God, no longer veiled; or the divine reaction to the murder of the beloved Son. The extinguishing of the light of the sun draws all creation into the salvific action; the tombs give up their dead proclaming the resurrection of the just and the centurion executioner proclaims his faith in the one he has executed.

is another window on the divine plan of salvation unfolding throughout the scriptures. This specific statement of witness to the blood and water following on the handing over of the Spirit, forms an inclusion with the emphasis on the witness of the Baptist to the coming of the Spirit on Jesus at the beginning of the ministry.[135] The reader recalls the occasion at the feast of Tabernacles when Jesus proclaimed: 'If anyone is thirsty let him come to me. Let the one come and drink who believes in me. As scripture says: "From his breast shall flow fountains of living water".' The narrator went on to explain: 'He was speaking of the Spirit which those who believed in him were to receive; for there was no Spirit as yet because Jesus had not yet been glorified.'[136] Now Jesus is glorified and the Spirit has been given.

The central point is summed up by W. Harrington: 'The drama of the cross does not end in death but in the flow of life that comes from death. The death of Jesus on the cross is the beginning of Christian life.'[137] In the words of F. J. Moloney: 'Despite his *physical* absence, Jesus is still present in the blood and water of the practices of a worshipping community.'[138] St Augustine, in the tradition of the Peshitta and Vulgate, translates the 'piercing' as an 'opening'. He comments: 'He did not say *pierced through*, or *wounded*, or something else, but *opened*, in order that the gate of life might be stretched wide whence the sacraments of the church flow.'[139]

The liturgical tradition of the church has given prominence to the sacramental interpretation of the blood and water that flowed from Jesus' side, the water of baptism (cf Jn 3:5) and the blood of the Eucharist (Jn 6:53, 54, 55, 56). The Preface of the Mass of the Sacred Heart speaks of the blood and water as 'the fountain of the sacramental life of the church'. This is in keeping with the frequent use of water as a symbol of the life-giving power of the Spirit which the neophyte receives through the sacraments of initiation. The blood of Christ is mentioned in the eucharistic teaching where Jesus says: 'He who eats my flesh

---

135. Jn 1:32-34. This seems most likely to have been the inspiration for the text of 1 Jn 5:6-8: '... there are three witnesses, the Spirit, the water and the blood'. This reference in 1 John was later transformed by the inclusion of the Johannine comma, a Trinitarian interpretation of the text, not in any of the early mss.
136. Jn 7:37-39.
137. W. J. Harrington, *op. cit.*, 90.
138. F. J. Moloney, *The Gospel of John*, 506.
139. Augustine, *In Joh.* CXX 2; PL 35:1953.

and drinks my blood will has eternal life and I will raise him up on the last day. For my flesh is real food and my blood is real drink. He who eats my flesh and drinks my blood lives in me and I live in him.'[140] The blood from his side is seen as symbol of the Eucharist. It is also the anointing and saving blood of the Lamb. It recalls the blood of the Passover lamb which in the celebration of the Exodus-Passover became a sign of life given and protected by God, an anointing, symbolising Israel's position as God's children. 'The blood will be a sign for you upon the houses where you are; and when I see the blood, I will pass over you, and no plague shall fall upon you to destroy you.'[141] Because life was seen to be contained in the blood, blood symbolised life and was central to the atonement rituals. 'This blood I myself have given you to perform the rite of atonement for your lives at the altar.'[142] The blood signifies also the atoning, sacrificial nature of Jesus' death, and the gift of life it bestows.

This gift of life draws all to him. 'When I am lifted up I shall draw all to myself.' He drew them to himself as he hung dead on the cross. 'They looked on the one they had pierced.' Zechariah's description of the murder of an only son among his own is recalled with its powerfully poignant description: 'But over the House of David and the citizens of Jerusalem I will pour out a spirit of kindness and prayer. And they shall look on the one they have pierced and mourn for him as for an only son, and weep for him as people weep for a firstborn child … When that day comes, a fountain will be opened for the House of David and the citizens of Jerusalem, for sin and impurity … and if anyone asks "explain the wounds on your chest" he will reply "with these was I wounded in the house of my loved ones".'[143]

Throughout the gospel Jesus has been portrayed as the locus of God's presence and revelation among the people. The *Logos* became flesh and pitched his tent of presence and revelation among us. The first disciples asked 'Where do you live?' The disciples are promised that they would see the heavens open and the angels of God ascending and descending on the Son of Man, an image of a new Bethel or House of God. The Temple of Jesus' body would be built up in three days, a victory of God over the destroyers of his body, temple of the divine presence.

140. Jn 6:53, 54, 55, 56.
141. Ex 12:13 (JB).
142. Lev 17:11.
143. Zech 12:10; 13:1, 6.

We have seen his glory, no longer a cloud, but the grace and truth accompanying his presence as the Word made flesh. The Temple imagery of God's presence opens onto the theology of the salvific power of God's presence symbolised graphically in Ezekiel by the water flowing from underneath the right side of the altar and bringing life from the Temple of God's presence to all the land. This water symbolism was graphically symbolised in the promise of living water to the Samaritan woman and the water ceremonies in the Temple at the celebration of the feast of Tabernacles where Jesus said : 'Let anyone who thirsts come to me.' From the Temple of his body the water of life now flows as he is glorified.

The statement of fulfilment of the scripture, 'Not a bone of his will be broken', reflects two traditions. One refers to the Paschal lamb. Ex 12:46 (and its parallel in Num 9:12) is a ritual instruction for the preparation of the Paschal lamb. It states: 'It is to be eaten in one house alone, out of which not a single morsel of the flesh is to be taken; *nor must you break any bone of it.*' It fits into the Paschal lamb motif of this gospel which is alone among the gospels in setting the crucifixion on the Day of Preparation and so canonises the allusions to the death of the Paschal lamb. The other tradition is that of the Just One, exemplified above all in the Suffering Servant. Ps 34:20: 'Hardships in plenty beset the virtuous man, but *YHWH* rescues him from them all; *taking care of every bone, YHWH* will not let one be broken.' This description of *YHWH*'s protection of the Just One, the Suffering Servant, reflects closely the Suffering Servant as described in Isa 52:13-53:12, the one led as a lamb to the slaughter, but also the one of whom it is said: 'See my servant will prosper, he shall be lifted up, exalted, rise to great heights. As the crowds were appalled on seeing him – so disfigured did he look that he seemed no longer human – so will the crowds be astonished at him and kings stand speechless before him; for they shall see something never told and witness something never heard before'.[144] From the point of view of Isaiah's Songs of the Suffering Servant, Pilate's 'Behold the Man' has a fitting sequel in 'They looked on the one they had pierced' when the unjust sentence they called for has been carried out.

---

144. Isa 52:13f.

Scene Six : Royal Burial (Jn 19:38-42)
The synoptic accounts of a hurried burial are a far cry from the
burial of Jesus in John's gospel. It is better to seek out the theological intent of the different traditions than to argue endlessly
about harmonising details between them. In the Johannine account the huge amount of spices and the linen cloth betoken a
royal burial like the burial of Asa the king, whose royal burial is
described in 2 Chr 16:14. Jesus is buried as a king. The tomb in
which no one had previously been buried can be interpreted on
two levels, theological and apologetic. It was newly prepared
and fit for a royal burial and a holy place uncontaminated by
previous burials. In addition there is the apologetic motive in
the detail. Being new there was no possibility of confusion with
other bodies buried there when the tomb was found to be
empty.

Two pious Jews come to render due honour to Jesus in his
burial. Nicodemus, who appears only in St John's gospel, had
stoutly defended Jesus' right to a fair hearing before the
Sanhedrin and suffered mocking opprobrium for his efforts. He
had first come to Jesus by night. Had he finally come into the
light of day as a disciple or is he still a representative figure of all
the good people in Judaism who could not accept Jesus' claims?
Joseph of Arimathea had become a disciple, but like many of the
people who first read this gospel account, he was afraid of the
consequences of an open profession of faith. Is his final action on
Jesus' behalf a sign of his coming out into the light of day? Has
Jesus finally drawn them to himself when he was lifted up?
Burying him with the honours due to a king certainly points in
that direction.

The extraordinary account of the earthly life and ministry of
Jesus, the Word made flesh, ends with shocking simplicity in
just three words, *ethêkan ton Iêsoun,* 'They laid Jesus (there).'

The Risen and Glorified Lord (Jn 20-21)

The Appearances in Jerusalem (Jn 20:1-31)

1. INTRODUCTION

'They laid Jesus there.' With these few words the story of the 'earthly' life of Jesus, the Word made flesh, is brought to its conclusion. The work given to him by the Father has been completed and brought to perfection. He has been lifted up from the earth to draw all to himself and to manifest the profound truth of his 'I am' proclamation. He has been glorified. The Spirit has been given. The prolepses or promises and foreshadowings in the account of the ministry have been fulfilled. Now the story of the risen and glorified Lord, present for all time through the gift of the Spirit, is about to begin. It is, however, not only the story of the risen and glorified Lord, but also the story of the disciples and their coming to experience the new presence of their risen Lord. 'The gospel ends with new-found faith ... but it is faith that must now go out into a new world, a new day, and attempt new tasks without knowing in advance where it will all lead.'[1]

S. Schneiders sums it up very well:

> ... the fourth gospel does not need a resurrection narrative in the same sense as the synoptic gospels do, because in John the death of Jesus, his lifting up on the cross, is his glorification, and he does not, therefore, require divine vindication after a shameful execution. In fact ... the primary purpose of chapter 20 is not to tell the reader what happened to Jesus after his death but to explore, through the paradigmatic and foundational experiences of the disciples, the effect on and meaning for believers of Jesus' glorification ... *glorification* is what happens to Jesus on the cross; resurrection is the communication to Jesus' disciples of his paschal glory through his return to them in the Spirit.[2]

The characters in the Easter story in John are well rounded, a fact brought out in their dialogues and reactions. Mary Magdalene, Peter and Thomas show evidence of confusion, grief, doubt, searching, finding and finally accepting and believing. Mary Magdalene weeps, turns and recognises Jesus on

1. N. W. Wright, *The Resurrection of the Son of God,* 662.
2. S. Schneiders, *op. cit.*, 190.

being addressed by her name. Peter is eager, blustering and confused. Thomas loudly professes his doubts but, on seeing Jesus,
instantly comes to faith and makes the great christological statement of the gospel. The Beloved Disciple manifests the love-en-
gendered vision and faith one associates with the intuitive faith
of the contemplative/mystic.

2. THE READER

Approaching the stories of the resurrection, each reader must be
conscious of the personal presuppositions that may be a deter-
mining factor in understanding or misunderstanding the text
and the truth it conveys.

The resurrection of Jesus is unique. There are no other examples with which it can be examined for the purpose of compar-
ing such experiences and how they came to be understood,
explained and articulated. The New Testament witness is therefore of crucial importance and must be the departure point and
continual referent for all discussion on the resurrection.

Faith experience is independent of philosophical and scientific presuppositions, though philosophy and science can legiti-
mately bring their questions to bear on the witness of faith. The
action of God is free and not subject to human approval or
immediate understanding. The argument, often put forward
directly or indirectly, that one's contemporaries and oneself
have not directly experienced a miracle and therefore God does
not perform miracles, denies the freedom and power of God and
elevates one's personal experience or scientific theory in a way
that denies the freedom of God's action and the special status of
God's chosen envoys in ancient or contemporary society. Above
all it overlooks the incarnation as the unique, once for all, salvific
action of God.

To assume that people in a pre-scientific age before the
Enlightenment were naïve or gullible in respect to God's presence and action in the world is to overlook the intelligence, insight and religious sense of people of another and possibly more
enlightened age. It is the arrogance of cultural imperialism,
imposed across historical and intellectual boundaries. It is a
counterpart to the politically incorrect variety of such imposition across cultural and ethnic boundaries in contemporary society. It is incumbent therefore on the reader to desist from impos-
ing *a priori* conclusions, or harassing the text to speak only in

terms of contemporary intelligibility. The onus is on the reader to become as sensitive as possible to the nature of the texts and the experience they are articulating.

In contemporary western society, an unusual series of experiences that produced such a radical change in people's lives would most likely be the subject of a report of several thousand pages, with tens of thousands of footnotes, from experts in all fields. It would not be read by most people and would be selectively and sensationally quoted in the popular media. Those who read it may even be mesmerised by its jargon, lulled to sleep or bored to death. The biblical storytellers and writers had a much simpler, more effective, and possibly far more sophisticated, approach. They communicated spiritual and theological insight in the details of an apparently simple story. They wanted, for example, to make the point that they were not expecting Jesus to reappear after his death and that there was no possibility that their experiencing him was a self fulfilling wish, auto-suggestion or induced hallucination sparked off by the more susceptible members of the group. They made their point by emphasising the fact that they did not recognise him, they doubted, and they had to be convinced. They emphasised the fact that he was the same Jesus who had been crucified, by drawing attention to the marks of the passion on his body. They emphasised the fact that he was not just physically resuscitated but living in a whole new glorified way, by the manner of his appearing, the doors being closed, their thinking he was a ghost and his disappearing from their sight. The commission to carry on his work also highlights the fact that he is same person who had been with them all through the ministry. These apparently simple details contain profound theological insights into the Risen Christ.

The fact that the churches generally put so much emphasis on the empty tomb, proving that it was empty, that the disciples did not steal the body, that the women had not gone to the wrong tomb by mistake, and so forth, meant that the rich theology of the resurrection, emphasising the presence of the Risen Christ and its implications for the lives of his followers and the mission of the church, were often lost in the labyrinth of apologetics. Reaction to this caused the opposite mistake to be made, where scholars and preachers began to adopt the attitude that the empty tomb, and the stories dealing with it, were to a greater or lesser extent, depending on the outlook of the individual, irrelevant. All four gospels, however, emphasise the empty tomb, which in turn needs the words of the angel(s) and/or the appearances of the Lord for explanation. R. E. Brown adds a serious word of caution:

> How did the preaching that Jesus was victorious over death ever gain credence if his corpse or skeleton lay in a tomb known to all? His enemies would certainly have brought this forward as an objection; yet in all the anti-resurrection argumentation reflected indirectly in the gospels or in the second-century Christian apologists we never find an affirmation that the body was in the tomb. There are Christian arguments to show that the body was not stolen or confused in a common burial, but the opponents seem to accept the basic fact that the body can no longer be found.[3]

Concerning these Easter stories, N. W. Wright states wisely: 'There is no reason to imagine that they were generated either by a newly invented apologetic for the fact that the word "resurrection" was being used of Jesus, or out of a desire to provide legitimisation for particular leaders or particular practices.'[4] He goes on to say that if it were so the storytellers 'would have done a better job'. The witness to the resurrection is manifold. First of all there is the emergence of the believing community and its two thousand year life of faith-filled witness, originating from a handful of powerless friends and frightened disciples. The entire New Testament is shot through with resurrection faith. The vestiges of early preaching in the Acts emphasise the victory of God over the apparent power of his enemies: 'You put him to death/God raised him to life.'[5] This traditional kerygma of God's victory is theologised in Paul, showing the divine plan and the salvific nature of the death and resurrection of Jesus: 'Christ died *for our sins, according to the scriptures* … he was raised on the third day *according to the scriptures.*'[6] Statements of victory and exaltation appear in the various documents of the New Testament. His being at the right hand of the Father, entering the heavenly sanctuary, becoming Lord and Christ, all these acclamations reflect the resurrection faith of the believers, and much of it is earlier than the writing of the canonical gospels.

The gospels articulate in story form the significance of the

3. R. E. Brown, *op. cit.*, II, 976.
4. N. W. Wright, *op. cit.*, 680.
5. Acts 2:23 et al.
6. 1 Cor 15:4.

resurrection for the life of the believers and engage in apologetic argumentation against their opponents. Against this background the gospel accounts of the empty tomb and the post-resurrection appearances of Jesus are formed. N. W. Wright sets the Johannine accounts in the New Testament context, showing the contrast in approach with the tightly argued approach of Paul:

> John's two Easter chapters rank with Romans 8, not to mention the key passages in the Corinthian correspondence, as much as most glorious pieces of writing on the resurrection. John and Romans are of course utterly different in genre and style. Instead of the tight argument and dense phraseology of Paul, we have John's deceptively simple account of the Easter events, warm with deep and dramatic human characterisation, pregnant with new possibilities. Instead of the strong QED, or the bracing 'Therefore ...' at the end of a long and gritty Pauline argument, we have John's disturbingly open-ended final scene: 'What is that to you? Follow me.'[7]

These experiences of the Risen Lord were probably more profound and varied than the articulated accounts can convey. The accounts that have survived have been interpreted and theologised in the various traditions and are in many ways incapable of harmonisation. One therefore needs to take each account and each New Testament document in its own context and on its own terms. The alternative is fragmentation of the texts and endless discussions about contending historical and traditional detail. A clear approach is spelled out by S. Schneiders in her introduction to her treatment of the Mary Magdalene episode on Easter morning:

> First I aim to achieve a (not the) complete or integrated reading of the whole text rather than an exegesis of fragments, which means that my reading of the Mary Magdalene episode should make sense of that episode in itself but also in the context of the whole of the resurrection narrative in John (chap 20) and eventually within the whole of the gospel.[8]

This is a very sound and fruitful approach when applied also to the various other accounts, individually and taken together, without attempts at forced harmonisation. Approached in this way they leave very clear impressions of the experience of these first followers of Jesus, that open onto the inexhaustible wonder of the resurrection.

7. N. W. Wright, op.cit., 662.
8. S. Schneiders, op. cit., 189.

3. AT THE TOMB (Jn 20:1-18)

Mary Magdalene, Peter and the Beloved Disciple (Jn 20:1-10)

It was the first day of the week and there was still darkness when Mary Magdalene went to the tomb. The imagery is striking. The day is described as the first day of the week, not 'the third day' as in the kerygmatic proclamation of the resurrection. The light had not yet shone through the darkness of the night of Judas' betrayal and the choice of darkness over light by those who had rejected the light of the world. The 'first day of the week' and the imagery of light and darkness recall the creation story and form an inclusion with the opening of the gospel. Mary Magdalene made her way through that darkness to the tomb.[9] She saw the stone rolled back and in confusion, ran away from the tomb to Simon Peter and the other disciple, the one whom Jesus loved, and said to them: 'They have taken the Lord from the tomb and *we* do not know *where* they have put him.'[10] Throughout the gospel the words *where, where to* and *where from* have been recurring ever since the first question of the disciples 'Where do you live?' *Where he comes from* and *where he is going* were repeating themes throughout the ministry.[11] Now the quest for the whereabouts of his body opens onto the experience of his return to the Father and his return to the disciples. '… the where of Jesus in John is not primarily spatial or geographical location. It denotes indwelling, the communion between Jesus and God and between Jesus and his disciples.'[12]

Unlike the account in the synoptics, Mary is the only woman mentioned at this point, though subsequently she says, '*we* do not know where they have put him', perhaps reflecting an older story where the other women are mentioned.[13] The 'we do not know' may also include the puzzlement of Peter and the Beloved Disciple at this point in the story. This gospel singles out Mary, probably because of the subsequent appearance to her of the Risen Lord. The gospel has shown a strong tendency towards singling out an individual as representative of an experience, attitude, or group. It will subsequently single out Thomas

---

9. The scene reminds one of the Song of Songs where the lover seeks the beloved in the garden at dawn. cf Song 5:6-8.

10. Jn 20:2. Here for the first time 'the other disciple', mentioned again in the next verse, is identified with 'the disciple whom Jesus loved'.

11. *Pou, hopou*. Between them they appear forty eight times.

12. S. Schneiders, *Written that You May Believe*, 191.

13. cf Mt 28:9f. The women having found the empty tomb, were on their way to

as the doubter, though the broader New Testament tradition speaks also of other doubting disciples.

Movement has been important throughout the gospel. Now Peter is setting out on a new journey.[14] The verb is in the singular, emphasising Peter's setting out to the tomb (possibly reflecting an earlier version of the story which spoke only of Peter, as in Luke's account[15]). The Beloved Disciple joins him in this journey. Here again the Beloved Disciple 'upstages' Peter, both in the physical journey in which he outruns him, and in the journey in faith in which he is the first to realise the significance of the empty tomb and of the presence and position of the gravecloths. As they ran to the tomb, the other disciple outran Peter and came to the tomb before him. Bending down he saw the linen cloths lying there, but did not enter. He waited for Peter who entered and saw the linen cloths, and the napkin that covered Jesus' head lying apart, folded up. Peter's reaction shows no sign of faith, like the reaction of Mary Magdalene earlier on seeing the stone rolled back. Then the other disciple, who reached the tomb first, entered. Whereas Peter saw only the empty tomb and the grave-cloths, the Beloved Disciple *saw* and he *believed*. The Beloved Disciple is the only witness to the empty tomb who *sees* and *believes* before an angelic announcement or an appearance of the Risen Lord explains its significance. Here the narrator, as on previous occasions, relates how they had not understood the scripture that stated that he must rise from the dead. In typical literary form, the scene ends with their returning home.

Unlike Lazarus who emerged from the tomb still bound to a future death, signified by the cloths that others had to unbind to set him free, Jesus emerged without human help and left the trappings of death behind. Perhaps also an apologetic motive lies behind the emphasis on the cloths and the folded napkin. Had the rumour that the disciples had stolen the body, as re-

---

tell the disciples when Jesus met them on the way. He used the epiphany formula 'Do not be afraid' and they fell down before him, clasping his feet. He told them to tell his brothers to go Galilee where they would see him.

14. cf Lk 24:12. Peter runs to the tomb, bends down to look into the tomb, sees the gravecloths and returns home 'amazed' at what has happened. There is no reference to the beloved disciple here and the description of the gravecloths is not detailed. It is like a primitive 'skeleton' account, focused on Peter, that has been fleshed out in John with the story of the Beloved Disciple and the detailed account of the gravecloths.

15. Lk 24:12.

ported in Matthew, been current, it would have been necessary
to point out that they were unlikely to have removed the cloths
from the body and carefully folded the napkin during a night
raid on the tomb. Had the gardener removed the body he too
would not have removed its wrappings.

Mary Magdalene: ' I have seen the Lord' (Jn 20:11-18)
Now the focus shifts back to Mary Magdalene. Matthew and
Mark, as pointed out above in relation to the scene on Golgotha/
Calvary, pointedly emphasise the presence of the women who
witness the death and burial of Jesus and their subsequent finding of the empty tomb. Matthew and the Marcan Appendix describe a first appearance of the Risen Lord to these women, including Mary Magdalene. John, in keeping with the approach
throughout the gospel of focusing on an individual as representative of a group, focuses on Mary Magdalene as the first one to
whom the Lord appeared. Various groups preserved the tradition of their 'founder' figure's experience. In his handing on of
the testimony he had himself received, Paul's 'kerygma' in 1 Cor
15:3-8 singles out the appearances to Cephas (Peter) and James
as though they were 'premier' experiences followed by the
shared experience of their followers. Then for his own disciples
Paul emphasises his own personal experience. The priority
given to these 'premier' appearances can be explained in terms
of rank and importance of the individual concerned, Peter for
the broad church, James for the Jerusalem church, Paul for his
communities. These were all 'politically correct'. The Johannine
tradition/community, however, in spite of its 'canonisation' of
the Beloved Disciple, clearly emphasised the priority of the appearance to Mary Magdalene, an appearance not only private
and personal to herself, but involving a commissioning to proclaim the resurrection to the *adelphoi* (an inclusive term representing brothers and sisters, all those constituted family of Jesus by
the gift of his 'Mother' to the Beloved Disciple on Golgotha). The
embarrassment of accepting a woman as witness in a society
that did not value the testimony of women, not to mention the
testimony of just one woman, is the strongest claim to the actual
historical accuracy of the account.[16]
    The essential steps in 'conversion' are present in the story.

16. Zefferrelli's film 'Jesus of Nazareth' makes the point very well as it shows the
reaction of the disciples to the 'hysterical' woman!

She 'weeps' for the death of Jesus and the disappearance of his body, a human reaction showing love and loss. She 'turns away', 'converts' from that hopelessness focused on a tomb, to seek further, and having found, and been found by, the Risen Lord she becomes the delegated witness or apostle of the good news to the *adelphoi*.

She stood outside the tomb weeping, and when she bent down and looked into the tomb she saw two messengers/angels,[17] in white, one at the head the other at the feet of where the body of Jesus had been lying. Replying to their question about the reason for her weeping, she said: 'They have taken my Lord and I do not know where they have put him.'[18] As she turned round and saw Jesus, not knowing who he was (like Luke's story of the disciples' not recognising the stranger on the Road to Emmaus),[19] and mistaking him for the gardener, she responded to his question as to why she was weeping, with the request: 'If you have removed him, tell me where you have laid him and I will take him away.' Again the *where* is in evidence. Jesus, just called her by name, 'Mary', and she recognised him, responding with *'rabbouni'*. Here again, as with Mary of Bethany and Lazarus, Jesus, the Good Shepherd, calls his own by name, they recognise his voice and respond to his call. Mary responds by calling him *rabbouni, 'my* teacher'. Hers is now a deeply personal faith. The address is an acknowledgement that for her he is the teacher *par excellence*, the revealer.

The Easter stories focus on the relationship of Jesus of Nazareth and the Risen Lord and how believers relate to both. Those who knew Jesus of Nazareth now have to adjust to knowing him in a whole new way. John focuses on Mary Magdalene to illustrate this challenging process of adjustment. At first she comes seeking a dead body in the tomb, then she wonders where that dead body might now be. In this search she is continuing the 'human' relationship through visiting the tomb and mourning the loss of a loved one. When she finds him, or rather he finds her, she reacts to him as to the returned friend and

---

17. The symbolism of the two angels may well be an allusion to the cherubim, adorning the divine presence at either end of the mercy seat of the ark. cf N. W. Wright, *op. cit.*, 668.

18. The singular verb here probably shows that this was intended to be the main story about Mary, and the preceding story of her finding the tomb was adapted to it with the elimination of the reference to the other women.

19. Lk 24:13-35.

teacher, but then has to 'let go' of 'a worldly relationship' as Jesus points ahead to his going/ascending to the Father, and all that means for his followers and their new relationship with him.

At first sight, not yet recognising his glorified state, she wishes to hold on to him in his former capacity, to which Jesus responds: 'Do not touch (*haptou*) me for I am not yet ascended to my Father.' Both the 'do not touch' and 'I am not yet ascended to my Father' pose problems for translation and interpretation. Because Matthew speaks of the women 'clasping' (*kratein*) his feet, translators are inclined to see *haptou* also as meaning the same as *kratein*, 'clasping, grabbing hold of and clinging onto someone'. However, the only other place where *haptein* is used in the Johannine writings is in 1 Jn 5:18 where it says that the Evil One *does not touch* anyone who has been begotten by God. 'Touch' in this sense means 'get involved with' or 'relate to' as in the expression 'being touched by someone's kindness or malice'. Understanding *haptou* in this way, it is clear that Jesus is directing her attention away from her former style of attachment to himself in his earthly life, to a new presence and relationship with him in his glorified state, in communion with his brothers and sisters.[20] The emphasis is also on the call to witness and mission. 'Don't be clinging to me, trying to hold on to what is past, but instead get on with the business of witness and mission, beginning with the brothers (and sisters).' There may also be an apologetic dimension to the encounter. The fact that she wanted to cling on to Jesus emphasises that she saw him as the very same person, Jesus of Nazareth and not as a wraith or ghostly apparition of a kind familiar to a Greco-Roman from reading the Homeric literature,[21] or to a modern reader familiar with Shakespeare's ghost of Hamlet's father.

Jesus' remark about ascending to the Father can be translated as statement or question, just like the statement or question at Cana, 'My hour has not yet come' or 'Has not my hour come?' Following Albert Vanhoye's proposal that 'John uses double-meaning or ironical questions whose answer is both positive and negative to lead the reader into theological reflection, S. Schneiders comments: 'In this case Jesus *appears* to be not yet ascended because he is interacting with Mary, but what she (and

---

20. S. Schneider,*Written That You May Believe*, 197f.
21. N. W. Wright, *op. cit.*, relating Teresa Okure (1992), 181f.

the reader) must realise is that *in reality* he is now in a very different state, that is, glorified.'[22] The translation then should be: 'Am I still not ascended?', a rhetorical question designed to elicit the response from Mary Magdalene and the reader, 'You are ascended, glorified.'

Mary Magdalene is the apostle to the apostles, the one sent to them, and hers is the first proclamation of the resurrection, 'I have seen the Lord.' The expression 'I am ascending to my Father and your Father, to my God and your God' recalls the words of Ruth, 'Your people will be my people and your God my God' as she took her place among the covenant people.[23] The believers, Jew and Gentile, are now bonded with the glorified Christ in his relationship with the Father, whom he can now define as 'my God and your God'. The significance of the representative role of the Beloved Disciple in becoming 'son' to Jesus' mother is here made manifest. Being children of his mother the disciples are now his brothers and sisters. Now his Father is their Father, and in being his disciples his God is their God. Up to this point in the gospel Jesus has spoken of 'the Father' and 'my Father'. Now he speaks of 'your Father'. They are now 'children of God, children of the Father' in their own right.

4. WHERE THE DISCIPLES WERE GATHERED (Jn 20:19-29)
In the Absence of Thomas (Jn 20:19-23)
Again the imagery is striking. It was evening, twilight, the half light. Anxiety and insecurity hung over the group and the doors were locked for fear of the Jews. The witness of the Magdalene had not dispelled the darkness. Coming unexpectedly into their midst, Jesus returned to them bringing the final gift he promised before his trial and execution. 'Peace to you' re-echoes his words: 'Peace I leave with you, my peace I give to you, not as the world gives peace do I give peace.' To assure them that he was the same person who had been crucified, he showed them his hands and his side – his hands which had been outstretched as he was lifted up and drew all to himself, and his side from which there flowed the blood and water, the fountains of the sacramental life of the church in baptism, Eucharist and forgiveness of sin; the atoning sacrificial blood of the lamb and the life-giving

---

22. S. Schneider, *Written that you may believe*, 197f, n 18. cf A. Vanhoye, 'Interrogation johannique et exégèse de Cana (2:4)', *Biblica* 55 (1974), 157-67.
23. Ruth 1:16.

water, symbol of the Holy Spirit. The hands and side also showed the personal continuity between the Jesus who had been crucified and the glorified one now standing miraculously in their midst. They rejoiced, as he had promised they would, when he said: 'I will see you again, and your hearts will rejoice, and no one will take your joy from you.'[24] Now the disciples rejoiced on seeing the Lord and Jesus repeated his reassurance: 'Peace be with you.' The disciples had heard the testimony of Mary Magdalene, but they still needed the appearance of Jesus to confirm their faith.[25]

The appearance accounts reflect the narratives of the call and commissioning of a prophet in the Old Testament. In the midst of a divine encounter of some kind, the prophet was commissioned. Here the disciples in their encounter with the Risen Lord are commissioned: 'As the Father has sent me, so I am sending you.' They will carry on Jesus' own mission from the Father. He breathed on them and said: 'Receive the Holy Spirit.' Breathing on them evokes again the imagery of creation, recalling how God breathed life into the first man and he became a living creature.[26] The ministry of Jesus opened with the witness of the Baptist to the Spirit coming on Jesus and remaining on him. John proclaimed that Jesus would baptise in Holy Spirit. The Spirit was given to the nascent church at the foot of the cross. Here is the manifestation of the gift of the Spirit for the universal mission. Just as Jesus was proclaimed by the Baptist as the one who would 'baptise in Holy Spirit' and described in terms of 'the Lamb of God who takes away the sin of the world', here too the disciples are given the gift of the Spirit and their commission to carry on Jesus' work is described in terms of the forgiveness of sin. The expression 'forgive/retain' is a typical example of a Semitic parallelism which signifies complete control or authority in an action or situation, (as for example in the case of a person

---

24. Jn 16:22.
25. cf Lk 24:36-49. There are striking similarities with Jn 20:19-23, though not closely in wording. Jesus appears unexpectedly to the assembled disciples, on the first day of the week, the day of the discovery of the empty tomb and the appearance in the garden; Jesus wishes them peace; draws attention to his hands and his feet. He gives them the gift from the Father, i.e. the Holy Spirit and commissions them for their task in the world. Luke and John seem to have developed in their own individual ways an earlier story. Notice how John draws attention to Jesus' hands and *side*, Luke to the hands and the *feet*. This ties in with John's piercing of the side and the significance for John of the flow of blood and water.
26. Gen 2:7.

who has authority to *open and shut* a door). Jesus has 'taken away the sin of the world', he has 'overcome the world', and now the disciple-apostles are empowered by his victory and invested with his authority. They will have a mission to a world that may or may not accept their ministry and the one who sent them, just as they had accepted or rejected Jesus and the Father who sent him. As in the case of Jesus, people's reaction to them by way of acceptance or rejection will itself incur the judgement, in which forgiveness or retention of sin will be the outcome.

The Disciples, including Thomas (Jn 20:24-29)
Thomas was absent. The testimony of Mary and the other disciples 'I have seen/we have seen the Lord' still does not convince him. Though he does not deny the possibility, he insists on seeing for himself, and on his own strict terms: 'Unless I see … I refuse to believe.'

'We *have seen* the Lord.' This was the great proclamation of the resurrection faith. Mary had proclaimed 'I *have seen* the Lord.' Paul reassured the Corinthians: 'I am an apostle and I *have seen* Jesus our Lord.'[27] The only one of the disciples who *had not seen* but had believed was the Beloved Disciple, founder figure of the Johannine faith community/tradition. He was unique in that he alone of the original disciples has come to faith without *seeing* the Lord. Thomas is the antithesis of the Beloved Disciple. His story is representative of the other disciples, and of the early Christians who had difficulty in believing *without having seen*. Not being present with the disciples when Jesus had appeared he doubted their testimony and retorted with the stock argument of the doubter or non-believer demanding concrete proof, verifiable to the senses. He graphically proclaimed that he would not believe unless he saw the body of Jesus mangled after crucifixion, the holes in hands and feet and the wound in the side – a very physical and graphic depiction, though Jesus had already shown his hands and his side to the other disciples. When Jesus appeared again Thomas was present. However, he did not approach to touch his wounds, when Jesus invited him to do so,[28] but made the great profession of faith, the fullest christological statement of the New Testament: 'My Lord and

---

27. 1 Cor 9:1.
28. Contrary to the impression sometimes conveyed in artistic representations of the event.

my God.' This is the proclamation of the church's faith and Jesus proclaims blessed all those who believe it without having seen the Lord. This second 'macarism' in the gospel reaches out to all Christians who have come to faith in Jesus without having seen the Risen Lord.

Though Thomas' road to faith was rocky, he is credited with 'the supreme christological pronouncement of the fourth gospel.'[29] In the context of the Roman Empire and its attitude to Christians at the time, this was a very significant proclamation. When the Samaritans gave Jesus the title 'Saviour of the World' it resembled very closely the imperial title *restitutor orbis terrarum,'* originally bestowed on Augustus for bringing the God-given peace, the *Pax Deorum,* after the ending of the civil wars. Now Thomas bestows on Jesus the title 'My Lord and my God', a title reflecting the demand of the Emperor Domitian, persecutor of the Christians in Asia Minor, that he be styled *Dominus et Deus* (Lord and God).[30] As in the case of Mary Magdalene, Thomas' faith in Jesus is now seen to be deeply personal as he confesses, *'my* Lord and *my* God'. It rings out in the gospel like a challenge to the Lord and God of this world, the emperor Domitian.

5. ORIGINAL CONCLUSION AND STATEMENT OF INTENT (Jn 20:30-31)
There is widespread acceptance of the fact that Jn 20:30-31 represents the conclusion of the gospel at an earlier stage of its composition. The statement 'Jesus did many other signs in the presence of the disciples, which are not written in this book' acknowledges, here at the conclusion to the gospel in an earlier stage of formation, that a selection of Jesus' 'signs' had to be made. The actual conclusion (Jn 21:25) states: 'There are also many other things that Jesus did; were every one of them written, I suppose the whole world itself could not contain the books that would be written.' The clear impression given by both comments is of a severely curtailed selection among a vast body of traditional material. The selection was not made for purely historical purposes but, to quote the narrator or editor, 'These are

---

29. R. E. Brown, *op. cit.,* II, 1047.
30. Jn 20:28; cf Suetonius, *Lives, Domitian,* x-xxiii reads like a litany of victims. He twice expelled the philosophers from Rome, including Dio Chrysostom and Epictetus. In such a climate the gospel of John is making a strong statement to the Christians about ultimate power and divinity.

written that you might believe that Jesus is the Christ, the Son of God, and that believing you may have life in his name.'[31]

It is not surprising then that many historical questions are left unanswered and many details remain unclear. Like the search for the body of Jesus, the quest for the 'historical' Jesus is overtaken by the faith experience of those who believe in the glorified Lord. Jesus is not only 'the Resurrected One', he is 'the resurrection and the life' for all believers for whom his story is recalled in the light of the resurrection and its promise of eternal life.

There is ... nothing about John 20, seen in the context of the gospel as a whole, and particularly of the prologue which it balances so well, to suggest that these stories originated as, or would have been heard by their first hearers as, an allegory or metaphor of spiritual experience. Of course, like virtually everything in John's gospel, they function at multiple levels of meaning simultaneously; but the meaning which grounds everything else is the Word becoming flesh. To deny that in respect of John 20 is to leave the symphony without its closing coda, its final crashing chords.[32]

... chapter 20 forms a frame at the end of the gospel that corresponds in several ways to the prologue (1:1-18) at the beginning; and by tracing the themes which, important already in the body of the gospel, find their eventual destination in this chapter.[33]

---

31. Interestingly, Mark opens his gospel with a similar christological statement: 'The beginning of the good news of *Jesus Christ, Son of God*.'
32. N. W. Wright, *op. cit.*, 668.
33. N. W. Wright, *op. cit.*, 666.

Appearance in Galilee (Jn 21:1-25)

1. INTRODUCTION

The final words of Jesus in chapter twenty: 'Blessed are they who have not seen and yet have believed', combined with the statement of purpose of the gospel: 'that believing you may have life in his name', leave the reader with the very definite impression that this was originally intended to be the conclusion of the gospel. Such a conclusion would have been typical of contemporary literature both as a summing up of content, restatement of purpose and final acknowledgement of the contribution made by the protagonist. The reader is therefore somewhat surprised to find another chapter with substantial content. However, there are no known early texts of the gospel without chapter 21 and, furthermore, the story of an appearance in Galilee is in keeping with the broader picture in the gospels. Matthew, like John, has the Risen Jesus appear to his disciples both in Jerusalem and Galilee. Mark has Jesus promising an appearance in Galilee.

This chapter focuses on Peter and the Beloved Disciple. The rehabilitation of Peter takes place through his triple affirmation of his love for Jesus, manifesting his repentance and resulting in his reconciliation and restoration to leadership in the community. The Beloved Disciple is a major focus of interest in the chapter because a report had circulated in the community that Jesus had said he would not die before his (Jesus') return. This misunderstanding may have been compounded by his exceptionally long life, if the tradition of such a long life is true, and the consequent shock to the community when he actually died. The gospel corrects the misapprehension. His death, probably still a recent event when the account was written, had raised a serious question. The account addresses the question and explains it as a misunderstanding. This may also reflect, and address, a more general expectation of a return of the Lord in the not too distant future.

The chapter is ecclesial and missionary. It is ecclesial in so far as it reflects the story of the faith and inter-relationship of the traditions and/or communities represented by these foundational figures. It is missionary in that it has emphasis on the drawing together into the following of Christ of every kind of person, represented by the catch of fish, and the maintaining of the unity of all, represented by the untorn net. It involves also the possibility of witnessing in a hostile world and paying the ultimate price, as Peter is told when Jesus reminds him that 'follow me' entails a following that leads to places he would rather not go, specifically to martyrdom.[34]

2. THE RELATIONSHIP OF CHAPTER 21 TO CHAPTERS 1-20

There are pointers to continuity and discontinuity with the rest of the gospel. There is general agreement among scholars that chapter twenty one contains genuine Johannine tradition showing another hand, and it is usually associated with the final editing of the work which may also have seen the inclusion of the prologue.

Among the pointers to continuity with the rest of the gospel one first notices that the appearance of the Risen Jesus in this chapter is counted as the third appearance to the disciples, putting it in a line of continuity with the two appearances to the disciples in chapter twenty. The stories of Peter and the Beloved Disciple are also in direct continuity with chapters 1-20 and are brought to completion in chapter 21. Furthermore the 'competition' between Simon Peter and the Beloved Disciple is a feature both of Jn 1-20 and Jn 21.

Chapter 21 completes the story of Peter, both restoring his good name and returning him to his discipleship and leadership role. Jesus called Peter 'Rock' when his brother Andrew brought him along with the declaration: 'We have found the Messiah.' When challenged by Jesus amid the falling away that took place after the discussion on eating his flesh and drinking his blood, Peter made his confession of faith: 'Lord, to whom shall we go? You have the message of eternal life, and we believe; we know that you are the Holy One of God.' At the Last Supper he blustered his way through the washing of the feet before his avowal of loyalty to die with Jesus. Then he denied him three times when the pressure was on, around the charcoal fire in the courtyard of the high priest. Now the charcoal fire by the Sea of Galilee recalls the setting of his triple denials. In another setting around a charcoal fire Peter is again questioned three times, this time by Jesus. Peter affirms his love for Jesus, and Jesus entrusts his flock, both lambs and sheep to Peter's care. Chapter 21 was necessary to complete the story of Peter and to emphasise the continuity of Jesus' shepherding role among the flock.

---

34. Jn 21:18.

Chapter 21 completes also the story of the Beloved Disciple. Having reclined on his bosom at the Last Supper and shared his confidence about the identity of the betrayer, the Beloved Disciple's love for Jesus was tested when, far from denying him, he remained with him at the cross, and as representative of all disciples, received the Holy Spirit as Jesus bowed his head and handed over the Spirit. He witnessed the blood and water from Jesus' side, symbolising the sacramental and Spirit-filled life of the new-born church. He received the gift of Jesus' Mother and was constituted her son in Jesus' place. Now chapter 21 clears up the misunderstanding about his death and at the same time sets the scene for the solemn declaration that his witness stands behind the gospel.

The solemn declaratory formula 'Amen, amen I say to you' occurs twenty five times in chapters 1-20 and appears again in Jn 21:18, but is nowhere else in the New Testament. There are also striking similarities in vocabulary and idiom typical of the rest of the gospel, but rare in the New Testament as a whole. These are words used in ordinary narrative where other words and idioms could easily have been used, rather than contexts requiring technical vocabulary. Several examples present themselves. Peter is called Simon Peter, not just Simon or Peter, twelve times in chapters 1-20 and five times in chapter 21. Elsewhere in the New Testament he is called Simon Peter only twice, in association with the miraculous catch of fish in Luke 5:8, and his commissioning by Jesus in Mt 16:16, both incidents with parallels here in Jn 21. In the body of the gospel, the verb *helkuein*, 'draw/pull/drag', is used three times and twice in Jn 21. Elsewhere in the New Testament it is used only once (Acts 16:19). The verb *piazein*, 'catch', is used six times in the body of the gospel and twice in Jn 21. Elsewhere it is used only twice in Acts and once each in 2 Cor and Rev. The gospel has a penchant for using the double diminutive, *paidarion, ploiarion, opsarion*.[35] The last mentioned, a word never used elsewhere in the New Testament, appears twice in chapter six and three times in Jn 21. The use of *oun* which normally means 'therefore' is used 195 times in Jn 1-20 without a sense of inference (as in 'therefore'), but simply as a conjunction meaning 'so, then, next'. It is so used nine times in Jn 21. *Meta tauta*, 'after these things' and *ou ... mentoi* , 'though ... not' are also frequently used in the body of the

---

35. little boy, little boat, little fish.

gospel and also in Jn 21. All these examples serve to set the chapter firmly within the vocabulary and style of Johannine tradition.

There are also a number of features which point to an additional source/tradition and a different individual hand. The fact that the story of the appearance at the Sea of Galilee comes after the apparent conclusion of the gospel, with its climactic christological formula, its clear statement of intent, and the utterance of the beatitude for all those who, though not having seen, would believe, leads the reader to expect that the episodes of 'seeing' the Lord were concluded in Jn 20. Furthermore, the story of the appearance in Jn 21 shows the difficulty of the disciples in recognising Jesus. This is difficult to understand when they had already seen him twice. It sounds like a story about a first appearance that comes to the gospel of John from another tradition.

In addition to the above, there are differences in *personae*, vocabulary and idiom. Leaving aside the more technical vocabulary associated with fishing, and concentrating on the ordinary narrative, the following differences emerge. The sons of Zebedee are never referred to in the body of the gospel and turn up in Jn 21:2 as *hoi tou Zebedaiou*. The verb *ischuein*, 'to be able', never appears in Jn 1-20, where *dunasthai* is used thirty-six times for 'to be able', but *ischuein* is used in Jn 21:6. Luke-Acts uses *ischuein* thirteen times. Jn 1-20 uses the verb *erôtan*, to ask, twenty-six times and its cognate *eperôtan* twice, but in Jn 21:12 *exetazein* is used.

3. THE MIRACULOUS CATCH OF FISH (Jn 21:1-14)

The story of the miraculous catch of fish is associated with the special role of Peter both in Luke's gospel, where it occurs during the ministry, and here in this gospel, where it is in the context of an appearance of the risen Lord. It is so similar in Lk 5 and Jn 21 that one suspects that a common source/tradition stands behind both. It illustrates the effectiveness of the disciples' mission when undertaken at the behest of Jesus. It reflects the futility of even their best efforts when relying on their own expertise. It is a perfect illustration of Jesus' teaching: 'I am the vine, you are the branches ... cut off from me you can do nothing.'

The 'competition' between the impetuously active Peter and the intuitively perceptive Beloved Disciple is highlighted again as the Beloved Disciple recognises the stranger on the shore and

THE GOSPEL OF JOHN

Peter jumps into the water to come to him. Just as Peter went running to the tomb and the Beloved Disciple went running with him, a priority given in the sentence structure to Peter, it was the Beloved Disciple who arrived at the tomb first, and while Peter was still puzzled by the grave cloths and the empty tomb, the Beloved Disciple *sees* and *believes*.

The story of the miraculous catch of fish in Luke leads into the calling and commissioning of the disciples with special emphasis on Peter.[36] It describes Peter confessing that he is a sinful man. Here in Jn 21 it leads on to Peter's repentance, reinstatement and commissioning as shepherd. In both gospels Peter is called 'Simon Peter' in this episode. Significantly, the only scene in Matthew's gospel where Peter is called 'Simon Peter' (Mt 16:16-19) is where he is commissioned to exercise pastoral authority in the community. In the episode in Matthew's gospel (Mt 14:28-33) where Jesus comes to the disciples in the boat, Peter leaves the boat and gets into the water, as here in Jn 21. Having failed in courage as he experienced the wind and the waves and began to sink, he calls out to Jesus to save him. The scene ends with Peter and his companions acknowledging him as Son of God, just as here in the Johannine story Peter acknowledges his love/loyalty to Jesus.

In Lk 5:10 Jesus tells Peter and his companions that they will be 'fishers of people'. The same idea is contained here in the allusions embedded in the text. The theme of 'drawing in' the nets reflects Jesus' teaching that the Father draws people to him in faith (*helkuein*), and that he (Jesus) would draw all to himself when he was lifted up and glorified.[37] It further emphasises the all-embracing nature of the mission to all people. It is very likely also that the number of the fish, one hundred and fifty three, represents the totality of human kind. The zoologists at the time believed there were one hundred and fifty three species of fish in the sea. In its statement that the nets were not torn, the same verb is used, *schizein*, which is used throughout the gospel for 'division' among the authorities and the people about Jesus. It is most significantly used in the statement about the seamless robe, how it was not divided/torn at his crucifixion, signifying the undivided community of believers he had drawn to himself

37. Jn 6:43; 12:32.

as he was 'raised up'.[38] Peter's role as leader who draws people and maintains unity comes through. This will be made explicit in his appointment as shepherd.

The theme of abundance, brought about by Jesus' word, as a sign of the kingdom, is in evidence in the wine at Cana, the multiplication of the loaves in Galilee and here in the abundance of fish on the Lake of Tiberias. At the multiplication of the loaves in Galilee the bread was supplemented by the fish (*opsarion*). Here the fish (*opsarion*) is supplemented by the bread, surprisingly since the whole emphasis has been on the fish. The words *elaben /lambanei, artos, opsarion* and *homoiôs* occur both in Jn 6:11 and 2:13. The eucharistic formula 'takes the bread and gives it to them' is evident in both.

4. PETER THE SHEPHERD (Jn 21:15-19)

The meal with its eucharistic overtones and the charcoal fire (*anthrakia*) serve to evoke memories of the Last Supper where Peter protested his willingness to die with/for Jesus and the subsequent scene in the courtyard of the high priest where Peter three times denied being his disciple (Jn18:18). Here he has three chances to reaffirm his love for Jesus and this leads to the scene where Jesus reiterates the call to discipleship, 'Follow me', and predicts that in so following he will in fact lay down his life as a disciple.

The three questions put to him parallel his three denials. In fact they seem carefully crafted to make up the number three. Together lambs and sheep make up the flock. Two instructions would therefore have covered the commission, and formed a perfect Semitic parallelism. 'Do you love me? Feed my lambs; Do you love me? Feed my sheep.' In the first two questions Jesus uses the verb *agapân* (love) and Peter responds with *philein* (love), again a parallelism. However, the text says that Jesus asked him the third time 'Do you love me?' but this time using the verb *philein*. This bears the hallmarks of an addition to the more simple, original parallelism, for the purpose of emphasising the triple opportunity to repent for the triple denial.

Doubts about Peter's role in the wake of his denials are set aside, the ecclesial community is assured of Jesus' forgiveness and reinstatement of the leader. Jesus works through, and in spite of, the human failure of his followers, even that of their

---

38. *schisma, mê schizômen, ouk eschisthê.*

leader. Feeding the lambs and sheep is reminiscent of the work of the shepherd in Ez 34. When the shepherds fail, God promises to take over the shepherding himself, and to raise up a good shepherd, a new David. The good, or model, shepherd is described by Jesus in chapter ten as the one who knows the sheep by name, and whose voice the sheep recognise and follow. He is the one who lays down his life for the sheep, because the sheep are his own, and he is no hireling who abandons them when danger comes. Jesus speaks in the discourse on the model/good shepherd of 'my sheep', and his own role. Now Peter is inserted into that role, and is to look after *my* lambs, *my* sheep, that is, to shepherd the flock of Jesus. Peter also will lay down his life for his sheep.

5. PETER AND THE BELOVED DISCIPLE (Jn 21: 20-23)

Now the futures of Peter and the Beloved Disciple, the one who had reclined on Jesus' breast at the supper, are brought under scrutiny.[39] Peter had proclaimed at the supper that he would follow Jesus, and lay down his life for him. Jesus said he would deny him three times, but also foretold that 'You will follow me afterward.'[40] Now Peter, confirmed in his leadership and experience of the Risen Lord, is told by Jesus about how he will follow him afterward. He will be bound like a criminal and led to execution. Like the Good Shepherd, Jesus himself, Peter will lay down his life for his flock. In this his love for Jesus is definitively proved true.

A report had circulated in the community that Jesus had said that the Beloved Disciple would not die. This misunderstanding may have been compounded by his exceptionally long life, if the tradition of such a long life is true, and the consequent shock to the community when he actually died. The gospel corrects the misapprehension by pointing out that what Jesus had said was: 'If it is my will that he remain until I come, what is that to you?' His death, probably still a recent event when the account was written, had raised a serious question. The account addresses the question and explains it as a misunderstanding. The text again refers to how he reclined close to the breast of Jesus at the Supper.

---

39. Note the identification of the Beloved Disciple with the one who leaned on Jesus' breast at the supper. Above (20:22) the Beloved Disciple, and 'the other disciple' are identified.
40. Jn 13:36-38.

Maybe questions were being asked also about different types of discipleship, different community experiences, and different ways of witnessing. Why did the Beloved Disciple go on living so long and people like Peter (and Paul and so many others) die as martyrs (witnesses)? That question may well be another element in the sub-text to Peter's question: 'What about him?' which created the context for the prophecy about Peter's death.

Excluding the narrator's explanatory statement in v 23, Jesus' final words in the gospel are: 'Follow me.'

6. Verifying the Witness (Jn 21:24)

Referring to the Beloved Disciple just mentioned, the community vouches for the witness and writing of 'the disciple who is bearing witness to these things'. 'This is the disciple who is bearing witness to these things, and who has written these things; and we know that his testimony is true.'

7. Conclusion (Jn 21:25)

The vastness of the experience of Jesus is such that a selection of his deeds had to be made. This seems a very small percentage of his life's work, judging by the comment that if all were written even the whole world could not contain the books that would have to be written. This statement challenges all attempts to enclose Jesus in neat categories and to make over confident statements about the 'historical Jesus'. Far from 'minimising' him, one should remain open to the vastness of his impact and the sheer inability of any written document or group of documents to capture it in full.

The Jewish Calendar

Nisan (Abib)	March-April
Iyyar (Ziw)	April-May
Sivan	May-June
Tammuz	June-July
Ab	July-August
Elul	August-September
Tishri (Ethanim)	September-October
Marheshvan (Bul)	October-November
Kislev	November-December
Tebeth	December-January
Shebat	January-February
Adar	February-March

The oldest liturgical calendars in the Hebrew Bible, Ex 23:14-17 and Ex 34:18-23, presuppose a year that began in autumn. In early Israel the months were distinguished by number. Four Canaanite names appear in the Bible (in brackets above). Under Babylonian influence after 587 BC the months took on the Babylonian names, and possibly also the custom of reckoning the beginning of the year in spring was introduced, though the feast of the New Year continued to be celebrated in autumn, at Tishri, the seventh month (September-October).

List of Abbreviations

ABD	Anchor Bible Dictionary, NY Doubleday, 1992
Ant	Josephus: Antiquities of the Jews
ATR	Anglican Theological Review
BA	The Biblical Archeologist
Bel	Josephus: The Wars of the Jews
Bib	Biblica
BVC	Bible et Vie Chrétienne
BZ	Biblische Zeitschrift
CBQ	Catholic Biblical Quarterly
CC	Corpus Christianorum
CD	Damascus Document
De Somn.	Philo: De Somniis
De Agr	Philo: De Agricultura
HE	Eusebius: Ecclesiastical History
HTR	Harvard Theological Review
IDB	The Interpreter's Dictionary of the Bible, Nashville, Abingdon, 1962.
In Joh	Augustine: Tractatus in Joannis Evangelium
JB	Jerusalem Bible
JBC	Jerome Biblical Commentary
JBL	Journal of Biblical Literature
JSNT	Journal for the Study of the New Testament
JSOT	Journal for the Study of the Old Testament
JTS	Journal of Theological Studies
LumVie	Lumière et Vie
LXX	Septuagint
LSJ	A Greek-English Lexicon (ed. H. G. Liddel, R. Scott and H. S. Jones)
NovT	Novum Testamentum
NRSV	New Revised Standard Version
NTA	New Testament Abstracts
NTS	New Testament Studies
OCD	Oxford Classical Dictionary
PG	Patrologia Graeca-Latina (Migne)
PL	Patrologia Latina
IQH	Qumran Hymns (from cave I)
IQM	Qumran War Scroll (from cave I)
4QF	Qumran Florilegium (from cave 4)
4QT	Qumran Testimonia (from cave 4)
IQS	Qumran Manual of Discipline (from cave I)
Qdp	Philo: Quod Deterius Potiori insidiari soleat

RB	Revue Biblique
REJ	Revue des Études Juives
RSV	Revised Standard Version
SNT	Supplements to Novum Testamentum
SNTSMS	Society for New Testament Studies, Monograph Series.
StB	H. L. Strack and P. Billerbeck, Kommentar zum Neuen Testamentum aus Talmud und Midrasch (vols 1-5, Munich, Beck,1922-55)
Tg. Onk.	Targum Onkelos
Tg. Neof.	Targum Neofiti
Tg. Neb.	Targum of the Prophets
Tg. Ps-J	Targum Pseudo-Jonathan
Tg. Isa	Targum of Isaiah
TS	Theological Studies
TDNT	Theological Dictionary of the New Testament, G. Kittel and G. Friedrick, Vols 1-10, Grand Rapids, Eerdmans, 1964-76.
TS	Theological Studies
ZNW	Zeitschrift für die neutestamentliche Wissenschaft

Rabbinic Literature Prefixes

m.	Mishnah
t.	Tosefta
j.	Jerusalem Talmud
b.	Babylonian Talmud

Comprehensive Bibliographies
on St John's Gospel

Malatesta E., *St John's Gospel,* 1920-65. Rome. PIB, 1967.

van Belle, G., *Johannine Bibliography* 1966-85, Louvain, Leuven University Press, 1988.

Mills, W. E., *The Gospel of John, Bibliographies for Biblical research*, NT Series. Lewiston, NY, Mellen, 1995.

NT Gateway http://www.ntgateway.com/featured.htm

Just, F. SJ., Loyola Marymount University, The Johannine Bibliography Web Pages:

http://clawww.lmu.edu/faculty/John/Bibliog-Gospel.html

Select Bibliography

COMMENTARIES

Barrett, C. K., *The Gospel According to St John: An Introduction with Commentary and notes of the Greek Text*, SPCK London/ Philadelphia, 1955/1978.

Beasley-Murray, G. R., *John*. World Biblical Commentary 36, Waco: Word Books, 1987.

Bernard, J.H., *A Critical and Exegetical Commentary on the Gospel according to St John*, 2 vols, International Critical Commentary, Edinburgh, T & T Clark, 1928.

Brodie, T. L., *The Gospel According to John: A Literary and Theological Commentary*, NY, Oxford University Press, 1993.

Brown, R. E., *The Gospel According to John*, 2 Vols, Chapman, 1966-70.

Brown, R. E., *The Gospels and Epistles of John*: *A Concise Commentary,* The Liturgical Press, Collegeville, 1988.

Bultmann, R., *The Gospel of John: A Commentary*, Oxford, Blackwell/ Westminster, 1971.

Craddock, F. B., *John*, Atlanta, John Knox *Press*, 1982.

Culpepper, R. A., *The Gospel and Letters of John. Interpreting Biblical Texts,* Nashville, Abingdon, 1998.

Dodd, C. H., *The Interpretation of the Fourth Gospel,* Cambridge University Press, 1980.

Haenchen, E., *A Commentary on the Gospel of John*, 2 vols, Hermeneia, Philadelphia: Fortress,1984.

Leon-Dufour,X., *Lettura del Vangelo secondo Giovanni*, Vols I-III, Cinisello Balsamo-Milan, 1989, 1992, 1995.

Lindars, B., *The Gospel of John,* Eerdmans/Marshall, Morgan & Scott, 1972.

Lightfoot, R. H., *St John's Gospel: A Commentary*, Oxford University Press, London/ Oxford, New York. First published 1956, several reprints.

McPolin, J., *John*, New Testament Message 6, Veritas, Dublin / Glazier 1979/1990.

Michaels, J. R., *John,* New International Bible Commentary. Peabody, Mass: Hendrickson, 1989.

Moloney, F. J., *The Gospel of John*, Sacra Pagina 4, The Liturgical Press, Collegeville, 1998.

Moody Smith, D., *The Gospel of John*, Cambridge University Press, 1995.

Ridderbos, H., *The Gospel of John: A Theological Commentary*. Grand Rapids: Eerdmans, 1997.

Schnackenburg, R., *The Gospel According to St John*, 3 Vols, NY: Crossroads, 1968, 1980, 1982.

Stibbe, M. W. G., *John's Gospel*, London, New York, Routledge, 1994.

Stibbe, M. W. G., *John as Storyteller: Narrative Criticism and the Fourth Gospel*, SNTSMS 73, Cambridge (Eng.); New York, Cambridge University Press, 1992.

Witherington, B., *John's Wisdom. A Commentary on the Fourth Gospel*, Louisville: Westminster/John Knox, 1995.

OTHER RECOMMENDED WORKS

Ashton, J, ed., *The Interpretation of John*, SPCK, 1986.

Ashton, J., *Understanding the Fourth Gospel*, Oxford Clarendon Press, 1991.

Ashton, J., *Studying John, Approaches to the Fourth Gospel*, Oxford, Clarendon, 1994.

Ashton, J., ed, *The Interpretation of John*, T&T Clark, Edinburgh, 2nd ed 1997.

Ball, D. M., *'I am' in John's Gospel: Literary Function, Background, and Theological Implications*. Journal for the Study of the New Testament: Supplement Series 124. Sheffield: Sheffield Academic Press 1996.

Bammel, E., ed, *The Trial of Jesus. Cambridge Studies in Honour of C F D Moule*, Studies in Biblical theology, Second Series 13, SCM Press, London, 1970.

Bammel, E., 'The Trial before Pilate', in *Jesus and the Politics of His Day*, ed. E. Bammel and C. F. D. Moule, Cambridge, Cambridge University Press, 1984.

Baucham R. J., ed, *The Gospels for All Christians: Rethinking the Gospel Audiences*, Grand Rapids: Eerdmans, 1998.

Baucham, R. J., *Gospel Women, Studies of the Named Women in the Gospels*, W. B. Eerdmans, Grand Rapids, Michigan,/Cambridge, UK, 2002.

Betz, O., *Der Paraklet: Fürsprecher im häretischen Spätjudentum, im Johannes Evangelium und im neugefundenen gnostischen Schriften*. Leiden: Brill, 1963.

Beutler J., and Fortna R. T., eds, *The Shepherd Discourse of John 10 and its Context*, Cambridge University Press, Cambridge,1991.

Bishop, J., 'Encounters in the New Testament', in *Literary Interpretations of Biblical Narratives*, 2 vols, ed. K. R. R. GrosLouis, Nashville, Abingdon, 1982.

Blinzer, J., *The Trial of Jesus*, Westminster, Md, Newman Press, 1959.

J. Blinzer, 'The Jewish Punishment of Stoning in the New Testament', in *The Trial of Jesus*, ed E. Bammel, 147-161.

Bodson, J., SJ, *Regards sur l'Evangile de saint Jean*, Éditions Beauchesne, Paris, 1976.

Boismard, M.-E., *Du Baptême à Cana*, Paris, Cerf, 1956.

Boismard, M.-E., *St John's Prologue*, Westminster: Newman, 1957.

Bornkamm, Günther, *Geschichte und Glaube, Gesammelte Aufsätze*. Erster Teil, Band III, München: Kaiser, 1968, esp pages 68-89, 'Der Paraklet im Johannes-Evangelium'.

Borgen, P., *Bread from Heaven: An Exegetical Study in the Concept of Manna in the Gospel of John and the Writings of Philo*, Supplements to Novum Testamentum 10. Leiden, Brill, 1965.

Braun, F. M., *La Mère des Fidèles*, 2nd ed, Paris, Casterman, 1954.

Brownlee, W. H., 'Whence John?' in *John and Qumran*, ed, C. H. Charlesworth, Geoffrey Chapman, London 1972.

Burney, C. F., *The Armaic Origin of the Fourth Gospel*, 1922.

Burridge, R. A., *Four Gospels, One Jesus?.*, SPCK, 1996.

Busse, U., 'Open Questions on John 10', in *The Shepherd Discourse of John 10 and its Context*, ed, G. N. Stanton, SNTS, Monograph Series, Cambridge University Press, 1991.

Carter, W., 'The Prologue and John's Gospel: Function, Symbol and the Definitive Word', JSNT 39 (1990), 35-58,

Cassidy, R. J., *John's Gospel in New Perspective: Christology and the Realities of Roman Power*, Orbis Books, Maryknoll, New York, 1992.

Casey, M., 'The Corporate Interpretation of "One like a Son of Man" (Dan 7:13) at the time of Jesus', NT 18 (1976), 167-180.

Charlesworth, J. H., ed, *John and Qumran*, Geoffrey Chapman, London, 1972.

Chester, A., *Divine Revelation and Divine Titles in the Pentateuchal Targumim*, Texte und Studien zum Antiken Judentum 14. Tübingen, J. C. B. Mohr (Paul Siebeck), 1986.

Collins, R., 'The Representative Figures of the Fourth Gospel', Downside Review 94 (1976).

Coloe, M. L., *God Dwells With Us, Temple Symbolism in the Fourth Gospel*, The Liturgical Press, Collegeville, Michael Glazier, 2001.

Crossan, J. D., *In Parables: The Challenge of the Historical Jesus*, New York, 1963.

Culpepper, R. A., *Anatomy of the Fourth Gospel*, New Testament Foundations and Facets. Philadelphia: Fortress, 1983.

Culpepper, R. A, and C. Clifton Black, *Exploring the Gospel of John: In Honor of D. Moody Smith*, Louisville, Westminster/John Knox, 1996.

Culpepper, R. A., 'The Pivot of John's Prologue', NTS 27 (1980-1):1-31.

Dahl, Nils. A., 'The Neglected Factor in New Testament Theology', in *Jesus the Christ: The Historical Origins of Christological Doctrine*, edited by D. H. Juel, Minneapolis, Fortress, 1991, 153-63.

de Jonge, M., 'Jesus, Stranger from Heaven and Son of God', Missoula, 1977.

de la Potterie, I., 'Naître de l'eau et naître del'Esprit', *ScEc* 14 (1962) 351-74.

de la Potterie, I., 'Structure du Prologue de Saint Jean', *NTS* 30 (1984), 354-81.

de La Potterie, I., 'The Truth in St John', in *The Interpretation of John*, ed, John Ashton, Philadelphia, Fortress Press, 1986.

de La Potterie, I., *The Hour of Jesus*, St Paul Publications, 1989.

Dunn, J. D. G., *The Partings of the Ways between Christianity and Judaism and their Significance for the Character of Christianity*, London: SCM/Philadelphia: Trinity, 1991.

Dunn, J. D. G., *Christology in the Making: An Inquiry into the Origins of the Doctrine of the Incarnation*, 2nd ed, London: SCM, 1989.

Dunn, J. D. G., *Baptism in the Holy Spirit*, London: SCM Press, 1970.

Epp, E. J., 'Wisdom, Torah, Word: The Johannine Prologue and the Purpose of the Fourth Gospel', pages 128-46 in *Current Issues in Biblical and Patristic Interpretation*, ed, G. F. Hawthorne, Grand Rapids: Eerdmans, 1975.

Fehribach, A., *The Women in the Life of the Bridegroom: A Feminist Historical-Literary Analysis of the Female Characters in the Fourth Gospel*, Liturgical Press, Collegeville, Minn, 1998.

Forese, P., *Jesus: His Last Will and Testament, Meditations on Unity, Faith, Hope and Charity*, London: New City, 1986.

Fortna, R. T. and Thatcher, T., *Jesus in Johannine Tradition*, Westminster John Knox Press, Louisville/Leiden, 2001.

Gächter, P., 'Maria in Kana', ZKT 55 55 (1931), 351-402.

Giblin, C. H., 'Suggestion, Negative Response and Positive Action in St John's Gospel', *NTS* 26 (1979-80), 197-211.

Giblin, C. H., 'Two Complementary Literary Structures in John 1:1-18', *JBL* 104 (1985), 87-103.

Graffy, A., *Trustworthy and True: The Gospels beyond 2000*, The Columba Press, Dublin 2001.

Grassi, J. A., *The Secret Identity of the Beloved Disciple*, Paulist Press, Mahwah, 1992.

Grelot, P., 'L'Interpretation pénitentielle du lavement des pieds', in *L'Homme devant Dieu, Mélanges H. de Lubac*, 2 vols, Paris: Aubier, 1963, vol 1: 75-91.

Hanson, A. T., *The Prophetic Gospel*, T & T Clark, 1991.

Harrington, W. J., *John, Spiritual Theologian: The Jesus of John*, The Columba Press, Dublin, 1999.

Harris, M., 'The Dead Are Restored to Life: Miracles of Revivification in the Gospels', in *Gospel Perspectives*, vol. 6, ed, D. Wehnam et al., Sheffield: JSOT Press, 1986, 310-317.

Harris, M., *Jesus as God: The New Testament Use of Theos in Reference to Jesus*, Grand Rapids: Baker, 1992.

Harsh, P. W., *A Handbook of Classical Drama*, Stanford, CA: Stanford University Press, 1944.

Harvey, A. E., *Jesus on Trial: A Study in the Fourth Gospel*, London: SPCK, 1976.

Harvey, A. E., 'Christ as Agent', pages 239-50 in *The Glory of Christ in the New Testament: Studies in Christology in Memory of George Bradford Caird*, ed, L. D. Hurst and N. T. Wright, Oxford: Clarendon, 1987.

Hogan, M. SSc., *Seeking Jesus of Nazareth: An Introduction to the Christology of the Four Gospels*, Dublin: The Columba Press, 2001.

Jeremias, J., *The Prayers of Jesus*, Philadelphia: Fortress, 1967.

Jeremias, J., *Poimên*, *TDNT* 6, 487, 8.

Johnston, G., *The Spirit-Paraclete in the Gospel of John*, *SNTSMS* 12, Cambridge: Cambridge University Press, 1970.

Kealy, S. P., *John's Gospel and the History of Biblical Interpretation*, Books I and II, Lampeter: The Edwin Mellen Press, 2002.

Kilmartin, E.J., 'The Mother of Jesus was there', *ScEccl* 15 (1963), 213-26.

Lamarche, P., 'Le Prologue de Jean', *RSR* 52 (1964), 497-537.

Lane, D. A., *The Reality of Jesus: An Essay in Christology*, Dublin: Veritas, 1975.

Lindars, B., 'The Son of Man in the Johannine Christology', in *Christ and Spirit in the New Testament: Studies in Honour of C. F. D. Moule*, ed, B. Lindars and S. Smalley, Cambridge: Cambridge University Press, 1973, 43-60.

Lindars, B. and S. Smalley, *Christ and Spirit in the New Testament: Studies in Honour of C. F. D. Moule*, Cambridge: Cambridge University Press, 1973, 43-60.

Loader, W., *The Christology of the Fourth Gospel: Structure and Issues*, Beiträge zur biblischen Exegese und Theologie 23. Frankfurt am Main: Peter Lang, 1989.

Luibhéid, C., *Exploring John's Gospel: Reading, Interpretation, Knowledge*, Arlen House, Galway and Dublin, 2001.

Lund, N. W., 'The influence of Chiasmus upon the Structure of the Gospels', *ATR*, xiii (1931), 42-46.

Lund, N. W., *Chiasmus in the New Testament*, Chapel Hill, NC: University of North Carolina Press, 1942.

Malina, B. J., *The Palestinian Manna Tradition: The Manna Tradition in the Palestinian Targums and Its Relationship to the New Testament Writings*, Leiden: Brill, 1968.

Manns, F., *L'Evangile de Jean à la lumière du Judaïsme*, Studium Biblicum Franciscanum Analecta 22, Jerusalem: Franciscan Printing Press, 1994.

Marsh, T., *Gift of Community: Baptism and Confirmation*. Message of the Sacraments 2. Delaware: Michael Glazier, 1984.

Martin, F., *The Feminist Question: Feminist Theology in the Light of Christian Tradition*, Grand Rapids: Eerdmans, 1994.

Martini, C. M., *Il Caso Serio Della Fede*, Edizioni Piemme, 2002.

McMullen, R., *Enemies of the Roman Order*, Cambridge: Harvard University Press, 1966.

Meeks, W. A., 'The Divine Agent and his Counterfeit in Philo and the Fourth Gospel', pages 43-67 in *Aspects of Religious Propaganda in Judaism and Early Christianity*, ed, E. Schüssler Fiorenza, Notre Dame: University of Notre Dame Press, 1976.

Meier, J. P., *Vol 2: Mentor, Message, and Miracles*, Anchor Bible Reference Library, New York: Doubleday, 1994.

Moloney, F. J., *The Johannine Son of Man, BSRel* 14, 2nd ed, Rome: LAS, 1978.

Moule, C. F. D., 'The Meaning of "Life" in the Gospels and Epistles of St John: A Study in the Story of Lazarus, John 11:1-44', *Theology* 78 (975): 114-25.

Mullins, M., *Called to be Saints, Christian Living in First Century Rome*, Dublin: Veritas, 1991.

Mussner, F., *The Historical Jesus in the Gospel of John*, Quaestiones Disputatae, Herder Freiburg/Burns & Oates, London, 1966.

Neyrey, J., '"My Lord and My God": The Divinity of Jesus in John's Gospel', pages 152-71 in SBL *Seminar Papers, 1986*, Society of Biblical Literature Seminar Papers 25, Atlanta: Scholars Press, 1986.

O'Grady, J. F., *According to John: The Witness of the Beloved Disciple*, NY: Paulist Press, 1999.

O'Rourke, J. J., 'The Historic Present in the Gospel of John', *JBL* 93 (1974), 585-90.

Otto, R., *The Idea of the Holy* (E. T. of *Das Heilige*, 1917), Oxford: Oxford University Press, 1923, 1950, paperback edition 1958, 1976.

Painter, J., 'Theology, Eschatology and the Prologue of John', *Scottish Journal of Theology* 46 (1993), 27-42.

Potin, J., *La Fête juive de la Pentecôte*, Lectio Divina 65, Paris, Cerf, 1971.

Pryor, J. W., *John, Evangelist of the Covenant People*, London: Darton, Longman and Todd, 1992.

Rochais, G., *Les récits de résurrection des morts dans le Nouveau Testament*, SNTSMS, Cambridge: Cambridge University Press, 1981.

Rossé, G., *The Spirituality of Communion: A New Approach to the Johannine Writings*, New York: New City Press, 1998.

Sabbe, M., 'John 10 and its Relationship to the Synoptic Gospels', in *The Shepherd Discourse of John 10 and its Context*, ed, G. N. Stanton, SNTS, Monograph Series, Cambridge University Press, 1991.

Sanders, E. P., *Judaism: Practice and Belief, 63 BCE-66CE*, London: SCM/Philadelphia: Trinity, 1993.

Salmon, V., *The Fourth Gospel: A History of the Text*, Collegeville: The Liturgical Press, 1976.

Saxby, H., 'The Time-Scheme in the Gospel of John', *ET* 104 (1992), 9-13.

Schneiders, S. M., *The Revelatory Text, Interpreting the New Testament as Sacred Scripture*, Collegeville: Michael Glazier/ Liturgical Press, 1999.

Schneiders, S. M., *Written That You Might Believe: Encountering Jesus in the Fourth Gospel*, NY: Crossroad, 1999.

Scott, M. A., *Sheffield: JSOT Press, 1992*. Journal for the Study of New Testament: Supplement Series 71.

Segovia, F. F., *The Farewell of the Word: The Johannine Call to Abide*, Minneapolis: Fortress, 1991.

Senior, D. CP., *The Passion of Jesus in the Gospel of John*, Gracewing/ Fowler Wright Books, UK/Collegeville: The Litrurgoical Press, 1991.

Sloyan, G., 'The Samaritans in the New Testament', *Horizons* 10 (1983), 10.

Stauffer, E., *Jesus and His Story*, London: SCM, 1960.

Stenning, J. F., *The Targum of Isaiah*, Oxford: Clarendon Press, 1953.

Thompson, M. M, *The God of The Gospel of John*, Grand Rapids: Eerdmans, 2001.

Thompson, M. M, 'The Historical Jesus and the Johannine Christ', pages 21-42 in *Exploring the Gospel of John: In Honor of D. Moody Smith*, ed, R. A. Culpepper and C. Clifton Black, Louisville: Westminster/John Knox, 1996.

Thurian M., *Mary Mother of All Christians*, NY: Herder and Herder, 1964.

Treanor, O., *This is My Beloved Son, Aspects of the Passion*, London: Darton, Longman and Todd, 1997.

van den Bussche, H., *Giovanni: Commento del Vangelo Spirituale*, Assisi: Cittadella Editrice, 1971.

Turner, J. D., 'The History of Religions Background to John 10', in *The Shepherd Discourse of John 10 and its Context*, ed, G. N. Stanton, SNTS, Monograph Series, Cambridge University Press, 1991.

Vanhoye, A., 'Interrogation johannique et l'exégèse de Cana', Bib 55 (1974), 157-77.

Yee, Gale A., *Jewish Feasts and The Gospel of John*, Zacchaeus Studies: New Testament, Delaware: Michael Glazier, Wilmington, 1989.

Westermann, C., *The Gospel of John, in the Light of the Old Testament*, translation by S. S. Schatzman of *Das Johannesevangelium Aus der Sicht des Alten Testaments*, Stuttgart: Calwer verlag, 1994.

Wijngaards, J., *The Spirit in John*, Zaccheus Studies, Wilmington: Michael Glazier, 1988.

Windisch, H., *The Spirit-Paraclete in the Fourth Gospel*, Philadelphia: Fortress, 1968.

Witherington, B., *Women in the Ministry of Jesus: A Study of Jesus' Attitude to Women and Their Roles as Reflected in His Earthly Life*, Cambridge: Cambridge University Press, 1984.

Wright, N. W., *The Resurrection of the Son of God*, London: SPCK, 2003

Zimmerli, W., *I am Yahweh*, ed, W. Brueggemann, trans. D. W. Scott, John Knox Press, 1982.